The Making of Twenty-First-Century Richmond

The Making of Twenty-First-Century Richmond

Politics, Policy, and Governance, 1988–2016

THAD WILLIAMSON

JULIAN M. HAYTER

AMY L. HOWARD

THE UNIVERSITY OF NORTH CAROLINA PRESS

Chapel Hill

© 2024 Thad Williamson, Julian M. Hayter, and Amy L. Howard

All rights reserved

Designed by Jamison Cockerham
Set in Scala and Libre Franklin
by codeMantra

Cover art by Brian Palmer. Used by permission.

Manufactured in the United States of America

LIBRARY OF CONGRESS CATALOGING-IN-PUBLICATION DATA
Names: Williamson, Thad, author. | Hayter, Julian Maxwell, author. | Howard, Amy Lynne, 1971– author.
Title: The making of twenty-first-century Richmond : politics, policy, and governance, 1988–2016 / Thad Williamson, Julian M. Hayter, Amy L. Howard.
Description: Chapel Hill : The University of North Carolina Press, [2024] | Includes bibliographical references and index.
Identifiers: LCCN 2024023915 | ISBN 9781469681283
(cloth ; alk. paper) | ISBN 9781469681290 (pbk. ; alk. paper) |
ISBN 9781469681306 (epub) | ISBN 9781469681313 (pdf)
Subjects: LCSH: Racism—Social aspects—Virginia—Richmond. | Richmond (Va.)—Politics and government—20th century. | Richmond (Va.)—Politics and government—21st century. | Richmond (Va.)—Race relations. | Richmond (Va.)—Social conditions. | Richmond (Va.)—History. |
BISAC: HISTORY / United States / State & Local / South (AL, AR, FL, GA, KY, LA, MS, NC, SC, TN, VA, WV) | SOCIAL SCIENCE / Sociology / Urban
Classification: LCC F234.R557 W55 2024 |
DDC 320.97552309/05—dc23/eng/20240709
LC record available at https://lccn.loc.gov/2024023915

For

LILLIE A. ESTES

and

JOHN V. MOESER

In a place like Richmond, where history is steeped in unfathomable human suffering, planning must concentrate on rebuilding what was lost and uniting all that was torn asunder.

JOHN V. MOESER (1942–2022)

My goal is total community transformation, which is a work in progress.

LILLIE A. ESTES (1959–2019)

Contents

LIST OF ILLUSTRATIONS   *ix*

1   Overview: A Laboratory of Democracy in the Shadow of Jim Crow   *1*

2   Richmond City Politics, 1988–1994: Decline, Disarray, and Dissatisfaction   *23*

3   Richmond City Politics, 1994–2016: The Road to Reform and Beyond   *51*

4   Education and Governance in Richmond, 1988–2016   *85*

5   Poverty, Inequality, and Economic Development, 1988–2016   *135*

6   The Persistence of Segregation: Housing Richmond, 1988–2016   *183*

7   Toward a Just Twenty-First-Century Richmond   *223*

ACKNOWLEDGMENTS   *249*

APPENDIX: ORAL HISTORY SOURCES   *257*

NOTES   *261*

INDEX   *333*

Illustrations

MAPS

1.1 City of Richmond in state and regional context
5

1.2 Notable locations, City of Richmond
19

3.1 Richmond city council districts, 2002
69

5.1 Poverty by census tract and council district, 1999
137

6.1 Black and white populations by council district, 2000
186

6.2 Latino and Asian populations by council district, 2000
187

6.3 Black and white populations by census tract, 2000
218

6.4 Black and white populations by census tract, 2015–2019
219

TABLES

2.1 Basic demographics in Central Virginia localities, 1970–2016
28

4.1 Race of and economic disadvantage among students in Greater Richmond school districts, 2003–2004 and 2013–2014
88

4.2 Academic outcomes, Central Virginia Public Schools, 2002–2016
89

5.1 Employment by locality in Central Virginia, 1980–2015
143

5.2 Ratio of employment share to population share by locality in Central Virginia, 1980–2015
144

5.3 Total employment by Standard Industrial Classification sector in City of Richmond, 1980–2000
146

5.4 Total employment by North American Industry Classification System sector in City of Richmond, 2001–2015
147

5.5 Total employment and manufacturing employment in Richmond metropolitan statistical area, 1980–2016
148

6.1 Race and residential patterns by census tract in City of Richmond, 2000
185

6.2 Housing and demographic trends in City of Richmond, 1990–2020
215

6.3 Demographic changes by census tract in City of Richmond, 2000 and 2015–2019
216

The Making of Twenty-First-Century Richmond

1

Overview

A Laboratory of Democracy in the Shadow of Jim Crow

In the summer of 2020, a diverse set of protesters toppled several of Richmond, Virginia's long-standing colonial and Confederate monuments. On the evening of June 10, protesters spray-painted and pulled down a statue of Jefferson Davis, the president of the Confederacy, on the city's famed Monument Avenue; a night earlier, demonstrators had torn down a statue of Christopher Columbus and unceremoniously dumped it in Byrd Park's Fountain Lake. Protesters had already spray-painted a statue of Robert E. Lee, transforming it into a Black Lives Matter memorial. The *New York Times* later deemed this BLM memorial as the most powerful piece of protest art in American life since World War II.[1] These actions took place during five consecutive weeks of nightly, often volatile protests against police brutality and systemic racism, in which Richmond's long-standing monuments became a prime target.[2] The activism in Richmond mirrored hundreds of other BLM protests nationwide following the murder of George Floyd by a white policeman in Minneapolis, Minnesota—at that time, the most recent of many police killings of Black Americans caught on film.[3]

Protesters in Richmond—and throughout the American South— directly associated Confederate iconography in public spaces with continuity of racial segregation and state-based violence against Black bodies. Indeed, just hours after an enabling state law went into effect on July 1, 2020, Richmond city government formally took up the work the protesters had already begun of removing the city's Confederate monuments, starting with Stonewall Jackson, as a multiracial throng of onlookers cheered. These Richmonders recognized the inextricable link between the commemorations of former slaveholders, which stood uncontested for most of the twentieth century, and the perpetuation of African American serfdom during Jim Crow segregation. The Confederate memorials stood not just as relics but as visible reminders of the systemic white supremacy long operative in Richmond and central Virginia—systemic inequality that even decades of formal control of the city's political apparatus by Black leadership had yet to eradicate.

Richmond, Virginia, has been known—and commonly referred to—as the former capital of the Confederacy. Slavery and segregation shaped Richmond's development well into the twentieth century.[4] Richmond's central role in the American Civil War is both well-known and deeply contested.[5] By 1860, slavery and slave trading played an essential role in Richmond's economic, political, and social life, the legacy of Black bondage that had been part of Virginia life from the earliest days of the colonial era. Virginians waged war for independence from Britain on the backs of enslaved labor.[6]

Less well-known is Richmond's history after the Civil War, a story of both courageous Black community building and vicious white backlash to African Americans' upwardly mobile aspirations.[7] After a brief Reconstruction era moment of multiracial democracy—epitomized by the populist, biracial Readjuster Party, which pushed for expanded public education for whites and Blacks—elitism and oligarchy reasserted itself in Virginia by century's end.[8] Limited interracial political cooperation continued to characterize Virginia's color line at the turn of the twentieth century—even as the commonwealth's whites began to enact some of the South's most draconian race laws.[9] Indeed, throughout most of the twentieth century, attenuated representative government characterized Richmond and the commonwealth's political development. Richmond, like many cities farther South, came to rely on a form of government in which "powerful political leaders created and preserved" undemocratic institutions that made Black dehumanization (as well as exploitation of poor whites) an inevitability.[10] There is now growing scholarly and public understanding of the ways that racial segregation perpetuated Black serfdom and defined Richmond life well into the twentieth century.[11]

Understanding contemporary Richmond requires a thorough examination of how the forces of racial restriction shaped life during and after the American civil rights movement.[12] The pages below demonstrate that the triumphal narrative that so often defines the story of race in America after the civil rights movement needs substantial revision.[13] Local accounts are essential to understanding national trends. The more recent antipathy toward Confederate iconography might very well be a national story.[14] But that record also has intense significance and layers of meaning specific to Richmond. For most of the twentieth century, local and state governments were the primary executors of Jim Crow segregation.[15] Local governments also served as the architects of many unresolved problems that define contemporary unrest.[16] Using the tools of both state and local government, and in some cases federal assistance, Richmonders themselves designed and controlled housing segregation, maintained racial apartheid in public schools, and razed Black neighborhoods in the name of modernity and progress.[17] The impact of these policies survived the segregationist system and came to define Richmond long after Blacks first obtained majority political control in the City of Richmond in the late 1970s.[18] Any understanding of America in the twenty-first century must consider how people met (or failed to meet) the challenges of structural racism locally.

This book uses Richmond's recent history (1988–2016) as a means to understand contemporary urban crises and responses to them.[19] This periodization covers the city's development following the fracturing of the civil rights coalition in the mid-1980s through the early twenty-first-century push for political reform and finally the initial consequences of that reform for the city's ability to tackle its deepest problems. There has been, leading historians argue, a "productive movement to deploy historians' analytical tools on contemporary structures and problems."[20] To this end, this book examines the operation of power and the pursuit of community problem-solving within the context of institutionalized, structural inequality and racism.

The picture that emerges is neither a straightforward story of government futility nor one of linear progress. Segregation has cast a long shadow over contemporary Richmond, including the period of this study. Policy responses favored by elites—including the 2004 change in the city's form of government—almost always avoided direct confrontation with structural inequality, even as the city and region continued to be defined by entrenched patterns of housing and school segregation. Nonetheless, by the turn of the century white elites had accepted the reality of Black political power in Richmond, and there was significant evidence at both the grassroots and elite level of a desire to build a city not defined by its racial divide. While race continues to loom large over the city's identity (both real and imagined), for the first time in the city's long and often tortured history, everyday politics are generally no longer characterized by zero-sum racial polarization. In fact, the capital city has taken numerous significant steps toward "racial reconciliation" (or more recently, "racial equity").[21] Some 160 years after the Civil War, both Richmond residents and its leadership class are at last ready for the city to claim a different identity than the "Capital of the Confederacy."

Such optimism about Richmond's future, while not wholly unwarranted, masks fundamental continuities. Political and civic leadership have struggled to address the city's most enduring social and economic conditions in more than cosmetic ways. In fact, citizens blamed political leadership almost exclusively for the city's decline in the post-segregation era.[22] In many ways, Richmond remains a city divided—economically, racially, socially, and culturally. It persists, well into the twenty-first century, as a city where life expectancy is often inextricably linked to one's census tract.[23]

In the recent past, larger regional inequalities have shaped the city's divisions. In 2016, the City of Richmond's population of roughly 225,000 persons accounted for less than one-fifth of the over 1.25 million people in the Richmond metropolitan area.[24] The bulk of the remaining population resided in either of the two counties immediately adjacent to Richmond—Chesterfield and Henrico (over 664,000 persons combined in 2016)—or in affluent Hanover County (104,000 persons) to the north. The remaining population was sprinkled among thirteen additional localities, ranging from predominantly rural Goochland and New Kent Counties (to the west and east of Richmond, respectively) to the impoverished, overwhelmingly African American city of Petersburg (population 31,000) to the south.[25] The poverty rate in Richmond in 2016 was 25.4 percent, compared with just 8.6 percent in Chesterfield, Hanover, and Henrico Counties combined.[26] In 2016, African Americans made up 48.4 percent of the city's total population but totaled just 23.4 percent of Chesterfield, Hanover, and Henrico residents. Importantly, these numbers also reflected increases in white and Latino residents in Richmond since 2005 and growing racial diversity in the counties; by 2016, some 177,000 African Americans lived in Chesterfield, Hanover, or Henrico compared with 105,000 African Americans in the City of Richmond.[27]

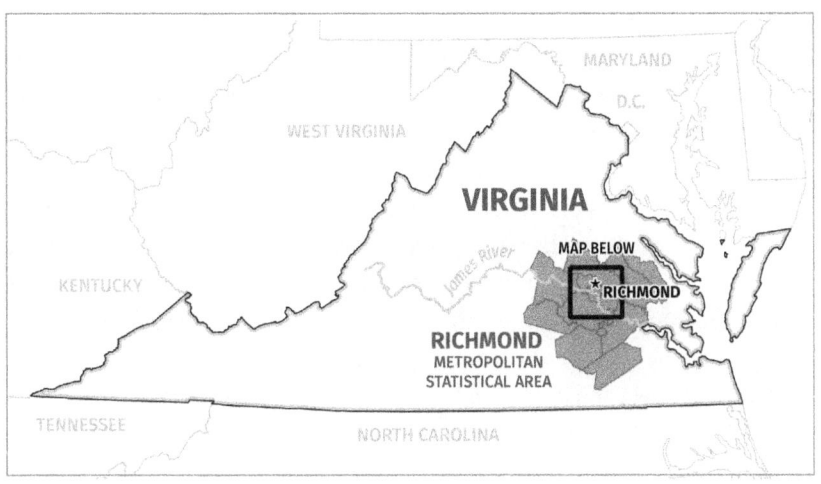
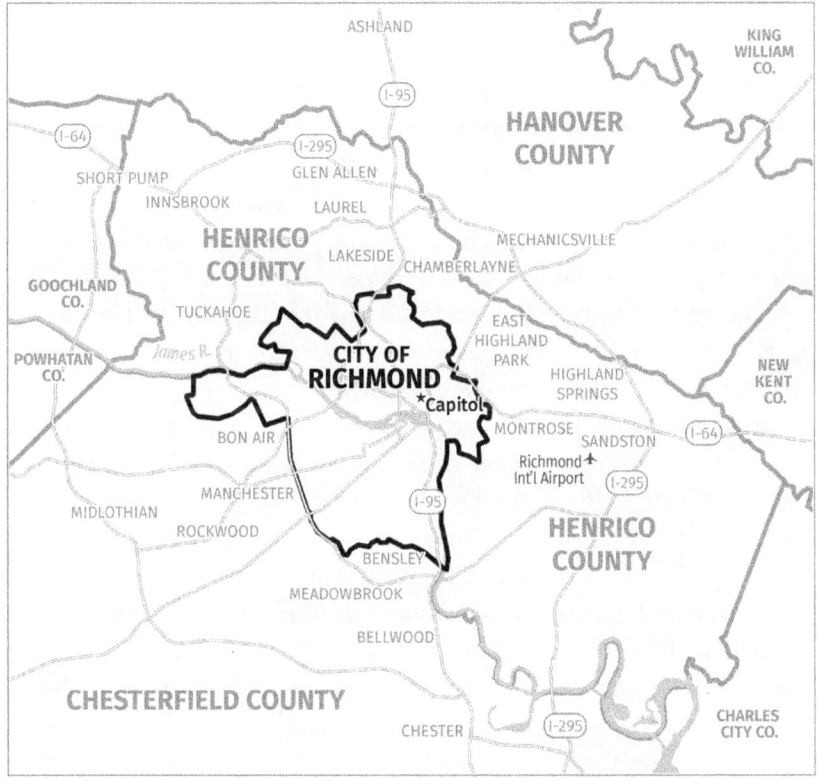

Map 1.1. City of Richmond in state and regional context.
Map by Riley D. Champine of the University of Richmond Digital Scholarship Lab, based on data from the U.S. Census Bureau and OpenStreetMap.

Such inequalities between central city and suburban areas are of course commonplace in the United States—but unlike regions in the United States where there have been at least sporadic attempts to create region-wide political alliances aimed at correcting such inequalities (driven by both elite and grassroots groups), the peculiar political structure of Virginia localities strongly militates against meaningful metropolitan-wide cooperation.[28] Cities are not, as in every other contiguous state, subsets of counties in Virginia. Instead, designated cities are themselves equivalent to counties.[29] While this arrangement assures the "independence" of particular localities, it also means that the City of Richmond, encompassing just sixty-three square miles, has its own separate—and unequal—school system and city government. Historically, there have been no fiscal mechanisms in place for channeling suburban resources back into city neighborhoods. Likewise, cities in Virginia are constrained in their ability to act creatively in the face of these restraints without an explicit mandate from the commonwealth's General Assembly, which affords cities only those powers specifically enumerated in the city charter or in general state law. The only possible site of redress of intra-metropolitan inequalities is the state government itself. But city and urban interests were, to say the least, weak players in Virginia's state politics over the period of this study. The importance of this arrangement to Richmond's development (or lack thereof) cannot be overstated. The aggregated political clout of populous suburbs and large rural areas with vested interests in the status quo have constrained and frustrated urban development in Richmond since the mid-twentieth century.[30]

In examining the historical legacy of structural political and economic forces, our purpose is twofold. African American leadership in predominantly Black cities often inherited decaying cities yet were blamed for the decay itself.[31] While we acknowledge the shortcomings of post–civil rights era leadership, we also recognize the complexity of the problems these leaders inherited.[32] First, we seek to demonstrate the ways leadership from the 1980s through the 2010s in Richmond largely failed to redress—and in some cases failed to even engage—the city's most serious structural problems (racism, poverty, educational inequality). Second, we attempt to explain *why* this was the case: that is, more specifically, why, despite widespread agreement across the spectrum of the community on what the key issues were, there has been to date only limited and sporadic success in addressing these pressing matters. Finally, we note that Richmond had greater success in tackling a key symptom of those problems, violent crime, which fell over the period of this study, and in undertaking a variety of policies aimed at attracting new investment and eventually people back into the city. Those efforts did not bring about equity, but they did help sustain Richmond as a viable city and set the stage for its eventual resurgence. A major question for the future is whether that resurgence will take the form of modern-day gentrification or instead shape a twenty-first-century Richmond that better exhibits the inclusive vision often voiced by both residents and leaders but rarely delivered in practice.

We begin by providing a detailed account of the evolution of politics and governance in Richmond between 1988 and 2016, establishing a baseline understanding of the key political events that shaped policy development before and after the 2004 political reform. We then proceed with in-depth analysis of three key *issues* that defined the city and continue with an assessment of how city leadership did and did not address these issues. These central issues, taken together, represent in our judgment (and in that of many Richmonders) the most serious intersecting problems facing Richmond's communities: *public education*; *jobs and job-related issues* (such as workforce development, transportation, and economic development); and *housing* (including affordable housing, public housing, and housing redevelopment).

Interwoven with our discussion of these three issues are five ongoing *themes*—features of Richmond's civic and political culture that have shaped and often distorted the approaches the city has taken to any number of pressing issues. Pervading significant public and political activity in Richmond, these themes are, first, *the weight of Richmond's history, particularly its racial history*; second and relatedly, *ongoing racial mistrust and racial inequality*; third, a pattern of *civic participation* (including voting, neighborhood advocacy, and policy advocacy) that has been highly skewed toward white, well-educated residents and in which powerful civic groups, especially diverse groups addressing multiple issues, have been generally absent; fourth, a *regional and state context* that leaves the city isolated and persistently short of resources to take up major initiatives on its own; and fifth, *the limited capacity and uneven effectiveness of local government itself*.

Leadership in the Shadow of Segregation

Our starting point and claim is at once both moral and empirical: the most fundamental structural problem facing the City of Richmond and its residents is its large, heavily racialized prevalence of poverty, much of it highly concentrated geographically.[33] Poverty is visible across all racial groups in Richmond, but it is by far most prevalent among Blacks and Latinos in the city, persons with less than a high school education, and the city's children. At the end of the period under study, the 2016 American Community Survey indicated that over one-quarter of the city's population, including over two-fifths of the city's children, lived in poverty, and the city's median income of $41,200 far trailed the national median of $55,300.[34] Poverty in Richmond was and continues to be unevenly dispersed across the city; it is mostly highly concentrated in Black and Latino neighborhoods of the East End and Southside. There are, in fact, two Richmonds: a more affluent city where residents occupy corporate spaces by day and spacious neighborhoods by night, a city that is disproportionately (but not exclusively) white; and a predominantly Black and Brown city of substandard housing, underemployment and unemployment, vacant lots, high crime, sparse retail, food deserts, and often visible signs of decay and despair. This divide reflects decades-long patterns of racialized inequality, encoded and reinforced by public policy (both actions and inactions). Indeed, by almost any statistical measure, the problem of poverty in the city worsened or stayed consistent over the twenty-eight-year time frame of this study. Relatively recent efforts to address poverty in a more direct way and the tangible but limited progress that has resulted since 2016 need to be placed against the larger backdrop of inertia, inaction, and ineffectiveness relative to the scale of the problem.

We advance four arguments to explain both the reasons Richmond has generally failed to redress poverty and racial segregation and these issues' impact on housing, schools, and economic opportunity, and also to suggest the possibility (not certainty) of more than cosmetic change in the near future. First, many of Richmond's most pressing problems (including racialized poverty) are the predictable result of anti-urban national and statewide policies that made it extremely difficult for local leaders to address deepening economic dispossession. Second, the specific structure of local government in Virginia, derived from the segregationist era, limits the capacity of Richmond leaders—legally, politically, and resource-wise—to address the city's problems at the scale they exist. Third, over the period of our study there have been significant localized obstacles to effective problem-solving in Richmond, including a palpable amount of skepticism and distrust of civic and political leadership—skepticism that often had racial overtones—and a relatively weak culture of civic activism. Finally, we argue that some of these obstacles have weakened in most recent years, as a result of both profound demographic changes and a greater willingness from many Black and white leaders to speak bluntly about the city's fundamental challenges. These changes create the possibility that Richmond residents and leaders will seek to confront the long shadow of racial domination in more fundamental ways, whether through existing institutional channels or by demands for bolder and more far-reaching reform at the local, regional, and state level.

National and State-Level Anti-urban Policies and the "Ungovernable" City

Richmond at the dawn of the twenty-first century represented a caricatured version of postwar metropolitan development in the United States. For most of the late twentieth century, two stark suburban and urban stories played out—a perpetually under-resourced, majority-Black city surrounded by predominantly white, much more affluent suburbs, each with their own distinct school systems and governance structures. Many urban scholars today stress the ways in which this traditional picture has evolved over the past generation, with many suburbs becoming steadily more diverse racially, poverty increasing in older suburban communities, and growing interest among the middle class (especially the young) in moving back to central cities.[35] These trends have been evident in the Richmond region as well, and in the past twenty years the rapid growth of the Latino population, although yet to tangibly impact city politics, portends a future for Richmond that necessarily moves beyond the traditional Black-white axis. But the dominant picture in Richmond over the course of this study was that of a high-poverty city surrounded by generally more affluent suburbs. Moreover, some of the most rapid growth in the region occurred in outer suburban counties, even more distanced from the city than the inner suburban rings in Henrico and Chesterfield Counties.

The legacies of postwar federal policies, namely the racialization of homeownership and subsequently racially homogeneous suburban growth, have shaped the last seventy-five years of urban life in Virginia and Richmond. These policies, well documented in the urban history and policy literature, include federal subsidies for homeownership through the Federal Housing Administration, the mortgage interest tax deduction for homeowners, federally funded construction of interstate highways and generous subsidies for road maintenance and automobile use, and federal support for urban renewal policies that destroyed many urban neighborhoods deemed "undesirable" by white elites in the 1950s and 1960s nationwide.[36] Richmond's modern development as a city was profoundly shaped by discriminatory anti-urban policies that razed Black neighborhoods to construct highways serving white suburban commuters, concentrated Black poverty in certain parts of the city, and systemically steered investment away from remaining Black neighborhoods.[37]

From the 1970s forward, Virginia's General Assembly demonstrated little political appetite for initiatives aimed at seriously ameliorating urban poverty or related problems facing central cities.[38] The legislature has long been dominated by a coalition of suburban and rural interests. To be sure, in the 1980s and early 1990s a string of centrist Democratic governors—Chuck Robb, Gerald Baliles, and L. Douglas Wilder—managed to expand public investments in education, transportation, and environmental protection.[39] But anti-urbanism persisted well into the late twentieth century. By the first decade of the twenty-first century, northern Virginia had become (relative to the rest of the state) markedly more progressive, and remarkably, Richmond's immediate neighbors Henrico and Chesterfield Counties began shifting from red to blue in national and statewide elections between 2006 and 2016. But over the course of this study Virginia progressives rarely challenged the traditional fundamentals of the Virginia creed: low taxes, a business-friendly environment, hostility to labor unions, a miserly (by national standards) state safety net, and strong aversion (beyond support for public education) to redressing systemic inequalities of either educational opportunity or economic outcome.[40]

In addition, Virginia had (and continues to have) peculiar state laws that impeded the ability of cities to launch innovative policy responses to their predicaments and often exacerbated city-suburban inequalities. Cities and counties in the Commonwealth of Virginia are legally separate, meaning there is no overlap of tax base. Over the last five decades, this has put cities and their surrounding suburbs in a zero-sum competitive relationship on key issues, particularly the pursuit of economic development and new residents. It also, as we will outline in detail, has precluded meaningful integration of public education and provided the counties with perverse disincentives to offer social services. Virginia is a Dillon Rule state, meaning the City of Richmond's only powers are those specifically granted by the state in the city charter or in Virginia general law. Any change in the charter must be approved by the state legislature. Such change is not impossible, but the Dillon Rule tends to put a dampening effect on proposed innovative urban policies, especially those with a revenue-raising function or that might potentially threaten private business interests. This 150-year-old doctrine also provides a convenient excuse for local politicians seeking to dismiss certain policy proposals ("We can't do it because of the Dillon Rule").[41] Finally, cities in Virginia since the 1970s have been, in effect, barred from pursuing expansion through annexation.[42] Cumulatively, these policies helped shape

Richmond as a city that is landlocked, with essentially no greenfield space for commercial development, no capacity to expand its tax base through annexation, and limited ability to pursue innovative local policies that might creatively respond to this predicament.

The net result of this convergence of federal and state policies is that city officials repeatedly find themselves trying to deal with large, entrenched, and interconnected problems without regional allies or adequate resources. Predictably, this situation was exacerbated in times of fiscal austerity. During the period under study, the annual budget process often came down to deciding on a series of tragic trade-offs: Money for schools, or money to finance needed economic development and job training? Money to protect seniors from rising property assessments, or money to support disadvantaged youths?

City leaders who were conscientious realized that to make good policy in this context of overloaded demand and limited resources required a strategy and a prioritization of which problem to tackle first—trying to deal with the pressing issues all at once would spread limited resources too thin and prove ineffective. Those choices in turn exposed officials to criticism from advocates frustrated that their favored program or priority was not adequately supported. From the outside, city elected officials often were portrayed as hapless figures too confused to get out of their own way, lurching from one policy strategy to another yet failing to address the city's underlying realities. The self-portrait of city officials themselves tended to be quite different, understandably: they tended to view themselves as heroically tackling the nearly impossible, trying to do the best they could to keep a good, beautiful city viable, trying to help the city outgrow its painful past, and trying to do right by their constituents, many of whom were in dire need, all with limited resources and a series of challenges their suburban counterparts could barely imagine.

Ultimately, Richmond policymakers have been placed in a chronically disadvantageous situation by factors outside their control. We hold that despite these larger structural limitations, city leaders might have done much better as policymakers—and might in fact do much better in the future. At the same time, we demonstrate that city government had limited but important policy successes that are insufficiently recognized.

The Virginia Rules and the City of Richmond

In addition to the structural challenges common to central cities across the United States, Virginia's tortured history of integration and its segregated institutional structures have often thwarted progress in Richmond. The city was an important site of struggle during the civil rights movement, particularly with respect to education and racial integration.[43] The notorious strategy of "Massive Resistance" emerged in 1956 out of Virginia senator Harry F. Byrd's widely promoted "Southern Manifesto" opposing integrated schools, with the support and inspiration of editorialist James Kilpatrick of the *Richmond News-Leader* in the 1950s.[44] After the collapse of Massive Resistance, Virginia leaders then successfully employed a strategy of token integration to preserve the basic structure of white schools and Black schools for as long as possible. The city's so-called freedom of choice plan offered Black students the opportunity to apply for admission to white schools, if they could provide their own transportation and would agree to forfeit any right to transfer back to their previous school—no matter how much intimidation and harassment they faced in majority-white schools. Federal judge Robert Merhige finally overturned Richmond's glacial approach to integration in critical decisions rendered in 1970 and 1971. Merhige ordered the comprehensive integration of city schools via a busing scheme, to be fully implemented in the 1971–72 school year.[45] Many white families at this point left either the public school system or the city entirely, joining the many other white families who had already escaped the specter of integration throughout the previous decade, often by moving to federally subsidized suburban homes. Between 1950 and 1960, Richmond's population declined overall by over 10,000 people, even as the city's Black population increased by nearly 19,000 people over the same time period.[46] By the time the courts enacted effective integration of Richmond schools, the city was already well on its way to becoming a high-poverty, overwhelmingly Black school system. Meanwhile middle-class whites had already built up an infrastructure of alternatives to the city schools, including numerous private schools within the city limits.[47]

Recognizing that suburbanization had become a mechanism for perpetuating de facto racial segregation of schools, Judge Merhige, in a subsequent 1972 decision, ordered the merger of the Richmond, Henrico, and Chesterfield school systems in order to achieve effective metropolitan-wide racial integration. To the relief of most whites in greater Richmond, this decision was reversed by the Fourth Circuit Court of Appeals, a reversal upheld by the Supreme Court.[48] The continuity of hyper-segregation in Richmond public schools by race and class all but ensured that generations of Black children would continue to receive a substandard education. Yet by the early twenty-first century, many Richmonders were unaware of this history and regarded the substandard conditions of Richmond city schools and the presumed superiority of suburban schools as normal (or even natural).

The segregationist era had a lasting impact on Richmond in numerous other respects beyond schools, including neighborhood displacement, the creation of highly concentrated public housing in the city, the racially motivated annexation of part of Chesterfield County in 1970 that led to a federal intervention in Richmond city politics, and more. Richmonders still live with a legacy of racial mistrust resulting from the segregationist era—including a lack of shared understanding of Richmond's racist history—that has hampered efforts to build multiracial coalitions in the city and continues to impact public discourse and public perceptions in a variety of policy areas, especially housing and education.

"Can't Get Out of Their Own Way": Localized Obstacles to Progress

The ability of local leadership to address Richmond's pressing challenges was also commonly impeded over the course of this study by more specific local features of Richmond civic culture. White elites (including many in the business community, some *Richmond Times-Dispatch* editorialists, and some politicians) often focused on problems and projects that did not fundamentally affect the well-being of most citizens, especially the economically disadvantaged. Favored strategies for redressing education and poverty discussed in elite circles were heavily voluntarist and largely failed to speak to the fundamental structural and policy arrangements that defined Black and Brown portions of the city. Many city residents (regardless of race) during this time period instinctively distrusted both city hall *and* perceived elite actors.

At the same time, outside of its legacy civil rights organizations, Richmond generally had a weak culture of civic activism. Over the period of this study, there simply were not strong multiracial, cross-cutting civic organizations capable of acting independently to both educate citizens and hold elected leaders accountable.[49] To be sure, a number of organizations engaged in local political and policy advocacy, but they were relatively small in scale and clout, and none successfully organized and sustained a strong multiracial, multiethnic, cross-generational, citywide base. This fact is somewhat ironic given the pathbreaking role of the Richmond Crusade for Voters in organizing African American voters in the 1950s and 1960s, prior to the Voting Rights Act.[50] These traditional civil rights organizations continued into the 1990s and beyond, but in weakened form compared with their mid-century heyday (though some individual leaders associated with the groups were recognized civic voices). This relative lack of political organization resulted in failure to offset the default influence of business groups and in insufficient grassroots pressure to steer elected leaders in a consistently progressive direction. When Black political leaders who were aligned with civil rights organizations successfully attained elected office, they found they had few outside civic partners capable of offsetting the influence of the business community. While there were some deliberate efforts to create multiracial civic organizations during this period, these also generally steered away from bold political stances.

The specific governance structures in place in Richmond—the city council, the school board, and, since 2004, the directly elected mayor—also have frequently frustrated aspirations for coherent governance and problem-solving, making it difficult for the city to develop and sustain a concerted attack on its most serious problems. Many residents invested hope in the major political reform of 2004 to create the directly elected "strong mayor" as a potential turning point for the city. We find that this reform did relatively little to directly impact the major challenges facing the city with respect to racial segregation and educational and economic inequality; it altered municipal governance but did nothing to alter the regional and statewide arrangements that systemically disadvantage the city. The reform did, however, create the possibility for developing a more coherent citywide strategy focused on racial equity and reducing poverty—while also introducing new governance problems on issues from schools to the mechanics of city administration.

Demographic and Generational Change and the New Richmond Waiting to Be Born

Despite severe and ongoing challenges, there have been important positive developments in the city and to some extent the region that suggest the future may not (and need not) be like the past. First, the racial dynamics of city politics have changed markedly since the 1970s, creating the possibility of a genuine multiracial progressive regime in the city. While race remains highly relevant, Richmond politics by the 2010s could not so easily or adequately be categorized in terms of racial coalitions. In the civic sphere, decades of "trust-building" work to create conversations between whites and Blacks in Richmond have helped incubate growing spaces in which multiracial civic conversation can take place.[51] More generally, many newcomers to the community as well as young people in the city do not have direct experience or consciousness of the epochal racial conflicts of the 1960s, 1970s, and 1980s. This cuts both ways: while to be ignorant of this history is to be profoundly ignorant of why the city is the way it is today, it does mean that these newcomers and young people generally regard racial polarization as harmful, not a default norm.

Second, significant demographic changes in the region, particularly the growing racial and economic diversity of Richmond's immediate neighbors (Chesterfield and Henrico Counties), have helped change the tone of suburban politics in Richmond, enhancing prospects for serious regional cooperation on issues such as transportation. Third, there has been slowly growing consciousness, even among many elite groups, of the desirability of "doing something" about entrenched poverty and inequitable education in Richmond. Taken together, these changes have created the promise of a more equity-focused and productive local politics that takes square aim at Richmond's most severe problems. This promise was partly symbolized in the events of 2020—including the popular push to tear down the Confederate monuments, the endorsement of that push by elected officials, and the minimal pushback from "Old Richmond" as those events unfolded.

These observations should not be confused for a naively optimistic prediction about the city's future, however. Growing support for ongoing action to address poverty does not mean that the city will be able to implement and sustain policies likely to make a major impact on poverty and economic inequality. Growing attention to public schools does not mean the city will be able to reverse decades of poor educational outcomes for the city's most vulnerable children. There is a possibility of a different kind of politics in Richmond's future, one that both aims at serious poverty amelioration and reduction and is more participatory in content. But there is also the possibility any such emergent politics will simply be overwhelmed by the many negative countervailing trends and factors that continue to afflict Richmond. Moreover, achieving a serious breakthrough on Richmond's fundamental problems would require, eventually, a more robust and more successful challenge to the existing structural obstacles than most city and state politicians have been willing or able to muster in recent decades. In chapter 7, we consider possibilities for positive change in considerable detail.

Richmond's Outsize Significance

Why does any of Richmond's recent history matter? What can Richmond's story tell us about the nature of American cities at the turn of the twenty-first century, or about larger-order questions concerning social justice and democracy in twenty-first century America? We offer four answers to these questions.

First, midsize cities matter.[52] As of 2016, Richmond was the center of the nation's forty-fifth-largest metropolitan area, home to over 1.25 million people, and capital city of a historically and politically significant state.[53] The challenges facing the Richmond metropolitan area—how to revive a struggling city and curb suburban sprawl, how to rectify place-based and race-based inequalities of opportunity and outcome, how to revive a broad-based politics of the public interest—are common, in one flavor or another, to nearly all of America's metropolitan areas.[54] Put bluntly, Richmond's problems are America's problems—many of the issues Richmond faced in the last several decades mirror those found in other American cities with sizable minority populations.

Second, Richmond is important for its uniqueness, in particular its historic status as the former capital of the Confederacy and one of the crucial locations in the history of American slavery. Richmond is where slaveholders sold enslaved people "down the river," effectively breaking apart families.[55] Richmond is the city whose fall heralded the end of the Civil War, punctuated by Abraham Lincoln's solemn but triumphant march through the defeated city in April 1865. Much later, Richmond also became a focal point for the crucial racial conflicts of the 1950s and 1960s, including Virginia's "Massive Resistance" to racial desegregation, sit-ins to desegregate restaurants and stores in the 1960s, and conflicts over annexation and metropolitan-wide school integration.[56] For much of its history, Richmond has been a symbol of the ideology and practice of white supremacy and the treatment of African Americans as second-class citizens. It has also been the site of sustained Black resistance. The struggle of city residents today to both come to terms with and transcend that history—and shape a new, more equitable one—has ramifications for the nation at large that are indeed outsize compared to the city's size and relative standing among Southern metropolises. Change in Richmond and in Virginia reverberates throughout the South and yet resonates throughout the entire nation.

Third, Richmond is significant as a case study in urban injustice. Our ultimate concern in this book is with the quality of the lives in Richmond's low-income and working-class communities. Richmond (like other central cities) is a geographic container for a disproportionate amount of human suffering. Over the last several decades, considerable numbers of Richmond's residents struggled to meet the challenges of the twenty-first century. This theme asks, What obligation do cities have, not merely to address historical wrongs but also to fashion public policies for the good of all residents? Just societies provide for and promote the human flourishing of all and do not permit one group to dominate other groups. Unjust societies waste human potential by failing to equally value lives—these are societies where material deprivation and economic instability, which also give rise to high and continual violence, characterize or even define many people's lives.[57] We use the term "just society" instead of "just city" deliberately here, because there can be no fully just city in the context of a fundamentally unjust society. Local institutions and local political leadership *can* and must attempt to redress (and avoid exacerbating) such suffering, but the fundamental structural conditions concentrating suffering in the city are beyond local control.

Fourth, Richmond is an important example of the significance of civic history. The long-dominant Lost Cause narrative that held sway in Richmond for most of the twentieth century has been decisively rejected, but there is not as yet a shared, deep understanding of how structural racism continued to debilitate the city even *after* Black leaders obtained majority control of the city's political offices in the 1970s.[58] In the absence of such clear understanding, Richmonders may default to simplistic explanations for the city's current condition rooted more in ideology or assumption than in fact. Fact-finding, storytelling, and ultimately truth-telling are essential to understanding how we got to now. Rather than delineating a history of blame, we set out to elevate civic consciousness and civic discourse by outlining historical shortcomings and challenges to promote cross-racial, generational, and socioeconomic civic participation toward a more just Richmond.

The authors of this book are all Richmond residents. And as Richmond residents, we are unapologetic in our concern for the welfare of the city and its residents. Recognition is essential to reconciliation. More importantly, policies done purposefully require equal (if not stronger) intentionality to undo. In delineating the City of Richmond's recent history, we hope that readers in the Richmond region will have a greater understanding of the city and region's civic, social, and political condition. Even more optimistically, we hope that this account of the city's recent political and urban history engenders greater and more compassionate civic engagement. We also hope that readers outside Richmond will come to have a greater understanding of the realities of American society and how those realities play out in real time, on the ground in one urban context. Perhaps this book will inspire people outside of Richmond to think critically about the history and nature of their own urban spaces and creatively about possibilities for action and change.

Methodological Overview

This work stands at the fruitful intersection of policy history, policy analysis, urban studies, and leadership studies. Our assessment of late twentieth-century and early twenty-first-century Richmond and how it came to be employed several research methods. First, we used *historical methods*: reviewing the existing scholarly literature on mid- and late twentieth-century Richmond and analyzing a range of primary and secondary sources in an effort to track the evolution of Richmond politics since the 1980s in a detailed way, from newspaper accounts to contemporary assessments by scholars and observers to official plans, budgets, and policies. Next, we employed *social science* methods by bringing to bear detailed data on the demographics and economy of contemporary Richmond (city and region) and how it has evolved since the late 1980s. In some cases, this involved comprehensive examination of neighborhood-level and school-level data for the purpose of identifying trends and linkages; in other cases, our aim was simply to provide broad descriptive data to orient the discussion.

Oral histories also shaped our findings. Over a two-year period early in the project (2010 and 2011), we conducted some sixty structured interviews with business, civic, political, and grassroots leaders, ranging in length from thirty minutes to two hours. We selected subjects to reach a broad cross-section of the Richmond community, while at the same time covering many individuals widely acknowledged in Richmond to wield substantial formal and informal power. Interview locations ranged from local coffee shops and back porches to high-rise suites in downtown office towers and inner sanctums within city hall and county government offices. Interviewees were asked a common set of questions pertaining to general impressions of the City of Richmond and the surrounding region, their perceptions of the city's problems and how the city goes about addressing them, and their perceptions of who wields power within the city. Follow-up questions then focused on the subjects' areas of expertise and experience. Taken as a whole, this body of interviews provided us with an array of perspectives on Richmond as well as important insights into power and leadership in the city.

Fourth, when relevant, our narrative and analysis drew on our personal experiences as citizens engaged in different capacities with local government. While participatory research was not a primary mode of analysis in this book, we do utilize insights gained from our experiences at various points in the narrative.

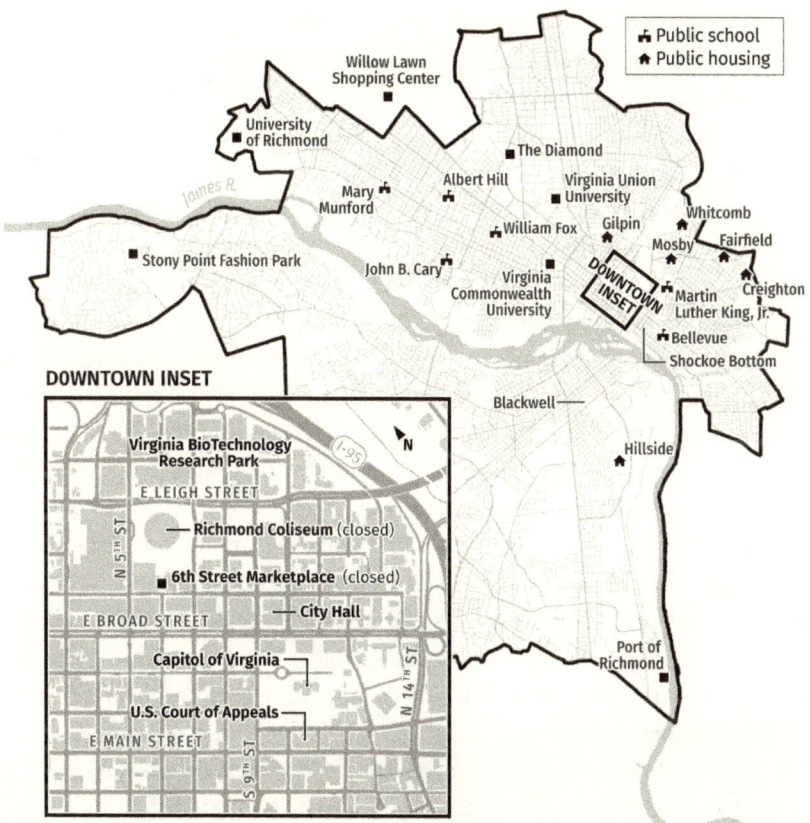

Map 1.2. Notable locations, City of Richmond.
Map by Riley D. Champine of the University of Richmond Digital Scholarship Lab, based on data from the City of Richmond.

Outline of the Book

Chapters 2 and 3 provide a detailed account of the city's political history since the mid-1980s, from roughly 1988 to 2016. This account has a fourfold focus: telling the story of who got elected and why during this time period; discussing the specific issues that dominated policy and public debate during this time; telling the story of how accumulated public discontent with the performance of Richmond local government led to major local political reform in the early aughts; and finally, examining the consequences of that reform once enacted. The book then goes on to examine three specific policy areas in greater detail: public education (chapter 4); poverty, employment, and economic development (chapter 5); and housing policy (chapter 6). Map 1.2 notes several of the specific places and institutions noted in those chapters.

In each case we examine in greater depth baseline trend changes over the 1988–2016 period and the successes and failures of local policies in each area. Here we demonstrate that despite some notable steps and discrete policy successes and accomplishments, the bigger picture is that Richmond failed to seriously redress its most important problems. On issue after issue, problems identified by community leaders going back to the 1980s (and beyond) often became even more entrenched. This is particularly true of issues related to poverty and the well-being of low-income residents in the city, although by the end of this period city leaders had moved to adopt a more intentional and strategic approach, framed as "community wealth building."

Chapter 7 examines future possibilities for change. First, we spell out the substance of a bold "Marshall Plan" focused on education, housing, and community wealth-building policies that aim to meet Richmond's poverty-related challenges at the scale they exist, with the goal of effecting positive changes and potentially improving the lives of tens of thousands of residents in the near and mid-term future. In some cases, this policy agenda draws on existing initiatives and programs, and in other cases it involves embracing entirely new approaches. Altogether, the agenda would require levels of investment in a holistic poverty-fighting and affordable housing agenda an order of magnitude larger than current efforts. An implicit question in sketching an agenda of this kind is whether city government has not only the requisite resources but also the organizational capacity to implement a multipronged plan successfully. With that question in mind, we turn to assessing the pros and cons of Richmond's unique experiment with a directly elected mayor and consider possibilities for both mild and major reforms to the system. We then look at several state-level policy shifts that could substantially help Richmond and other Virginia cities, most importantly by directing more resources to Richmond to help pay for the costs associated with a comprehensive poverty-fighting initiative.

Richmond is a critical locale not just for engaging national discussions about racism and its long shadow but for understanding and critically assessing the efforts of local leaders and citizens to redress racial inequality. Many Richmond residents and observers default to a racially coded narrative frame of dysfunctional governance to explain past and current city woes and problems, from the condition of schools to poverty. We emphasize—and paint in the following pages—a more nuanced picture in which many Richmond leaders, particularly Black leaders, strived with the imperfect tools at their disposal to make good on the promise of an equitable, racially inclusive city, often against overwhelming odds and daunting obstacles. Richmonders are not used to viewing their own city as a laboratory of democracy (however imperfect), let alone one on the cutting edge of wrestling with the deep legacies of institutionalized racism, embedded in local institutions. Perhaps this book will allow readers near and far to see new meaning, including new possibilities for the future, in Richmond's journey, even as it recounts the struggles and frustrations of a difficult and often tragic past.

2

Richmond City Politics, 1988–1994

Decline, Disarray, and Dissatisfaction

The modern era of Richmond city politics began in 1977. In the early 1970s, the U.S. Department of Justice suspended local elections in the city for a seven-year period as a major legal controversy played itself out. On January 1, 1970, Richmond had annexed a predominantly white portion of Chesterfield County, adding some 47,000 new residents and thereby precluding African Americans from gaining expanded representation on the city council in the 1970 municipal elections. The DOJ and the Supreme Court eventually ordered the city to implement nine single-member districts for city council elections, replacing the at-large voting system that had been in place since 1948. Richmond's district system instituted a revolution in the complexion of local politics that exists, like the district system itself, to this day.[1]

The district system saved and even institutionalized racial politics in Richmond.[2] In mandating majority-minority districts (that is, districts made up of predominantly African American voters), Washington created the possibility of an Atlanta-like governing alliance between Black political leadership (with little economic power) and the white business community (with both political and economic power) to advance city interests.[3] But this regime failed to emerge in Richmond in any stable sense during the 1980s and 1990s, despite considerable effort. The new governance structure proved ill-equipped to contend with the shadow of segregation. It turned out that Monument Avenue and its Confederate iconography were not the only relics of Jim Crow to survive segregation—poverty, substandard public education, inadequate housing, and exposure to crime came to characterize much of Black life in Richmond in the last decades of the twentieth century.

For many whites in the Richmond metropolitan area (especially outside the city), the ongoing drama, corruption, and dysfunction at city hall in the late twentieth century affirmed a long-held racist contention of the segregated era: Black leaders were incapable of effectively running the city.[4] Black Richmonders, in turn, felt that they had inherited a "hollow prize": a declining city without the resources or power to address its most fundamental problems.[5] If Richmond's African Americans closed ranks during segregation, the urban woes of the late twentieth century challenged their coalition. By the 1980s, Black Richmonders no longer agreed on how to solve the city's problems. Economic pragmatism eclipsed the optimism of the civil rights movement. The fallout from the collapse of the Black governing coalition on the city council in the 1980s also led to searching and at times scathing internal critiques within the Black political community.

As this chapter illustrates, policy failures and political dysfunction reinforced one another, leading to growing frustration with local government on the part of both Black and white residents in the early 1990s. By the next decade, many Richmonders would come to believe that cleaning up the city required political reform: namely, replacing the council-manager model established in 1948 with a strong mayor.

Federal imposition of Richmond's district system in 1977 led immediately to the historic election of the first majority-Black council and first Black mayor. The federal government had already suspended local elections in the city following a legal challenge to the 1970 Chesterfield annexation filed by local activist Curtis Holt, a Black public housing resident. In response to widespread efforts to dilute Black political power following the 1965 Voting Rights Act, federal policymakers spent the better portion of the late 1960s and early 1970s implementing safe minority districts throughout the South, which allowed African Americans to vote free of white interference.[6] The election of Henry L. Marsh III, Willie Dell, Walter Kenney, H. W. "Chuck" Richardson, and Claudette McDaniel to the city council in March 1977 and their selection of Marsh as Richmond's first Black mayor represented a major triumph for civil rights activism and public policy. In this moment of profound hope and optimism, Black Richmond looked to these officials to address deepening problems in their community.[7]

The Black-majority council struggled to meet the challenge of high expectations, as realizing the promises of the rights revolution proved easier said than done. Marsh and the majority-Black council faced stubborn opposition from the white business community, white politicians on the council, and their allies in the press, namely the *Richmond Times-Dispatch* and the *Richmond News Leader*. As the majority council transitioned into power, they almost immediately exercised their political muscle by changing the complexion of city hall. Mayor Marsh's removal in 1978 of the holdover white city manager, William Leidinger, enraged white elites and their media outlets. (The decision also perplexed some African Americans.) By the city council election of 1982, the city suffered the fatigue of years of political fighting, decades of white flight, a declining tax base, and urban retrenchment from the Reagan administration. That year, an African American technocratic, conservative-leaning school principal, Roy West, defeated incumbent Willie Dell, an activist social worker, in the Third District city council race. Four white council members and West, who voted for himself, then elected the newcomer mayor. West's ascension brought an abrupt end to civil rights era politics in Richmond.[8]

West ushered in an era of political conciliation that characterized Richmond politics for most of the 1980s. As mayor (and also as a Richmond Public Schools administrator), West often cooperated with white business interests and power brokers to secure selective benefits for Black Richmonders, especially in the Black business community.[9] The share of local public contracting dollars going to Black-owned businesses grew rapidly in the 1980s under an aggressive affirmative action contracting policy championed by West, with partial support from white leadership as well as Black members of the council. At the same time, West routinely voted with white members of the council on an array of issues.[10] West's election, in many ways, demonstrated that three coalitions were now vying for power in Richmond:

whites and the business community; a progressive African American coalition steeped in the civil rights movement aligned with working-class and poor Blacks; and middle-class African Americans willing to form pragmatic, economic alliances with whites in exchange for material benefits. These groups dominated Richmond politics in the following years.

Significant examples of interracial cooperation and selective economic gains for Black business interests abound in the 1980s. Marsh cited the completion of Project One, a downtown economic development plan launched by city officials in the 1970s, and the formation of Richmond Renaissance, a partnership of businesses and city government to promote economic development, as evidence that the majority-Black council had acted responsibly to save the core of Richmond at a time when, "like most central cities, Richmond was and is in a precarious situation, surrounded by affluent suburbs, in a state which seriously limits the right of a city to tax." Richmond Renaissance, Marsh added, represented "blacks sharing the political power they had gained over many years with the white business community."[11] Richmond Renaissance represented Richmond's best effort at forging a cross-racial coalition between Black elected officials and white corporate interests, modeling the Atlanta-style partnership of Maynard Jackson and Andrew Young.[12] Richmond also embraced a particularly aggressive approach to affirmative action in contracting, requiring city construction contractors to subcontract at least 30 percent of their work to minority-owned suppliers. In this fashion, Black interests could concretely benefit from economic growth driven by white business investors. The Supreme Court shot down this approach in a 1989 decision that struck a fatal blow to the most distinctive policy initiative in Richmond of the 1980s, favored by Marsh and West alike.[13] In *City of Richmond v. J. A. Croson*, the Court held that the historical legacy of racial discrimination was not sufficient reason to justify racial quotas in public contracts.[14] The *Croson* decision effectively closed the door on the primary wealth-broadening strategy favored by Richmond's Black leaders in the 1980s.[15]

Richmond in the late 1980s was unquestionably in social and economic decline. Both Black and white civic leaders recognized the basic facts: Richmond continued to be a declining city amid a suburban boom. Former city manager and council member William Leidinger of the Second District articulated this dilemma in explaining why the city's property tax rate was so high ($1.53/$100 of assessed value). "Richmond is an older city," said Leidinger.

It's like a very large old house. It needs a lot of upkeep and repair and constant attention. That includes streets, sewers, water lines, parks and everything else. Secondly, we have the largest concentration of poor folks in the metropolitan area. Those folks have the largest requirements for social services. They are undertrained, undereducated, underemployed, undernourished and require a great deal of care. [Third], there's a fundamental difference between the way the state shares its revenues between cities and counties. The cities in the state control about 25 percent of the votes in the General Assembly, so it's harder for us to get larger shares of state revenue. How does that play out? In Chesterfield County, for example, all road maintenance, repair and construction is done at 100 percent state expense. In the city, while we do receive state assistance, we have to pay out of our local tax revenues large portions of our own street costs. I'd guess we probably pay half. [It's] more expensive to operate the government in the city than it is in the county.[16]

Indeed, troublesome population, employment, and poverty trends did not bode well for the present and future of the capital city, particularly as adjacent Chesterfield and Henrico Counties and nearby Hanover County outpaced Richmond growth between 1970 and 2016. Richmond's population and employment base declined steadily over three decades—from a peak of nearly 250,000 at the moment of annexation in 1970 to a low of some 197,000 in the early aughts—even as the greater Richmond region's population expanded and employment rose.[17] White flight during the 1970s and 1980s was inextricably associated with the integration of public schools and the ease with which white families gained access to majority-white public schools simply by living in the counties (even while continuing to work in the city).[18]

A Short Political History of Richmond, 1988–1994: Governance without Coherence

By the end of the 1980s, the optimistic spirit of the 1977 political revolution was a fading memory. As the spring 1988 municipal elections approached, Roy West's alliances with Richmond's white power structure withered African Americans' confidence in his governance. At the same time, his strong support for minority set-asides placed him at odds with some of his white allies. Controversies stemming from West's overall leadership style as well

TABLE 2.1. Basic demographics in Central Virginia localities, 1970–2016

	POPULATION (IN THOUSANDS) AND AREA						
	1970	1980	1990	2000	2010	2016	Area[a]
Chesterfield	76.9	141.4	209.3	259.9	316.2	338.5	437.0
Henrico	154.4	180.7	217.9	262.3	306.9	325.9	244.6
Hanover	37.5	50.4	63.3	86.3	99.9	104.3	474.1
Richmond	249.6	219.2	203.1	197.8	204.2	225.4	62.6
Total population	518.3	591.7	693.5	806.3	927.2	994.1	
	PERCENTAGE OF POPULATION BLACK[b]						
Chesterfield	11.2	9.8	12.9	17.6	21.6	22.7	
Henrico	6.6	14.9	20.0	24.5	29.1	29.6	
Hanover	17.9	12.9	10.1	9.3	9.2	9.1	
Richmond	42.0	50.8	55.0	56.9	50.1	48.5	
	PERCENTAGE OF POPULATION IN POVERTY, 1970–2016[c]						
Chesterfield	7.1	4.6	4.3	4.5	6.4	7.1	
Henrico	5.4	6.3	5.5	6.2	10.5	10.0	
Hanover	9.9	7.9	4.3	3.6	5.1	5.6	
Richmond	17.4	19.3	20.9	21.4	26.7	24.5	

Source: U.S. Census Bureau, Decennial Census (1970–2010) and Current Population Estimates (2016), via Social Explorer; Decennial Census (1980–2000) and American Community Survey (2010 and 2016), via Social Explorer. Poverty data from 1970 derived from U.S. Census Bureau, *1972 City and County Data Book* (Washington: Government Printing Office, 1972), table 2, items 3 and 64.

[a] Area in square miles post-1970 annexation.

[b] Except for 1970, the percentage of the population that was Black excludes Black residents of Latino origin.

[c] 1970 data not exactly comparable to subsequent dates as denominator is based on total population, not total population minus institutionalized population and persons living in college dormitories, as in subsequent years. Poverty data for 2010 and 2016 refer to the 2008–12 and 2014–18 American Community Survey Five-Year Estimates. (The Decennial Census after 2000 stopped collecting detailed socioeconomic information, which is now undertaken by the American Community Survey.)

as his dual role as a middle school principal also impacted his standing with both Black and white members.[19] When West announced he would give up the mayoral role while remaining on the city council after the 1988 municipal elections, council members selected Geline B. Williams, a white Republican woman from the First District, as mayor. That development raised new questions for Richmond politics. On the surface, little had changed: voters reelected eight of nine council members in the 1988 municipal elections, and again the council consisted of five Black and four white members.[20] But the seemingly improbable selection of Williams to lead a majority-Black council and a majority-Black city underscored the fact that substantive policy leadership from the council had stalled. With the council unable to shape a policy-based consensus, effective power defaulted to the city manager position.

Some Richmonders began to raise fundamental questions about the efficacy of the city's political structure. One concern was that the single-member system compelled council members and candidates to focus on neighborhood issues at the expense of citywide concerns. In a prescient analysis in 1988, political scientist Bob Holsworth wrote, "If one gauged the importance of the issues by what is being discussed in [the 1988 council] campaigns, you would think that leaf collection on Northside and traffic in Westover Hills are the most pressing matters calling for council's attention in the immediate future. Is there any serious discussion of downtown development, of the problems with the 6th Street Marketplace, of declining sales tax revenues and of the Main Street Station debacle[?]" He continued,

> What about poverty? Studies have shown that Richmond is one of the most economically bifurcated middle-sized cities in the nation. There are neighborhoods of enviable wealth. Yet in some areas of the city, the poverty indicators rival that of the worst places in the country. And by now we should be well aware of the crime and despair that normally accompany abstract statistical measures of poverty. But is anyone talking about this? Is any candidate proposing how we might locally or in tandem with the state and national government address these problems? Is there serious public debate about the alternative approaches that might be chosen?[21]

Echoing a widely held view, in a subsequent piece Holsworth added that the "petty bickering on City Council and the personal behavior of some of its members have been a source of embarrassment rather than pride."[22] The district system, critics held, incentivized council representatives to focus on neighborhood-specific issues and municipal services from the bureaucracy rather than to consider broader citywide concerns such as poverty, let alone develop and implement a strategy to address them.

A second, closely related worry was the mayor's role and responsibilities. Because Richmond's mayors were not directly elected by the people but by the city council itself, mayors often did not have experience developing and defending positions on citywide issues or running on those positions before a citywide electorate. Geline Williams's election to the role in 1988 exacerbated these concerns. Williams, a Republican, pro-life, anti-ERA activist from one of Richmond's wealthiest neighborhoods, the West End, had served two terms on the council; she made it clear that she viewed the mayor's position primarily as a ceremonial role and not as the driver of policy. "The [Roy] West years began the trend of downplaying the role of the mayor as a major agenda-setter in the city," warned Virginia Commonwealth University political scientist John Moeser. "That is likely to accelerate in Geline Williams' term." Moeser went on to assess what would become a central fault line of local politics over much of the following decade: the role of the city manager as default policy leader. "One of two things is likely to happen," stated Moeser. "Either we will continue with the city manager playing an increasingly pivotal role in setting the city's agenda, or there will be a growing chorus to change the charter." Added Moeser, "When much of the agenda-setting in the city is coming from an appointed official like the city manager and not elected officials, there is always the question of accountability. There is no direct check on the city manager."[23]

The city manager in question was Robert Bobb, who had been hired in 1986 from the same position in Santa Ana, California, describing himself as an "'I-make-things-happen-and-get-things-done' type of city manager."[24] Bobb's work ethic, take-charge assertiveness, and competency in financial matters quickly won over both white and Black members of the council.[25] For over a decade, until his departure in 1997, Bobb, and not the five mayors and twenty-seven council members he served, was the pivotal figure in city hall policymaking.[26] The city's institutional structure contributed to this predictable result. But it was also in part because none of the intervening mayors had sufficient stature to fill the shoes of Henry Marsh as both leader of a political coalition and architect of a strong, coherent policy agenda. Bobb, in contrast, actively set the policy agenda and often had better knowledge of the details of policy and local government than his counterparts on the council. He was also widely respected personally as a Black administrator with good professional relationships with the business community and other civic actors.[27] Over time, however, some of those relationships caused mistrust: Bobb's critics felt he took his direction from establishment Richmond rather than from elected representatives.

The council-manager model, in effect, prioritized *professional* administrative competence over *political* leadership. This model made it more likely that the basic machinery of city hall would function in an acceptable fashion but less likely that the same machinery could be oriented toward broad political goals such as reducing economic inequality or redressing systemic racial disadvantage. The political personality during this time period potentially best suited for a policy leadership role, Henry Marsh, not only had made his political bones litigating against segregation but had spent the better portion of his mayoralty trying to refashion the city council to address Richmond's intensifying racial problems.[28] Marsh's critics argued that he governed more like a lawyer than a politician; nonetheless, Marsh remained the most obvious candidate to fill the role of a strong, policy-driven mayor and he decried the lack of leadership provided by his successors.[29] Yet while Marsh continued as an active and influential council member as well as a practicing lawyer, he could not muster the five needed votes to regain the mayoralty, so long as West held the Third District seat. In the end, Marsh left the city council after his election in 1991 to the Virginia Senate, where he served until 2014.

In the absence of strong mayoral leadership, Bobb frequently stepped into the void with policy proposals, many of which aimed at creating a more favorable environment for business investment. The most systemic effort to generate a sustained citywide policy strategy in his tenure was the "Richmond Tomorrow" strategic initiative, formed by the city council on Bobb's recommendation in 1988.[30] Five task forces including representatives from the civic, business, and government sectors provided recommendations in the areas of municipal finance, economic development, education, human services, and regional relations, informed by the expectation that improving city services and quality of life would "depend largely upon the future *management of our financial resources rather than the growth of such resources.*"[31] The final recommendations emphasized finding ways to reduce fiscal strain without raising already-high real estate taxes though the regionalization, elimination, or privatization of services, as well as through improved human resources and fiscal management. The wide-ranging final report identified a total of sixty-six strategies across the five major policy areas, including giving school principals more autonomy, creating "neighborhood-based delivery systems" for social services, encouraging the rehabilitation of housing units through tax incentives, and beginning to "aggressively package and market Richmond's place in history, including the Civil War and the city's role in the early development of Black entrepreneurship."[32] A ten-person steering committee appointed by the council guided the entire effort, with over 130 additional residents participating on one of the task forces.

Altogether the Richmond Tomorrow initiative laid out a substantial, pragmatic agenda that helped inform policy development in Richmond in the 1990s and beyond. It also showed that the council-manager system, at its best, was capable of articulating a holistic strategy for the city and could do so in a participatory manner that invited community engagement. However, it failed to be the "turning point for our city" that a pleased Henry Marsh envisioned when the city council received the report in June 1991. All of the strategic challenges identified by the report—"a high crime rate, the negative image of the school system, higher taxes than the surrounding counties, decline in the downtown retail core, scarcity of land, and a lack of a unified, positive city image"—would persist in the city for the rest of the decade and beyond.[33]

As city manager, Bobb well understood the adverse circumstances facing the city and periodically challenged existing regional arrangements. The closure of long-standing downtown shopping landmarks Thalhimers and Miller & Rhoads, along with mounting woes at the 6th Street Marketplace, symbolized a sense that downtown Richmond was dying—at the same time suburban Richmond was booming. Recognizing this dynamic, Bobb stated in late 1992 that for the city to flourish, "we need a plan for the city equivalent to the Marshall Plan, and we need to focus on the revitalization of the neighborhoods." Bobb took his case directly to the counties, calling for a tax-base sharing arrangement "so that we can eliminate the need to compete between localities."[34] Not surprisingly, officials in the suburban jurisdictions showed no interest in such resource sharing.

By the late 1980s, then, Richmond's political structure was already subject to serious criticism. The city's most enduring policy concerns were widely recognized. These included the city-county divide, the question of regional cooperation, concern with entrenched poverty and inadequate employment opportunities in poor neighborhoods, the condition of Richmond Public Schools, downtown economic development, the living conditions of public housing communities, provision of adequate social services, and crime. To reexamine the political history of Richmond's recent decades means confronting the fact that most of these problems have persisted, despite their being widely recognized by city leaders of all stripes.[35]

Naming the city's problems was far easier than developing effective and enduring strategies to overcome them. For starters, marked divisions remained in the city's African American political community. One wing consisted of more conservative-leaning African Americans such as Roy West and Leroy Hassell (a West ally who served as chair of the Richmond School Board, then an appointed body). Hassell, a Harvard Law School graduate, criticized

Marsh (and others) for attempting to run Richmond simply as a "Black city."[36] A second prominent wing consisted of the remaining members of the Marsh coalition—Marsh, Chuck Richardson, and Walter Kenney, all of whom remained on the council—as well as a young Baptist minister who had already served as school board chair and was increasingly seen as a potent political force on the Southside, Rev. Dwight C. Jones.[37] Finally, Black nationalists also emerged as an increasingly powerful political voice, including the talented lawyer Sa'ad El-Amin, a Yale Law School graduate who had moved to Richmond during the civil rights era, and later the young field secretary of the Virginia NAACP, King Salim Khalfani. El-Amin and Khalfani found in Richmond plenty of targets for their critiques of white supremacy. El-Amin reserved particular scorn for African American politicians perceived as collaborating opportunistically with whites to advance their own political interests. Black nationalist criticism of established Black leaders exemplified a growing trend in Richmond politics—grievances within the Black community that might have been aired privately during the heyday of the civil rights movement were more frequently aired openly in the 1990s.

No one knew the fractures in Richmond's body politic like the Black press. In 1992, a new publication emerged in Richmond premised on the idea that African Americans had a distinct political identity and set of interests that Richmond's white newspapers systemically disparaged. Raymond Boone returned to Richmond from a position teaching journalism at Howard University and launched the *Richmond Free Press*, a weekly free newspaper emphasizing detailed reporting on city hall, along with editorial commentary from a Black perspective. From day one, the newspaper enjoyed the support and commanded the attention of Black (and before long, white) political leaders. During the 1960s, Boone had edited the *Richmond Afro-American* and worked closely with the Crusade for Voters and hence maintained deep connections to Richmond's Black political community. Boone was also closely allied personally with Wilder, though his editorials typically staked out a more unabashedly progressive position. Columnists for the paper initially included Preston M. Yancy, a widely respected professor at Virginia Union University who articulated a mainstream progressive analysis of local politics, and A. Peter Bailey, a Black nationalist and former associate of Malcolm X who consistently made appeals for Black economic empowerment. A yet wider range of views found expression on the letters page, including from regular correspondent Sa'ad El-Amin. The *Free Press* succeeded in reinvigorating robust political debate in a city often skeptical of political actors.

In its inaugural issue in January 1992, the paper published a statement of purpose observing that "Richmond, long stagnated in the information and ideas department by a monopolistic daily press, desperately needs a strong gust of fresh air to vigorously fan the expression of ideas about public policy and, in the process, to encourage wide-opened, uninhibited debate.... The *Free Press*," the statement continued,

> will not shy away from the hard problems—including racism, holding politicians (black and white) accountable to the people, and what needs to be done—immediately—to revitalize Downtown Richmond.
>
> The *Richmond Free Press* believes that the cause of racial justice can be served best if society has a better understanding of the entire complex picture of race relations (the good and the bad, the facts and the distortions, yesterday's mistakes and today's solutions). The *Free Press* will focus reliably on the status of racial justice in Richmond.... The result, we believe, will be a Richmond armed with enlightenment and, thus, in a better position to build a brighter future for our city.[38]

The paper successfully established itself as a prime venue not only for journalistic coverage of city hall but for passionate debate among Black political and civic voices about Richmond politics. Notably, also in 1992, the daily *Richmond Times-Dispatch* made one of its staff reporters, Michael Paul Williams, the newspaper's first Black columnist.[19]

The fracturing of Black political coalitions inhibited prospects for progressive political change. As poverty deepened in Richmond, the city's Black activist community came to view putative interracial coalitions as a double cross. Even Richmond's Black middle class was exhausted by the continuity of institutionalized bigotry. Some also noted that the class divide in Black Richmond tended to undermine needed solidarity. In a 1990 interview, Reverend Jones of First Baptist Church of South Richmond offered a critique of the disengagement and political apathy of the Black middle class:

> The Reagan years sent signals that the days of fighting for social justice were past, that it's all right not to care about poor people, about the hungry and to cut funding for programs that serve them because the truth of the matter is if these people wanted to work they could work. And oddly enough, that mentality seeps into not just white middle class but also black middle class. And an insensitivity begins to build, and individual prosperity begins to cloud the issue of our responsibility to our fellowman. We become complacent.... So our

goal today is to continue to sensitize those who have been able to escape that they are not free, that black people must take their destiny in their own charge. If we're going to do something about teen-age pregnancy, drugs, the high rates of blacks in prison, the tragic mortality rate of our people, it's going to require all of us together in some consensus about our destiny. We've got to come back into Blackwell [a low-income neighborhood on the Southside] and work.[40]

In Jones's analysis, class divisions within the Black community directly hampered the possibility of mustering a strong response to long-standing community problems—with the consequence that the community continued to suffer.

The declining hope of sufficient Black political unity to sustain a strong policy agenda over time would raise this question: Could progressive Blacks ally with progressive whites in Richmond to push forward a shared progressive agenda? At the start of the 1990s, relatively few people saw this as immediately likely. Bob Holsworth, who had written a book about the antinuclear peace movement in Richmond in the 1980s, faulted the city's white progressives for failing to engage the political arena. "The absence of an organized progressive presence in the electoral arena impoverishes the political debate in the city and makes the goals of the progressive groups themselves more difficult to achieve," wrote Holsworth in 1988.[41] This critique of weak progressive organizations in Richmond (outside the traditional civil rights groups) would remain valid for decades to come, but by the end of the 1990s multiracial political alliances in Richmond had begun to emerge, with tangible impact.

The first step toward effective interracial political coalitions manifested during the elections of 1990. Richmonders elected four new council members, with John Thompson replacing the retired Leidinger in the Second District; Carl Prince, associate minister at Dwight Jones's First Baptist Church, defeating McDaniel in the Eighth District; William Golding replacing Carolyn Wake in the Ninth District in an open seat race; and Charles Perkins defeating Joyce Riddell in the Fourth District. The racial composition of the council remained unchanged (five Blacks, four whites), but John Thompson, who was white, cast the deciding vote to elect Walter Kenney, a member of the original Marsh coalition, over the incumbent Geline Williams on a 5–4 vote (tallied as 6–3 officially after Perkins switched his vote).[42]

Thompson surprised some Richmonders with his vote. Both the *Richmond Times-Dispatch* and the *Richmond News Leader* endorsed Williams, dismissing Kenney as Henry Marsh's "loyal footman."[43] But Thompson himself represented something new in Richmond politics—a willingness on the part of some white leaders to begin to thaw the frozen racial politics of the 1980s. Both the Teams for Progress (targeting predominantly white voters) and the Crusade for Voters (targeting primarily Black voters) endorsed Thompson, and he had made a point of attending Election Night victory celebrations with Marsh and Kenney. But eventually Thompson came to realize just how entrenched racial politics were in Richmond—his effort to negotiate a compromise in a racially charged debate about designating Church Hill a historic district (favored by white residents, opposed by Blacks) ended in failure. Thompson stated later that fall that serving on the council had made him more aware that "sensitive issues impact one race in a different way than they do the other. . . . Black-white politics are very much alive. It's more true than I realized going into this."[44] Thompson served just one term on the council, but subsequently the Second District continued to show a willingness to elect officials who sided with the Black community on at least some key issues, most notably future mayor Tim Kaine.

Efforts to develop interracial political coalitions continued to grow. Mary Tyler Freeman Cheek, a daughter of a prominent West End family with deep roots in patrician Richmond, evolved into an increasingly progressive activist tackling issues of poverty and housing in the city. Cheek founded the Richmond Urban Forum, a social club for Black and white leaders to gather for dinner, as well as the Better Housing Coalition, which would grow into an important community development organization focused on affordable housing production.[45] At the more grassroots level, the organization Hope in the Cities gained traction in the 1990s. The nonprofit began paying deliberate attention to recognizing Richmond's painful past, dating to slavery, as a strategy for building trust and relationships across racial lines.[46] Even so, these efforts paled against the continuing reality of extreme polarization between affluent and impoverished Richmond and the consequent racial divide.

Drake versus Crupi: Contrasting Analyses of Richmond's Predicament

By the early 1990s, very few Richmonders believed that the outcome of municipal elections would change the city's fortunes or begin to address Richmond's most persistent problems. Declining voter turnout in the city reflected this lack of public confidence. Turnout in 1992, although sharply up from the 1990 elections, still was nearly 30 percent lower than turnout ten years earlier.[47] More importantly, internal voices within the Black political community began questioning why Black political leadership had not led to stronger policies benefiting all African Americans. Richmond, though, was about to put itself on the proverbial couch in several scathing analyses of the city's political identity.

No one better encapsulated these hyper-racial frustrations in the early 1990s than Virginia Commonwealth University professor Avon Drake. In the spring of 1992, Drake, an African American political scientist, published an in-depth critique of Black political leadership in the *Richmond Free Press*. "Black leaders," wrote Drake, had been allowed "to define the interests of the black middle class to be representative of the overall black community. Consequently, African-American leaders have been ideologically wedded to a black progress strategy of affirmative action and minority set-asides without fully considering the differential impact that it has on the life chances of the more advantaged blacks vs. those who are lower income or locked in inner-city poverty."[48] Drake cited data showing that Richmond's set-aside program, despite all the attention it received, had limited impact on the broader community, with just two firms capturing roughly half of total contracts. In fact, the advent of Black political control over local politics had done little to help the Black poor, Drake argued.

> Richmond has traditionally had a dynamic black middle class. It benefitted significantly from the Civil Rights Movement. The ascendancy of blacks in local politics in the late 1970s helped to expand the opportunity structure for middle class African-Americans. But the ability of black leaders to racially redistribute public benefits did not significantly help poor inner-city blacks.
>
> Today Richmond politics is driven by a majority black city council, a black mayor, a black city manager, a black school superintendent, a black police chief, several strategically located black delegates and senators in the state legislature and a capable African-American governor with numerous African-Americans in his administration as department heads or cabinet members.
>
> Still, the plight of poor inner-city blacks has worsened while that of the more advantaged blacks has improved. This view can be corroborated by examining patterns of city employment (high paying administrators vs. lower paying non-professionals); effects of Richmond's set-aside plan (later ruled unconstitutional by the Court of

Appeals and the Supreme Court) and black demographic patterns (flight of stable working class and professional families to the counties and border suburbs).⁴⁹

Black leadership, critics held, were beginning to behave like white leadership—they demonstrated political favoritism, failed to address the concerns of impoverished African Americans, and, more generally, proved ill-equipped to come to terms with the city's more pressing issues—ranging from public schools to public policy.

Drake, who later published an expanded version of this analysis, *Affirmative Action and the Stalled Quest for Black Progress*, coauthored with Bob Holsworth, went on to call for "thoughtful African-Americans in Richmond to begin formulating new and more effective political arrangements between the black professional and leadership class and the broad rank-and-file in our community. It is necessary for the more advantaged blacks in Richmond to cease mistaking their own interest for those of all African-Americans here." He suggested that if future debates about policy initiatives set clear expectations about who was to benefit, in particular policies' impact on "various sectors of the black community," that would "contribute to the political education of the African-American community and generate more informed debate by a wider spectrum of black opinion."⁵⁰

In order to make change, Drake called on Black political leadership to identify and adopt "racial advancement strategies . . . designed to help uplift those in our community most in need." Echoing critical comments made by Dwight C. Jones about the Black middle class (see above), Drake added, "The time has come for black leaders and the black middle class in metropolitan Richmond to see their own future as being directly related to the status of the larger African- American community. It is a moral imperative and a political necessity."⁵¹

Black political leadership was not alone in receiving criticism. White leadership had also failed to address Richmond's deepening problems. In a parallel analysis, white corporate leaders in Richmond increasingly expressed frustration about the direction of the city and region. This perspective, however, framed Richmond's problems, in particular the lack of regional cooperation, as a failure of elite mobilization. Dr. James Crupi, a Texas business consultant hired by the white business community, crystallized these concerns in an influential 1993 report. Colloquially known as the "Crupi Report," this analysis had a substantial and lasting impact on the way many Richmonders, especially whites, thought about the city and region's problems.

Formally titled *Back to the Future: Richmond at the Crossroads* Crupi's report focused on fifty interviews with business leaders (mainly chief executives) in greater Richmond over a two-week period in December 1992 and January 1993. These leaders reflected on where Richmond likely would be relative to where it should be five years hence, commented on the state of business and political leadership in Richmond, and compared Richmond with other southern cities. Crupi did not identify by name any of the interviewees in his analysis, but the short, declarative report struck a nerve with the business community and had an outsize impact on local political imagination.

Crupi offered a direct and blunt critique of Richmond's local business culture and its failure to constructively engage in local politics. He held, "What is striking about Richmond is that the business community's almost total agreement on the nature of the challenges facing the metropolitan area is surpassed only by its inability to reach a consensus on how to solve its problems and take advantage of its opportunities." Crupi went on to describe the business community as in transition, between an "older generation . . . whose influence over the city's political process was pervasive" and a newer group that lacked political influence yet nonetheless were "increasingly frustrated with traditional Richmond ways; ways that emphasize political caution and social activity over results." Business leaders in Richmond had failed "to accept that economic development is a political responsibility," a responsibility that had been evaded "in order to avoid a political confrontation that might be cast in racial terms."[52] Crupi had, in essence, articulated the frustrations of more forward-thinking business leaders at the time with an older, more conservative mindset. Rather than withdraw from the city and its challenges, Crupi called for Richmond's business elite to reengage and act with greater intentionality, including cooperation with Black elected officials.

Yet even as he challenged Richmond's conservative climate, Crupi invoked stereotypical views about Richmond's African American political leadership. He also, as business communities often do, viewed government as the distinctly junior partner in local economic development. Black political leaders, wrote Crupi, "lack the economic and business skills of their predecessors" and found themselves "presiding over a political 'island' in economic and social decline." The city council under the ward system had resulted in "fragmentation that shows itself as constant infighting over the future of the city." Crupi then went on to describe the eclipse of the city by its suburban neighbors and observed that "there is little sense of community unity as a metropolitan area and almost no cooperation on such critical regional issues as water, the environment, government services, or mass transit." He further warned that the city was losing ground to other regional competitors like Jacksonville and Raleigh/Durham. But, Crupi said, "There is a growing realization [among business leaders] that somehow old formulas don't work and that the alternative to trying to change is worse." These leaders were "baffled by the lack of regional government cooperation, puzzled by the lack of a compelling community vision, perplexed by the scarcity of an organized effort to solve community problems and capitalize on economic development opportunities, frustrated by the lack of political leadership in the city, and determined to tackle the increase in crime."53

Crupi went beyond critiquing Richmond's political paralysis. He further held that the business community and its prevailing culture were significantly responsible for Richmond's relative failure to progress. First, Crupi argued that Richmond's business culture proved resistant to change because of its attachment to tradition and history; further, "there is no compelling picture of Richmond's future and certainly no sense of urgency." Rather, the "status quo is recognized to the point where it becomes a virtue." Second, Crupi wrote that the "business style of conventional Richmond is aristocratic, conservative, genteel, and reserved." Those who were "out-front" leaders were like a nail sticking out that would get "hammered down." The emphasis on politeness and avoiding confrontation made direct communication difficult. Crupi also faulted the business community for its shadowy presence in government and for not using government as a tool to enhance economic development; what was needed was "more of a 'can do' attitude by the business community. It needs to believe that it can get things done and that getting things done is expected of the business leadership." Third, Crupi argued that business leaders were "well connected, but not well-coordinated." But, in his estimation, they were also out of touch. Fourth, the business community repeatedly critiqued the political leadership in Richmond as being fragmented and inefficient yet ignored the fact that the business community itself was fragmented rather than organized on coherent regional lines. Fifth, the business community lacked diversity that might be commensurate with the city more broadly, and "with the exception of Richmond Renaissance, little social interaction takes place between blacks and whites."54

Indeed, commentary on Richmond's strained race relations were a key theme in the report. While he resorted to large-scale racial generalizations and hackneyed racial tropes to help explain the prevailing dynamic, Crupi made some critical observations about the nature of Richmond's Black and business communities. African American leaders, he held, tended to interpret problems "in light of their social consequences," owing to their training in education, the ministry, and medicine, and often employed "emotional expression" in communication. White leaders, in contrast, were said to be concerned with "economic consequences," action-oriented, and averse to emotional expression. Hence, Black-white communication remained "at an elementary level" that had "not moved to the next step of social compatibility." Further, whites often had stereotypical views of Blacks, and these views were often less informed by personal interactions with their counterparts and more informed by media accounts of inner-city problems such as "crime, welfare dependency, illegitimacy, and educational failure." Consequently, whites were unwilling to underwrite the costs of central cities and "fear the social underclass threatens to violate or corrupt their children." This in turn left cities with poverty-related "social costs not experienced by the counties." These were the types of problems that impinged upon both racial reconciliation and the urban difficulties that defined much of Richmond.[55]

Despite the use of stereotypes and generalizations (as well as sparse and opaque documentation), most readers of Crupi's report at the time believed he had accurately captured at least part of the dynamic in Richmond, including racial distrust at both the elite and the popular level. The proposed response, however, did not address tackling the structural problems of poverty or the city's social problems. Crupi treated poverty and related issues as obstacles to economic development rather than as fundamental policy priorities in their own right—in large part because he emphasized economic, rather than political, solutions to Richmond's problems. Crupi concluded by introducing several recommendations aimed at making Richmond more politically effective and enhancing prospects for economic development:

- Create a collective community vision.
- Form a single metropolitan ("Greater Richmond") business organization to "plan, coordinate, and execute its blueprint for the region."[56]
- Create a better organized business community to engage in the political process. "The political structure," Crupi wrote, "needs to focus on running Richmond like a business, rather than engaging in social experiments."[57]
- Address regional divisions and promote regional cooperation through leadership training and by lobbying the state to create regional governance structures, such as new authorities to handle environmental and water issues.

- Pursue "aggressive economic development" focusing on existing strengths, emerging industry/technology clusters, and infrastructure, with an intentional focus on Black business development.
- Address Richmond's "image" problem. The report urged Richmond to create an image to market both to itself and nationally, one based on high quality of life with shared appreciation by the localities for each other's successes.[58]

Crupi also recognized that forces outside of politics and business exacerbated local progress—namely, he argued that the *Richmond Times-Dispatch* often acted as a force of divisiveness. He stated, "Richmond is not perceived as having a responsible press by the majority of those interviewed for this report. The *Richmond Times-Dispatch* is perceived by many as right-wing and racist." Crupi went on to quote a business leader who asserted, "There is a major difference between what the Charlotte paper does for Charlotte and what the Richmond paper does to Richmond." Crupi called on business leaders to use their advertising influence to make the paper more responsible and attentive to their views.[59]

The report had its limits. Notably, even though Crupi stated that 80 percent of his interviewees cited changing "the structure of county and city government to force regional governmental cooperation" as the one change they would make to Richmond, he stopped far short of recommending any fundamental change in the government structure.[60] Nonetheless, the Crupi Report laid Richmond bare and offered an analysis that resonated profoundly within the city's leadership circles. He faulted the parochialism, vestigial racism, and inherent conservatism within the dominant business culture; pointed to real problems in racial and regional cooperation; and warned that the region was in serious danger of falling behind competitively.

In this sense, the report issued a blunt challenge to Richmond's elite yet reinforced prevailing ideas about the ineffectiveness of government and the presumed ineffectiveness of Black political leaders. (This was ironic, insofar as many of Crupi's themes had in fact been clearly articulated by the city hall–commissioned Richmond Tomorrow project completed two years earlier.) Underlying Crupi's analysis of local decision-making was the assumption that the business elite needed to be the primary force in shaping the region as a whole, including in politics. He offered, in effect, a blueprint for consolidating business political power in Richmond and making it more engaged and effective. In short, Crupi delivered what his (unnamed) sponsors requested:

an assessment of why Richmond had fallen so far behind other southern cities (such as Atlanta and Charlotte) and an outline of what business leaders might do to change course. The possibility of democratic empowerment from below—something like the agenda Avon Drake recommended—simply was not on Crupi's conceptual screen.

In the end, Crupi's business-oriented approach to problem-solving contained significant blind spots. His account is of historical interest not just because of its pointed observations about Richmond's political and economic culture but because it reflected (and expressed) the views of numerous Richmond leaders who felt frustration at the city's path. It also gave rise to heated discussions about the nature of the city. In fact, Richmond City Council passed a resolution protesting "certain comments disparaging black politicians" in the report. But the *Free Press* praised the report, crediting Crupi for "point[ing] out in straightforward language that the 'aristocratic, conservative, genteel and reserved' nature of the white business community was the major impediment to moving Richmond forward in the areas of economic and political progress and improved race relations." The *Free Press* called on offended Black politicians to set aside "misplaced victimization" and use the report as an occasion to "address the hard questions that cry out for attention in our crisis plagued community."[61]

The report did not in fact lead to addressing all of these hard questions, but there was little doubt that it helped set the agenda for the business community over the subsequent decade. It is impossible to understand the many subsequent efforts by the business community to engage with Richmond without reference to Crupi's original and still-remembered report. The report also offers an instructive mirror to the contrasting analysis of Avon Drake: both white and Black civic leaders in the 1990s were dissatisfied with the overall shape of Richmond's trajectory *and* with the nature of leadership offered by (white) business and (Black) political leadership, respectively.

Despite this, a large disconnect remained between Drake's and Crupi's analyses. Crupi envisioned Richmond finding its way to an Atlanta-style coalition between forward-looking white business leaders and "responsible," "moderate" Black political leaders. But Crupi failed to acknowledge, first, that whites (when Marsh was mayor) had rejected such a coalition, and second, that many Black Richmonders, echoing Drake, had now concluded either that such a coalition was impossible or that it would provide few tangible benefits for low-income and working-class Blacks in Richmond. The notion that white business (and civic) leadership might need to commit explicitly to prioritizing the demands of low-income Black residents as a precondition for a thriving city and for forging a sustained partnership between the business and political communities still seemed beyond the political horizon.

Some business leaders took the Crupi Report to heart and brought its recommendations to bear on reform: namely, they developed a strategy of selectively cultivating and supporting Black political leaders who might be willing to partner with whites (and the business community itself) rather than adopt an adversarial stance. The first fruits of this effort came in the 1993 commonwealth's attorney race. Unlike council members, the commonwealth's attorney (chief prosecutor) was elected in a citywide race. The incumbent attorney, Joseph (Joe) Morrissey, was a charismatic white man who had built strong support from Black constituencies. But Morrissey had repeatedly attracted controversy for his conduct in the office, including a courthouse brawl with attorney David P. Baugh.[62] David M. Hicks, a New Jersey native with undergraduate and law degrees from the University of Virginia, resigned from Morrissey's staff in order to run against his former boss. Hicks, an African American, found support from influential white donors such as businessman Jim Ukrop who had tired of Morrissey and his problems, as well as from prominent Black leaders such as Dr. Allix James of Virginia Union University.[63]

In the spring of 1993, a dramatic primary race unfolded featuring a white candidate with strong Black support and a Black candidate with strong white support, inverting traditional expectations about race and politics in Richmond. Hicks printed up two sets of campaign posters: one with his picture on it, which was aggressively posted in African American communities, and one without his picture for placement in the white West End. (Under Virginia election laws, registered Republicans could vote in the Democratic primary, and these voters strongly opposed Morrissey.)[64] In the end, Hicks's well-financed campaign was able to break through, and he won the race with well over 60 percent of the vote; five felony charges unveiled against Morrissey just days before the primary, including alleged misuse of public funds, helped seal the result. (None of those charges ultimately led to a conviction.)[65] Hicks remained the commonwealth's attorney for twelve years and became a key figure in anti-crime efforts as well as in the prosecution of prominent criminal cases in Richmond over the next decade. From a political point of view, the Hicks-Morrissey race demonstrated the possibility of a Black candidate carrying a contested citywide vote, as well as the inherent potential of an electoral coalition of prominent white and Black boosters electing a candidate citywide.

Meanwhile, tensions between the city council and the city manager began building as council members sought to reassert their authority. In September 1992, the city council held a special closed-door meeting with Robert Bobb for the purpose of "[making] it clear to all that City Manager Bobb reports to council—and that it is not the other way round."[66] New Seventh District council member Leonidas Young II stated, "It has been determined that this City Council would plot the course for districts and the city as a whole. We are determined to lead. Mr. Bobb is going to follow our lead."[67] The *Free Press* praised the council for taking the initiative but added that "City Manager Bobb isn't entirely to blame for his [low] assessment of council. Council's actions haven't always been the most enlightened."[68]

In the closed-door meeting, the council pressed Bobb to be more responsive to its requests and to be more respectful in interactions with citizens. The *Free Press* continued over the next five years to be a relentless critic of Bobb, taking him to task for fostering a "high-horse" attitude among city hall employees, for inefficient service delivery, and even for the dirty condition of city hall.[69] But Bobb continued to get strong support from the white business community and from some African Americans. A letter writer to the *Free Press* argued that

> while the rocket scientists on City Council have been busy showboating, bickering about the pettiest issues, taking trips to Switzerland, and framing every issue in racially divisive terms, the city manager has been diligently trying to build partnerships and implement strategies on economic development, housing, crime and a myriad of difficult social problems. . . . While new, enlightened direction by City Council is certainly welcome, a continuation of the Keystone Cops style of leadership and the loss of an enlightened and dedicated city manager seem the most likely results of the executive session [focused on the council's conflict with Bobb].[70]

Commentary of this sort reflected the widespread sense that the city council had become political theater for airing grievances rather than a deliberative, problem-solving body that could be entrusted to effectively tackle the city's problems.

Emblematic of the tension between Bobb and local activists was a long-running dispute between the city manager and the city's Human Relations Commission. The commission, charged with improving race relations in the city, took Bobb to task in a December 1993 letter to the council for repeatedly bypassing the city's minority contracting policy by issuing waivers.[71] At a January 1994 public meeting, NAACP member Alvin Adams ripped Bobb, stating, "This city is tired of you and other members of City Council and your arrogance. . . . It bothers me when we have elected officials and city administrators that come and they have no feelings of remorse for anything that they do. I think that most of us in Richmond are really sick of it." Bobb responded, "It's not about arrogance. It's about facts as they are. I'm not going to change my personality, sir." Marty Jewell of the Richmond Crusade for Voters then replied to Bobb, "You won't change your personality. You just told us that. But something's got to change if we want to bring some sanity to this city. You've got to be a lot more sensitive to the fact that black people feel they have been hurt in the process of our own government."[72] The city council attempted to restrict Bobb's ability to waive the minority contracting requirement in response to the commission's charges, but that effort was shot down by the city attorney in the spring of 1994.[73] Later in 1994, Bobb faced additional fierce criticism from the Human Rights Commission for slashing the commission's budget (while also failing to redress the minority contracting issue).[74]

The conflict between Bobb and the city council proved a major issue in the 1994 councilmanic elections. Again, political analysts saw the Bobb controversy as a by-product of the lack of an elected mayor. With council too fractured to provide coherent policy direction, Bobb was left to fill in the gaps, in turn raising questions of accountability; after two years of concerted effort by the city council to redefine its relationship with Bobb, the sense that Bobb still called the shots persisted.[75] Local political analysts such as John Moeser decried the lack of continuity on the council and worried that with the decline of both the Crusade for Voters and Teams for Progress as potent slate-making organizations, "there doesn't seem to be any political gyroscope on council, setting the direction for this city."[76] Doug Wilder, months removed from the governor's office, echoed this complaint, stating, "Now we have six black people on council, [it] would appear to me, that it doesn't make sense for blacks to have to come down to council and be arguing and fussing all the time about 'we can't get anything done.' Why? It just doesn't make sense. So let's have an agenda. And let's carry that out to the people and say this is what we're going to do."[77]

There was, however, a concerted effort to reshape the council in the May 1994 elections. The Crusade for Voters, on advice from a research committee headed by future legislator Donald McEachin, endorsed no less than five challengers to sitting incumbents, including Shirley Harvey over Mayor Kenney in the Sixth District, Viola Baskerville over ex-mayor Roy West in the Third District, Tim Kaine in the Second District over Ben Warthen, Anthony Jones over Gwen Hedgepeth in the Ninth District, and Carl Prince over Larry Chavis in the Eighth District. Crusade president Marty Jewell stated that there was "a need for a change in Richmond. We feel that this slate will do it better without the old division."[78] Chuck Richardson in the Fifth District was the only incumbent to receive a Crusade endorsement. A *Free Press* editorial cited the Crusade's stance as "further evidence of the widespread citizen dissatisfaction with the sad, embarrassing performance of a City Hall that holds an outstanding record for inefficiency and the lack of vision. It also represents a strong community yearning for city leaders who possess the ability to fully take advantage of opportunities for positive change, not blow them practically every time."[79]

On Election Day, Richmonders elected five new council members, including four of the challengers endorsed by the Crusade: Kaine, Harvey, Baskerville, and Jones, as well as John Conrad, winner of an open seat race in the First District. The 1994 elections thus marked a watershed, with the three most recent former mayors leaving council simultaneously: Kenney (the first sitting mayor to lose reelection in his district), Geline Williams (retired), and Roy West. The results—in a low-turnout election—reflected not only the efforts of the Crusade but also the efforts of the multiracial coalition that had elected David Hicks as commonwealth's attorney in 1993, with Jim Ukrop playing a key role in supporting candidates. It was later reported that one of Ukrop's business entities had directed some $3,500 to support the Crusade for Voters slate in the campaign.[80] Indeed, while the *Free Press* and the Crusade exulted in the result, columnist Peter Bailey was far more skeptical:

> The elections of Tim Kaine, Viola Baskerville, Anthony Jones, L. Shirley Harvey, John Conrad, and the re-election of Larry Chavis were no accident. They were the result of major league politics backed by major league money. . . .
>
> As for [Roy] West, he seems to have gotten a dose of the same bitter political medicine that he gave Willie Dell in 1982. . . .
>
> The election of West then completely derailed the black political/economic movement that was emerging in Richmond. The local daily

noted, "His tenure as mayor turned Richmond away from the precipice." A "precipice," according to Webster's New Unabridged Dictionary, is a "hazardous situation."

That hazardous situation was the possibility of a serious, effective black political/economic movement emerging in this city. Many of the same operatives who backed West in 1982 unceremoniously dumped him in 1994. Black members of the much-heralded new "coalition" would be smart to take note.[81]

Other African Americans, however, welcomed the election results and emphasized that grassroots activism, not just white money, had made the overhaul possible.[82] Despite the attention to the city council races and the presence of the first-ever school board election on the ballot, voter turnout remained low in 1994, a fact emphasized by skeptics such as Bailey.[83] Underscoring the challenges the new council would face, between the election and the start of the new council term on July 1, the city's bond rating was downgraded by Moody's from AA to A1 in response to the council's action to cut taxes and its failure to increase reserves.[84]

Into this new council landscape, Rev. Leonidas Young, following reelection to a second term out of the Seventh District, successfully lobbied to become the new mayor. Young, in a platform statement published in the *Free Press* just prior to the new council taking office, distanced himself from Henry Marsh and expressed support for an at-large mayor, four-year council terms, and greater regional cooperation. "If I were to be given the honor of serving this council and the people of the city of Richmond as mayor, my first and foremost agenda would be to bring all of Richmond's elements—black and white, rich and disadvantaged, old and young, business and community—together for the benefit of all of Richmond," wrote Young. "The unification of black and white, business and community, for a common betterment has been accomplished in cities as once polarized as Atlanta and beyond—and we *can* do it in Richmond."[85] Young's broad comments expressed the hope that it might yet be possible to respond to the kinds of concerns raised by both Drake and Crupi and forge a productive forward path for the city.

Other members of the new city council expressed a desire to turn over a new leaf upon taking office, in hopes of rebuilding respect for the institution. These newly elected officials unanimously endorsed a code of conduct drafted by newly elected councilman Tim Kaine from the Second District.[86] Kaine, a Harvard-educated lawyer with strong social justice commitments, had married Anne Holton, the daughter of former governor Linwood Holton, a liberal Republican who had sent his children to integrated public schools in Richmond in the early 1970s in a major symbolic statement of acceptance of racial integration. Like many Richmond politicians in the early 1990s, Kaine identified greater "regional cooperation" as a crucial goal. During the campaign, echoing Robert Bobb's call for regional tax-sharing, he stated, "Ultimately, there is not a viable city without some form of regional government. But that is not a first-term issue."[87] The first order of business was to get the city council's house in order and begin operating as an effective deliberative body. To that end, the approved code of conduct called for a dramatically higher level of civility:

> To achieve the measure of unity needed to address the challenges that face us today, we will:
>
> - Respect the full range of opinion by our citizens as they seek to guide, inform and criticize our deliberations;
> - Demonstrate regard for one another as we pursue the good of the city, recognizing that difficult issues call forth legitimate differences of opinion that can and should be expressed in a dignified way;
> - Pledge to be informed, dedicated, prudent, ethical, creative and compassionate in addressing the needs of our citizens, with a primary focus on the good of the entire community rather than any particular segment within it;
> - Promote an attitude that all public employees are servants whose primary role is to treat citizens in a courteous, prompt, and responsive manner; and
> - Commit special attention to the needs of our youth, who stand to inherit the community we have made for them and are entitled to a safe future marked by strong educational and economic opportunities.
>
> Finally, we acknowledge that this dedication is merely one of words that will be hollow unless our actions match the commitments we have made here. We encourage the right of every citizen to have high expectations of our performance and we state these principles publicly so that we might be judged against an exacting standard.[88]

This statement reflected Kaine's hope that moral commitment and goodwill could change the fundamental nature of council politics and how the body governed. In practice, it would not take long for the principles to be compromised by personal and political conflicts (followed in time by revelations of high-level corruption). Eventually, most Richmonders (including Kaine) would conclude that not just high-minded statements but structural political reform was a requirement of forging a more effective city government.[89] These questions, and many more, came to define city politics in the 1990s.

3

Richmond City Politics, 1994–2016

The Road to Reform and Beyond

Richmond's political paralysis in the 1990s was not simply inconsequential theater.[1] The city's governance challenges coincided with the descent of much of the city into a period of deep suffering marked by both violent crime and a growing sense of hopelessness and frustration shared by leaders and residents alike. Time and again, promising developments were offset or overshadowed by highly visible setbacks. Ultimately, city hall's collective failure to gain traction on the city's problems gave rise to a veritable political reformation in local government. Seeking to turn the page on years of infighting, perceived ineptitude, and corruption, voters in 2003 embraced a new form of government: a directly elected mayor, to act as the city's chief executive officer. People hoped, perhaps desperately, that a "strong mayor" could reshape the direction and performance of city government.[2] In calling for an executive branch directly accountable to them, voters responded to years of dissatisfaction with the ability of the council-city manager system to address the city's ongoing needs.[3] Changing leadership responsibilities, voters believed, might right the ship.

The new system—enacted following General Assembly approval in 2004—followed a decade of failed reform proposals as elected officials tried hard to make the existing system work, with at best mixed results. In July 1994, the newly elected city council took office with high hopes and a brief season of optimism that fresh faces might produce a new dynamic. The body soon faced several major challenges: the working relationship between the council and city manager Robert Bobb; the council's internal issues, including acrimonious political rivalries and personal problems; and, most urgently, the declaration of a crime crisis in the city.

Crime and Tragedy

Immediately after being selected by council colleagues in July 1994, Richmond's new mayor, Leonidas B. Young II, sought to revive the policy leadership role of the mayoral position. A Richmond native, Young earned a bachelor's degree from Virginia Union University and a master's degree from Drew University before rising to prominence as the pastor of Richmond's Fourth Baptist Church and winning election to the council in 1992 from the Seventh District.[4] Young began his mayoral tenure by launching a major community and police effort to tackle crime. He sought help from the commonwealth's attorney, David Hicks. Both recognized the imperative to address a spike in violent crime, especially homicide, in the previous years. Murders in the City of Richmond rose from 100 in 1988 to a peak of 160 in 1994.[5] As in many cities in the 1990s, crime necessarily became city hall's dominant policy concern. Some local pundits deemed the spike in crime a result of Richmond's location as a convenient way station on Interstate 95 between New York and Miami for the illegal drug trade, with Richmond's public housing communities seen as a relatively easy place for drug transactions. Others attributed the crime to the general effect of concentrated poverty.

At the end of July 1994, Young and Hicks announced a crime summit to be held in August at First Baptist Church and the formation of a panel charged with developing new anti-crime responses. By design, the panel was racially diverse and represented a variety of sectors, including city council and school board members, pastors, judges, college presidents, business leaders, civic organizations, and key administrative officials.[6] Employing a playbook that city leaders would periodically return to in years to come, the commission aimed to focus public attention on a single issue and develop a consensus for coordinated action, to which each of the city's key institutional players (schools, city government, housing authority, legal system, business leaders, and civic organizations) might contribute.

Testimony before the city council and at the crime summit was poignant in its emotion, anger, and calls for more police protection. By the early 1990s, Richmond public housing communities had grown into areas of profound disappointment, and Richmonders came to associate most of the city's violence with its deeply concentrated public housing.[7] The mother of a seventeen-year-old male who had been murdered in 1993 told the council, "You have not lived horror until you approach the scene of the murder of your child."[8] Statistics showed that 71 percent of the victims in Richmond murder cases dating back to 1980 were Black males and that one-third of the city's murders happened in just seven census tracts containing or adjoining public housing communities. The *Free Press* reported that "the profile of the killers strongly suggests that they tend to live for the moment, have an 'us vs. them' mentality, hold life cheap, take offense easily, are survival oriented but have little success in school, church or work, and find easy solutions in violence."[9] At the summit, citizens called for a variety of interventions, most related to preventive measures to address the causes of crime. These included investments "in human services and low-income neighborhoods by improving the quality of life," providing "more job opportunities and economic development in the black community," "mandatory educational and rehabilitation programs for inmates to prevent repeat offenders," "job opportunities for ex-convicts," and "more drug treatment and rehabilitation centers" to address "the lack of bedspace and long waiting lists at existing facilities." But Richmonders also voiced support for more "police protection and visibility in high-crime areas."[10] Overall, the recommendations confirmed the view that crime was inextricably linked to poverty and economic disempowerment. They also demonstrated that many Black residents favored stronger and more effective policing in high-crime neighborhoods.

Proposed solutions to crime in the 1990s nationwide mirrored this opinion. Most cities focused on increased police presence in the highest crime areas. While Richmond's anti-crime panel prioritized attention on both policing and the deeper roots of crime, implementation centered primarily on policing strategies that were easier to organize and seemed to promise immediate results. The city's plan, released in September, focused heavily on increasing police presence in high-crime neighborhoods. In a highly unusual step, Governor George Allen (R), U.S. senator Charles Robb (D), Commonwealth's Attorney Hicks, and Mayor Young announced a bipartisan plan at a council meeting.[11] Specifics included a "full alert" police crackdown in seven neighborhoods, involving periodic stop-and-frisks of drivers, use of police dogs to locate narcotics, helicopters, police on horseback, and the establishment of two "juvenile care centers" for violators of a new teenage curfew. Targeted neighborhoods for the increased police presence included locations adjoining public housing communities or other low-rent, high-poverty areas. Allen pledged to assign sixty state troopers to the effort, and additional policemen were eventually brought in from Henrico County.

The city also committed significant resources. The council approved nearly $1 million in expenditure for the four-month initiative, including $580,000 for police overtime.[12] While some observers were skeptical of this approach, others believed even stronger police action was mandated in the wake of so many murders: *Free Press* columnist Jean Morris called for a citywide declaration of martial law, and school board chair Melvin Law called for deployment of the National Guard in Richmond.[13]

In the initial two-week period of "full alert," Richmond recorded just one murder.[14] But in mid-October, the city was rocked by a tragedy of seismic proportions—a quintuple homicide that seemed to encapsulate the social disaster of Richmond's highest-poverty communities. The tragedy took place in Gilpin Court, the city's largest public housing community located just north of Jackson Ward, where U.S. attorney general Janet Reno had taken a walking tour just weeks before.[15] Twenty-year-old Christopher Goins had impregnated his former girlfriend, fourteen-year-old Tamika Jones. Goins had been raised in an abusive home as a young child. At the age of twelve, Goins moved to New York City to live with his grandmother. After the death of this grandmother, Goins relocated to Richmond, where disturbing events unfolded that resonated well beyond the periphery of public housing and poverty.

On October 14, 1994, Goins entered the Jones family's apartment and murdered five people: three of Tamika's younger siblings—Robert Jones, David Jones, and Nicole Jones, three, four, and nine years old, respectively, and Tamika's parents, Daphne Jones (age twenty-nine) and James Randolph (thirty-five). Goins also shot Tamika nine times, killing the seven-month-old unborn child. Tamika, along with a toddler sister, Kenya, who had also been shot, survived the shootings. Each of the deceased victims had been shot at point-blank range in the head.[16] In the aftermath of the shooting,

Goins and his new girlfriend fled town and remained at-large for five weeks before finally being apprehended and arrested in a New York City apartment. The murders became a referendum on long-standing problems in public housing.

Gilpin Court was, as the *Richmond Free Press* noted in a page 1 headline, gripped with fear in the weeks after the crime.[17] The city kept Tamika Jones under twenty-four-hour police protection for fear of reprisals against the one surviving competent witness of the murders.[18] Gilpin Court Civic Association president Robin Andrews, mother of four children, described an atmosphere where "nightmares dominated by the fear of being killed fill the minds of little children. They hear gunfire, almost nightly, but rarely do they hear police sirens in response. Mothers and children worry about whether each other will live." Andrews appealed to the city council "not to allow the Gilpin community to return to business as usual."[19] She emphasized, "We are not trying to insult anyone or hurt anyone. We [just] want you to know what we are going through and the pain. Our children cannot sleep at night. Our children wake up in the middle of the night, crying, with nightmares, with fear in their hearts."[20] The *Free Press* published a front-page article by Richmond child psychiatrist Dr. Wesley Carter on how to cope with the violence and help youth affected by it. Carter urged "adults in our community [to] begin to spend more time interacting with and paying closer attention to our youths, whether they are a parent, other family member, professional or friend." Carter concluded his article by arguing that "such adult involvement with children will plant seeds of hope, which will sprout when watered by socio-economical changes that we as adults must continue to pursue."[21]

Community reaction to the murders was intense and emotional. A memorial service presided over by Rev. Dwight C. Jones drew 3,000 mourners, who watched a procession of six coffins (including one for the fetus). Mayor Young delivered an impassioned speech vowing "war" against crime and the social forces that led to Goins's actions. "We as a people have been through much . . . as a people we have survived slavery, as a people we have survived the Civil War, as a people we have been through the Great Depression, as a people we have been through massive resistance, we have been through the voting rights struggle . . . but now, we face an enemy far greater than any other. . . . We have determined we will take it no longer! We declare war!" Denoting a conservative strain in his thinking, Young described the enemy as a welfare system that had "seduced our people for too long" by encouraging irresponsible behavior by fathers and financial reliance on drug money and government assistance. Concluding the service, Reverend Jones stated, "We have heard the clarion cry that war has been declared.... In order to fight this war, you've got to put on the whole armor of God."[22] In a pattern that Richmond leaders would repeat numerous times in decades to come in the wake of gun violence, Jones and Young sought both to express collective grief and to use the event to muster the moral and political will needed for a meaningful policy response.

Richmond Juvenile and Domestic Relations Court judge Alton E. Bryant offered a complementary analysis of Richmond's crime predicament in the *Free Press*. Bryant, a white man, stated that "changes in the economy have reduced job availability and really put a squeeze on families.... It is very difficult to have a true partnership in rearing children if a parent isn't able to offer some income."[23] Bryant, who oversaw roughly 1,000 cases a year involving broken families in Richmond, went on to argue that "discord, anger, abuse, tension, drug abuse and depression increase in resource-short households ... and the results can be seen in broken relationships, battering, abuse and neglect."[24] Wesley Carter and Alton Bryant's observations demonstrated an understanding of the systemic connection between traumatic violent crime and economic inequality—an understanding shared by many local Richmond officials but still deeply at odds with prevalent thinking about race and crime in late twentieth-century Virginia. The murders seemed to encapsulate not just the problem of violent crime in Richmond but anomie brought on by the compounding stresses of poverty in public housing developments. Richmond was in a state of triage.

Richmond City Council was not immune to the problems of crime. Almost immediately after the 1994 election, a recall campaign emerged against long-serving councilman H. W. "Chuck" Richardson. Richardson, a decorated Vietnam War veteran, returned from Southeast Asia with a heroin addiction that got the better of him during the 1990s.[25] In early July 1994, Richardson announced he had relapsed and entered a rehabilitation program.[26] Even the African American *Free Press* called for Richardson's resignation. Richardson refused to resign, and the recall campaign ultimately failed when a local jury ruled there were no grounds for expelling Richardson from office.[27] But the shoe finally dropped in September 1995 when Richardson was caught in the act of heroin distribution during a police sting.[28] Richardson promptly resigned office, ending the tenure of the last remaining member of the Black council majority elected in 1977.

False Start: The First Push for an At-Large Mayor

Tough-on-crime initiatives were not specific to Richmond—in fact, these strategies characterized many American cities with sizable minority populations during the 1990s.[29] African Americans, whose communities were often directly affected by crime, were sometimes at the vanguard of late twentieth-century punitive populism. So too were their conservative white counterparts. Crime made for strange bedfellows, and Richmond was no exception.

In 1994, Leonidas Young became one of the few Black politicians in Richmond to actively support Republican governor George Allen's proposal to ban parole in Virginia.[30] At the same time, Allen pledged cooperation and use of state resources for the city's anti-crime crackdown.[31] Over the next two years, Young and Allen forged a working political relationship—a relationship Young hoped might enhance his stature and influence and advance his ambitions to become Richmond's first "strong mayor."

That ambition ultimately helped undo Young. His political downfall was linked to the first major effort at political reform in Richmond since the shift to district elections in 1977: a proposal to create a directly elected mayor, beginning with the 1996 elections. Upon taking office, Young identified this reform as a major priority and made it clear that he planned to run for the position should the initiative pass. In a November 1995 referendum, voters overwhelmingly approved a proposal to keep the nine-member district system for the city council *and* the city manager's position and to add an elected, at-large mayor, who would preside over the council and act as its de facto leader.[32] To become law, however, the proposal needed approval by the Virginia legislature. Advocates of the proposal, including a majority of the city council, hoped the proposal would pass in the General Assembly prior to the 1996 local elections. Allen and many of the assembly's Republican leaders favored the proposal and endorsed (with some modifications) its implementation, beginning with a November 1996 mayoral election.[33]

Opposition from Black political leadership in Richmond stopped the proposal in its tracks. Richmond's legislative delegation, led by now-senator Henry Marsh, as well as most of its Black political class, were highly skeptical of the proposal. Advocates such as Marty Jewell of the Richmond Crusade for Voters worried that the proposal could lead to a dilution of Black political power in the city.[34] Other leaders simply argued that the proposal made no sense from a governance point of view. What role would the mayor actually play? How would the council conduct its business? How would the role of the city manager change under the new system? Citing these concerns, the majority of African American leaders in Richmond, including Marsh himself, state senator Benjamin Lambert, former governor L. Douglas Wilder, former mayor Roy West, the editors of the *Richmond Free Press*, and others coalesced in opposition to the plan during the 1996 legislative session.[35]

The most prominent exception was Leonidas Young. In an impassioned State of the City address early in January 1996, Young made the matter personal. He accused state senators Marsh and Lambert of opposing the proposal because of their personal objections to him and because they feared they could not defeat him at the polls. Both Marsh and Lambert dismissed the mayor's claim, with Marsh stating that Young was "being absurd."[36] The mayor's comments undermined the proposal and heightened already prevalent anxieties about a strong mayoralty by turning the debate into a matter of ego.[37] The legislature eventually shelved the plan, concluding that the matter had not been thoroughly vetted.[38]

Young's stance and his alliance with Allen led to a precipitous decline in his political standing. In 1996, the Crusade for Voters, which still held considerable sway with Black voters, endorsed challenger Reggie Malone in the Seventh District council race. Many of Young's previous supporters chose to remain silent during the race, while the *Free Press* pointedly refused to issue an endorsement for the seat. In the run-up to Election Day in 1996, speculation mounted that Young's reelection was in jeopardy.[39] Young in fact retained his council seat, collecting some two-thirds of the vote and demonstrating the continued strength of his base in the district's Church Hill neighborhood.[40]

District-level support, however, did not lead to an extension of Young's citywide leadership. When Young announced his intention to serve as mayor again, respected one-term councilwoman Viola Baskerville of the Third District threw her hat into the ring. Tim Kaine publicly stated he would not contend for the position but would be willing to serve if selected as a compromise candidate. Negotiations concerning the new mayor took place in late June in private discussions among council members. The decisive blow to Young's bid apparently came when Vice Mayor John Conrad, previously a Young supporter, became convinced of the imperative need for a leadership change. Surprisingly, the council member who emerged as the "compromise" choice was neither announced candidate Baskerville nor Kaine but a lower-profile council member, Larry Chavis of the Eighth District. The council unanimously elected Chavis mayor in July 1996, with Baskerville replacing Conrad as vice mayor.[41]

Chavis, a forty-five-year-old African American native of Richmond who operated a trucking company, was in some ways a surprising choice. He was first elected in 1992 in the Eighth District and had narrowly survived a strong challenge for reelection in 1996 from white anti-crime activist Reva Trammell. Chavis had not played a leading policy role in his four years on council, though he was respected by his peers and had acquired a reputation as a blunt straight-shooter, and as a champion of racial justice and regional cooperation. Chavis's service-oriented approach, moreover, marked a welcome contrast to the ego-laced drama of the Young years. He was also married to the widely respected city clerk, Edna Keys-Chavis. In his inaugural speech as mayor, Chavis focused on crime and promised a crackdown on open-air drug markets in the city. "When they move, we move," stated Chavis, to applause. "And when we move, we move with a vengeance. We kick butt and take names . . . and I don't care which comes first." Chavis went on to add that "the precious fiber that holds our neighborhoods together is threadbare and covered with blood. . . . We have heard many excuses. No more. No more. Our precious city cannot take any more."[42]

But Chavis was largely unable to deliver on the rhetorical promises. Significant financial problems undermined his capacity to serve effectively as mayor—Chavis's trucking company had accrued over $500,000 in unpaid back taxes before it declared bankruptcy in 1998.[43] In time, Richmonders noted that he made fewer public appearances than previous mayors. In early 1998, Chavis announced he would be stepping down from the city council altogether rather than seek reelection.[44]

While Chavis exited city hall with his personal reputation intact, his predecessor Leonidas Young experienced a more dramatic fall from public grace that for many encapsulated the corrupt nature of Richmond politics. In February 1998, Young's former mayoral aide and right-hand man, Joel Harris, was sentenced to prison on cocaine distribution and racketeering charges, following his conviction the previous September.[45] Young followed Harris a year later. In February 1999, Young resigned his council position after pleading guilty to federal charges of mail fraud (two counts), tax fraud, and obstruction of justice.[46] All of this had occurred while Young served both as mayor and as pastor of Fourth Baptist Church. He was sentenced in May 1999 to two years in federal prison. "My presence here today is a result of my own personal misjudgment and, I shudder to say, stupidity," stated Young during his sentencing. Admitting that he had been "dazzled by the heights" of political power, Young added, "I have learned more in the fall that is of value than I learned in the climb."[47] After leaving prison in 2001, Young launched a new ministry in the Northside section of the city, where he served until his death in 2016.[48]

Assessments of the accomplishments of the city council in the mid-1990s by contemporary observers were almost entirely negative. From the Richardson debacle to Young's indictment and conviction, claims of corruption and ineptitude stained city hall. A bitter assessment by Hazel Trice Edney of the 1994–96 council term enumerated a long list in the *Free Press* of "broken promises," running the gamut from failing to confront Robert Bobb and a substandard record on minority contracting to procedural problems. "Near silence has been the hallmark of the current City Council on economic justice issues," wrote Edney, who provided a list of specific examples, such as weak minority business contracting requirements on a $56 million deal with Crestar Bank and lack of progress on promised commissions addressing police conduct, crime, and "'race-specific' economic and social problems pertaining to the city's African American males."[49]

Edney's assessment, consistent with Avon Drake's critique of Richmond political leadership (see chapter 2), again spoke to the view that Richmond City Council had failed to effectively redress inequities and act effectively on behalf of Black Richmonders. Council members also failed the city more broadly. These claims were exacerbated by apparent egoism, corruption, and infighting within city hall.

New Mayor, New Manager

Richmond local government in 1997 was presented with both a new challenge and a new opportunity when Robert Bobb finally left the city manager post to take a similar position in Oakland, California. Bobb's departure left a void at city hall: despite his intermittently rocky relationship with the city council and enduring years of sharp criticism from the *Free Press*, Bobb provided policy continuity at a time when mayoral and council leadership was largely ineffective. In the eyes of the counties and the white business community, Bobb was the only force keeping city hall financially solvent and politically respectable. Bobb's departure and Chavis's abdication as mayor formed the backdrop for the 1998 city elections. The new council would not only elect a new mayor but also hire a new city manager.

The 1998 council elections saw several unusually competitive and close races. Council candidates offered a variety of interesting diagnoses of Richmond's problems. Some of the most incisive analyses came from voices outside the city's political mainstream, on both the right and the left. Below is a sample of their commentaries, in response to a questionnaire issued by the *Richmond Free Press*. Jeanne M. Bridgforth, a challenger in the First District to incumbent John Conrad, stated that

> Richmonders are taxed higher than residents of other jurisdictions in the state on real estate, phone, utilities and food. Yet, we rate our services as less than satisfactory. In short, Richmonders aren't getting value and service for our hard-earned tax dollars. My dealings with City Hall have revealed widespread mismanagement, a gap in the chain of accountability and a lack of responsiveness. This explains why Richmonders are strapped with so much waste. Things aren't so good for a lot of Richmonders. City employees are demoralized and too many Richmonders live in poverty and fear. The decline will continue unless we restore accountability to city government.[50]

In the Sixth District, Sa'ad El-Amin, challenger to incumbent James Banks, wrote,

> I am dedicated to changing our daily reality in the 6th. Reality: Crime and violence, gunfire, theft of anything which is not chained down, filthy and garbage-strewn streets and alleys. Also, drug dealers hawking and selling their drugs in open sight, young men on our streets, disrespecting and threatening residents. More often than not, the police fail to remove these people from the streets. We are paying more to live in the city and we get a whole lot less. We pay far more for the natural gas which we use to cook and heat our homes than county residents who get the same gas we get. A hamburger at McDonald's costs at least 12 cents more in the city than it does in the county. All of these hardships are compliments of a City Council which cares more about West End and county residents than it does about us. We must change our representation on Council.[51]

Community activist Torey Edmonds, one of five challengers to Leonidas Young in the Seventh District, stated,

> I became involved with the East District Initiative about five years ago because I could not tolerate the high incidence of crimes, the concentrated poverty, the educational deficits of our youth and the high rate of health-related problems. I had to get involved in order to do battle with "business as usual." We had program initiatives to address those issues, yet needed someone who was competent and would

not be self-serving, to lead the charge to move these programs to the next level—sustainability! This district needs a councilperson who is present, aware and cares about the concerns of the community.⁵²

Finally, in the Eighth District, Reva Trammell, a self-employed landlord, stressed the problem of crime:

> I have lived nearly my entire life in the 8th. I watched as businesses left because of rampant crime. Deterioration of our neighborhoods followed. And there was fear, especially with our citizens. I became angry. Why should those of us who obey the law be victimized by lawbreakers? I decided to do something about the drugs and the prostitution that were so openly available. And I have, with the help of a lot of concerned people, made a difference. As a council member, I can make an even greater difference. Our citizens need a voice that will combat crime so that new businesses, new housing such as HOPE VI and its other improvements will be possible.⁵³

In short, both successful and unsuccessful city council candidates expressed deep dissatisfaction with the direction of the city and the performance of the city council—just as they had in 1992, 1994, and 1996. White candidates tended to focus on inefficiency and waste; Black candidates focused on the lack of tangible progress on equity. Violent crime also cast a pall over the entire city (while creating a political pathway for anti-crime activists like Trammell).

Election Day in May 1998 produced two razor-thin contests, in the Fifth and Sixth Districts, between activist Black leaders and more moderate Black candidates. Sa'ad El-Amin defeated by fewer than ten votes Sixth District incumbent James Banks, who had been backed by business leader Jim Ukrop as well as by numerous prominent Black elected officials. In the Fifth district, Rudolph (Rudy) McCollum survived a recount to hold his seat against challenger Marty Jewell. Reva Trammell also won her open-seat election against former council member Claudette McDaniel, becoming the first white elected in a majority-Black district since the adoption of the councilmanic system in 1977.⁵⁴

The 1998 elections made history in another manner as well. Tim Kaine, from the Second District, became Richmond's second white mayor since the reorganization of city government in 1977 and the first to be backed by a majority of the Black members of the council. Kaine's selection as mayor was not straightforward: the Richmond NAACP, the Crusade for Voters, and the Baptist Ministers' Conference of Richmond and Vicinity held a press conference calling for selection of a Black mayor.[55] But the most plausible Black candidate for the job, Rudy McCollum, announced he would not be in consideration for the role due to time demands. (Former vice mayor Viola Baskerville had vacated her city council seat upon election to the Virginia House of Delegates in 1997.) The *Free Press* then followed with an editorial that endorsed Kaine as mayor and McCollum as vice mayor:

> We do not buy the proposition that the election of a black person guarantees the representation of black people. Examples to the contrary are in abundance in Richmond.
>
> The better approach, in judging black and white politicians, is to review their records. Records are the best yardstick for measuring what a candidate will do in the future. . . .
>
> The Kaine-McCollum team represents the enlightened, committed brand of leadership that Richmond needs at this time.[56]

The *Free Press* endorsement of a white candidate transcended racial politics, marking a watershed in Richmond's political development. It mirrored John Thompson's decisive vote for Walter Kenney as mayor in 1990. Richmond City Council elected Kaine mayor on an 8–1 vote (with El-Amin objecting) and McCollum vice mayor on a 9–0 vote at the first meeting of the newly elected council.[57]

Kaine's initial challenge was to assuage public skepticism and reassure residents that city hall intended to move beyond the problems of the 1990s.[58] His first significant action was pushing through the hiring of Calvin Jamison, a human resources executive at Ethyl Corporation, as city manager in the fall of 1998. The hire was controversial, since Jamison (an African American) was new to city politics and lacked formal training in public administration and management, though he had facilitated several strategic leadership retreats with the council beginning in 1995.[59] When Jamison's name emerged as the leading candidate, Virginia State University professor of public administration Earl H. McClenney wrote a public letter to Kaine urging the mayor to reconsider the appointment, stating, "The issues facing this city are too complex and urgent for on-the-job training. . . . It would be a travesty for Richmond to lower its standards in hiring a new manager."[60] McClenney's assessment was echoed by numerous Black organizations and leaders over the next several weeks, although Jamison also received expressions of support. In November, the council confirmed Jamison on an 8–1 vote, with

Sa'ad El-Amin dissenting.[61] Subsequent news reports indicated that not a single sitting manager from a comparable city had applied for the position.[62]

In practice, close observers believed that the Kaine-Jamison partnership functioned reasonably well, with Kaine taking on expanded responsibility and acting to some extent as a "strong mayor."[63] Kaine drew on his mastery of the details of city government and embraced an out-front role in speaking on behalf of the city (such as in annual State of the City addresses, following a precedent established by Leonidas Young in 1995).[64] In Kaine's first month as mayor, Richmond established the Slave Trail Commission to officially recognize and physically commemorate the city's painful history with slavery.[65] The council under Kaine also established an innovative community development program, "Neighborhoods in Bloom," that successfully revitalized several urban neighborhoods by concentrating available community development funds into select areas (see chapter 5). In his private legal practice, Kaine won a historic lawsuit in October 1998 filed by the local organization Housing Opportunities Made Equal against Nationwide Insurance for racially discriminatory home loan practices in the Richmond area.[66] (Nationwide eventually settled with HOME for $17.5 million in April 2000).[67] The city's homicide rate also fell markedly during Kaine's tenure and did not again return to the levels of the mid-1990s. (See below for discussion.)

Kaine brought to the position a keen awareness of the regional context shaping the City of Richmond and of the ways Virginia's structure of government upheld and reinforced racialized inequalities in education, housing, transportation, and economic opportunity. For example, at various points, Kaine challenged the status quo by pushing for greater regional transit and a regional approach to public housing provision (see chapters 5 and 6). In his initial bid for office in 1994, Kaine had flatly said that a Richmond isolated from the suburbs was not a viable structure, but by the end of that decade, prospects of structural change toward some form of regional governance model were as dim as ever.[68] As mayor, Kaine entered office with an extensive list of priorities, starting with "educational excellence and youth success" and including "African-American economic development; regional breakthrough in transportation; revitalized neighborhoods; international focus; safety; and city employee empowerment."[69]

While the city made progress on some of these issues during his tenure, such as neighborhood revitalization (see chapter 5), Kaine also found that the mayoralty offered few avenues for meaningfully tackling larger-order regional inequities. Indeed, Kaine soon reached the same conclusions about Richmond politics that many city politicians had before and since: most of the fundamental obstacles to the city's progress could be addressed effectively only at the state level. Kaine left the mayor's office on September 10, 2001, and that fall was elected Virginia's lieutenant governor. Kaine's own view of his tenure echoed that of many other observers: the mayor's office in the council-manager system was simply too weak to have any likelihood of impacting the city's structural problems. Indeed, before exiting the scene Kaine made clear that he favored political reform and establishing a directly elected mayor.[70]

The city's success in reducing crime in the late 1990s—a critically important development for the city's future—merits further discussion. The Richmond Police Department, under highly respected police chief Jerry Oliver, instituted two signature initiatives widely credited with reducing both street-level drug narcotics activity and levels of violence. In 1997 the city launched "Project Exile" in partnership with federal prosecutors. The concept was to charge individuals involved in drug transactions, while also possessing guns, with federal firearms charges. In theory this would reduce the likelihood of bail and increase the likelihood of offenders receiving federal minimum sentences. In announcing the program, then assistant U.S. attorney James B. Comey cited the success of similar initiatives in other cities and said the approach could make a "substantial difference" in reducing violent crime in Richmond. "We expect to indict about 50 of these cases in the next week or so," Comey said to a reporter. "And then we're going to indict 50 more, and then 50 more, and then 50 more."[71]

In 1998, under Chief Oliver, the Richmond Police Department implemented the "Blitz to Bloom" program, building on several previous street-level initiatives. Blitz to Bloom aimed at moving police resources to specific neighborhoods intensively for a set period while also making tangible improvements to the target community's appearance. A description stated that "the idea behind the program is to use as much police force as needed to chase drug dealers away, one city neighborhood at a time, while using building inspectors, trash collectors and other workers to clean up the community."[72] Richmond launched Blitz to Bloom campaigns in several neighborhoods, including Highland Park, Blackwell, Jackson Ward, and Gilpin Court between 1999 and 2000 before facing cutbacks the following year due to budgetary concerns.[73]

By 2000, Oliver and other city leaders received significant national attention for their novel strategies to address unprecedented crime. Homicides in Richmond had declined from 140 in 1997 to 94 in 1998 and 74 in 1999. Oliver stated in early 2000 that to decrease the rate to 20 or 25 homicides a year, in line with similarly sized cities, the department would have to go beyond Project Exile and Blitz to Bloom to focus on prevention. The police chief floated an idea called "Project Embrace," intended to "bring together the police department and a variety of social service and nonprofit agencies" with a focus on reaching "potential criminals" and reducing recidivism among returning citizens. "Right now we are very good at locking people up," Oliver said. "I want to be known for lifting them up as well."[74]

The Project Embrace concept exemplified Oliver's unusually reflective approach to policing, articulated in a series of op-eds he penned for the *Richmond Times-Dispatch* addressing issues such as racial profiling and the proper role of police in society. In a June 2000 column on "Community Oriented Policing," Oliver wrote, "I'm concerned about our increasing dependency on police to fill the growing number of holes in the fabric of our society—to do what other social institutions such as the family, the church and schools rightfully should be doing. . . . Have we as a society allowed our well-intentioned police officers to exceed their legitimate mission?"[75]

Oliver's Project Embrace idea never reached full fruition. In December 2001, he was appointed chief of police in Detroit. Oliver left Richmond one month later, and his departure was widely recognized as a significant loss for the city.[76] Richmond had again lost a capable and productive leader in a key role. Indeed, Oliver's exit and its aftermath contributed to the narrative of city hall failure.[77]

From Corruption to Reform

Problems continued to besiege city hall in the early aughts. Rudy McCollum became mayor in September 2001 after Tim Kaine moved on to state office, with Calvin Jamison remaining as city manager. McCollum and Jamison maintained the work of government, making progress in some areas.[78] Within two years, however, public focus shifted from questions about policy and agency performance to a more fundamental one: Just how corrupt was city hall? In 2003 in quick succession, council members Sa'ad El-Amin and Gwen Hedgepeth were ensnared in scandals that would drive both from office. El-Amin pled guilty to a felony charge related to federal tax evasion in July 2003 and resigned from office; less than a month later federal bribery charges surfaced against Ninth District representative Hedgepeth.[79] Equally serious, in late 2003 revelations of large-scale embezzled funds by a high-ranking city hall employee came to light. The scheme involved an assistant to the city manager creating false invoices to send city funds to two shell companies.[80] The details of the embezzlement scheme, echoing the machinations that led to the conviction of Leonidas Young, helped further people's belief that city hall was rife with systemic corruption. The Hedgepeth matter, too, struck at the heart of Richmond's system of government: the charges concerned illegal efforts to influence Hedgepeth's votes in filling the seat vacated by El-Amin in the Sixth District and in the council's selection of mayor in January 2003.[81] (Hedgepeth was convicted and left office in April 2004.)[82] This latest round of high-profile problems cemented public support for wholesale political reform.

Thomas Bliley, the last white mayor under the pre-1977 system, and Doug Wilder, the former Virginia governor and Richmond native, took up the charge. In fact, it was Wilder himself who famously termed city hall "a cesspool of corruption and inefficiency."[83] Over the course of 2002 and 2003, Bliley and Wilder devised a proposal to establish a directly elected mayor in the City of Richmond in place of the council-manager system. A dozen Richmond-based corporations contributed $5,000 each to support the work.[84] In the spring and summer of 2002, Wilder wrote a series of op-eds for the *Richmond Times-Dispatch* laying out the case for a directly elected "strong mayor," characteristically mixing sharp criticisms of various Richmond officials with a call for charter reform as the path to a better future. Wilder put these criticisms to print just prior to the formal launch of the Wilder-Bliley Commission in August 2002, an eleven-member commission called on their own authority. Few were spared Wilder's criticisms; he charged former mayor Tim Kaine, now in statewide office, with having run off accomplished city manager Robert Bobb to the detriment of city government and having hired Calvin Jamison despite his lack of experience.[85]

Wilder initially envisioned a mayor elected at-large with "appropriate powers to run the city," including the ability to hire and fire department heads.[86] Subsequent discussion led to compromise on both parts of that vision. Following the recommendation of Virginia Commonwealth University political scientist Nelson Wikstrom, direct mayoral power in the administration would consist primarily of the ability to hire (with council consent) a chief administrative officer who would serve at the mayor's behest. In an opinion piece for the *Richmond Times-Dispatch*, Wikstrom argued that it would be unlikely to find a leader who could both lend effective political and policy leadership to the city and successfully run the city's complex bureaucracy. That latter job would fall to a professional chief administrative officer, who would assume powers previously held by the city manager. The proposal aimed to combine the benefits of clear and effective political leadership with the benefits of professional city management.[87] Indeed, the referendum questions placed on the 2003 ballot (drafted by Paul Goldman, the longtime adviser to Wilder and former state Democratic chair who served as a consultant to the commission) called for replacing the city manager with a chief administrative officer to be hired by the elected mayor.[88]

The initial proposals for a directly elected mayor attracted opposition from numerous Black politicians. Both mainstream figures like Henry Marsh and more radical voices like Salim Khalfani rejected the proposal on the grounds that it weakened Black political power. (Khalfani termed the proposal a "power grab.")[89] Wilder initially dismissed the concerns, pointing to the citywide election of Black leaders (including David Hicks) to the constitutional offices of commonwealth's attorney, sheriff, and treasurer.[90] Nonetheless, Black leaders understood well the fragility of Black voting power: whereas Black residents made up about 57 percent of the city's overall population in 2000, they made up only 52 percent of the voting-age adults.[91] Differences in voter registration and turnout rates across district and racial lines, exacerbated by Virginia's draconian policies that disenfranchised former felons, could easily produce a majority-white electorate. Further, the new mayoral position would be a far more consequential position than the constitutional offices cited by Wilder.

When it became clear that the issue would become a major sticking point, the Wilder-Bliley Commission pivoted to accept a proposal originated by political scientist John Moeser, educational expert Tom Shields, and community leader Ernest Brown. Instead of being elected by the popular vote directly, the winning mayoral candidate would need to win five of nine council districts, either in the general election or in a runoff election if no candidate initially garnered five districts. The citywide popular vote came into play only in the event of a runoff: in that instance, the citywide vote, not number of districts won, would determine the top candidates to be included in the runoff.[92]

The five-of-nine district system to elect the mayor strengthened Black voting power in two ways. First, the district maps themselves, largely unchanged since the 1991 redistricting, "packed" white voters into the First, Second, and Fourth Districts. Whereas white voting-age adults at the time of the 2000 census constituted 43 percent of voting-age adults citywide, nearly two-thirds of white adults resided in those three districts. Black adults constituted a solid majority of the other six districts, ranging from 60 percent in the Fifth District to some 90 percent in the Sixth District.[93]

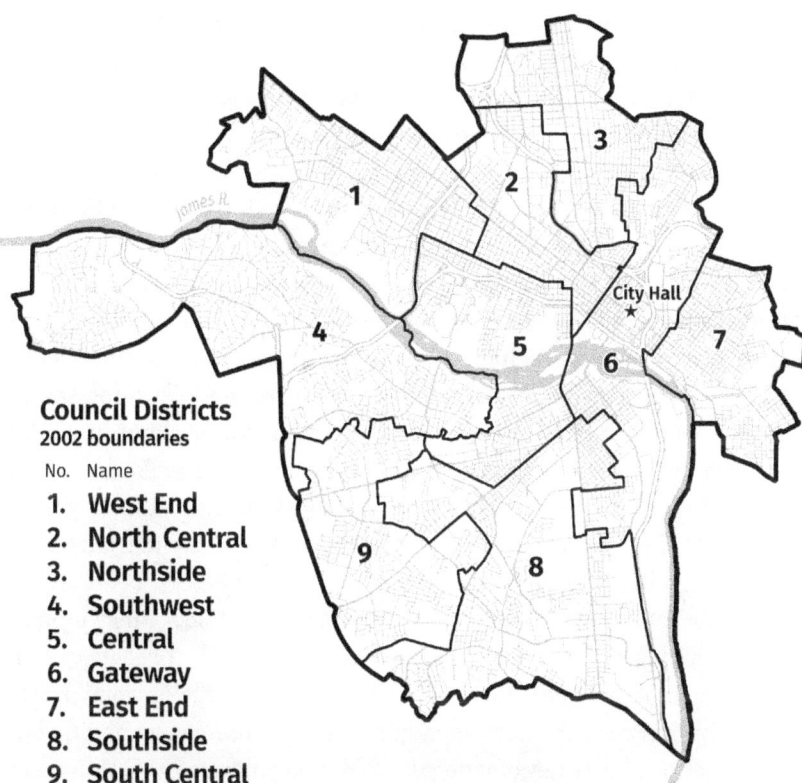

Map 3.1. Richmond city council districts, 2002.
Map by Riley D. Champine of the University of Richmond Digital Scholarship Lab, based on data from the City of Richmond and IPUMS NHGIS (University of Minnesota, www.nhgis.org).

Second, the new system offset the fact that voter registration and actual voter turnout were markedly higher in the majority-white First and Fourth Districts than in the majority-Black districts. First and Fourth District voters in fact accounted for over 36 percent of citywide votes cast in elections between 2000 and 2010—a greater share than the majority-Black Sixth, Seventh, Eighth, and Ninth Districts combined over that same time.[94]

Given that Richmond's municipal elections were (and remain) nonpartisan, with the possibility of large candidate fields, and given ongoing political divisions within Black Richmond, adoption of the district-based system did not preordain a particular result or preclude a white candidate from gaining election. It did, however, all but preclude a candidate from winning the mayoral seat without significant support from at least part of the Black electorate or without appealing to a wide geographic cross-section of the city beyond its more affluent neighborhoods.

The Wilder-Bliley Commission moved briskly to adopt this plan, finalized in a closed-door meeting in the offices of the influential McGuireWoods law firm downtown in early 2003, thereby setting the terms for subsequent debate. In contrast, a competing seventeen-person body established by the city council in late 2002 to also study governance issues was slow getting out of the gate, struggled to build consensus, and was effectively marginalized by the corporate-backed Wilder-Bliley effort.[95] The Wilder-Bliley Commission had earlier declined to include council appointees on the panel.[96] Rather than go through city hall, Wilder in effect went around it by going straight to the General Assembly. A long-standing provision of the city charter that permitted revisions to the charter to be brought to the General Assembly via an advisory referendum made Wilder's strategy viable and ultimately highly effective. The "strong mayor" effort simply did not need buy-in from current leaders at city hall to move forward.[97]

Richmond Times-Dispatch editorialists praised the Wilder-Bliley proposal at launch and offered up its editorial pages for pro and con debate over the next several months. Debate in the *Times-Dispatch* was largely favorable to the plan, with several commission members writing columns in support of the proposal, offering a variety of rationales: building renovator Robert Congdon contended that "great cities have great leaders" and "a committee has never led people to greatness"; businessman Michael Byrne argued that "a mayor elected at large has to act as a visionary for the entire city and can be held accountable for his or her performance"; most poignantly, former school board chair Melvin Law praised the commission proposal for "[respecting] the need for a unified city in a most creative manner," predicting that "if this proposal is approved, Richmond can move into the future with a quality of grace and harmony that can be a model for America."[98]

Discussion in the Black media was far more contentious. Henry Marsh formed a new coalition, "Citizens Alert: At-Large Mayor," to oppose the proposal. The effort won support from a variety of current and former Black elected officials, including Vice Mayor Delores McQuinn, delegate Dwight C. Jones, U.S. congressman Bobby Scott, former mayor Walter Kenney, and current mayor Rudy McCollum. Grassroots criticism of the proposal described it as a vehicle for restoring white business influence over city hall. On this view, it would be easier for business interests to influence, bargain with, or cut a deal with a single official elected in a big-dollar campaign compared with multiple officials elected in largely grassroots, small-dollar campaigns.

McCollum and allies also stressed the city's progress on various issues, including an improved financial position, and argued that changing the form of government would not resolve Richmond's structural disadvantages.[99]

Ultimately, the mini–electoral college system represented sufficient compromise to ensure the initiative's success.[100] Interestingly, while political scientist John Moeser publicly endorsed the proposal as a way to increase accountability to voters, in an October 2003 public forum he cautioned against the idea that the directly elected mayor would be a panacea. Moeser instead called for a broader regional effort to address the city's challenges. The *Free Press* reported Moeser asking, "Is a mayor elected by the people enough? Enough to solve the most pressing problems of this city?" and answering, "Of course not."[101] Moeser called for changes in state funding policies as well as regional cooperation to help the city.

Richmond voters went to the polls in November 2003 to vote for or against creating a directly elected mayor and a mayor-council form of government, following a massive petition campaign organized by Paul Goldman to put the advisory referendum on the ballot. City voters sent a clear message: the proposal garnered 80.2 percent support citywide, while carrying every district and sixty-five of seventy-one precincts citywide.[102] Political scientist Nelson Wikstrom observed that African Americans' criticisms of the proposal were rooted in fears of vote dilution. These claims, though, failed to resonate beyond Black political actors. Instead, qualified Black and strong white support produced a veritable landslide.[103] The proposed charter change passed the Virginia legislature in early 2004, setting the stage for direct elections of Richmond's mayor that November.[104]

The adoption of the mayor-council form of government, particularly its support from the business community, in part reflects the continuing resonance of the 1993 Crupi Report (see chapter 2). The Crupi Report had two central recommendations regarding politics: first, the city should adopt a "strong mayor elected at-large . . . who will look after the best interests of the city and not succumb to district parochialism"; and second, the white business community should reengage in city politics by supporting diverse candidates, including "black leaders cast in the mold of an Andrew Young, Barbara Jordan, Tom Bradley, or Arthur Ashe."[105] Having authority over the city administration reside in a single figure, elected in a presumably more expensive election, would make the task more manageable and predictable than having authority reside in a nine-member council.

Wilder's association with the effort, including some residents' hope that he would run for mayor, lent comfort as well: as governor, Wilder acquired a reputation for fiscal moderation. (His first speech to the General Assembly as governor in 1990, in which he called for limiting spending and rejecting new taxes, was described by one Republican senator as "the best Republican speech I've ever heard spoken by a Democrat.")[106] Potentially handing control of city hall to a "strong leader" who largely shared white residents' predominant critique of city hall as a cesspool of corruption and who was at the same time a historic Black icon was an appealing proposition. Opponents of the proposal, including Marsh, the sitting city council, and several Black community and political organizations, were left to defend the status quo: a losing hand in the Richmond of the early aughts.

While the shift to a mayor-council form of government resulted from the initiative of determined and well-organized political actors, that initiative tapped into dissatisfaction across the city with local government. Specifically, the white business community and many white residents were unhappy with local government; activist African Americans were sorely disappointed at the practical results generated by Black political empowerment; the city manager was viewed critically by a considerable portion of Richmonders, as was the city council itself; city hall had a well-earned reputation for corruption; and the manifest, interlocking problems of violent crime, poverty, low educational achievement, racial distrust, and population decline remained largely unaltered since the political revolution of 1977. Further, there was no plausible avenue for substantial increased resources from state or local government or for an improved arrangement of the city's position vis-à-vis its growing suburban neighbors. Like other American cities in the late twentieth century, Richmonders found that local democracy is easier work and generally does better under conditions of affluence and economic security as opposed to poverty, scarcity, and constant infighting for resources. In view of the seemingly self-inflicted failures of city government highlighted by the local media, it became easy for most observers and participants alike to forget that many of Richmond's problems were a predictable result of statewide and regional political constraints that made the city nearly ungovernable.

Conversely, after years of frustration with local public leadership, Richmonders began to invest a wide range of hopes into the new position of mayor: the mayor might provide a single point of accountability to voters while reining in and cleaning up the bureaucracy; the mayor might articulate a community-wide vision for change and persuade other actors to join that vision; the mayor might be a stronger, more credible advocate for the city in the regional and statewide political arenas, thereby garnering Richmond more resources and a measure of beneficial cooperation with the counties;

and, in the context of resource scarcity, the mayor might develop a strategic plan to marshal and develop over time the city's resources to focus on its most crucial goals and then impose and enforce the discipline needed to execute the plan. The "strong mayor" position, then, provided possibilities for driving much-needed change in Richmond.

To the surprise of few, after the General Assembly approved the new government structure for the city in 2004, Doug Wilder, who had previously denied rumors he was interested in the position, announced he would run for mayor.[107] While four candidates appeared on the ballot, including incumbent mayor Rudy McCollum, Wilder's entry into the race made the result a foregone conclusion. What Wilder intended to *do* with the position of mayor, given the various possibilities, was not entirely clear. What was clear was that Wilder, based on a lifetime of experience in politics, understood the concept of power, and he intended to assert that power to its fullest possible extent once in office.

Enter Mayor Wilder

L. Douglas Wilder is one of the most extraordinary and complex figures in the past half century of American politics and a signature personality in modern Virginia history.[108] The arc of Wilder's political career can be summarized as follows: Wilder, a Richmond native and grandson of formerly enslaved persons, was a Korean War veteran and a self-made lawyer, having worked his way through Virginia Union University and then attending Howard Law School on the GI Bill. He was elected to the state senate in 1969 in a special election and over time consolidated his position as one of the most influential figures in that body.[109] Despite the magnitude of this accomplishment—Wilder was the first Black person elected to the Virginia state senate in the twentieth century—he also held a complicated relationship with Richmond's mainstream civil rights organizations, banking on their support in his statewide efforts but making it very clear that they would not control his agenda.

Wilder also carried a long-standing political rivalry with Henry Marsh, his former law school roommate. Wilder and Marsh's often antagonistic relationship helped define Richmond politics from the 1970s well into the twenty-first century.[110] Marsh, as city council member, mayor, and later state senator, remained a stalwart champion of a progressive civil rights agenda throughout his political career. Wilder, in contrast, remained far less predictable, partly because of his ambition for higher office but also due to his desire to show himself to be personally independent of the Democratic Party and to distance himself from the adamant liberalism of national Black political figures like Jesse Jackson.[111]

By the mid-1980s, Wilder had attracted critics who charged him with placing personal ambition over commitment to any cause or group. But the sheer magnitude of Wilder's political accomplishments in the 1980s—election in 1985 as the state's first Black lieutenant governor and in 1989 as the nation's first elected Black governor—allowed him to brush aside or win over those critics.[112] Wilder remained an influential voice in Richmond and Virginia politics after his gubernatorial term expired, but following his aborted run for the U.S. Senate as an independent in 1994, he did not run for another elected office until 2004. Even in 2004, however—after a decade out of office—the bulk of Richmond voters saw Wilder as a vastly more substantial figure than anyone on the council. Many believed he had the political clout to exemplify what a "strong" mayor in Richmond could do. On Election Day, Wilder won 79 percent of the vote, sweeping the nine districts and assuming a seeming mandate to inaugurate dramatic changes in the city.[113]

Here it is important to consider the context Wilder was addressing: Richmond's power structure and existing style of politics in the early aughts. A detailed examination of Richmond's networks of power published by the *Richmond Times-Dispatch* in the summer of 2005 concluded that a relatively small number of white men—in particular, corporate leaders Jim Ukrop, Beverley W. "Booty" Armstrong, William H. Goodwin Jr., and Virginia Commonwealth University president Eugene Trani—held disproportionate influence over civic affairs.[114] The analysis noted that

> this small, tightly knit group of leaders seems to be at the center of most decisions about what direction the region should take and in the middle of many of the changes happening downtown. . . .
>
> Richmond, like many cities, has been shaped in large part by small, interconnected groups of the very wealthy. They've paid for museums, parks, hospitals and colleges. Often, it is their interest and money that keep nonprofit social-service agencies going.
>
> In some places, their business interests have quietly dictated what city or county governments do. Some critics say that happens in Richmond, too.[115]

Wilder, newly minted as mayor, was seen as a potential counterweight to this long-standing elite network. Wilder had long expressed frustration with the state of political leadership in city hall, especially from Black leaders. The *Times-Dispatch*'s power analysis attributed to Wilder the view that "the pattern over time has been for power brokers to take advantage of a system under which elected officials—the City Council—were relatively weak and instead go directly to the appointed officials who really could get things done."[116] But Wilder also believed that Richmond's corporate community was too complacent and self-congratulatory and indeed complicit in ongoing city hall dysfunction.[117] Such complacency belied good governance, especially given Richmond's failures to meaningfully address a wide variety of issues, including municipal service delivery, public education, and poverty.[118] Wilder thus believed he had a mandate and a responsibility to take on *both* the (predominantly Black) bureaucratic and political structure of city hall and the (overwhelmingly white) business community in order to forge a more functional government that actually addressed problems.[119]

That assessment of Richmond's issues and the need for dramatic change was cogent and, to many Richmonders, convincing. City residents and leaders alike expressed excitement that a political figure with national stature would devote attention to cleaning up his hometown city hall. Even so, many questions remained unanswered about just how Wilder would take on this daunting mission. Some advocates of the new political system imagined that Wilder might act as a strong advocate for the city in dealings with the suburban counties and the state and forge new regional agreements on key issues such as transportation, economic development, possibly even public education. Instead, Wilder took a different path—one that focused on consolidating the position of the mayor, seemingly against all comers, inside and outside of city hall.[120] He challenged the corporate community by demanding renegotiation of what he described as a sweetheart deal subsidizing the city's new downtown performing arts complex, a major priority of corporate leaders, and attempting to cut grants to city arts organizations in his first budget (cuts that were reversed by the council).[121] Strong Wilder supporters in Black Richmond cheered when he pointedly said that Jim Ukrop "doesn't own, nor will he own or buy me."[122]

Likewise, Wilder generally won applause for his efforts to rationalize and improve accountability in the city bureaucracy, sending the message to department heads that they no longer had nine "mayors" but one mayor to report to.[123] Wilder stated publicly that "if you trace every political issue to its core, it all comes back to who controls the money, how it is being spent, and—most important—who benefits and who doesn't." Arguing that city taxpayers received too little return and that special interests had claimed too large a share of city resources without producing tangible benefits, Wilder sought nothing short of a full reset of city government, on his terms.[124] In addition to city manager Calvin Jamison and four of his top five aides, twelve agency directors left city hall in Wilder's first nine months in office, a development welcomed by some but lamented by others who saw a loss of talent and institutional knowledge.[125] Meanwhile Wilder appointed, with the council's approval, the lone holdover from Jamison's staff, deputy city manager William Harrell, to the interim and then permanent role of chief administrative officer, which under the revised charter held formal authority over the bureaucracy.[126] But Harrell understood well the true reality: Wilder himself, fully embracing his charter-designated role as the city's chief executive, was the lead actor in the new city hall.[127]

Initially, members of the city council such as Vice Mayor Manoli Loupassi and Second District representative Bill Pantele sought cooperation with Wilder, reaching agreement on procedural changes to the workings of the city council so that proposed legislation received more vetting before reaching the council floor. Pantele later credited the change with improving both the process and the public perception of the council.[128] But such moments of cooperation were soon overshadowed by a series of skirmishes between the mayor and other branches of government.

The very first budget process under the new system of government, in fact, illustrated Wilder's determination to be the dominant actor in city hall. (It also highlighted remaining ambiguities in the city charter following the change in form of government.) Wilder's FY 2006 budget proposal, including a five-cent drop in the real estate tax from $1.38/$100 to $1.33/$100, had zeroed out numerous "non-departmental" grants to organizations outside city hall, including payments related to past economic development projects as well as a variety of nonprofit organizations. His proposal also cut $5.5 million from Richmond Public Schools' budget request. City council members noted that some of these cuts were actually contractual obligations, and hundreds of community members attended budget hearings in early May to demand restoring funding to schools and to the nonprofit and social service organizations that helped schools meet the demands of daily life. By mid-May, the council had reached a set of amendments to restore the school and nondepartmental funding, assisted in part by a 1.5 percent across-the-board cut to city agencies' operating budgets and adding a requirement that city employees contribute to the retirement system. Manoli Loupassi, vice mayor and council leader and a Wilder ally, praised the agreement, stating that Wilder was correct to at least raise the question regarding the nondepartmental expenditures. The mid-May budget agreement even included a $25,000 raise for Mayor Wilder.[129]

That apparent agreement was short-lived, however. Wilder (after making it clear he had not asked for and would not accept a raise) wrote a sharply worded letter to the council attacking its amendments for cutting funds for social services and the police as well as adding the required employee contributions to the retirement system, to the astonishment of Loupassi and the anger of others on the council. Council members responded with another set of amendments that scrapped the employee contribution but imposed significant cuts on the mayor's office and canceled a plan to relocate the mayor's office to the seventeenth floor.[130] The additional amendments led the council to schedule a special meeting for May 31, the last day before the body was required to adopt a balanced budget or else have the mayor's proposal be adopted as originally presented. Wilder first argued that he would be the sole judge of whether the council had in fact balanced the budget (a position undercut by his own finance director, who stated that the council had done so) and then argued that adopting the budget at a special meeting rather than at a regular meeting of the council violated the city charter—a claim that city attorney Norman Sales rejected. Citing Sales's opinion, the council adopted the amended budget on May 31.[131]

Wilder continued to insist that the budget was invalid and chief administrative officer William Harrell stated on June 1 that he intended to follow Wilder's initially proposed budget. That stance created a procedural impasse, since, to take effect, the law required the approved budget to be certified by both the city clerk and the chief administrative officer. City clerk Edna Keys-Chavis certified the council-approved budget, but Harrell did not.[132] Over two tense weeks, council leaders prepared to take Wilder to court to resolve the matter; at the same time, Wilder, while insisting he would prevail in court, also sought to reopen negotiations over the budget. Those negotiations ultimately led to a deal on June 13 by which the administration would introduce on July 1 a series of negotiated amendments to the May 31 budget, including restoring positions in the mayor's office, to be approved by the council.[133]

In short, what might have been a relatively routine set of budget negotiations instead escalated to brinkmanship, narrowly averting formal legal action. That was, some believed, the entire point. At this early stage in the new governing model, numerous council members, including Loupassi, Pantele, Ellen Robertson, Jackie Jackson, and Delores McQuinn, sharply criticized Wilder's actions, as did members of the school board. They believed that the city was still a democracy and not under the "rule of 'one man.'"[134] Widely read *Richmond Times-Dispatch* columnist Mark Holmberg, while stressing the positive potential of Wilder and the strong mayor system, commented that the city did not need Wilder to become a "Lone Ranger."[135] Other veteran observers of Virginia politics such as Larry Sabato of the University of Virginia suggested that no one should have been surprised: "If you want to elect a committee chairman who gets along with everyone and who is conciliatory, you don't elect Doug Wilder."[136] The die was cast.

Wilder's more promising policy steps—such as the ambitious "City of the Future" initiative that sought to refurbish or rebuild fifteen city schools by borrowing against future tax receipts—were largely overshadowed by the continuing practice of confrontation.[137] In the fall of 2006, Wilder weighed in on several city council races, saying, "There are Council members who just don't understand their role. They think it is to oversee me and the administration." That statement drew a rebuke from the *Richmond Times-Dispatch* editorial board, which opined that "if members of the City Council see part of their responsibility as checking—and checking up on—the administration, they seem to have a pretty good grip on one of their major responsibilities to the public."[138]

Undaunted, in 2007 Wilder took on not just individual council members but the council as an institution. He moved to fire the council's legislative staff on grounds they had been improperly hired; fifty-four council-hired staffers were told to reapply for their jobs or face dismissal.[139] One staff member who refused was in fact terminated.[140] The other staff members eventually kept their jobs after the state court ruled against Wilder following legal action by the council, but conflicts of this nature led to a poisonous atmosphere inside city hall.[141] For its part, the city council also sought to exert its power by refusing to confirm Wilder's preferred choice for the key chief administrative officer role, Harry E. Black, in May 2007.[142] As detailed in chapter 4, Wilder also dramatically clashed with the school board, in an astonishing series of events that ultimately damaged Wilder's political standing altogether.

Despite these high-profile conflicts, Wilder entered 2008 sounding like a mayor seeking reelection. Alongside his blowups he had several clear or perceived successes to point to: a sharp reduction in homicides under the popular police chief Rodney Monroe; the appointment of an unusually bold and charismatic city planning director, Rachel Flynn, who had galvanized citizens (particularly middle-class whites) in support of an ambitious new downtown master plan; and the leveraging of future revenues to secure a $300 million credit reserve to underwrite infrastructure improvements and construct several new schools.[143] Particularly significant was the improvement in violent crime, with reported homicides falling from ninety in 2004 to fifty-five in 2007 and then thirty-one in 2008, an accomplishment lauded by even Wilder's harshest critics.[144] In his January State of the City address, Wilder laid out his achievements in front of a largely supportive audience at city hall.[145] Over the next three months, however, several high-profile credible politicians, including veteran state delegate Dwight C. Jones, made clear their intentions to run for mayor in the fall. The shoe dropped in May when Monroe, now more popular than the mayor himself, announced that he had taken the position of police chief in Charlotte, North Carolina.[146] Shortly after that announcement, Wilder declared he would not seek reelection but would instead bring his remarkable political career to a close at the end of 2008.[147]

Wilder had made the definition and assertion of the mayor's role in the new system the overriding theme of his tenure. But by the end of his term, few citizens believed Wilder was claiming power for the sake of future mayors or in order to help forge a better political system or advance a tangible policy goal.[148] In the end, it turned out that Richmonders did not want *that* kind of strong mayor; Wilder's inability to convince the public that his various assertions of power served a larger, rationally defensible goal led to a spectacular collapse in his political standing. By the fall of 2007, a poll showed just 35 percent of Richmond voters would support reelecting Wilder. (Notably, the poll also showed that self-identified Republicans remained Wilder's most supportive constituency.)[149] Bluntly put, Wilder overplayed his hand and failed to strike, or to even attempt to strike, the right balance between confrontational and cooperative approaches to constructive change.

The mayoral race in the summer and fall of 2008 featured three major candidates, each of whom pledged to take a different approach to the role than Wilder had.[150] Bill Pantele, the city council president and Tim Kaine's successor in the influential, majority-white Second District seat, had strong business support and was widely admired both for his command of city issues and for standing up to Wilder. Pantele ran on an agenda of competent city government and effective economic development. Dwight C. Jones, longtime pastor of a prominent African American Baptist church on the Southside, state delegate, and former chair of the city school board, was perceived as the inheritor of Henry Marsh's political base. Jones ran on a social justice platform, emphasizing poverty reduction. Robert Grey, a prominent and accomplished Black lawyer, ran with strong backing from influential downtown law firms. These backers saw Grey as a better and more appealing version of Wilder—a quasi-patrician African American with credibility in both the white and the Black community but with far humbler affect.[151] A fourth declared candidate, Wilder's former political adviser Paul Goldman (a white New Yorker), dropped out prior to the election and endorsed Jones.[152] Grey stayed in the race but never gained traction among a broad base of voters. This left Pantele to run against Jones in what had become a two-person race. The tone of the race was cordial, and both men were careful not to make race an explicit issue. Nonetheless, support for the two candidates was clearly driven by race, as the subsequent vote would show.

Jones rode strong support from Black voters to a close but decisive victory. On Election Day, Pantele carried the First, Second, and Fourth Districts, all predominantly white, with ease. As expected, Jones carried the predominantly Black Sixth, Seventh, Eighth, and Ninth Districts by wide margins, bolstered by the historically large turnout in support of Barack Obama. The expected battleground was the Fifth District, the city's most racially diverse district, where Pantele had concentrated much of his effort.[153] Jones carried the district with a plurality of 43 percent and also won a narrow victory in the Third District, where Pantele had been expected to win, likely benefiting from strong Black turnout for Obama. Citywide, Jones won 39 percent of the vote, compared with 33 percent for Pantele and 21 percent for Grey.[154]

Jones took office in January 2009, taking pains to ally himself as closely as possible with the most popular man in Richmond—Barack Obama—and to distance himself from Wilder's tactics. Indeed, Jones's victory represented a stunning reversal of fortune: like Marsh, Jones had criticized the mayor-council proposal from his position in the House of Delegates. Now a leading representative of the Black political class that had been marginalized in the 2003 "strong mayor" debate would take the helm of the very office they had opposed—and would have the opportunity, perhaps, to mold it in a different direction. Jones pledged to forge a much more productive relationship with the city council and to prioritize the needs of low-income residents.

Recasting the Mayoralty: The Jones Era, 2009–2016

Dwight C. Jones, a Philadelphia native, moved to Richmond to attend Virginia Union University in the late 1960s. He never left the city, earning his bachelor's degree at VUU in 1970 and then a master of divinity degree in 1973 from VUU School of Theology. In 1973, he became pastor of First Baptist Church of South Richmond, a large and influential congregation with televised worship services.[155] By the time of his election as mayor, Jones had been visible in Richmond public life for over a quarter century, dating to his tenure on the appointed Richmond School Board in the 1980s and fifteen years of service as a delegate in the General Assembly.

Over the course of his two terms, Jones recast the mayoralty by working within the limitations of the charter-defined elected mayor role, avoiding direct legal confrontations with the council on constitutional issues. Yet Jones (and his senior advisers) also held the view that it was the mayor's responsibility to seek to impact policy matters citywide, with full use of both the formal powers provided by the charter and the informal influence provided by the position itself. Given the many institutional forces beyond one's control, to move policy in a meaningful direction in Richmond, a mayor must push and pull every available lever. Doing so meant giving mayoral attention not only to the budget and to maintaining a majority coalition on the council but also to board appointments, to partnerships with business and philanthropic actors, and to using the bully pulpit to build community-wide support for (and political leverage on) major policy priorities—including Jones's signature policy issue, poverty reduction.[156]

Jones's first order of business was to set a new tone at city hall. In his first term, he focused on mending fences with the city council and rebuilding a city bureaucracy that had seen rapid turnover during the Wilder years.[157] Jones hired as chief administrative officer Byron C. Marshall, a veteran public administrator who served as chief executive of the Austin Revitalization Authority in Texas, and began filling other key leadership positions in his first two years.[158] After the constant drama of Wilder's term, many on the city council and in the corporate community appreciated the low-key style Jones projected publicly.[159] The largest project undertaken in the first term was the reconstruction of the city jail as a new "Justice Center." Given the dilapidation of the old jail and its inhumane conditions, Jones and city officials viewed the project as a moral imperative.[160] Jones then launched an Anti-Poverty Commission in 2011, which eventually helped shape his second term (revisited in chapter 5).[161] In 2012, Jones began taking a tougher stance vis-à-vis the school board (which he had chaired in the 1980s), saying that Richmond needed to stop "celebrating mediocrity" and refusing to fund the school board's budgetary request for an additional $24 million in FY 2013. Jones eventually created a committee to make recommendations on operational cuts and efficiencies within Richmond Public Schools, bringing in former city manager Robert Bobb as a consultant to conduct an analysis and develop specific proposals. (See chapter 4 for further discussion.)[162]

While Jones's stance on school funding had a mixed public reception, no serious candidate emerged to challenge his reelection bid in 2012. Political neophyte Michael Ryan did appear on the ballot, but Jones, with relatively light campaigning on his own behalf, was reelected with 73 percent of the popular vote, carrying all nine council districts. Indeed, Jones's coattails and political machinery led to his most vociferous city council critics on the left and the right—Marty Jewell in the Fifth and Bruce Tyler in the First—losing their seats to newcomers Parker Agelasto and Jonathan Baliles.[163]

In his second term, Jones continued to battle the school board on funding issues while pushing forward other initiatives. Much of 2013 and early 2014 was consumed by the debate over Jones's proposal for a new downtown minor league baseball stadium in Shockoe Bottom, in proximity to a historic slave trade market regarded as sacred ground by numerous activists, a proposal that was ultimately withdrawn. Other second-term economic development projects, including high-profile deals with the Washington NFL franchise and a privately owned brewer, received council approval but also significant public criticism (see chapter 5). In 2014, Jones also took two (quite different) steps to secure his legacy: first, in June he established the Office of Community Wealth Building to lead implementation of policy recommendations generated by the Mayor's Anti-Poverty Commission (see chapter 5); and second, in September he made the seemingly abrupt decision to request the resignation of Marshall as chief administrative officer, leading to the appointment the following spring of Selena Cuffee-Glenn (previously the city manager of Suffolk, Virginia).[164] Jones's second term also saw the city secure federal funding for a bus rapid transit line and establish a new partnership with the Commonwealth of Virginia to increase investment in the Port of Richmond, among other policy developments (detailed in chapter 6). The successful staging of the Union Cycliste Internationale world cycling championships brought global attention to Richmond in September 2015 and a needed burst of civic pride.

Yet by 2016, Jones's popularity had declined markedly. The annual political battles with the school board over budgets took a toll, and problems with the implementation of financial reporting software, leading to the city falling badly behind on its required annual financial reports, were widely publicized as evidence of continued city hall dysfunction.[165] An investigation into allegations of corruption after it was revealed that the city's public works director was simultaneously doing volunteer work on the construction of a new building (in Chesterfield County) for Jones's church cast a pall over his final year in office. Ultimately, the investigators sternly criticized Jones's administration for not drawing sharper lines between church business and city business but concluded that no laws had been broken.[166] Jones left office in December highlighting a laundry list of specific achievements, emphasizing his efforts on poverty.[167]

The 2016 mayoral election started as a free-for-all with over a dozen declared candidates before the field of legitimate contenders shrank to five and then three candidates. In an odd echo of the Jones-Pantele-Grey race of 2008, 2016 became the first mayoral contest in which three candidates won at least one district: veteran politician Joe Morrissey (Eighth and Ninth Districts), downtown booster and former city administrator Jack Berry (First and Fourth Districts), and newcomer Levar M. Stoney, the former Virginia secretary of the commonwealth, who surpassed expectations by winning the Second, Third, Fifth, Sixth, and Seventh Districts (and also narrowly carrying the popular vote) to gain election as Richmond's youngest mayor. Stoney pledged to continue and extend Jones's work to fight poverty through the Office of Community Wealth Building, but he also pledged to take a far friendlier stance toward schools and to pursue meaningful action to improve the city's operations. Still unclear to most citizens at the time of his election was whether the city, having invested great effort in changing its form of government, would be able to move from promising starts to breakthrough progress on its most entrenched and enduring problems.

4

Education and Governance in Richmond, 1988–2016

You can't build a system that is plagued with constant controversy and upheaval and strife.

RICHMOND PUBLIC SCHOOLS SUPERINTENDENT
LOIS HARRISON-JONES, JULY 1988

There is no clearer example of the practical consequences of Richmond's collective failures in governance than its continued inability to educate and graduate public school students at rates comparable to its county neighbors or to the rest of Virginia. Richmond residents and observers often pointed to the condition and ineffectiveness of the city public schools as both symptomatic of and a contributing cause of the city's decline and stagnation from the 1970s to 2004, when the city's population bottomed out. Even after 2004, the struggles of Richmond's public school system were widely regarded as the leading obstacle to the city's revival.

Contemporary Richmonders, be they political leaders or everyday citizens, frequently opine that "the schools" remain the community's largest challenge.[1] Untangling the problems in Richmond schools remains a complex and daunting task, raising numerous difficult questions. Is poverty itself the problem? Are the problems of Richmond Public Schools (RPS) attributable to poor administrative leadership, or perhaps ineffective instruction, or inadequate funding? Do middle-class families, and their continued reluctance to send their children to public schools with children in poverty, bear some of the responsibility for the continuity of educational challenges? How does the historical legacy of racial discrimination continue to hamper Richmond's efforts? Has the national emphasis on test results as the barometer of "school quality" helped or harmed schools in Richmond?

Answers to these questions are not obvious, and in the period of this study, leaders and organizations in Richmond tended to give significantly different responses. However, historical investigation, discussion with contemporary educational leaders, and analysis of data on school performance suggest some broad points on which there was wide agreement.[2]

Few people disputed the harm done to Richmond city schools by the legacy of Massive Resistance and the subsequent failure of metropolitan-wide school integration in the 1970s. Both accelerated white and middle-class flight out of Richmond for a generation. Some Richmonders also recognized the profound challenges the city schools faced in educating a population with a disproportionate number of not only impoverished but also special needs children with acute emotional or mental difficulties, often related to the impact of traumatic experiences. The age and condition of the city's school buildings were a serious concern, as was a state funding formula that for decades has been unfavorable to the City of Richmond. In Virginia, as elsewhere in the United States, schools are funded primarily by local property taxes, thereby straining Richmond's ability to provide an education sufficiently high in quality to overcome the numerous challenges many Richmond students have faced. While there were pockets of educational excellence, many outstanding individual teachers, and some outstanding schools, as a *system* Richmond Public Schools had numerous difficulties. In particular, the lack of a coherent strategy for academic improvement or an overall strategic plan for much of this time period, alongside bureaucratic inefficiencies and, in some cases, neglect or malfeasance, proved overwhelming.

There was much more dispute—politically and educationally consequential—concerning just how much progress the RPS system has made in overcoming both structural and "self-imposed" challenges. As shown below, in the 1980s and 1990s, school leadership seemed to lurch from one strategy to another as a consequence of instability in senior administration. The 1994 transition of the school board from an appointed body to an elected body would in time have far-reaching impacts on Richmond politics but did not immediately alter the fundamental operations of RPS or its educational outcomes. During the first decade of the twenty-first century, the schools, responding to the new demands of accountability emanating from state mandates and the national No Child Left Behind legislation (especially its focus on testing), made substantial progress in implementing a coherent academic program and in significantly raising student achievement as measured by test scores, while at the same time reducing the dropout rate.[3] But by other measures of academic success, particularly middle school and high school achievement, graduation rates, enrollment in college, and preparation for work, the school system continued to see poor results into the 2010s, by both Virginia and national standards, and still struggled to convince middle-class "families with choices" to embrace the city school system. Nor did anyone seriously claim that RPS had closed the gap between the quality of education in city schools and the education available in Henrico or Chesterfield Counties. On the contrary, claims that the city schools were a "mess" continued as a commonplace and widely held belief, both inside and outside the city limits.

Further, the school system continued to be a magnet for political controversy rooted in a series of ongoing disputes about where authority and responsibility for the schools' operation should lie. In the 1990s and early aughts, debates over city schools often were three-pronged, with the school administration, the school board, and the city council as the main players, but starting in 2005, a fourth major player came on the scene: the office of the new directly elected mayor, in the persons of Doug Wilder and Dwight Jones, both of whom invested significant energy in attempting to influence educational policy. Ongoing jousting and debates over schools and school policy, as well as a nearly continuous string of crises and controversies, often overshadowed the substance of what was taking place in the educational process itself.

This chapter considers Richmond's educational challenges, showing how they were both a predictable by-product of the regionalized segregation of public schooling in the Richmond metropolitan area *and* the result of significant internal dysfunction, within both the school system and the institutional architecture of city government. Day-to-day attention of parents, teachers, administrators, and citizens were inevitably drawn to the ongoing conflicts and dysfunction, too often without awareness of their connection

TABLE 4.1. Race of and economic disadvantage among students in Greater Richmond school districts, 2003–2004 and 2013–2014

	Percentage Black	Percentage Latino	Percentage ED[a]
2003–4			
Richmond	90.0	2.3	69.0
Chesterfield	25.0	4.2	12.9
Henrico	35.4	2.9	26.4
2013–14			
Richmond	78.3	10.0	77.9
Chesterfield	26.3	11.5	29.4
Henrico	36.5	7.7	41.4

Source: Virginia Department of Education, Fall Membership Reports, accessed February 6, 2024, https://p1pe.doe.virginia.gov/buildatable/fallmembership.
[a] Economically disadvantaged (ED) refers to a student's eligibility for free or reduced school lunch or other federal antipoverty programs.

to the mandated inequities inherent in the Commonwealth of Virginia's organization of public education. More specifically, the Richmond Public Schools system was charged with educating students in the context of high rates of child poverty, with many schools that were both nearly 100 percent African American and extremely high-poverty, whereas neighboring counties educated primarily middle-class, economically stable students. (See table 4.1.) Because Richmond as a locality was continually fiscally stressed compared with its neighbors and already had a significantly higher local tax rate, its capacity to make the investments needed to provide the quality of facilities and intensive family and educational support that might give more Richmond children a realistic chance of educational success was limited. Because the majority of children in the Richmond public school system were Black and the majority of children in neighboring counties were white, the result from a regional perspective was the reproduction of severe racial inequality from one generation to the next. (See table 4.2.) Likewise, the extreme challenge of delivering educational success in the context of high poverty, limited resources, and numerous political pressures has created a continual narrative (and, often, reality) of dysfunction around Richmond Public Schools. That narrative, along with implicit acceptance by many Virginia legislators of racialized educational inequalities as normal, has dampened demands for

TABLE 4.2. Academic outcomes, Central Virginia Public Schools, 2002–2016

	2001–2	2009–10	2015–16
Richmond			
Percentage that graduated on time	62.7[a]	60.0	75.0
Percentage that earned an advanced diploma	20.0	16.5	23.8
Percentage that planned to attend a two- or four-year college	31.9	37.8	48.7
Chesterfield			
Percentage that graduated on time	80.7	87.7	92.0
Percentage that earned an advanced diploma	44.8	48.9	53.2
Percentage that planned to attend a two- or four-year college	60.0	68.3	71.0
Henrico			
Percentage that graduated on time	81.6	83.3	89.6
Percentage that earned an advanced diploma	35.9	39.4	47.7
Percentage that planned to attend a two- or four-year college	59.2	64.8	71.2

Source: Virginia Superintendent's Annual Report, table 5, 2001–2, 2009–10, 2015–16, accessed February 6, 2024, https://www.doe.virginia.gov/data-policy-funding/data-reports/statistics-reports/superintendent-s-annual-report.

[a] Denominator for all percentages is cohort size of entering ninth grade class within each system three years prior to the graduation year. Graduation rates differ from official Virginia graduation rates, which take into account student mobility between districts.

dramatic change (including but not limited to more equitable funding) to address regionalized patterns of inequity.

Regional and statewide politics have influenced the way local government can and cannot dictate educational outcomes. Generations of Richmond educational leaders have worked within this imbalanced dispensation to try to improve outcomes for Richmond's children and to reverse the historic dynamic of white and middle-class flight from the school system, in hopes of creating a school system integrated by class and race that fosters achievement and upward mobility for all students. The specific challenges those leaders have faced—including no small amount of internal conflict—are considered in the following narrative, which illustrates the painful consequences of the inequitable organization of public education in central Virginia.

Separate and Unequal, the Sequel: Richmond Public Schools in the Post–Civil Rights Era

The modern era of Richmond Public Schools dates to 1986, when U.S. district judge Robert Merhige put an end to court-mandated crosstown busing in the city. Most historical accounts understandably stress Merhige's pivotal role in the epochal events of the 1970s. In 1970, Merhige ordered Richmond city schools to finally set aside token integration. During the 1960s, Virginia had moved beyond the caustic politics of Massive Resistance (such as school closures and legislation designed to undermine the Supreme Court's 1954 *Brown v. Board of Education* decision) toward passive resistance. Whites slowed down meaningful racial integration in local public schools by bogging down the court system with litigation. They also moved with their feet to private schools and predominantly white counties with predominantly white schools. By creating genuinely integrated public schools within the city limits, Merhige's 1970 court order accelerated this process of white flight from the city and inaugurated a long period of declining enrollment and transition to an overwhelmingly African American city school district.[4]

Merhige understood these consequences: indeed, in January 1972 he ordered the consolidation of the Richmond, Henrico, and Chesterfield school systems in order to achieve effective metropolitan integration. He held that the constitutional obligation to comply with *Brown v. Board of Education* outweighed local boundaries, especially when such boundaries had been used as mechanisms to achieve racial segregation in housing and hence schools. His decision was overturned on appeal in June 1972 before going to the Supreme Court, which upheld the reversal on a 4–4 vote in in May 1973, without ruling on the underlying constitutional issue. (Justice Lewis Powell, a former Richmond School Board chair, recused himself.) When the city's bid for a rehearing was denied by the Supreme Court that October, Chesterfield County attorney and state senator Frederick T. Gray triumphantly stated, "Forever is a long time; but I think we've got them licked forever."[5] A year later a similar case in Detroit that was fully argued consolidated the Supreme Court's view (on a 5–4 vote) that states are not obliged to overturn local boundaries in order to create racially integrated schools.[6]

Accounts by James Ryan, Robert Pratt, and other scholars rightly stress the decisive importance for the Richmond region of the court rulings in *Richmond School Board v. Board of Education* (1973) and *Milliken v. Bradley* (1974).[7] But Judge Merhige also played a critical, less-remembered role in the mid-1980s with two consequential decisions impacting the trajectory of Richmond schools well into the twenty-first century.[8]

First, Merhige ordered an end to district-wide busing in April 1986 for the purposes of achieving racial integration.[9] While many parents of all races applauded the order, the decision hardly marked the end of racial segregation within Richmond's local schools. Indeed, decades later, after many cycles of superintendents and school boards, RPS leaders continued to face the same dual challenges as their predecessors in the 1980s and 1990s: how to make the school system attractive to racially diverse, middle-class families and as a result bolster enrollment and create the possibility of more socioeconomic and racially integrated schools, while at the same time strengthening performance in the many schools in the city that remained extremely high-poverty and virtually all-Black.

The end of busing as a tool for desegregation did lead to changes in enrollment procedures, changes intended to encourage middle-class families of all races to return to public schools. Enrollment procedures in the era of court-mandated busing had created anomalous situations in certain parts of the city: most notably, for a time, over 90 percent of students at Mary Munford Elementary School in the white West End (First District) were African Americans.[10] White families in the area, and citywide, largely abandoned the public school system rather than risk having their children attend majority-Black schools.[11] In the years after the Merhige ruling ended busing, RPS settled upon the twofold enrollment procedure that has continued to guide policy ever since: assigning all students a neighborhood school and then allowing them to apply to designated schools "out-of-zone" for acceptance on a space-available basis. By 1991, RPS had designated twelve elementary schools as "model schools," meaning they could accept out-of-zone applicants, and extended the concept to the middle and high school levels. These policies, designed to make RPS more attractive to middle-school families by offering a range of options not tied to geography, sat in inherent tension with RPS's embrace of neighborhood schools, adopted formally in 1992 by the school board on a 4–3 vote.[12] A subsequent analysis by scholar Genevieve Siegel-Hawley and her colleagues showed that this cluster of policies, post-court-ordered desegregation, led to an increase rather than a decrease in racial segregation within RPS.[13]

Legal battles over integration survived passive resistance. Prior to the end of court-ordered busing in 1984 the school board sued the Commonwealth of Virginia, demanding substantial funds—$48 million—to compensate for the harms of metropolitan school segregation and to permit an upgrading of school programs and facilities at sufficient scale to attract middle-class families, Black and white, back to the system.[14] Here again, Judge Merhige played a critical role. In a July 1986 ruling, confirmed on appeal in 1987, Merhige rejected the school board's claim. Merhige acknowledged that the state had played an affirmative role in promoting segregated schools, that the city's educational attainment was hampered by high poverty, and that the city's high poverty rate was directly impacted by the inadequate education that many Black Richmonders had received under segregation. But he contended that the state actions significantly impacting segregation had taken place prior to the implementation of the school desegregation order in 1972 and rejected five of six specific claims made by plaintiffs of discriminatory actions taken by the state since that date. These included accrediting private schools that may have engaged in discriminatory admissions policies, the site selection of a Governor's School, state limitations on consolidating school districts, state limitations on annexing county land, and use of federal funds by the state. In each rejected case, Merhige found the charge unproven or unwarranted and that school funding increases could not properly remedy the problem. (Merhige agreed with the claim that inclusion of private school teachers in the public teacher pension plan was problematic but argued this could have had only a very slight impact on patterns of segregation in Richmond schools.) Merhige further held that while poverty was a factor historically impacting achievement in Richmond schools and that the city's poverty level was in part a consequence of the prior segregated system, "it is not within the Court's power to remedy either the poverty itself or the ancillary effects of such poverty." Finally, Merhige pointed to the high levels of funding that city schools already received relative to other localities.[15]

In rejecting the claim that Richmond Public Schools might be entitled to a constitutional remedy in the form of increased state payments, Merhige's decision painted a distressing picture of the condition of RPS in the mid-1980s but at the same time gave a curiously optimistic interpretation of that picture. First, Merhige observed that "it is undisputed that RPS is currently racially isolated. Approximately eighty-seven percent of RPS' students are black. Of RPS' twenty-nine elementary schools, fourteen are ninety percent or more black. Similarly, four of RPS' eight middle schools are ninety percent or more black, and three of the six high schools are more than ninety percent black."[16] But Merhige then cited testing and dropout data to argue that since 1972, there was no clear correlation between shifts in the proportion of the school system that was Black and positive outcomes.[17]

Merhige then considered Richmond's school outcomes vis-à-vis those in the counties. In 1984–85, the RPS dropout rate of 8.6 percent was nearly double the state average of 4.4 percent and more than double the 3.9 percent average obtained in both Henrico and Chesterfield Counties; Richmond students failed grades at a much higher rate than in the counties; RPS graduates were less likely to go on to additional schooling than their suburban counterparts; and the on-time graduation rate for RPS high school students was just 53.5 percent, about 25 percent less than in the counties. Likewise, SRA (Science Research Associates) achievement test scores for Richmond students in grades four, eight, and eleven lagged far behind Chesterfield and Henrico students. For instance, eleventh-grade math scores for Richmond students were in the 44th percentile nationally, compared to the 72nd percentile for Chesterfield County and 69th percentile for Henrico. But Merhige held that these differences were not due to state-sponsored segregation and further argued that relatively high and rising test scores among elementary school students showed that Richmond was on its way to steady academic progress and a narrowing of the gap. Richmond fourth graders in 1985 scored in the 52nd, 57th, and 59th percentile nationally on reading, math, and language arts tests, nearly at the state level. From this evidence, Merhige optimistically concluded that "it appears likely that the current fourth graders will maintain their performance levels through graduation." He continued: "Further, given the steady improvement of RPS' test scores in recent years, there is no reason to suspect that the performance of future RPS students will not exceed that of those currently in the system. Accordingly, RPS appears to have already reached the point where its students can be expected to consistently equal or exceed the performance of students throughout the nation and in the state of Virginia."[18] Merhige went on to argue that most students in RPS were kindergarten-ready, that the system's teachers were well-trained (citing the proportion holding college and advanced degrees as well as Mayor Roy West's assertion that RPS teachers were "excellent"), and that the plaintiffs had not provided evidence that RPS facilities were actually inferior. Poverty, according to Merhige, largely accounted for the relative deficiency of school achievement:

> In 1984, for example, 51.1% of RPS' students came from low-income backgrounds. In contrast, low-income students comprised only 13.0% of Henrico's school population, and 7.3% of Chesterfield's. When RPS' test scores are compared, not to the nation as a whole, but rather to schools with a relatively high incidence of poverty.... RPS

students generally perform *better* than would otherwise be expected. When compared to schools with a high concentration of Title One students, the percentile rankings of RPS students on the 1984–85 SRA tests were as follows: fourth graders—nearly 75th percentile, fifth graders—55th percentile, eleventh graders—45th percentile.[19]

Class, not race, primarily explained Richmond's difficulties, Merhige wrote, but "segregation-related poverty is not a factor that can be used to justify the imposition of remedial programs in a school system."[20]

Merhige also argued that flawed teaching approaches within RPS were a significant cause of Richmond's low educational outcomes. His opinion approvingly cited Roy West's statement that RPS had practiced erratic educational philosophies based on "newfangled" techniques, as opposed to the "basics." He then went on to cite the increase in test scores at Albert Hill Middle School, where West was principal in the 1980s, as evidence that improvements could be attained "not through an influx of money, but rather through a change in the educational philosophy followed by the school." Taking the two points together, Merhige claimed that "a large part of the disparity between the achievement levels of students in RPS and those of students in the State as a whole and in Henrico and Chesterfield Counties is attributable to the high incidence of poverty in RPS and to the ineffective educational philosophy that was followed for some time in the district."[21]

Finally, Merhige provided an overview of seemingly robust RPS programs as part of his opinion. By the mid-1980s, RPS had a lower pupil-teacher ratio at both the elementary and the secondary levels than in the state as a whole or in Henrico and Chesterfield Counties, as well as more instructional support staff and administrative and service support staff per student than in the counties. RPS operated a full-time kindergarten, two pre-kindergarten programs, four year-round remedial programs for different age levels, and truancy prevention, in-school suspension, and comprehensive dropout prevention programs. Merhige further pointed to funding levels from state and federal sources showing that Richmond, despite receiving a lower amount of "equalized" funding from the state, overall received more state and federal resources per pupil than Chesterfield or Henrico.[22]

In shockingly optimistic terms, Merhige seemed to believe that the city was well on its way to solving the problem of local public schools. He drew a picture of a well-funded school system that offered students solid programs and had made progress that would eventually result in Richmond students performing at levels comparable to those in the neighboring counties and the state. Poverty remained as an obstacle, but not one subject to constitutional remedy. Merhige's decision is striking for its positive appraisal of the school system's ability to overcome the impacts of poverty and provide equal educational opportunity. Indeed, the judge closed his ruling by writing, "The Court commends the Richmond Public School System for the exemplary efforts and progress it has made since 1972."[23] Virginia attorney general Mary Sue Terry was also quick to pat the state on the back after the ruling, declaring that the case "proves Virginia has fully met its constitutional responsibilities to eliminate segregation, not only in Richmond but in schools across the state." Terry added that the ruling "shows the nation that our educational system is indeed colorblind."[24] The attorney general's triumphant remarks rendered invisible the very specific racial and class implications of Richmond's school failures.

Merhige's ruling in effect slammed the door on the era of civil rights litigation impacting Richmond Public Schools and normalized as acceptable the operation of an overwhelmingly African American, high-poverty, separate school system in Virginia's capital city. More surprising than his legal reasoning, however, was Merhige's rosy take on Richmond's ability to catch up in academic achievement, by continuation of its existing programs combined with application of sound educational teaching philosophy. This conclusion meant that in legal terms, the Commonwealth of Virginia had no further obligation for additional actions to address the historical legacy of racism in Richmond's schools. The evidence cited by Merhige in support of that conclusion—the relatively high test scores of fourth graders, the performance of Richmond students relative to other impoverished students, and the views of one elected official—seems in retrospect remarkably thin, particularly in light of overwhelming national evidence showing a systemic link between high concentrations of poverty and depressed school achievement. Merhige's decision and the positive reaction to it from top Democratic officials showed that neither the courts nor the state possessed either the analytical framework or the political will to address the growing disparities wrought by race-based segregation and poverty.

The Richmond School Board itself had a much more realistic assessment of the challenges the school system faced as a high-poverty district operating in a highly racialized context and did not share in Attorney General Terry's triumphant reaction to Judge Merhige's decision. Instead, the school board filed an ultimately unsuccessful appeal.[25] While school officials could take some satisfaction in the accomplishments and signs of progress cited by Merhige, their perception was that the city's schools were still avenues of failure for far too many students. These educators might have told Merhige that given the stresses and potential pitfalls of growing up in a high-poverty community, achievement of relatively good elementary school scores was hardly a firm guarantee of continued academic success at higher grades, let alone reason to think the youngest generation would be able to close the wide gap in high school graduation rates and college attendance. And they would have been correct.

Three decades later, in the 2010s, Richmond continued to do relatively well on test scores at the elementary level, and its economically disadvantaged third graders routinely matched or exceeded the statewide performance for poor children.[26] And yet the overall performance of the school system, as measured by graduation rates, college attendance, test scores for middle school and high school students, and virtually any other measure remained disastrous, leaving successive school boards in much the same situation as their predecessors in 1986: facing the dual challenge of attracting more middle-class families while also improving outcomes for high-poverty schools.

In some ways, however, the picture was even grimmer. Few people in the Richmond region, especially in recent decades, have thought it worthwhile to launch a legal or political challenge to segregated schools, or even to de facto racial segregation within RPS. The legal challenge of the Richmond School Board in the mid-1980s to the normalization of a highly unequal status quo may have failed, but at least that school board felt empowered to try. Virginia's inequitable legal and funding structure was generally taken as a given by those charged with improving the city's public education over the course of this study.

Further, Merhige's twin claims, that Richmond schools received substantial resources and at times failed to use them effectively, have echoed in the discourse on public schools in Richmond for decades. Merhige was almost certainly wrong to think that positive trends in test scores by fourth graders showed that Richmond was on its way to educational equality. But was he wrong to think that Richmond might and ought to have continued to achieve significant progress instead of backsliding? To answer that question, we need to examine in more detail the school system's policies and leadership since the late 1980s.

The Politics of Education in Richmond, Act 1

In the late 1980s and 1990s, Richmond School Board members—both before and after the shift to a directly elected school board in 1994—recognized that they were presiding over a troubled system with declining enrollments and below-average educational outcomes. In this context, they devoted enormous energy and attention to two inherently contentious issues: first, devising enrollment policies designed to make the school system as attractive as possible to middle-class families, and second, selecting facilities for closure in order to consolidate resources. The aim? To arrest enrollment decline (and boost funding, which was tied to enrollment) and to find savings that could be redirected to the classroom by operating fewer buildings.[27] Attention to the details of the educational program was generally left to the school administration. This division of labor (the school board focusing on broad policy, the administration on educational implementation) conceivably might have proven functional if RPS had enjoyed stable administrative leadership during the 1980s and 1990s. Instead, as education scholar Joshua Cole observes, the school system had a very high turnover rate of superintendents, with six individuals holding the role between 1985 and 2002, none of whom stayed more than five years.[28]

The case of Superintendent Lois Harrison-Jones embodies this problem: a three-decade veteran of Richmond Public Schools, Harrison-Jones in 1985 became the first Black woman to lead the system. She was credited with overseeing the transition back to neighborhood schooling, ending the notoriously unpopular experiment of having high school students attend multiple buildings simultaneously ("Plan G"), and generally being an effective leader and educator.[29] Yet she created a powerful adversary in August 1987 by reassigning Principal Roy A. West—then the city's mayor—from Albert Hill Middle School to Mosby Middle School after receiving numerous complaints from parents and students at Hill. This personnel move led West to call for her resignation.[30] (Over the course of the 1987–88 school year, West was sued, successfully, by six Hill students for ordering blanket searches of student possessions in the 1986–87 school year.)[31] The school board, at the time appointed by the city council, was led by Leroy Hassell, a Harvard-educated attorney and future Virginia Supreme Court chief justice viewed as a close ally of Mayor West.[32]

The situation worsened. In June 1988, a third-party consultant filed a previously commissioned report stating that the school system had administrative bloat and had not cut staff despite seeing a decline in enrollment.[33] The report came on the heels of a painful budget season in the spring of 1988, in which the school board was forced to cut $11 million from its budget when the council did not fund its original request; school board chair Hassell had publicly rebuked Harrison-Jones for a remark about the budget process he interpreted as critical of the council and Mayor West.[34] Harrison-Jones responded to the cost-cutting recommendations by saying that most of the consultants' recommendations were already in motion but in July announced she would not seek renewal of her superintendent contract when it expired in June 1989. Days later she told a local reporter she felt she could not win over the opposition of the school board and that the city did not prioritize education, citing conflicts with Hassell regarding the budget question and unnecessary finger-pointing in the wake of the third-party report, adding that "you can't build a system that is plagued with constant controversy and upheaval and strife."[35] Harrison-Jones's departure, and the circumstances leading to it, sparked indignant responses from the Richmond Crusade for Voters and other groups who called for Hassell's resignation, as well as from veteran school board member Melvin Law, who suggested the "crisis" was entirely of Hassell's making.[36] But by the end of July, a new fourteen-person search committee had formed to find a leader with the official job description of fostering educational progress in a challenged system and the unofficial job description of navigating Richmond's political complexities.[37]

School systems—their teachers and children and, more broadly, communities—benefit from institutional continuity and stability. The frequent changes, especially in the 1980s and 1990s, made it difficult for the Richmond school system to establish and stick with coherent philosophies or strategies long enough to make an impact. At the same time, organizational assessments described an insular administrative culture within RPS in which decisions were too often influenced by personal favoritism or political considerations. Related to this, editorialists and other observers blamed RPS (both the administration and at times the school board) for being resistant to change; and others pointed to blunders by the superintendents themselves.[38]

The short tenure of Albert Jones from 1989 to 1991 as superintendent exemplified how quickly a promising new hire could be undone. Jones, who had earned a doctorate at the University of Washington and served in Seattle-area schools for nineteen years before a two-year stint as associate superintendent in Wichita, Kansas, arrived to considerable optimism. That optimism proved short-lived, though, in part because of political and administrative missteps. Seeking to hit the ground running, Jones aggressively promoted a magnet school initiative in order to create academically attractive schools. He also took steps toward bringing a Governor's School to

Richmond, initially housed on one floor of Thomas Jefferson High School in often tense "coexistence" with the regular high school.[39] Like Harrison-Jones before him, Jones was compelled to spend political capital by transferring former mayor and sitting councilman Roy West, this time from his post as principal of Mosby Middle School to an administrative position, following a teacher's complaint that West had ordered the building's doors locked in violation of safety regulations.[40] Citizens also raised questions about expenses incurred by Jones on a school board credit card (Jones mixed business and personal expenses on the card and was late repaying the personal expenses) and about consulting work Jones performed for the Washington, DC, school system while serving as RPS superintendent.[41] In late June 1991, the school board dismissed Jones after just two years of service, with *Richmond Times-Dispatch* reporter Robin Farmer observing that he was "often perceived as an arrogant outsider" by the "closely knit" RPS community.[42]

The administrative transience continued. Following Jones's departure, the school board turned to an RPS lifer, Associate Superintendent Lucille Brown, to steady the ship. An employee of the city schools since the 1950s, Brown was widely respected and in her first year continued the magnet school initiatives piloted by Jones. But in her second year, the school system was convulsed by a complaint of the racial clustering of children in classrooms at Bellevue Elementary School in the Historic Church Hill neighborhood. Church Hill as a whole in the 1990s was predominantly African American, but Historic Church Hill also contained a substantial number of middle-class and affluent white families who prized the area's historic architecture and picturesque hilltop views of the James River. These two enclaves, despite their proximity to one another, for all intents and purposes lived in two different Richmonds. This polarization had implications for RPS. In 1992–93, 74 of Bellevue Elementary's 400 students were white, and Principal Sylvia Richardson systematically clustered whites together in classroom assignments. The practical effect was that at each grade level, the school had one or two classes that were all-Black and one class (two for kindergarten) in which the proportion of white students ranged from 24 percent to as much as 58 percent.[43] Richardson stated in a letter that this clustering was done for "social and emotional reasons" and was in the best interest of the students.[44]

Clustering led to a firestorm in December 1992. African American city leaders generally interpreted such clustering as evidence of separate and unequal education within the school.[45] Did white students clustered in a class get the best teacher in the grade? And with benefits of diverse environments understood, why were many Black students being denied the opportunities for daily interaction with other racial groups by being kept in all-Black classrooms? Likewise, why were whites in majority-white classrooms? In a court-ordered public hearing to address the issue in February 1993, legendary civil rights lawyer Oliver W. Hill, who played an integral role in the NAACP's litigation strategy that culminated in 1954's *Brown v. Board of Education*, offered public comment condemning the clustering practice and demanding its immediate cessation.[46] But some white parents expressed support for Principal Richardson and argued that the practice may have helped increase the number of white students attending the majority-Black school.[47] Indeed, soon after the Bellevue story broke, evidence emerged that Ginter Park Elementary School on the Northside also appeared to be practicing racial clustering—not as a result of administrative design but because of the principal's compliance with parents' requests for particular teachers.[48]

The racial clustering controversy laid bare the dilemmas that individual Richmond schools and the system faced: In seeking to make majority-Black schools comfortable and acceptable to white parents—and later, seeking to make majority-poverty schools comfortable and acceptable to middle-class parents (regardless of race)—how far could schools go without jeopardizing their commitment to provide an excellent and equal education to all pupils, including the majority who did not have a choice? Superintendent Brown and the school board were swift and emphatic in their judgment that the arrangements at both Bellevue and Ginter Park crossed the line. But Brown's handling of the situation provoked a backlash when she ordered, with board approval, changes in the racial composition of the classes at Bellevue midyear, leading to the reassignment of about sixty Bellevue students (Black and white) to new classrooms.[49] Many Bellevue parents, Black and white alike, vehemently opposed this remedy as disruptive and traumatic.[50] The decision also attracted criticism from the *Times-Dispatch* and other powerful voices.[51] Brown further upset many parents at Bellevue by reassigning the popular principal Richardson to another school at year's end.[52] Meanwhile, a U.S. Office of Civil Rights probe concluded in July 1993 found that clustering at Bellevue and Ginter Park had violated the Civil Rights Act but that the board's corrective action had resolved the issue.[53] The bad feelings generated by the entire episode negatively impacted systemwide morale and also led to a precipitous decline in white student enrollment at Bellevue, which fell from seventy-four in 1992–93 to just six by the end of the 1994–95 school year.[54]

Enter the Elected School Board

The discontinuity of personnel and lack of consensus in RPS continued. Brown retired as superintendent in 1995, giving Richmond's first elected school board the opportunity to put its stamp on the system. In 1992, the Virginia General Assembly had passed enabling legislation to permit elected school boards, and in a November 1993 referendum Richmond voters supported shifting to an elected board, with over 80 percent voting yes.[55] Many supporters of the change, including the Richmond Education Association (REA), the teachers' professional organization that led the petition drive, hoped school board elections would serve as a way to make the struggling school system more accountable to residents.[56] The REA, which in March 1993 had voted no-confidence in the appointed board as a protest against several of its policies and the overall direction of the system, also argued that an elected board would be more independent of the city council.[57]

Not everyone pushed for change, however. Foreshadowing the "strong mayor" debate ten years later, the Richmond chapter of the NAACP opposed the measure in an October branch meeting on the grounds that "the elected school board would lack taxing power, politicize education and allow special interest groups to push agendas."[58] School board chair Clarence Townes had earlier stated that an elected board without taxing power would merely be "minor-league training to run for council the next time around. It puts them in prep school to run for council and that's just increasing the politics of education."[59]

Richmond's plans for an elected school board were approved by the General Assembly in the spring of 1994, allowing the first school board elections to proceed in May with twenty-two candidates vying for nine districted seats.[60] After the 1994 elections, the new board included three veterans—holdovers Alexina Fagan and Delores McQuinn and former chair Melvin Law, who ousted an incumbent appointee to regain a seat on the board—as well as six newcomers (two of whom were elected without opposition).[61] In March 1995, a racially divided board hired newcomer Dr. Patricia C. Conn, then serving as deputy superintendent of schools in Rochester, New York, as superintendent, with the three white board members and two of six Black members favoring Conn over another finalist for the position.[62]

For a brief moment, Conn's hire seemed promising for Richmond Public Schools. Conn, a Black woman, impressed the *Times-Dispatch* and many others by embracing a comprehensive reform agenda and pledging to make

Richmond "the standard by which all other urban school districts are measured."[63] Her reform agenda included commitments to

- Change the name of the downtown offices from Central Administration to the Support and Accountability Center (SAC)
- Integrate and streamline SAC operations, emphasizing boundary-crossing teams
- Combine the Curriculum Materials Center and the Professional Developmental Center into a new entity: The Instructional Resource and Training Center
- Request four new Board policies: civic values and service learning; collaboration with community; student progress; site-based planning and management
- Begin planning the conversion of comprehensive high schools to theme-focused schools featuring small school units
- Restructure middle schools so that every child is connected to a group of caring adults in each school
- Change the employee appraisal system from an input-based to a results-based approach
- Implement (Total Quality Management) principles throughout the organization
- Intensify, focus and integrate professional development opportunities
- Align volunteer and partnership programs with new goals
- Establish pathways for sharing teaching ideas and teamwork
- Establish a peer support system for principals
- Identify a farm site where troubled youth can be educated using a hands-on approach
- Establish community-learning centers for children and families
- Seek relief from state and federal rules and policies
- Identify priority schools for intensive problem-solving support[64]

Conn's thoroughness initially won broad community support, before events in early 1996 spiraled into a series of conflicts that ultimately undermined her leadership. The turmoil began with a highly publicized dispute with teachers over their use of leave days. Conn caught wind of a long-standing practice where many teachers took a sick day on the Friday of the Central Intercollegiate Athletic Association (CIAA) conference basketball tournament in March to travel to the tournament site (in 1996 it was Winston-Salem, North Carolina). The CIAA event, featuring Black colleges from throughout the state and the South, was a significant social occasion for African Americans in Richmond. Conn viewed this practice as indefensible and sent a system-wide memo weeks before the tournament forbidding teachers to travel to the CIAA on sick leave and announcing that all teachers claiming absences due to sickness would have to produce a doctor's note verifying the illness and that no teacher would be allowed to take more than one day of personal time the week of the tournament.[65]

The media had a field day with this episode, especially after some teachers complained that Conn's actions were heavy-handed.[66] Upset teachers criticized the timing of the announcement, as some had booked hotel and travel arrangements already and even called for the Friday of the CIAA tournament to be designated as a built-in school holiday.[67] REA leadership also expressed resentment at teachers being portrayed as lacking commitment to city schools and found fault with the initial numbers Conn cited in announcing the policy, stating that Conn had "grossly exaggerated" the number of teacher absences in past years.[68] Eventually over 900 teachers filed a mass grievance against Conn.[69]

The turning point in Conn's tenure arrived, arguably, when the school board refused to fully back her in the dispute—some school board members, too, agreed with the REA that Conn's actions had been excessive and unnecessary.[70] Months later, Conn backed off her tough initial stance and withdrew proposed restrictions on teachers' use of personal leave time in an agreement with the REA.[71] That retreat led the *Times-Dispatch* to run a stinging staff editorial both denouncing teachers and expressing disappointment in Conn.[72]

The following year, in January 1997, the school board suspended Conn for "insubordination" and then officially dismissed her in March.[73] A two-page letter provided to Conn explaining the suspension listed numerous allegations that Conn had misled the board, ignored board directives, and made decisions and allocated funds without the knowledge of the board.[74] Prior to the suspension, the school board had stripped Conn of the capacity to make key personnel decisions, exemplifying a fatal breakdown of trust between the board and superintendent. A third-party attempt to defuse the conflict, including a private summit between board chair Melvin Law and Conn hosted by Virginia Commonwealth University professor Avon Drake, was unsuccessful in restoring the breach.[75]

Conn's perceived treatment by the board confounded many of her supporters, leading to the formation of a new coalition to protest the school board's actions.[76] Some observers took the entire episode as evidence that Richmond's educational community, including teachers, veteran administrators, the Richmond Education Association, and most of the elected school board, was incapable of embracing and supporting genuine reform. Others noted that Conn had failed to understand the city's complex racial politics: her handling of the CIAA affair doubly alienated many African Americans, partly because it was perceived as heavy-handed but much more so because it opened the door for white critics to rhetorically attack the city's predominantly African American corps of teachers.[77] The episode thus left Conn marked as an outsider, and without political support from either teachers or most Black leaders, she had little chance of staying long in the job.[78] The situation also called into question the notion that the elected school board would have the inclination or will to challenge the status quo when confronted with opposition, especially within the ranks of teachers.

In September 1997, the school board hired Virginia Beach assistant superintendent Dr. Albert J. Williams as its new superintendent.[79] Like Conn before him, Williams—a former military officer who still served in the reserves—initially made a positive impression with the public, pledging to collaborate with the REA to support academic progress.[80] Williams's initial message sought to both reassure and challenge multiple constituencies. Faulting low parental participation and student attendance, Williams described a "crisis of effort and commitment" enveloping city schools, quipping that "I can't teach algebra as they [truants] walk down Broad Street." But Williams also said he would demand not just "contributions" but "sacrifices" from those wishing to help city schools, and he criticized feel-good mentoring relationships that benefited adults more than children. Williams promised committed and immediate action but also called on students, parents, staff, and community members to do their part.[81] Immediate goals set included increasing the on-time graduation rate by 1999, improving attendance, assuring that third graders could read, and significantly boosting scores on standardized tests so that Richmond students exceeded national benchmarks.[82]

Lofty and laudable goals soon confronted hard realities. Williams's tenure coincided with the beginning of a new systemic testing regime in Virginia, the Standards of Learning (SOL) tests, resulting from legislation championed by Republican governor George Allen during his term (1994–98). The legislation mirrored national movements for "standards" and "accountability," heavily focused on standardized tests to measure learning. The first round of SOL tests took place in the spring of 1998, and the abysmal results came out that fall. The results for third graders: 35 percent of RPS third graders passed the English proficiency test compared with 55 percent of students statewide; 40 percent passed the math proficiency test compared with 63 percent statewide; 27 percent passed the history proficiency test compared with 49 percent statewide; and 36.5 percent passed the science proficiency test compared with 63 percent of students statewide. Similar achievement gaps were evident at the fifth grade, eighth grade, and high school levels. Conversely, third graders in both Chesterfield and Henrico Counties exceeded the statewide performance in all four subject areas.[83] This initial round of results illustrated the chasm between city and suburban schools in central Virginia and also established an annual rite of media commentary on the persistently low performance of Richmond schools.[84] More sophisticated analysts sometimes noted that Richmond's results were predictable when accounting for poverty, but the data confirmed and strengthened the widespread belief among Richmond metropolitan residents that suburban schools were "good" (and desirable) and urban schools were "bad" (and to be avoided if a family had a choice).[85]

Over the next three years, test scores improved in RPS but too slowly to alter the fundamental picture.[86] Steering clear of the debilitating controversies that had hampered his predecessors, Williams retained the support of the board, and he was offered and accepted a contract renewal in March 2001.[87] SOL results that fall showed Richmond continuing to struggle, however, with just five of fifty-five schools system-wide attaining full accreditation (compared with 40 percent of schools statewide).[88] In January 2002, to the surprise of the board, Williams shifted course and announced his retirement effective at the end of the year. Editorial critics credited Williams with stabilizing the system but faulted the slow academic progress on his watch.[89] A protracted national search for his replacement attracted just thirteen applicants. After unflattering news stories appeared about one finalist, the board settled on an unexpected internal candidate: Dr. Deborah Jewell-Sherman, associate superintendent for instruction. Jewell-Sherman, who had earned her doctorate in education at Harvard, had been hired by Patricia Conn in 1995. Few insiders considered her a likely candidate for the job, with some going so far as to describe her interview for the position as a "courtesy." But the school board hired her in the summer of 2002 after a 5–3 vote; observers immediately noted that three of the votes for Jewell-Sherman came from board members who were not seeking reelection and would be leaving the board at the end of the year.[90]

Gaining Traction, against the Odds

Deborah Jewell-Sherman thus came to the position amid considerable public skepticism of both RPS and her personally. Despite the apparent doubts,

Jewell-Sherman initially won plaudits by signing what at the time was a highly unusual performance-based contract, tying her salary and continued employment to the system's ability to achieve higher test scores. Specifically, by the end of the 2002–3 school year at least twenty schools were to be fully accredited (up from five in 2000–2001); the number of schools on full warning was to decline from twenty-nine to twelve; and sixteen elementary schools (of thirty-one) were to achieve 70 percent passing rates on the third-grade reading SOL. Some disbelievers questioned whether such rapid achievement was realistic, while others doubted the school board's willingness to follow through in enforcing the contract's provisions.[91] In signing the contract, Jewell-Sherman banked on the expectation that a significant alteration in the school system's curricular strategy already undertaken would show significant improvements in the 2001–2 tests scores. That expectation proved correct, as the 2002 scores showed an increase in the number of fully accredited schools from five to ten and a decrease in schools on full warning.[92] As superintendent, Jewell-Sherman moved to consolidate and accelerate those gains by implementing system-wide curricular coherence in association with newly promoted associate superintendent for instruction, Dr. Yvonne W. Brandon.

In a key decision, Jewell-Sherman and Brandon replaced site-based management of the curriculum with a centralized approach intended to assure quality control and to accommodate the high rate of mobility of individual students between schools. An initial survey by Brandon found that twenty-nine different reading programs were being used throughout the system. Brandon later recalled, "We were working hard, but we weren't working hard on the right things." Elaborating, she explained,

> We had an extremely dedicated staff of teachers, instructional staff, principals, but we did not have a clear definition of how to connect the pieces. We had no centralized curriculum alignment. We did not have any means of assessing our children to determine where they were and what they needed to do to get to the next level. The first step that we took was to look at an inventory of reading and mathematics products throughout the schools. We had previously been experimenting with site-based management. As a result, instruction became very, very varied. Each principal did what they wanted—it was varied in intensity and in product, which didn't quite match with having a 44% [student] mobility rate.[93]

To address this unevenness in curriculum across schools, Jewell-Sherman and Brandon moved to identify sound system-wide curricular products and at the same time institute a common instructional model to assure that schools consistently and correctly implemented the curriculum. Specific lesson plans were tied to the content of the SOL tests, both to help the students perform better on the tests but also to familiarize the teachers themselves with what would be on the tests, with teachers working closely with instructional specialists to devise each lesson. Jewell-Sherman and Brandon pushed the resultant detailed curriculum guides into each school building. For low-performing schools, Jewell-Sherman and Brandon selected the Voyager reading program and engaged the company in participating in teacher training and in monitoring the program's implementation. The administration also introduced baseline and frequent diagnostic testing to track individual students' progress and trained principals in the detailed use of data to assess and refine instruction, with the aim of having, as Jewell-Sherman put it, "a more explicit conversation about why someone may be having difficulties." Programmatically, the administration extended the school week for elementary students by ending early dismissal Wednesdays, created a "Twilight School" afternoon program to help high school students who had missed school time to make up courses, and introduced International Baccalaureate programs in secondary schools, among other initiatives.[94]

At the same time, in order to generate constructive feedback on the school system as a whole, Jewell-Sherman commissioned the Council of the Great City Schools to undertake an independent assessment of the system, which took place in 2003.[95] The council's report, released in January 2004, offered this diagnosis of the system Jewell-Sherman had inherited:

> [To make progress, Richmond] will need to change some bad habits. The school board has taken to fighting the superintendent rather than battling the forces of illiteracy. Until recently, the school system's administration had largely abdicated its responsibilities for spurring student achievement. The district's teachers are too often heard blaming parents. And the parents, for their part, have not been as actively engaged in the instructional process as they need to be. . . .
>
> In short, the Richmond school district has had trouble hitting its mark over the years because so many people in the system are aiming in different directions.

The council went on to issue nine broad recommendations:

1. Develop a coherent vision for what it [the school system] wants to achieve.

2. Set measurable goals for academic improvement.
3. Establish a new accountability system for attaining academic goals.
4. Standardize districtwide instructional strategies and curriculum.
5. Provide districtwide professional development on the implementation of the new curriculum.
6. Ensure that reforms are implemented at the classroom level.
7. Use data to monitor progress and decide on instructional interventions.
8. Incorporate literacy reforms into the preschool program and extend them through the high schools, grade-by-grade.
9. Focus on the district's lowest performing schools.[96]

These recommendations in fact mirrored and affirmed the agenda Jewell-Sherman had already established for RPS and appeared intended to strengthen the superintendent's standing with the board.[97] But the report itself offered a stinging, detailed critique of almost every aspect of Richmond Public Schools' academic program and decried the lack of a strategic plan to guide the district. While the report endorsed the start that Jewell-Sherman had made as a superintendent, it also made clear that the system still had a long way to go in becoming an effective, focused organization capable of delivering higher and higher levels of academic achievement.

The report focused particular attention on problems in governance, goal setting, and accountability. For instance, concerning governance, the report offered these observations:

- The district lacks a sense of urgency to accelerate student achievement.
- The board does not have a coherent vision or agenda for improving student achievement beyond its stated goals for 2002–2003.
- The school board is fractured on a range of issues and does not have a consensus around improving student performance.
- The board lacks strong leadership focused on student achievement. Agendas of school board meetings do not reflect a consistent focus on student performance.
- The school board is reported to make multiple requests of staff below the superintendent level that often distract staff from their administrative assignments.
- The school board does not have clear expectations for staff or student performance.

- Individual school board members fill the leadership void by pursuing their own agendas that sometimes correspond with higher student achievement but many times do not.
- The school board is more crisis-driven than strategic.
- The school board does not have a process for evaluating itself.
- School board support of the superintendent is fractured.
- The school board has a general plan for engaging the community in school improvement efforts, but it is not specific enough and has not spurred much action.[98]

The report also contained critical commentary on a variety of other topics, including curriculum, professional development and teacher quality, the reform process, assessments and data, early childhood and elementary education, middle and high schools, and low-performing schools.[99] In all, the report provided eighty-six specific recommended actions aimed at establishing clear goals and systematically reorganizing practices and procedures to achieve them. Separate sections evaluated RPS's use of Title I funds and its "Exceptional Education" (special education) department. Echoing a state report released earlier in 2003, this study identified systemic problems with adequately staffing special education with appropriately trained teachers and support personnel and also noted that "parents sometimes feel there is a lack of respect from the schools for the needs of their children and a disregard for what parents think are appropriate placements and services."[100] To correct issues in special education, the report offered an additional fifty-four specific action steps.

A brief conclusion from the Council of the Great City Schools recited the structural difficulties facing the schools (poverty, declining enrollment and tax base, leadership turnover, school behavior problems) but added that the "school district . . . had not made the situation much better for itself." They held further,

> The school board was marked by a fair amount of internal squabbling. The district did not provide the level of instructional direction and support for its schools that characterize other faster improving urban school districts. The district's instructional programs had become incoherent and subject to "program-creep." The district's staff members were not always well-versed on the latest reading and math research or prepared to implement it.
>
> The fact that the district had no strategic plan for improving student achievement was as emblematic of the challenges that Richmond faces as anything the teams saw.[101]

The authors closed by calling on the system to adopt a strategic plan drawing on the report's themes, with the aim of having the "board and administration . . . working off the same page and owning the same strategy for accelerating student achievement."[102] With this scathing report in hand, Jewell-Sherman aimed to leverage its findings to increase comprehension of and support for her academic initiatives and to provide an overarching direction for the system that could transcend the thicket of thorny day-to-day issues and problems.[103]

While Jewell-Sherman was focused on academic improvement, numerous other issues related to the school system's operation continued to command public attention. Chief among these were continued doubts about the operating efficiency of the system, incidents of violence in the schools, the system's continued high truancy rate, a scathing 2003 state report concerning special education in the system that led to the resignation of a deputy administrator, and boardroom politics.[104] The special education report particularly illustrated a disturbing legacy of institutional neglect. In her initial years as superintendent, Jewell-Sherman faced repeated criticism from two school board members, Vice Chair Stephen Johnson and Reggie Malone; in the fall of 2003, board member Charles Nance called for a vote of confidence in the superintendent to help quell the criticisms. Taken prior to the release of the finalized 2003 SOL results, the board gave Jewell-Sherman a 7–0 vote of confidence, with Johnson and Malone abstaining.[105]

The 2003 release of the finalized SOL results gave further credence to the vote. The number of schools receiving full accreditation shot up from ten to twenty-three, while the number of schools accredited with warning fell from twenty-three to nine.[106] System-wide, between 2002 and 2003 the pass rate improved from 57 percent to 70 percent for fifth-grade English and from 50 percent to 64 percent for fifth-grade math. Most grade levels (all but eighth-grade reading) showed two consecutive strong years of improvement in English and math, from 2001 to 2003.[107] The schools had thus met two of the three targets set in Jewell-Sherman's contract, and the superintendent proudly reported receiving a card from a board member reading, "I'm a believer now."[108]

Emboldened by these results, Jewell-Sherman called for the board to strengthen support for her initiatives. The *Richmond Times-Dispatch* offered her a guest commentary slot for twelve opinion pieces between February 2004 and January 2005 in which she laid out her philosophical principles and discussed specific school initiatives in response to the challenges of urban education.[109] She also initiated a working relationship with the

Partnership for Leaders in Education at the University of Virginia, with the aim of helping the school board become a more functional and focused body oriented toward academic progress. This partnership eventually led to the development of a new diagnostic tool, the "Balanced Scorecard," to evaluate progress and shortcomings at each school. The objective of the Balanced Scorecard was to provide the administration and school board a common framework for discussion and evaluation.[110] After the November 2004 election, the outgoing school board voted to offer Jewell-Sherman a new contract before learning this was prohibited by state law. Once the new board took office, a new contract was indeed offered and signed in March 2005.[111]

The New Politics of Education in Richmond: Schools versus Wilder

That vote of confidence, however hard-earned, provided Jewell-Sherman little breathing room. At the very moment the superintendent and school board had reached a long-sought accord, a dramatic new factor entered the equation of Richmond school politics: namely, Doug Wilder, in his role as popularly elected mayor. After passage of the 2003 advisory referendum to change the city charter, a second Wilder-Bliley Commission was formed to develop guidance on key policy areas in advance of the anticipated change in form of government.[112] Just weeks after Wilder's election, the education committee of that commission recommended that the new mayor be given the power to hire—with the "advice and consent" of the school board—the superintendent of schools.[113] In December, the school board met with mayor-elect Wilder to discuss his vision for schools; afterward, the board made clear that while it welcomed working with Wilder, it had no intention of giving up its constitutional power to hire the superintendent. Wilder also released a ten-point blueprint for school improvement, including closing underutilized schools, investing in vocational education, investing in after-school programs, cutting central administration, consolidating some school functions with the city, improving nutrition and fitness programs, enhancing transportation efficiencies, providing alternative schools for students with behavioral and truancy issues, engaging the business and religious communities, and combining financial incentives for high-performing employees with removal of low-performing staff. School board member Carol A. O. Wolf pointedly replied that the board already had been working on each item.[114]

Undeterred by this pushback, Wilder moved assertively to exert influence over the school system practically as soon as he settled into city hall. First, in

February 2005 Wilder announced a new initiative to seek some $690,000 in funds from the state legislature to underwrite the hiring of new truancy officers. Second, Wilder told the school board it would need to relocate its offices from city hall to the former Armstrong High School site in the East End. Third, Wilder requested that the school board cut its FY 2006 budget proposal, originally estimated in January at $271 million; in response, the board approved in March a slimmer budget proposal of $252 million. Fourth, on a tour of Richmond with U.S. secretary of education Margaret Spellings, Wilder announced his support for the formation of charter schools in Richmond.[115]

In this context, Jewell-Sherman began considering her own future. She was a finalist for superintendent jobs in St. Louis and Norfolk; after not getting the St. Louis job, she signed a new three-year contract in Richmond running to June 2008. The new contract also had performance incentives (a $10,000 bonus) tied to continued improvements on a range of metrics, including school accreditation, SOL scores, early reading, algebra enrollment for middle school students, PSAT and SAT test-taking and scores for high school students, attendance, and the dropout rate. Unlike the initial contract, the new contract did not stipulate specific numerical targets but allowed for targets to be determined year-by-year in consultation with the school board.[116]

Seemingly adding to the positive momentum, a March 2005 report by the Council of the Great City Schools highlighted Richmond as an urban school system making significant progress on elementary school testing. Pointing to changes in the curriculum and teacher training, Jewell-Sherman stated, "Our teachers, principals, and central-office staff took ownership of the [testing] results. . . . Before we used to say, 'The children did this, and the children did that.' Now, if the children don't succeed, then we failed."[117]

The new contract and positive review from the Council of the Great City Schools showed that Jewell-Sherman had won over the school board, but new challenges from within and without soon emerged. In the summer of 2005, a cheating scandal on the SOL tests at Oak Grove Elementary School on the Southside surfaced. Contrary to procedure, all students at the school were allowed to circle their answers in testing books rather than fill in circles on the answer sheets. School staff then filled in the sheets. But a review of the sheets and booklets showed significant discrepancies between what students had marked and what staff filled in as circles.[118] The issue led to the loss of Oak Grove's accreditation status and the firing of the school's principal.[119] As that scandal unfolded, Wilder announced the formation of a task force to provide oversight of the school board and RPS administration. In a July press conference, Wilder announced, "I am taking steps to end the complacency and dysfunctionality that plagues Richmond Public Schools," adding that RPS was "one of the best-funded yet poorest-performing" systems in Virginia.[120] Virginia Commonwealth University professor Robert Holsworth, now a Wilder ally, was tapped to lead the panel, and at the initial press conference Chesterfield County superintendent Billy Cannaday was also named as a participant. Cannaday quickly removed himself from the panel, claiming he had not understood that the panel would be exercising oversight over RPS. That misstep took the gloss off of Wilder's list of complaints about RPS: low SOL scores, the Oak Grove scandal, 135 disciplinary actions per day, and high truancy. Referring to statistics that showed over one-third of high school students were chronically truant (over ten unexcused absences), Wilder declared, "If these statistics are halfway right, I say if they are halfway right, what they tell me is that there are some people who are stopping the kids who want to learn, who really want to achieve. They can't get a good, decent education. That is not good enough for me."[121] Notably, Wilder made no reference to the 2003 Council on the Great City Schools report or the profound organizational issues it raised and made no acknowledgment of Jewell-Sherman's efforts to fundamentally reshape the system's curriculum and teaching.

The announcement of Wilder's panel drew battle lines that would shape the next three years of school, and indeed city, politics. "Why is Wilder attempting an end run around a pliable board whose chairman [Stephen B. Johnson] is staunchly aligned with him?" asked *Richmond Times-Dispatch* columnist Michael Paul Williams. "In the parlance of leadership, what Wilder is doing is called orchestrating conflict."[122] School board members' reactions ranged from diplomatic to hostile, with members defending the direction and progress of the school system and pointing to the difficulties of educating children in a high-poverty city. "Are we moving in the right direction? You bet. Are we where we want to be? No way," stated Carol Wolf. Less diplomatic was Chesterfield County school board member James Schroeder, who wrote a letter to the editor describing the task force as an "insult" to the citizens of Richmond whose impact would be to "[perpetuate] distrust and discord in [the] community."[123] But city council president Manoli Loupassi issued a statement supportive of Wilder's move, saying, "In many respects, I share the frustrations the mayor has. We spend a lot of money on schools, and you can see the results."[124]

In April 2006, Wilder's schools advisory committee held meetings decrying RPS's level of spending and recommending the consolidation of some administrative functions between the schools and the city.125 Later in the year, Wilder and the school board argued over who had the authority to approve the building of schools. The school board had approved a list of schools to be built under the "City of the Future" capital plan, but Wilder treated that recommendation as purely advisory and said (through a spokesman) the mayor's advisory committee would make final recommendations.126 Wilder, perhaps surprisingly, kept a relatively low public profile during the fall 2006 school board elections, which saw all incumbent candidates retain their seats, including George P. Braxton II, who would be elected as chair of the new board, as well as one of the most outspoken critics of the mayor's various stratagems, Carol Wolf.127

The mayor again moved assertively on schools in early 2007. The administration began to withhold one-half of the schools' non-payroll disbursements in the spring of 2007 on the grounds that Jewell-Sherman and the school board had not cooperated fully with requests for an independent audit. In February, city auditor Umesh Dalal had released an audit identifying potential savings of up to nearly $20 million, or 7.6 percent of the annual budget. But Wilder immediately stated the audit was incomplete, as Dalal had not been able to examine purchasing practices and several other areas and also had found some RPS staff to be "uncooperative."128 The mayor planned to spend $200,000 on a second audit by a Washington-based firm with a view to identifying additional savings. When school leaders did not immediately accede, he moved to begin withholding funds. This led the school board to file suit against Wilder in March for having withheld $4.7 million.129 Eventually the school board and Jewell-Sherman agreed to allow Dalal to perform a second audit with "unencumbered access" to school financial records.130

The battle between Wilder and Jewell-Sherman continued.131 Throughout the summer, Wilder and Jewell-Sherman sparred publicly concerning the proposed relocation of the school board away from city hall. Wilder first set a June 30 date for the board to leave and then scolded Jewell-Sherman by letter, stating, "I am appalled at your duplicity," after the superintendent announced plans to seek a private partner to develop a new permanent home while making it clear RPS could not vacate by June 30.132 The city council, in the meantime, announced an agreement to allow the school board to stay in city hall indefinitely.133

In this heated context, in August, twenty-six corporate leaders—overwhelmingly white and male—wrote a public letter to Wilder stating that the schools were in crisis and proposing an appointed school board as the remedy. The detailed letter is worth considering in full:

> Dear Mayor Wilder, President Pantele, and Members of Richmond City Council:
>
> We are writing today to offer our assistance as you work to establish the City of Richmond as a leading Virginia and American city. We represent a significant majority of the largest employers in the Metro Richmond area. All of us are proud of the recent momentum this city has achieved, and of the future plans envisioned for the arts, sports and recreation, and development along the river, including retail space and housing.
>
> Dramatic progress is being made in many areas. Reported crime rates have fallen each year since 2004. 2007 may yield the best statistics in decades. After years of decline, population in the city increased in 2006 over 2005, according to the Federal Bureau of Investigation.
>
> Cranes are visible all over the downtown area with new residential communities, a new Federal Courthouse, hotels, major new corporate buildings led by Philip Morris and MeadWestvaco, as well as renovation of the Carpenter Center, the National Theater, and plans for the Landmark.
>
> On the recreational front, plans have been announced to renovate or build a new Diamond, a new natatorium, a new indoor tennis facility for VCU along with new dormitories and a combined Engineering and Business School Complex. The VCU Medical Center is a hive of new construction. Discussions have begun for the proposed construction of a new Coliseum.
>
> We are convinced that the city is at a tipping point unlike any it has seen in over 150 years.
>
> ONE AREA continues to be of tremendous concern to us, however, and if it is not addressed now, will prevent the city from becoming a world-class place to live and work. This challenge is the performance of our city's public schools system, which continues to be one of the most expensive and least effective in Virginia—if not the nation. We know that all of you, the School Board, our teachers, and your constituents share our concerns.
>
> The educational statistics are alarming and constitute, in our view, an emergency situation that must be dealt with immediately and with

bold action. A few facts stand out (based on 2004 figures from the SchoolMatters, a service of Standard & Poor's):

— Richmond spends more than $10,500 a year for each student in its system, yet less than 57 percent of those funds actually go toward instruction rather than administration:

- Chesterfield $6,789, with 63 percent to instruction;
- Hanover $6,791, with over 66 percent to instruction;
- Henrico $6,801, with over 61 percent to instruction;
- [Similar figures for Norfolk, Petersburg, Portsmouth, Roanoke]

— . . . So while Richmond spends the most among its peer localities, its students see the lowest percentage of resources in the classroom. These figures do not take into account the enormous amount of unused space in underutilized school buildings.

— While Richmond spends the most of these comparative locales, the Virginia Department of Education reports that the city has the lowest graduation rate, except for Petersburg. . . . Similar statistics bear out in the SOL scores for children in elementary and secondary schools at all levels.

PERHAPS MOST alarming of all is the prevalence of serious violence in our schools, particularly when compared with other localities.

The state's Department of Education states that in the 2005–06 school year, there were 1,067 "serious incidents" in Richmond City schools or 4 for every 100 students. Other jurisdictions suffer a fraction of this violence. . . .

Recent studies indicate a concerted and focused approach to education, social services, and public health could significantly improve the lives of students who now begin their education destined to fail. Since Richmond has among the highest cost per pupil allocation of any Virginia jurisdiction, resources cannot be blamed for the poor quality of public education.

There are thousands of dedicated teachers in the Richmond Public Schools system. They are truly investing their lives in working hard to give each student their best efforts. But they will not succeed under the management and administration of the current Richmond School Board.

We have no quarrel with the members of the School Board who have done their best—rather, we believe a fundamental flaw exists in the governance structure which cannot be solved without a new approach to leadership and accountability for the success of the schools. For example, the mayor is responsible for proposing a budget for the city administration—but not for the schools. The City Council, with consent of the mayor, controls revenues through taxing authority. The School Board proposes a budget, yet has no control over raising revenues and, as we have learned recently, has no control over when they will receive their operating funds during the course of the fiscal year.

As a result, even the most well-meaning of public servants who serve on the School Board have little structural ability to make lasting decisions—particularly if subject to popular election. Neither do the City Council nor the mayor, because while they ultimately approve the budget, the School Board is responsible for policy decisions and selection of the superintendent. This mish-mash of accountability is doomed to failure—the proof is in the results.

WE BELIEVE those who have the revenue authority should be held responsible to the public for the performance of the city schools. With this in mind, we urge the mayor and the City Council to ask the city's General Assembly delegation to support amendments to the City Charter in the 2008 session that would make the following changes:

(1) An elected School Board would be abolished.
(2) A School Board Nominating Committee would be established composed of five members appointed by the City Council upon recommendation of the mayor. This committee would screen candidates much like the panel that recommends potential members of the various university Boards of Visitors to the governor.
(3) The Nominating Committee will present, to each member of the council, a list of three individuals. Each council member will select one person from the list of three who will represent the councilman's district for a three-year period.
(4) The School Board members' terms should be for three years and staggered so that three members would be appointed each year.

We believe this method of selection will result in a School Board composed of individuals who have good judgment and the required expertise to drastically reform the city schools. It will also place responsibility for the proper functioning of the schools with the elected representatives who control the purse strings—the mayor and the City Council. All of us would know who should be held accountable for the schools.

In addition to the Charter Amendments, we urge you to proceed as expeditiously as possible with the establishment of a Math-Science Magnet School and the proper funding and administration of the city vocational training program. The skills these two forms of education will enhance are critical to the present and future needs of our companies.

EACH OF OUR firms faces a rapidly aging workforce. Over the next decades, we will need thousands of new workers in Central Virginia—even tens of thousands.

The surrounding jurisdictions are producing better-qualified workers and a higher percentage of graduates. Richmond's schools are not producing the type of employees we need for the future in sufficient numbers.

We believe that extraordinary efforts are required to bring the Richmond Public Schools and the City of Richmond to the world-class level of which it is capable. Too many generations of children have already been lost.

We are eager and willing to work on this in a positive, productive, and candid partnership.

Together, we need to send a signal to the people of Richmond that its next generation of citizens will be successful, productive, and healthy, and that we will fight hard to make that promise come true. We stand ready to help.

Sincerely,
Thomas F. Farrell II, Chairman, President & CEO, Dominion.
Mike Szymanczyk, Chairman & CEO, Philip Morris USA.
Richard Cullen, Chairman, McGuireWoods, LLP.
Eugene P. Trani, President, Virginia Commonwealth University;
President & Chair of the Board of Directors, VCU Health System.
C. T. Hill, Chairman, President & CEO, SunTrust Bank, Mid-Atlantic.
William H. Goodwin Jr., President, CCA Industries, Inc.
John A. Luke Jr., Chairman & CEO, MeadWestvaco.
Robert J. Grey Jr., Partner, Hunton & Williams.
Michael D. Fraizer, Chairman, President & CEO, Genworth Financial.
James E. Ukrop, Chairman, First Market Bank.

Thomas E. Goode, Premier Executive Banking & Richmond Market President, Bank of America.
Thurston R. Moore, Chairman, Hunton & Williams.
Robert C. Sledd, Chairman, Performance Food Group Co.
Julious P. Smith Jr., Chairman & CEO, Williams Mullen.
G. Gilmer Minor III, Chairman, Owens & Minor, Inc.
Jon C. King, President & CEO, Exclusive Staffing.
Anthony F. Markel, President & COO, Markel Corporation.
Robert D. Seabolt, Administrative Partner, Troutman-Sanders, LLP.
Kenneth S. Johnson, President & CEO, Johnson Inc.
Clarence L. Townes Jr., Retired Executive [and past school board chair].
Patrick W. Farrell, President, HCA-Richmond Health System.
Robert W. Woltz Jr., President-Virginia, Verizon Communications.
Allison P. Weinstein, President & COO, Weinstein Properties.
John B. Adams Jr., Chairman & CEO, The Martin Agency, Inc.
Peter J. Bernard, Chief Executive Officer, Bon Secours Richmond Health System.
Theodore L. Chandler Jr., Chairman & CEO, LandAmerica Financial Group Inc.[134]

The corporate leaders' letter was notable for several reasons. Most obviously, the authors collectively formed a who's who of the established business power structure in Richmond. Few of these leaders had sent their own children to Richmond Public Schools, but they felt empowered to make this sweeping case for change. Second, the document provided no meaningful context for Richmond's school performance: it did not state the region's history of racial segregation in education or the political decisions that concentrated poverty and African Americans in the city, and it made only glancing reference to poverty and its impact on child development and learning. Third, the letter did not name Jewell-Sherman or recognize the substantial improvement in test scores that had taken place under her watch or mention the significant progress the board and administration had made toward creating a functional working relationship focused on long-term strategic goals. Fourth, the letter called on city leaders to take charter change legislation directly to the General Assembly as soon as possible, without giving the public the opportunity to weigh in via another advisory referendum.

Those who signed the letter quickly came to understand the politics of unintended consequences. They may have believed that they were following the spirit of the Crupi Report by engaging on a large civic issue, that by daring to tell tough truths they had shown how much they cared about Richmond, and that putting the elected school board on public notice would be as popular and successful an undertaking as establishing the directly elected mayor had been.

Instead, the gambit provoked an unprecedented level of public backlash. Columnists, letters to the editor, and most speakers at a public forum held by the *Times-Dispatch* in the following weeks strongly favored maintaining an elected school board. (One letter writer to the *Times-Dispatch* archly observed that the $10,500 per-student expenditure cited by the letter as evidence of waste "is almost a trifle compared to the $16,000-plus that many of these business leaders are probably spending to educate their own children at area private schools.")[135] Further, many observers assumed that the business leaders reflected Wilder's own views and interpreted the letter as yet another attempt by Wilder to expand his power. Some letter writers softened their stance in subsequent interviews, stating they simply wanted to start an urgently needed conversation about the condition of public schools.[136] But like many of Wilder's own statements, the letter showed little cognizance of the on-the-ground realities and struggles for improvement in city schools, instead settling for the view from 30,000 feet. As the second Crupi Report, released in late 2007, pointed out, Richmond business leaders were focused only on outputs of the system without attention to the inputs, in particular, poverty and "the condition of children entering the schools."[137]

Nonetheless, even observers who were taken aback by the tone and presumptiveness of the letter recognized that it had hit an important point: the inherent problem in Virginia's system of denying school boards taxing power, which created a disconnect between the body responsible for disbursing money (the city council) and the body responsible for determining how that money would be spent year-by-year on schools (the school board). By bringing school board membership under control ultimately of the council and the mayor, the letter's proposal would centralize authority and responsibility. Some observers agreed there was a disconnect but instead favored the opposite solution: giving the elected school board taxing power.[138]

Wilder's long-standing efforts to exert pressure on schools also undercut the letter's substantive arguments. The letter maintained that screening and then having the city council appoint school board members would lead to members with "good judgment and the required expertise" to make sound educational decisions—with the implicit conclusion that elected school boards would not. Elected school board members, as one favorable response to the letter put it, often "underestimate the time and effort required to do the job well." An appointed school board, in theory, might lead to nine members with experience and expertise while also strengthening accountability.[139]

But by August 2007, there was little reason to suppose Wilder (and perhaps some of the signers of the letter) held the city council in any greater esteem than the school board. Indeed, as noted in chapter 3, Wilder had moved assertively to claim powers previously thought to be under council purview already (such as the ability to fire the council's own staff). It was arguable that the (perhaps unintended) result of the logic the business leaders invoked would not be shared mayoral-council responsibility for the schools but something close to full mayoral control, giving Doug Wilder nearly unchecked dominion over Richmond's local government. At a minimum, the letter was an effort to redraw the lines of authority in the new form of government, so as to expand the mayor's power and influence. The lack of reference to the particularities of Richmond's recent academic progress in the letter and the failure to even attempt to undertake a balanced assessment of the system's progress under Jewell-Sherman did not inspire confidence among those involved in RPS that the business leaders who penned the letter truly knew what they were talking about. Indeed, rather than spark a productive civic debate about schools' governance, the net political effect of the letter was to increase public skepticism about Richmond's business elites and their vision for the city's future.[140]

The dramatic events of Friday, September 21, 2007, soon overshadowed the philosophical and governance issues raised by the letter. In the first act of what the *Richmond Times-Dispatch* characterized as a "blitzkrieg," Wilder's staff reported that a computer in city council president Bill Pantele's office had been used to search online pornography sites. Then the Wilder administration announced it would require all council liaisons to interview to keep their jobs and followed that up with a late afternoon email stating city hall would be closed to staff from 5 p.m. Friday to 7:30 a.m. Monday. Those actions proved the prelude for the main event: Wilder planned nothing less than the forcible eviction of the RPS offices from city hall. That evening, moving trucks assembled outside city hall on Broad Street while some 150 movers entered the building and for several hours began removing school system files and materials before being ordered to halt the eviction by a local judge, following the school board's request for an emergency injunction.[141]

The surreal scene, including file cabinets containing confidential school records left unattended outside City Hall, lasted for hours as the municipal version of a full-blown constitutional crisis played out. Deborah

Jewell-Sherman insisted that schools would open on Monday, September 24, as usual and gave administrative staff a pep talk before they went back to deal with the chaotically rearranged offices.¹⁴² Most Richmonders interpreted Wilder's precipitous actions as a wasteful and pointless overreach, an example of mayoral power run amok, exhibit A of what going "too far" looked like.¹⁴³ Furious council members described Wilder's action as an "attack on the city" (Bill Pantele) akin to an "orchestrated military attack" (Ellen Robertson).¹⁴⁴ The episode also irreparably damaged the relationship between Wilder and Jewell-Sherman, though this was not much of a relationship to begin with.

In the spring of 2008, Wilder's supporters found at least some justification of the mayor's attitude toward the schools with the release of city auditor Umesh Dalal's second audit of RPS, following up the initial audit released in 2007. The second audit was damning, presenting evidence that RPS lacked basic systems to adequately track purchasing and reimbursements.¹⁴⁵ Shortly after the audit's release, Jewell-Sherman announced her intention to leave office no later than the end of her contract in 2009.¹⁴⁶ (Ironically, Wilder would announce his plans not to run for reelection soon afterward.) Jewell-Sherman's departure date moved up to August 2008 once she landed a teaching and research position at the Harvard Graduate School of Education. Before leaving town, Jewell-Sherman was honored as Virginia's Superintendent of the Year. That honor and the Harvard appointment provided a measure of vindication to the embattled superintendent and contributed to the public perception that Wilder had run an effective educational leader out of town.¹⁴⁷ But the *Richmond Times-Dispatch* editorialized that Jewell-Sherman's departure in the wake of the scathing second audit was "the right thing to do."¹⁴⁸

The divided perceptions of Jewell-Sherman reflected a complex reality. Under her leadership, student achievement on the SOL tests continued to rise, albeit more slowly than the dramatic leap between 2001 and 2005, and by the end of her tenure over 80 percent of the city schools were fully accredited.¹⁴⁹ That improvement prevented the school system from being declared a failure and turned over to state control. But critics argued that RPS had not made comparable progress in other areas of the organization: operational efficiencies, effective communication with parents and community members, effective special education programming, and effective accountability for all teachers and principals. Other observers worried that the pedagogical strategies—reliance on the Voyager reading program, for example, or use of instructional specialists to guide teachers—had reached their limits in improving learning outcomes. While the Jewell-Sherman approach may have assured parents that a basic level of learning took place in all classrooms, critics charged it did so at the cost of restraining and over-programming the system's stronger teachers and students.[150]

The school board sided clearly with those who applauded Jewell-Sherman's tenure by appointing her lieutenant, Yvonne Brandon, as acting superintendent for the fall of 2008 and then permanent superintendent starting in January 2009. Brandon, who had worked in RPS almost continuously since 1977 in virtually every capacity, began her term the same month as incoming mayor Dwight C. Jones (himself a former school board chairman); Jones applauded the appointment, proclaiming, "She is an excellent educator. . . . The days before us are grander than the days behind us."[151] Jones and Brandon paired up in 2009 for a marketing campaign on behalf of city schools, titled "The Choice," which aimed to tell the story of RPS's success and progress in order to attract more parents to the school system.[152]

Jewell-Sherman's successes, as well as Wilder's departure from city hall, smoothed Brandon's transition. Brandon faced much less controversy than did Jewell-Sherman in the first three years of her term. Perhaps the most notable conflict concerned the relocation of some of the city's pre-kindergarten programs in 2010. In order to save money and create dedicated facilities for Virginia Preschool Initiative pre-K programs, Brandon recommended moving to create "regional" pre-K centers based in unused school buildings, relocating some of the programs that had previously been housed at individual elementary schools. Most notably, the proposal called for moving the pre-K program at Mary Munford Elementary School, an academically strong school with a majority-white student population located in Richmond's most affluent enclave, the West End, to the pre-K center at Maymont Elementary School, slated for closure at the end of the 2009–10 school year. The Maymont school building was located a short distance from the vast, publicly accessible Maymont Park and Nature Center and also a short distance from public housing units and other affordable housing properties. Students would be able to take a bus from Munford and other feeder elementary schools to Maymont. At public meetings in the spring of 2010, some Munford parents excoriated RPS over the change, citing the desire to keep siblings together in the same building and exposing the pre-K students to older students, with some also expressing concerns about safety. For some parents, the move was a typical example of poor communication and timing on the part of RPS.[153] But the pushback on what many recognized as a straightforward administrative decision offered a painful reminder of the continuing anxiety some Richmond parents felt about sending their children to socioeconomic- and race-integrated schools, outside of "safe" enclaves like Mary Munford Elementary and William Fox Elementary.154 The board ultimately approved Brandon's proposal on an 8–1 vote, and the Maymont preschool initiative program soon began winning rave reviews from parents.155

The New (and Old) Politics of Education in Richmond in the 2010s

Battles over the budget ultimately put an end to the era of "collaboration and cooperation" between the school board and the rest of city hall, with Yvonne Brandon ultimately paying the price. In his 2012 State of the City address, Dwight Jones kicked off his election year agenda by including some surprisingly blunt and critical statements about the condition of city schools, saying that the city could no longer engage in "celebrations of mediocrity."156 That statement seemed squarely aimed at the Jewell-Sherman/Brandon record of increasing accreditation levels in city schools, suggesting all that had been done was to create a baseline of mediocrity. Performance on SOL tests over the previous three years had consistently matched 2007–8 levels, Jewell-Sherman's final year, and in 2010 all schools reached full accreditation for the first time; meanwhile, the official graduation rate had gradually risen from 66 percent to 71 percent between 2008 and 2011.157 Achievement levels that from a certain vantage point represented clear progress—progress sustained even in the tight fiscal climate following the Great Recession—nonetheless fell far short of closing vast statewide and regional gaps. Jones's demand that the bar now be raised proved to be the opening skirmish in a yearlong battle between the mayor and the sitting school board.

The school board in February 2012, frustrated by years of flat budgets, declining state support following the Great Recession, and a flat annual contribution from the city, voted 8–1 to send a budget to the city council with a request for $24 million in additional funding from the city general fund.158 The bold request was conceived as a way to draw a line in the sand: the schools could not cut any more without cutting to the bone. The school board also launched a campaign to try to build public support for increased school funding. Jones responded by appointing a task force on accountability headed by several educational heavy hitters, including former Virginia secretary of education James W. Dyke Jr. and former secretary of health and human resources Eva Teig Hardy, who served as cochairs.159 That task force then hired a consulting firm headed by former city manager Robert

Bobb to undertake a review of RPS operations for the purpose of finding savings in the budget.[160] When the Robert Bobb Group released its preliminary recommendations, community pushback led Jones to agree to a partial compromise: $5.5 million were found for the schools primarily via a 1 percent across-the-board budget cut to other government operations.[161] Despite facing a massive shortfall, the school board completely rejected the Bobb Group's proposals to privatize transportation and custodial services. Instead it closed the remaining budget gap by placing teachers on five days' furlough, cutting twenty-eight noninstructional positions, and eliminating over 100 vacant positions.[162]

The showdown between Jones and the school board carried risks for both sides. Jones's tough line with the schools ran the risk not only of provoking community opposition—numerous residents testified on behalf of increasing the school budget in public hearings during the budget process—but also of handing an issue to a potential challenger for the mayor's job in the fall elections.[163] The school board, in turn, managed to claw substantial funds back into the budget, at the cost of being branded (by some) as irresponsible and lacking the courage to make the hard choices to close schools or implement fundamental changes to operational structures.[164]

In political terms, Jones's strategy paid off. No serious challenger emerged for the mayor's seat. Three of the nine members of the school board, including the influential former chair Kim Bridges, retired from public office. A fourth member, Adria Graham Scott, left town to follow her husband, Anthony Scott, the former Richmond Redevelopment and Housing Authority head who had taken a new job in Baltimore. A fifth member, sitting chair Dawn Page, gave up her seat in an unsuccessful effort to oust Reva Trammell from the city council in the Eighth District. That left just four incumbents running in the fall 2012 race, and with Jones free from serious competition for reelection, his political apparatus was able to influence the school board races. Incumbent Kimberly Gray from the Second District, the lone objector to the board's audacious budget proposal, won her reelection easily. Donald Coleman of the Seventh District also won without opposition. The other two incumbents were not so fortunate. Jeffrey Bourne, a William and Mary–trained lawyer, an African American, and a well-known deputy chief of staff for Dwight Jones, challenged Norma Murdoch-Kitt, Third District representative and a strong supporter of more school funding. Bourne's bid garnered numerous high-profile endorsements, and he won his race easily. In the Fifth District, Maurice Henderson, an African American NASA engineer and an outspoken critic of Jones and the accountability task force, faced a challenge from newcomer Mamie Taylor, a former RPS teacher. Buoyed by the endorsement of the influential Richmond City Democratic Committee, Taylor won the seat by a substantial margin. Finally, in the Eighth District, the mayor's son, Rev. Derik Jones, won election to the board to replace Dawn Page.165

When the newly elected school board was sworn in in January 2013, the city council elected Bourne board chair over Gray on a 5–4 vote, with Coleman elected vice chair. This result, combined with the presence of the younger Jones on the board and the November defeat of the mayor's two most outspoken critics on the city council (Bruce Tyler and Marty Jewell), prompted talk of a Jones political machine in Richmond.166 Internal divisions soon emerged, but the new school board agreed on the need for "change" and "reform" in RPS, challenging both the administration and decisions of the prior school board. After board members expressed dissatisfaction with the quality of information received from RPS administrators in response to board requests in the early months of 2013, Yvonne Brandon took the hint and announced her retirement in April, giving the new board the opportunity to place its stamp on RPS.167

Before the board could take action on hiring its next leader, however, it became ensnared in a prolonged debate about school closings and rezoning. Over half a century after Massive Resistance, this debate once again reopened fundamental questions about race and class and finding the proper balance between attracting middle-class students back into the system, operating efficiency, educational quality, educational equity, and the promotion of racial and economic diversity. The shadow of Jim Crow segregation and the problems between RPS and city government continued to loom large over public education in Richmond.

Race, Rezoning, and Retrenchment

The gains of the rights revolution and its emphasis on educational outcomes remained in jeopardy by the 2010s. In March 2013, the University of Richmond and Virginia Commonwealth University jointly sponsored a conference on educational inequality with the aim of calling attention to the need to nurture racially and economically diverse public schools and to begin undoing the long legacy of segregation and resistance to integration. While much of the conference focused on the regional dimensions of the issue, one of the conference conveners, Virginia Commonwealth University professor Genevieve Siegel-Hawley, presented data showing that racial segregation *within* RPS elementary schools had actually *increased* since the early 1990s. Siegel-Hawley, a Richmond native who had attended William Fox Elementary School as a child, showed that the Black-White Dissimilarity Index within RPS had risen from .47 in 1990 to .71 in 2010, meaning that 71 percent of white RPS students would have to change schools for the racial distribution of students within each school to match the system-wide racial average. By this measure, schools in the RPS system were *more* segregated than Richmond's neighborhoods, whose index score was .67 in 2010.[168]

Siegel-Hawley's data reflected more obvious measures of the distribution of students in RPS, as well as traditional middle-class folk wisdom. In 2011–12, roughly 70 percent of all white elementary school students in RPS attended just three schools out of twenty-eight: Mary Munford, William Fox, and Linwood Holton, which were 79 percent, 65 percent, and 30 percent white, respectively.[169] At the same time, fourteen elementary schools had populations at least 88 percent Black, including nine schools in which 94 percent or more of students were Black. The vast majority of elementary schools in Richmond were regarded as unthinkable educational options by white and Black middle-class families. Acceptable options included moving to the Munford, Fox, or Holton districts; trying to attain entrance into one of those schools via open enrollment; or sending children to Patrick Henry Elementary, a Southside charter school opened in 2010 that was nearly one-third white.

The study also showed that this segregated result was inextricably linked to politics. Siegel-Hawley found that school board policy, specifically the problematic way RPS combined the neighborhood schools concept with open enrollment, exacerbated neighborhood-level demographics to create intensely segregated schools. The provision of a large number of open enrollment slots—about 50 percent of total enrollment at William Fox in this period— created an incentive for white middle-class parents to apply to a school out-of-zone rather than invest in their neighborhood schools. In addition, in response to an audit recommendation, the school board in 2007 ceased providing transportation to students attending an out-of-zone school, creating a clear class bias in who could access open enrollment.[170] Consequently, the open enrollment system in practice facilitated the movement of white middle-class families to select schools. At the same time, the open enrollment process was also used by middle-class Blacks, who often enrolled in substantial numbers at select out-of-zone schools, particularly John B. Cary and Bellevue Elementary Schools.[171]

The case of John B. Cary merits analysis. From the 1970s to the 1990s, Cary, located just south of the I-195 expressway a few blocks west of the

Boulevard, was widely regarded as one of the city's best examples of a diverse, academically successful school.[172] But by the mid-aughts, the number of white students attending the school had fallen precipitously, stabilizing at about 10 to 12 percent. Many white families living in the Museum District, the affluent neighborhood located north of the school, sought to place their children at Fox or Munford in preference to Cary. At the same time, Richmonders continued to perceive the school as catering largely to middle-class African American families from the Southside and elsewhere. Hence by 2011, Cary was characterized by both high exit rates and high entrance rates from out-of-zone.[173] By 2011–12, the school had just 210 students—about one-half its building capacity.[174]

In 2011–12, the school board launched a comprehensive rezoning effort. Cropper Analytics, an Ohio-based consulting firm, produced several draft zoning proposals, using building utilization as its primary criterion. The firm did not consider the racial diversity of proposed districts or the academic achievement of the individual schools. In February 2012, the rezoning committee issued a preliminary recommendation to close John B. Cary and two other schools given the low building utilizations at these schools.[175] Community members pushed back on the proposal; Cary advocates argued that expanding the school to K–6 and eventually to K–8, as called for in the school's strategic plan, would help resolve the relatively low enrollment issue. Other community members argued that it would be a mistake to close academically successful schools for the sake of building efficiencies. The 2012 school board, persuaded by these arguments, passed a rezoning plan that closed one Southside school in order to allow students to move to the newly opened, state-of-the-art Broad Rock and Oak Grove Elementary schools, also on the Southside, in January 2013, while keeping the other schools (including Cary) open.[176] In a December 2012 action, the outgoing school board approved plans for Cary and J. B. Fisher (another school threatened with closure) to add sixth graders beginning in 2013–14.[177]

The new school board immediately revisited these issues, in dramatic fashion, in the first half of 2013. At its first working meeting in January, the board moved to reconsider the decision to allow Cary and Fisher to expand to add sixth graders, reversing the decision later that month.[178] Then in February, the board unanimously passed a preliminary budget that included a proposed $1 million in savings resulting from the closure of two unnamed schools.[179] Speculation at first focused on Cary and Fisher and then turned to Clark Springs Elementary School in the Randolph neighborhood as well as the Adult Career Development Center. Clark Springs' student body was

95 percent Black and had a reduced and free lunch rate of 94 percent.[180] Community members and Fifth District school board representative Mamie Taylor argued against closing Clark Springs, located in the Fifth District, citing data showing the school's strong academic performance relative to schools citywide, including stellar results on the 2011–12 math SOL tests. (The school's 93 percent math pass rate for fifth graders far exceeded the statewide average of 67 percent.)[181] In an April meeting, Taylor marshalled a 5–4 vote to postpone school closing decisions for one year so that the board would have time to adequately deliberate over different options and to provide ample advance notice to parents, staff, and community members of the forthcoming changes.[182]

That pause on the drive toward school closures proved short-lived. At the May 13 meeting, Newly elected First District representative Glen Sturtevant and Second District representative Gray surprised at least some of their colleagues by introducing a new proposal for school closures and rezoning. (Mary Munford and Fox Elementary Schools were located in the First and Second Districts, respectively.) The proposal called for closing Clark Springs and the Adult Career Development Center and relocating the Norrell preschool program. At the same time, the plan called for moving the bulk of Clark Springs students to Cary and none to Fox, even though Fox was geographically closer to Clark Springs, while also moving Museum District students from Cary to Fox. (Residents in the Museum District had circulated a petition requesting the area be rezoned to Fox or Munford.)[183] On the Southside, the plan considerably widened the Westover Hills zone to encompass several predominantly white neighborhoods, with the apparent aim of facilitating the transition of Westover Hills from an overwhelmingly Black school to one with a significant white presence.[184] After just a few minutes of deliberation, and over heated objections, the Board voted 5–4 to move forward with the plan (pending required public hearings), with swing vote Kristen Larson from the Fourth District pointing to the refusal of the city council to provide additional funds to keep schools open another year.[185]

Community reaction to the plan was overwhelmingly negative, with the vast majority of speakers at public hearings on May 28 and June 3 criticizing the proposal. Clark Springs staff and parents decried being singled out for closure despite strong academic scores. Many community members and the four dissenting board members argued it was impractical and inhumane to close schools so late in the year and only a few months before the start of a new school year.[186] Others were astonished that such a consequential plan could be voted in as policy with so little time for vetting by the board or the public. But what grabbed the most headlines was the charge that the rezoning plan would codify Fox as a majority-white school while undermining the possibility of Cary becoming a racially diverse school. Clouding the issue further was the fact that grossly erroneous data on the schools' racial composition had been presented by Cropper Analytics at a May 20 public meeting: critics pointed out that the board majority pushed the plan forward without even knowing what the effect would be on the schools' racial demographics.[187]

The data projections on economic disadvantage showed that while the ratio of reduced and free lunch children at Fox would remain just under 20 percent, the rate at Cary would jump from 50 percent to 74 percent. Further, analysis of the proposed boundaries showed that while the percentage of white students at Fox would stay nearly unchanged, the percentage of white and Hispanic students at Cary would fall sharply. Moreover, Clark Springs students coming to Cary would be moving, in effect, from one racially homogeneous environment to another.[188] As critics pointed out, the plan not only missed a chance to increase diversity at Fox by moving a substantial number of Clark Springs children there but also all but took Cary off the table, at least in the short term, as a diverse school environment. Critics also pointed out that as the virtually all-white Museum District began sending more kids to Fox, and as more families with children moved into the expanded Fox zone to take advantage of the opportunity to go to a "good school," prospects for bolstering racial diversity at Fox and bringing it closer to the citywide demographic would decline over time.[189]

Black and white parents from the affected schools and citywide rallied in opposition to the plan. The Richmond NAACP, Crusade for Voters, Genevieve Siegel-Hawley, former school board members, and an interracial coalition of white and Black parents from Clark Springs, Cary, and also Fox spoke out publicly against the proposal at the public hearings. (So too did two of this book's coauthors.) Despite the intense community opposition, the closure plan passed 5–4, with board chair Jeffrey Bourne and Derik Jones voting in the majority with Kristen Larson, Glen Sturtevant, and Kim Gray. Board vice chair Donald Coleman joined Mamie Taylor, Shonda Harris-Muhammed (Sixth) and Tichi Pinkney Eppes (Ninth) in strong opposition to the plan.[190] In apparent response to the criticisms, the board then voted to modify the rezoning plan slightly so as to keep in Cary part of one planning block slated to move from Cary to Fox, while also moving two planning blocks from the Carver zone into Fox.[191]

Nonetheless the overall plan smacked, critics charged, of segregationist strategies, where white parents again sought to stave off class- and race-based integration. On this view, adoption of the plan showed that the board majority was not serious about creating diverse, integrated schools in Richmond at every opportunity. Nonetheless, the board majority received praise from the *Richmond Times-Dispatch* editorial page for a difficult but financially responsible decision.[192] At an intuitive level too, many observers saw little wrong with the school board continuing to make policies and draw lines in ways designed to attract and retain middle-class residents in the school system—even if it came at the cost of RPS moving toward a two-tiered school system, *internally*. Some observers suspected this is what some school board members aimed for in the long term: to create a comfortable, clear path for white middle-class families to be able to go to "good" schools all the way through, from pre-K to twelfth grade, without having to learn in high poverty or majority–African American environments at any point along the way.

Such a plan created a profound moral question: Do privileged families that commit to an urban public school system have a moral responsibility to ensure that they push for policies and practices that take into account the needs of *all* children, including the disadvantaged? Consider two alternative reasons for wanting more white and middle-class families to invest in a setting like Richmond. One rationale would stress the higher enrollments, enhanced operating efficiencies, and stronger tax base that might result from a greater share of affluent children participating. A second rationale would stress the value of integrated schools as a good in itself and look to a greater racial and class mix in Richmond as the best way to not only provide the benefits of diverse schools to more and more students but also lift the performance of the 40 percent of the city's children living in poverty.[193] From this perspective, Richmond's ongoing policy of maintaining a school (like Fox) that was just 20 percent poor but was surrounded by schools with disadvantage rates ranging from 70 percent-plus to 90 percent-plus could only have had one real purpose: to provide an excellent education to some while denying it to others.

In the aftermath of the school closure and rezoning decisions of 2013, the future state of Richmond Public Schools remained uncertain. School board vice-chair Donald Coleman, in remarks at the June 3 public hearing, said that the old Richmond had not been in evidence that night, except in the actual vote of the board.[194] What he meant was that the outpouring across racial lines to demand that schools be closed only in a fair and humane way according to well-established criteria and that the school board prioritize the creation of *integrated* schools was something new and hopeful.[195] Despite this ray of hope, what remained clear was that any significant movement toward a balanced approach to the twin dilemmas of attracting the middle class while improving the performance of impoverished students would require much explicit and at times painful public discussion about the enduring realities of race and class segregation in Richmond.[196]

2014 and Beyond: Enduring Challenges

Over the course of this study, a recurring pattern of events played out in Richmond Public Schools, all fundamentally connected to the challenge of successfully educating a primarily disadvantaged student population. That challenge was often exacerbated by inadequate funding and aging facilities. The school system's serious problems made it increasingly difficult to attract or retain middle-class families. If these problems were not difficult enough, RPS was often characterized by frequent and localized conflict within the school board and on the city council. Nonetheless, at times Richmond witnessed glimpses of measurable progress. But the fundamental dynamics shaping the schools—and the large gaps in academic outcomes those dynamics produced—remained remarkably consistent across three decades. Paying the price for the perpetuation of the status quo were the large number of students who dropped out or graduated from the school system ill-equipped to meet the challenges of an increasingly complex work world. The story of education in Richmond, in this way, belied the spirit not only of public school integration but of the American civil rights movement itself.

The familiar cycle of hopeful starts followed by setbacks and resets played out yet again in the mid-2010s. The arrival of new superintendent Dr. Dana T. Bedden in January 2014 brought a revival of hope and interest in supporting Richmond Public Schools. Bedden stated that he wanted to be a major partner in Mayor Dwight C. Jones's battle against poverty, and he lent support to several collaborative efforts between RPS and the city's newly emerging Office of Community Wealth Building between 2014 and 2016. The overall relationship between RPS and the mayoral administration, however, soon turned frosty. Bedden immediately called attention to the sorry state of RPS facilities and the need for stronger financial support of schools from the city. The city administration in turn asked to see a clear academic improvement plan from schools' leadership as well as commitment to closing or consolidating underutilized buildings.

This conflict played out in early 2015 in what by this point had become ritualistic annual budget battles over school funding. The school board initially sent Mayor Jones's administration a request for $24.9 million in new operating funding for FY 2016. Jones countered with $2.1 million in new operating funding with a further $10 million to be made available in a special fund contingent on development of RPS's academic plans and demonstrated commitment to closing buildings. In this battle (paralleled by a similarly vast gap in the capital budget request), the mayor held the power of the purse whereas the school board held public sympathy and the capacity to mobilize public pressure on the city council for more funding. Bedden's direct approach galvanized support from many teachers and community members, and even the surprise announcement in February 2015 that he was a finalist for the Boston superintendent job after just a year in Richmond seemed to strengthen the school board's hand, generating a "Better with Bedden" campaign for the superintendent to stay. (Bedden withdrew from the Boston search after his in-person interviews.) The city council, again, ultimately brokered a compromise leading to Richmond schools receiving $9 million additional operating dollars for FY 2016.[197]

A similar dynamic played out a year later. In February 2016, the school board requested $18 million in additional funding, whereas Mayor Jones's final introduced budget proposed an increase of only $1.5 million in operating dollars. In response, Superintendent Bedden suggested RPS would have to close multiple schools to close the budget gap, including long-revered (and long-struggling) Armstrong High School in the East End. This in turn led to marches on city hall by students and another spring of activism pressuring the council to increase school funding. A Facebook-based group, Support Richmond Public Schools, grew to hundreds and then thousands of members and organized citizens to go to city hall during budget sessions and other meetings wearing red and holding signs to support RPS.[198] At the end of another tense spring, the city council ultimately approved a budget with a $5.5 million increase for the school system; no schools were in fact closed.[199]

This recurring dynamic of inadequate school funding, poor educational outcomes, and elected officials' frustration with both came to define the 2016 municipal elections. Increased support for the schools was a major theme for most mayoral candidates, coupled in some cases with a call for greater accountability. The ultimate winner, Levar M. Stoney, pledged to create an "Education Compact" to bring the city council, the school board, and the administration together around shared goals. The compact, adopted in August 2017, committed the council and the school board to quarterly joint meetings with the administration and established a team of community members, city agency representatives, and school staff representatives to discuss ways to support students and families inside and outside the classroom.[200]

Yet two other major events in early 2017 complicated that step forward. First, Bedden, who had vocally supported the Education Compact, was forced to resign his position by the newly elected school board.[201] Second, in the spring of 2017 the Virginia Department of Education notified Richmond Public Schools and the City of Richmond that RPS would be placed under a "memorandum of understanding" with the state board of education allowing the state board to exercise extensive, detailed oversight over school operations (including review and approval of superintendent candidates) until RPS achieved full accreditation of all schools. At the time, only seventeen of forty-four schools were so accredited.[202] This action resulted from a harsh, comprehensive review of the school system that had been requested by Bedden and the previous school board. In that review, the Virginia Department of Education assessed RPS in twenty-five specific categories and rated its implementation of best practices substandard (or nonexistent) in seventeen categories. RPS's leadership, governance, and human resources functions were singled out for particular criticism.[203]

In some ways, the story of RPS is exceptional; in other ways, it is typical of cities with large numbers of racial minorities. The state report echoed a long-recurring theme in Richmond: the cumulative impact of both severe structural challenges and vexing organizational and governance problems on student learning. In this sense, Richmond mirrored the challenges of many urban systems across the country—wherever there were large pockets of historically segregated African Americans and the compression of poverty, school systems suffered. And they suffered not merely from declining tax bases and a lack of resources but often from internal organizational issues that undermined efforts to break the link between concentrated economic disadvantage and substandard educational outcomes. In Virginia, just three decades earlier, when Judge Merhige ruled against Richmond schools' claims for reparations for segregation, state officials embraced the court's findings that the commonwealth had done all it was obliged to do to remedy racial inequalities in education and that Richmond schools were on the way to closing the achievement gap. History demonstrated otherwise. Here, Richmond's story mirrors the abandonment of state-level commitments to serious remedies for the legacy of educational segregation in the late twentieth century, both in the U.S. South and nationally.[204]

In the meantime, Richmond students continued to academically underperform students in neighboring counties, while dropping out at a much higher rate, all but assuring the reproduction of regionalized—and racialized—educational and economic inequality into the next generation.

5

Poverty, Inequality, and Economic Development, 1988–2016

If this is something we can't do, we don't deserve to be here.

MAYOR DWIGHT C. JONES, ON HIS
ANTIPOVERTY INITIATIVES, OCTOBER 2013

The continuity of African American poverty in Richmond stood in direct contrast to the goals of the American civil rights movement.[1] The shift among Black leaders from "protest to politics" was fundamentally concerned with community control and economic empowerment.[2] Indeed, the historic ascendancy of Richmond's first majority-Black city council in 1977 raised hopes that political control over city hall might yield tangible economic progress for low-income Black Richmonders.[3] Black politicians in Richmond (and throughout the United States) struggled to meet the demands of rising expectations—African Americans not only were concerned about voting for voting's sake but expected to see political power translate into a better quality of life. Black people in Richmond sought, like their white counterparts, to use politics as means to transform their communities. Yet a decade later, Richmond remained a center of concentrated, highly racialized poverty and post–Jim Crow racial antipathy. Any real understanding of the Black freedom struggle must come to terms with the bigotry that survived segregation, the continuity of poverty that outlived the rights revolution of the 1960s, and the election of Black officials who tried to combat these forces.

The numbers from 1989 demonstrate the manner in which reality tempered expectations in Richmond:

- The citywide poverty rate was 20.9 percent, but for Black city residents the poverty rate was 28.9 percent, and for children (of all races) it was an alarming 35.8 percent, nearly double the national average.[4]
- Nearly one-third of adult residents (32 percent) had less than a high school diploma, compared with 25 percent nationally.
- Eleven percent of residents, or over half of those living in poverty, had incomes of *less than 50 percent* of the federal poverty line, compared with 6 percent nationally.
- Fifty-four percent of residents were renters, compared with 36 percent nationwide. Median household income was $23,551 (1989 dollars), compared with $30,056 nationwide (1989 dollars).[5]

This chapter focuses on the interlocking, complex factors shaping access to quality employment in Richmond (and other urban areas) from the late 1980s onward: the quantity and quality of available employment opportunities, economic and community development policies intended to expand such opportunities, workforce development policies and initiatives to help economically marginalized persons access employment opportunities, and transportation systems and policies facilitating (or blocking) reliable access to job opportunities. We then consider a variety of strategies and initiatives that city officials and local actors undertook to foster economic development. Two of the most significant and effective institutional actors in stemming Richmond's decline and underwriting its gradual rebound of population were in fact public entities: the Commonwealth of Virginia and especially Virginia Commonwealth University (VCU).

While the commonwealth and its institutions may have "saved" Richmond, local government also remained an active and critically important player in economic development, as we will see. After 1980, rapid suburbanization

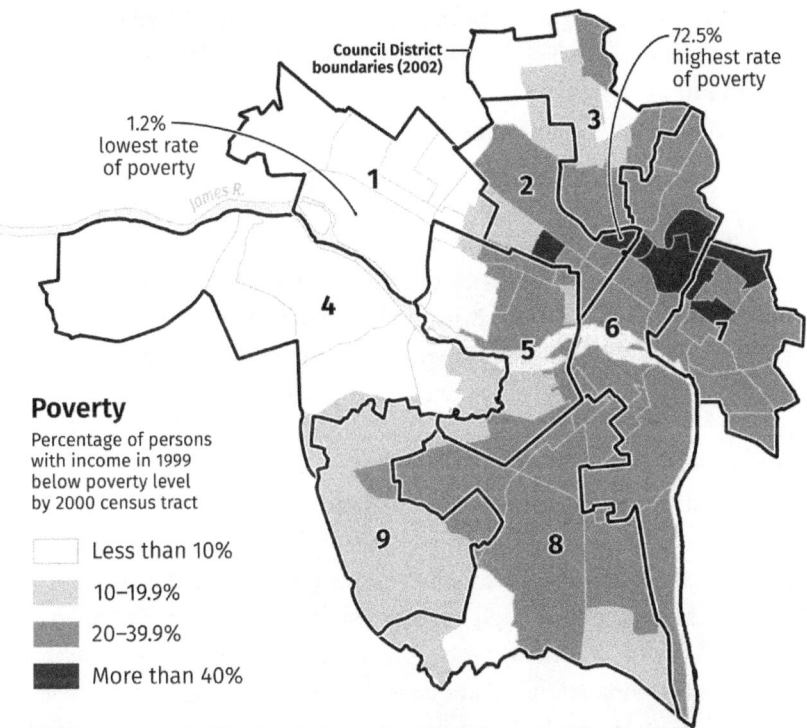

Map 5.1. Poverty by census tract and council district, 1999.
Map by Riley D. Champine of the University of Richmond Digital Scholarship Lab, based on data from the City of Richmond and IPUMS NHGIS (University of Minnesota, www.nhgis.org).

and center city decline partially, though not completely, displaced the City of Richmond as the economic center of the metropolitan area. The absence of a regional public transportation system contributed to an economic system in which low-income city residents were quite literally boxed out of suburban employment opportunities. Beginning in the 1990s, however, the expansion of VCU and the continued strength of the city's health care sector prevented Richmond from falling into an economic abyss: echoing a pattern found in numerous other American cities, "eds and meds" helped Richmond not only stabilize but revive as an economic entity.[6] Indeed, by the mid-aughts, the city began to show signs of a resurgence before the devastating impact of the Great Recession, which led to reduced activity and a sharp upward spike in the city's poverty rate. By the end of the second term of the Jones administration (2013–16), there were again ample signs of recovery and resurgence, as well as (in spite of the high-profile failure of Jones's most visible economic development proposal) several important policy developments that bolstered the city's long-term prospects.

Black poverty in Richmond outlived the segregated system. Twenty years after the protest movements of the 1960s, the city was still profoundly segregated by race and class. Black leaders struggled to meet the challenge of governing a declining and divided locality, years after they had been handed the proverbial keys to the city in 1977. Many whites contended (or implied) that Black leaders lacked the skills and knowledge to govern the city.[7] In reality, the Black-majority city council had been left to clean up a nearly century-long legacy of systemic and systematic disinvestment in Black communities, and to do so with relatively limited resources. During the mid-twentieth century, white Americans often resolved not to fix urban problems but to earn enough money to move away from them. In fact, white Richmonders, like white people in many American cities with sizable minority populations, abandoned so-called inner cities and invested considerable energy in building their way to better suburbs. Black leaders in Richmond sought to redress this pattern of escapism and retrenchment, both using established economic development tools and implementing new strategies aimed at expanding Black wealth and opportunity. Ironically, these policies may not have reaped immediate benefits, but they were, as this chapter demonstrates, fairly effective in helping revive the city. Yet while the economic pragmatism of Black politics paved the way for urban revival and gentrification, it often did little to move the economic needle for low-income Black city residents.

Anti-urbanism in Virginia shaped modern Richmond. After the 1960s, Virginia's leaders all but turned their backs on increasingly Black cities. Following the controversy over the City of Richmond's partial annexation of Chesterfield County in 1970, Virginia power brokers used the power vested in the General Assembly to hem cities in place geographically. By the late 1970s, cities were no longer permitted to use annexation as a means to expand, in effect locking in structural racial inequalities.[8] This seismic shift in state policy profoundly impacted Richmond.[9] Up until the 1970s, the city's boundaries and populations had routinely expanded throughout the nineteenth and twentieth centuries, a process that was long regarded as a normal part of urbanization and also necessary to maintain the viability of the city in the era of decentralization following the emergence of the automobile.[10] Richmond's white leadership sought a merger with Henrico County in the late 1950s and early 1960s, unsuccessfully, and then pivoted, with increased urgency, to annexing parts of Chesterfield in the late 1960s.[11] In short, what had been a widely accepted, legitimate expansionist economic tool (annexation) during the long era of white political control of Richmond suddenly became off-limits at the very moment in the late 1970s when Black people obtained majority control of the city council.

Richmond political leaders faced additional structural challenges in the following decades as they sought to expand the city's tax base from within. Public and nonprofit institutions, including the state government, VCU, hospitals, nonprofit organizations, and private colleges (Virginia Union University and the University of Richmond) held large amounts of city land. This meant that a large part of the city's property went untaxed, contributing nothing to the city's revenue.[12] At the same time, the state's tool for calculating a locality's capacity to pay for public schools, the Local Composite Index, was primarily based on that locality's taxable property value, not the economic need of its residents.[13] This meant that Richmond, in reality one of the poorest localities in Virginia, was classified as relatively rich and as a result received millions of dollars less in school funding from the state, year after year. It also meant that fiscal gains from a growing local tax base over time might be partly offset by reduced state educational aid.

There was more. By the 1970s and 1980s, the city's aging infrastructure created new challenges as roads, bridges, and sewers required high maintenance costs, adding to the tax burden and spurring high utility charges. The costs disproportionately hurt low-income residents. High crime created a demand for a large police force, and the older building stock increased the risk of fire emergencies. With one-fifth or more of city residents living in poverty, fewer residents could afford to pay significant city taxes, and demand and need for critical public services soared. Richmond committed to providing public transportation, health services, and social services often not available in the surrounding counties—including emergency support for the homeless and persons experiencing health or mental health crises. At the same time, the city sought to support various cultural activities and to provide public libraries, parks, and recreational facilities as a hallmark of an attractive, livable city. The city's financial situation, in short, was chronically strained by the turn of the twenty-first century.

Declining tax bases with increased needs gave rise to decades of economic pragmatism in city hall. The city council sought to meet revenue needs by imposing relatively high property tax rates: a rate of $1.53/$100 of assessed land values in the late 1980s, declining to $1.20/$100 by 2008 during the Wilder administration, where the city council kept it throughout the 2010s. The surrounding counties boasted tax rates well under $1/$100 over this entire period and continuing to the early 2020s—$0.87 in Henrico County (2021) and $0.95/$100 in Chesterfield County (2021) compared with $1.20/$100 in Richmond (2022).[14] These realities, and decades of neighborhood disinvestment, inspired local power brokers and politicians to promote economic development growth strategies. Politicians began to champion so-called silver bullet strategies that might reinvigorate the city by injecting new investments, often via public-private partnerships.[15]

Richmond, like many cities with sizable minority populations, attempted to grow and build its way to being a better city. Elected officials, including representatives of lower-income Black districts, largely accepted the proposition that growing a bigger economic pie was a functional imperative of sustaining and improving the city.[16] The logic was straightforward: more jobs would lead to more revenues for city government, allowing the city to sustain and expand services for low-income residents without further burdening Richmond's taxpayers. More jobs, in turn, might also (theoretically) reduce poverty directly, if underemployed city residents were hired in substantial numbers in the new positions. The aspirations of Richmond elected officials were little different from those of municipal officials nationwide who sought to keep or bring jobs to their communities. Nor were they different from the aspirations of leaders in other Black-led cities who keenly felt the urgency of improving economic prospects for Black residents.[17] Yet urban scholars have widely criticized conventional approaches to economic development as generally practiced in American cities for four main reasons:

- Economic development efforts are often too focused on attracting external private investment rather than better utilizing or developing existing assets (including underutilized human capital).
- Economic development efforts involving public subsidy often do not recoup the value of the public investment in the form of long-term tax revenues.
- Promised job benefits often do not materialize *or* do not lead to substantial opportunities for *existing city residents*, as opposed to newcomers (or in the Richmond context, county residents).

- Proposed projects reflect political pressures and the excessive influence of elite actors rather than reflect genuine community input. Consequently, many proposed projects may exacerbate gentrification and lead to the displacement of residents rather than build community wealth.[18]

Public pronouncements of "new investment" and "new jobs" associated with economic development projects rarely addressed these concerns, but they made for good politicking. What we know now, decades later, is that development projects often failed to deliver on many of their promises. Almost always, low-income communities benefited the least.[19]

Richmond's economic development efforts were not immune to these common pitfalls—in fact, they often embodied them. But the portrait that emerges is nuanced—and also reflects the fact that Richmond's local government (like other governments) at times demonstrated contradictory mindsets and promoted contradictory policies, depending on which actor, agency, or alliance was promoting any particular set of policies. The city underwent a period of relative economic growth in the early twenty-first century that reversed the downward trend of the previous decades. Overall economic activity and the city's downtown population grew substantially over a quarter century. But that growth and development failed to meet the types of post–Jim Crow challenges that cities such as Richmond faced: that is, these strategies often failed to meaningfully reduce the city's poverty rate, alter racialized disparities of wealth, or provide sufficient resources to lift Richmond out of its perpetual fiscal challenges.

In short, Richmond underwent a quarter century of development without equity. By the 2010s, citizens and some policymakers began to demand more. Richmond grassroots organizations developed the effective capacity to block certain elite-driven mega-projects, especially when they involved public subsidy. That work to stymie large initiatives flowed from widespread public skepticism about elite intentions as well as from harsh assessments of the results of previous endeavors championed by city leaders. What was missing was a model of economic and neighborhood development that more effectively embedded both fiscal responsibility and social equity concerns in ways that inspired public confidence that proposed projects would not only succeed but also deliver promised benefits to low-income city residents and the community more generally. Yet by the end of this time period, city leaders also sought to implement a new paradigm—community wealth building—with the intention of prioritizing the needs of the one-quarter of the city living below the poverty line.[20]

We begin, however, by reviewing the long-term economic trends that shaped Richmond and the region during and beyond the 1980s, trends that set the context for local economic development policymaking.

Overview of Broad Economic Trends, Richmond Metro Area, 1980–2015

Richmond experienced tremendous economic shifts between the 1980s and 2015, as encapsulated by four key trends: (1) Economic development increased in the region as a whole, yet (2) employment declined in the actual city itself. By the late 1980s, the capital city witnessed not just (3) deindustrialization but increases in specialized work that required better-educated workers. By the twilight of the twentieth century, Richmond's economic base had grown, yet (4) educational underachievement meant that the people who needed these jobs the most were often left in the economic lurch. The following section details these trends.[21]

First, economic development and growth steadily increased in the metropolitan region as a whole. Over this roughly thirty-year period, the number of jobs in the core Richmond region (the city and Henrico, Chesterfield, and Hanover Counties) expanded from roughly 386,000 in 1980 to about 614,000 in 2010.[22] The opportunities, however, were unevenly distributed, with many of these jobs located in the suburbs and not easily accessible to underemployed city residents. In fact, much of this growth took place *entirely* in the suburban counties; explosive growth in county employment levels in the 1980s would continue into the 1990s and beyond, while the city continued to lag behind.

Second, and more ominously, employment *within* the City of Richmond began to fall sharply after 1980, declining over 20 percent between 1980 and 2015. Taken together, these trends amounted to a stunning transformation: whereas in 1980, a solid majority (60 percent) of jobs in the core metropolitan area were located in the city, twenty years later only one-third of regional jobs were in the City of Richmond. Indeed, by 2010, Henrico County, which in 1980 had barely one-third as many jobs as the City of Richmond, became the region's largest employment base. (See table 5.1.) Speaking in 2010, longtime Henrico County manager Virgil Hazelett observed that when he began working for the county in the 1970s, he "got on [Interstate] 64 at Parham Road in the morning, [and] all of the traffic was going into Richmond and the out lanes were literally nothing as far as traffic; then it would reverse in the afternoon. Today it's balanced. . . . The development of the county over

TABLE 5.1. Employment by locality in Central Virginia, 1980–2015

Total employment[a]	1980	1990	2000	2010	2015
Chesterfield	50,509	96,849	137,184	156,644	180,774
Henrico	79,281	141,134	193,262	218,662	244,134
Hanover	22,243	36,236	48,327	60,646	67,710
Richmond	233,558	219,643	194,011	177,767	186,071
TOTAL	385,591	493,862	572,784	613,719	678,689

Percentage regional employment	1980	1990	2000	2010	2015
Chesterfield	13.1	19.6	24.0	25.5	26.6
Henrico	20.6	28.6	33.7	35.6	36.0
Hanover	5.8	7.3	8.4	9.9	10.0
Richmond	60.6	44.5	33.9	29.0	27.4

Source: Bureau of Economic Analysis (SIC series, 1980–2000; NAIC 2010–15), accessed February 6, 2024, https://www.bea.gov/data/employment/employment-county-metro-and-other-areas.
[a]Total number of jobs located within each locality (regardless of residence of employee).

these years has been dramatic."[23] Chesterfield and Hanover Counties also grew their employment bases, even as the city lost jobs.

Beginning in the 1980s, the Richmond region experienced both rapid decentralization of employment *and* a significant exodus of employers from the urban core. While the city continued, relative to population, to have a disproportionate number of jobs, it was no longer the sole economic pivot upon which the region turned. The ratio of the share of jobs in the city to the share of population among the four localities fell from 1.63 in 1980 to 1.22 in 2015 (see table 5.2). That same ratio rose in each of the counties over the same time period, and by 2000, the share of jobs in Henrico County rose higher than its share of regional population—meaning in economic terms that it no longer functioned as a traditional suburb.

The suburbanization of people and jobs had economic implications for the city. These economic facts in turn had significant political consequences. Many important employers in the Richmond region located outside the city, and while out-commuting from the city also increased dramatically in this period, suburban employers had little direct stake in the well-being of the city or city residents. Crucially, as the region's economic structure moved from being monocentric to polycentric, the region failed to develop an effective

TABLE 5.2. Ratio of employment share to population share by locality in Central Virginia, 1980–2015

	1980	1990	2000	2010	2015
Chesterfield	0.55	0.65	0.74	0.75	0.78
Henrico	0.67	0.91	1.04	1.08	1.09
Hanover	0.68	0.80	0.79	0.92	0.95
Richmond	1.63	1.52	1.38	1.32	1.22

Sources: Bureau of Economic Analysis (SIC series, 1980–2000; NAIC 2010–15), accessed February 6, 2024, https://www.bea.gov/data/employment/employment-county-metro-and-other-areas; U.S. Census Bureau, Decennial Census and Current Population Estimates (2015), accessed via Social Explorer.

Note: Figures greater than 1.0 indicate that a locality has a greater share of regional employment than regional population; less than 1.0 indicates the opposite.

mass transit system crossing jurisdictional lines (a topic detailed later in this chapter). These long-term economic trends dealt economically marginalized residents a double blow: the number of jobs available within the city limits declined sharply as jobs moved into the suburbs, but adequate functional transit to allow poor, carless workers to access those jobs was not provided.

The third major economic trend concerned the composition of jobs in the city and the region, with manufacturing jobs in the city declining by over 80 percent between 1980 and 2016. Mirroring urban trends nationally, manufacturing jobs in the city declined in the 1980s and 1990s, then began to decline regionwide after 2000. Richmond, for most of its history, was defined by tobacco cultivation and production. Tobacco, for centuries, was the bedrock of the city's prosperity. A major decline in tobacco employment characterizing the late twentieth and early twenty-first century helped drive the trend—by 2013, Philip Morris employed just 2,000 people, primarily at its Southside cigarette manufacturing plant, compared with 10,500 in 1993. But the decline proved broader.[24] Tables 5.3 and 5.4 illustrate trends in industrial composition in the city, first between 1980 and 2000 and then between 2001 and 2015. (Due to a change in industry classification systems utilized by the Bureau of Economic Analysis after 2000, the two trend lines are not exactly comparable.) In 1980, there were 33,824 manufacturing sector jobs located in the city (as determined by the government's Standard Industrial Classification system then in use); twenty years later, nearly 15,000 of these jobs disappeared, a 43 percent decrease. After 2001, manufacturing sector jobs declined even more precipitously, from 14,624 in 2001 (as determined by the North American Industry Classification System) to 6,063 in 2016, a 59 percent decrease. Concomitant with this decline, wholesale trade employment also declined sharply over this period: a 44 percent decline between 1980 and 2000, followed by a 30 percent decline between 2001 and 2015. Retail jobs also fell sharply between 1980 and 2000, declining by 37 percent over that time period, but declined more slowly between 2001 and 2015 (an 11 percent decline). Financial, insurance, and real estate jobs also declined sharply (41 percent) between 1980 and 2000, before stabilizing and indeed expanding after 2001.[25]

Other sectors of the city economy were more stable over time—namely, construction, the public sector, and service work. Construction employment fell 14 percent between 1980 and 1990 but after a trough in the mid-1990s held constant at about 8,000 jobs before plunging after the 2008 recession. The public sector—the anchor for the city economy—remained the most stable. Total government employment increased in the 1980s and remained at roughly 50,000–51,000 jobs between 1990 and 2000, before falling off 13 percent (6,400 jobs) between 2001 and 2005. Most of those job losses were attributable to a reduction in state government employees in the city between 2001 and 2005 following statewide budget cuts.[26] The city's service sector—a broad category encompassing labor or service provided for pay—exhibited not only stability but periodic increases in employment since 1980. Service sector employment increased 9 percent between 1980 and 2000 and 21 percent between 2001 and 2015. Even the 2008 Great Recession had little tangible impact on total service sector employment. Much of this gain was attributable to a sharp increase in health care sector employment in the mid-aughts, when employment in that sector rose from about 14,000 to 23,500 in a four-year period (2001 to 2005), increasing more slowly thereafter. Employment in professional services, education services, and hotel and restaurant services also increased after 2001.

The fourth major trend had educational and equity implications. Employers in Richmond's growing sectors increasingly required a skilled and educated labor force—workers that Richmond Public Schools had proved ill-equipped to provide. From the 1980s onward, the ability of Richmond residents with high school degrees or less to access good-paying, living-wage jobs declined sharply—leading to a perpetuation and deepening of poverty in the city, with many working-age residents dropping out of the formal labor market entirely. Large swaths of concentrated poverty in the city were virtually excluded from the bright economic times of the late 1990s; the

TABLE 5.3. Total employment by Standard Industrial Classification sector in City of Richmond, 1980–2000

	1980	1985	1990	1995	2000
Total employment	233,558	227,969	219,643	199,431	194,011
Construction	10,064	9,910	8,680	7,292	8,403
Manufacturing	33,824	32,070	28,523	23,395	19,145
Wholesale	16,016	13,970	11,600	10,042	9,011
Retail	29,431	30,412	22,428	19,265	18,614
FIRE[a]	28,251	27,783	24,362	18,667	16,605
Services	55,145	54,248	59,954	57,487	60,028
Government	47,139	45,954	51,092	50,733	50,480
—Federal civilian	5,328	5,765	7,471	7,150	7,183
—Military	1,390	1,591	1,737	1,376	1,358
—State	29,177	27,638	31,045	31,472	30,957
—Local	11,244	10,960	10,839	10,735	10,982
Transport/utilities	13,184	13,013	12,338	11,851	10,946

Source: Bureau of Economic Analysis, accessed February 6, 2024, https://www.bea.gov/data/employment/employment-county-metro-and-other-areas.

Note: Not shown: agricultural services and mining employment.

[a]FIRE = finance, insurance, real estate.

subsequent period of relative stagnation and then recession only worsened the economic plight of the city's most marginalized neighborhoods and residents, as reported reductions in the city's poverty rate proved temporary. Bright economic times alone were not enough to eradicate deep-seated inequalities. To be sure, strong public sector employment continued to bolster a strong middle class, including a strong Black middle class. But as in many American cities, the emergence of a robust Black professional sector with middle-class and affluent incomes did little to help low-income, economically marginalized and often geographically isolated residents (largely Black) in Richmond's deepest pockets of poverty. Indeed, jobs available to Richmond residents with a high school diploma or less often offered wages at or just above the poverty level. Workers at this level faced a precarious and fragile economic existence, in which one misstep or misfortune (either personally or involving a family member) could push a household back into poverty.

TABLE 5.4. Total employment by North American Industry Classification System sector in City of Richmond, 2001–2015

	2001	2005	2010	2015
Total employment	187,731	185,860	177,767	186,071
Construction	8,275	8,430[a]	6,583	7,557
Manufacturing	14,624	10,825	7,083	6,063[b]
Wholesale	6,698	5,902	5,008	4,675
Retail	10,641	10,297	9,402	9,443
FIRE[c]	12,882	13,821	15,189	17,252
Services	74,266	84,699	83,551	89,867
—Professional	12,271	11,968	12,892	13,460
—Management	10,195	12,280	10,390	9,764
—Admin/waste	12,144	11,127	10,067	10,398
—Education	3,714	4,042	4,422	4,894
—Health care/social	14,040	23,513	23,812	25,042
—Arts/entertainment	3,041	2,978	3,582	4,131
—Hotel/food	8,740	8,950	9,128	11,726
—Other	10,121	9,841	9,258	10,452
Government	50,098	43,692	44,024	44,166
—Federal civilian	7,055	6,418	5,072	5,436
—Military	1,325	1,174	1,277	1,203
—State	30,791	24,750	26,500	27,052
—Local	10,927	11,350	11,175	10,475
Transport	n/a	4,085	3,939	4,803

Source: Bureau of Economic Analysis, accessed February 6, 2024, https://www.bea.gov/data/employment/employment-county-metro-and-other-areas.

Note: Not shown: Forestry/fishing, utilities and mining employment. 2015 specific manufacturing figure not reported by BEA (but are included in 2015 total). Certain sectoral figures indicated by n/a are not reported in specific years by BEA for confidentiality reasons but are included in overall employment totals for those years. In these cases we report employment for the sector for an adjacent year, if available, as noted.

[a]Total is for 2004.
[b]Total is for 2016.
[c]FIRE = finance, insurance, real estate.

TABLE 5.5. Total employment and manufacturing employment in Richmond metropolitan statistical area, 1980–2016

	1980	1990	2000	2005	2016
Total employment	469,329	585,331	688,877	730,867	831,772
Manufacturing	71,342	69,244	63,590	43,730	33,937

Source: Bureau of Economic Analysis (SIC series, 1980–2000; NAICS, 2010–16), accessed February 6, 2024, https://www.bea.gov/data/employment/employment-county-metro-and-other-areas.

There were also parallels between the national economic landscape and long-term regional trends—including economic disruptions as well as the long-term national trend of increasing inequality—that shaped the City of Richmond's economy after 1990. In constant 2012 dollars, total domestic product in the City of Richmond in 2001 amounted to just over $20 billion, before falling to just under $17.5 billion in 2010 in the aftermath of the Great Recession; by 2016, production had rebounded to $19.6 billion (and continued to grow until experiencing a slight decline in the pandemic year of 2020).[27]

At the beginning of the twenty-first century, haves and have-nots continued to characterize Richmond. While the majority of Black people in Richmond were not poor—the Black poverty rate in the 2000 census was 28 percent—the majority of poor people in the city (nearly three in four) remained Black.[28] In contrast, the city's wealthiest residents were overwhelmingly white and lived almost entirely in the city's West End, in small enclaves on the Northside, and, to a lesser degree, in the Fan District or downtown. Consequently, the Richmond was (and is) one of the most unequal localities in the United States, measured by the ratio of the average income of the top 1 percent to the average income of the bottom 99 percent of households: forty-third out of 3,061 county units.[29] In 2015, the top 1 percent of households in Richmond earned $1.58 million annually, compared to about $42,400 for the bottom 99 percent. Interestingly, the top 1 percent in Richmond also earned significantly more than the top 1 percent of earners in Chesterfield ($803,000), Hanover ($898,000), or Henrico County ($1.05 million).[30] In short, both the wealthiest households and the highest concentration of poverty in the Richmond metropolitan area were disproportionately concentrated within the City of Richmond. By 2015, the richest 1 percent of city residents accounted for over 27 percent of total income in Richmond.[31]

Richmond's Response to Economic Decline: A Brief Overview

Upon taking office in 1977, Richmond's majority-Black council sought to use government to reshape the local economy. Council members aimed to move the civil rights revolution forward by harnessing the powers of government to save communities and businesses that had been torn asunder by Jim Crow segregation. After the 1989 *Croson* decision put an end to Richmond's affirmative action set-asides for Black contractors, the notion that local government could significantly impact the distribution of economic power along race and class lines waned. While not entirely abandoned, it took the city over two decades to reimagine a strategy that might redirect resources to communities that segregationists had purposefully underdeveloped. After 1989, Richmond struggled to meet the community demands to rebalance and redistribute wealth—a demand that was not fully acknowledged until Dwight C. Jones's administration occupied city hall.

Shoring up and revitalizing the city's economic viability in the wake of population decline and the rapid suburbanization of jobs struck most city leaders as the first order of business. Policymakers and power brokers spent the better part of the late twentieth and early twenty-first centuries devising a variety of strategies intended to combat Richmond's economic woes. These strategies might be best understood in four buckets, each with distinct institutional actors:

1. Attraction of business investment, via recruitment, public-private partnerships, and use of tax incentives. Key entities typically involved in these activities included the City of Richmond, the Richmond Economic Development Authority, the Greater Richmond Partnership (a regional recruitment entity), the Virginia Economic Development Partnership, the Greater Richmond Chamber of Commerce, Richmond Renaissance/Venture Richmond, and private business entities.
2. Development and expansion of existing assets and anchor institutions and focused strategic use of assets and resource streams. Key entities undertaking these activities included VCU, the VCU Health System, the Commonwealth of Virginia, and the City of Richmond.
3. Competitive and cooperative approaches to getting the city and city residents a greater share of the regional economic pie and greater access to regional economic opportunities. Key entities involved here included the City of Richmond, Greater Richmond Transit Company,

Henrico County, Chesterfield County, and (at times) private business entities.
4. Resource-steering and wealth-building policies aimed at ensuring low-income city residents and residents of color could access new and existing economic opportunities and build wealth over time. Key entities here included agencies of the City of Richmond (Department of Economic and Community Development, Office of Minority Business Development, Office of Community Wealth Building), the Metropolitan Business League, the regional Workforce Investment Board, and other entities (including, at times, the city's large anchor institutions).

The remainder of this chapter tells a more nuanced story, involving a complex web of activities and institutional entities—a story about a city that often met vulnerability paternalistically before finally beginning to embrace people-driven solutions to its problems. While this chapter examines several major projects (successful and unsuccessful), it is by no means a comprehensive review of the city's economic development efforts. Instead, this narrative illustrates that following the 1980s, Richmond often addressed problems in top-down fashion—institutions, businesses, and organizations were the architects of economic development solutions seemingly aimed at meeting middle-class and upper-class interests. Alleviating poverty was not a driving concern, and poor people were rarely brought to the policymaking table as civic equals with ideas to contribute.

In the 2010s, the Jones administration made a monumental pivot. Recognizing that improving the city in a more than cosmetic way required tackling poverty directly, Jones, with the support of the city council, formed a commission to study poverty in Richmond, developed strategies informed by the voices of residents most impacted by poverty, invested city resources into the resultant community wealth-building initiatives, and moved to institutionalize those initiatives. After decades of struggling with widespread vulnerability, Richmond, in 2015, became one of America's first cities to state as a matter of law that impacting the distribution of wealth and broadening access to economic opportunity is a *required*, ongoing function of city government.

1980s–2008: From Desperation to Stabilization

By the mid-1980s, cities with sizable minority populations had all but hollowed out. The suburbanization of people was followed closely by the suburbanization of jobs. Local leaders attempted to reinvigorate cities such as Richmond with pro-growth development strategies that might increase tax bases and, optimistically, draw suburban dollars back into cities.[32] Mayors and city managers argued that stadiums, coliseums, convention centers, and downtown markets might save their cities. They were, in many cases, wrong. Richmond joined other locales in looking for big-ticket economic development projects.[33]

To revitalize its status as a flagging economy and failing political entity, Richmond borrowed from Baltimore's Inner Harbor concept in the mid-1980s. Unlike Baltimore, where the Inner Harbor proved successful, Richmond's attempts to reinvigorate its downtown with a "festival marketplace" failed miserably. The 6th Street Marketplace, a high-profile public-private initiative intended to symbolize a new era of productive partnership between the city's Black political leadership and its white business community, over the course of the next two decades became an exemplar of the failures of pro-growth strategies.[34] But before its failure, city planners and Richmonders believed that a shopping center downtown could help save the city. The idea: not merely lure suburban shoppers back into the city but do so in grand fashion. As a bonus, the project also symbolized racial reunification, as the design bridged the long-standing racial divide on East Broad Street. The 6th Street Marketplace, opened for business in 1985, was also a signature initiative of Richmond Renaissance, the public-private entity cofounded by Henry L. Marsh as a vehicle to facilitate cooperation by the white business community with city government. Miller & Rhoads and Thalhimers department stores anchored the marketplace, which at opening included over fifty vendors across three wings.[35]

The ribbon cutting at 6th Street did not produce the economic windfall leaders had intended. The downtown enclosed mall, near the Convention Center and just blocks from city hall, never attracted a substantial base of retail shoppers, apart from downtown employees dining at the relatively successful food court in the building. The Marketplace offered not a genuine, walkable urban retail experience but a faux version of suburban shopping malls—only with less accessibility and more difficulty parking. The opening of major new retail centers in both Henrico (Short Pump Town Center) and Richmond (Stony Point Fashion Park) in the late 1990s (detailed below) struck a final death knell to the viability of the Marketplace. County residents came to associate the Marketplace, like Richmond more broadly, with crime and below-average retail options. They also found it much more convenient to shop in the suburbs than in the city center. In the end, the primary retail areas were demolished in 2003; by 2007, the food court had closed and the

Marketplace was shuttered altogether.[36] Over the subsequent decade (and beyond) the structure remained standing as the city failed to enact a redevelopment plan to repurpose or demolish the building, while the once-hopeful entrance message "Building a Brighter Future" served as a cruel reminder of the city's ongoing failures.

The legacy of the 6th Street Marketplace in many ways haunted economic development efforts, particularly downtown, over the next quarter century. For many Richmonders, the lesson drawn was not the error of attempting to replicate suburban space in an inherently urban context but the futility of local government as an architect of bold, successful plans. Research institutions filled the void.

VCU and the Revitalization of Downtown

Research revitalized Richmond—where the mall failed, the growth of the university succeeded. Over most of the twentieth century, Richmond had a relatively small academic footprint. Apart from Virginia Union University, which was a significant center for Black thought in the postwar era, Virginia Commonwealth University and the University of Richmond were primarily local and regional schools, respectively, until the 1970s. At VCU, the situation changed dramatically with the arrival of historian Dr. Eugene Trani in 1990. Trani's appointment proved a significant event for the city: as president, Trani embraced bold ideas to grow the university and further anchored it in downtown Richmond. In fact, it is difficult to imagine Richmond's modern core without VCU: over two decades, Trani spearheaded several major academic and nonacademic initiatives while changing VCU's emphasis from liberal arts to science and engineering. Trani's vision helped transform not just the school but the city's core. This transformation, though, came at a price.

VCU came to its role as an important anchor institution in the city through relatively humble beginnings. The school began as the Richmond Professional Institute in 1917, consolidated with the Medical College of Virginia in 1968 to become Virginia Commonwealth University, and grew in size and stature by building in areas that had been historically undervalued by the urban policies of the mid-twentieth century.[37] Following the merger, administrators reshaped the institution into a research university, with an increasingly significant footprint.[38] Efforts to expand VCU in the 1970s and 1980s provoked numerous conflicts with neighborhood organizations, especially in an adjacent neighborhood just south of the downtown expressway, Oregon Hill. Like many other urban universities, VCU employed its own police force to carve out a "safe" campus environment even amid an explosion of violent crime in the city during 1980s and 1990s.[39] VCU grew in size and scope, in the core of Richmond, at the very same time that Richmond had one of the highest murder rates per capita in the United States.[40]

Despite these challenges, Dr. Trani fully embraced VCU's urban identity and sought to raise the school's status by forging an unprecedented network of political and corporate connections. Over the course of his two-decade tenure (from 1990 to 2009), Trani, the fourth president of VCU, transformed the university from a provincial commuter school into a reputable locale of higher education with a dramatically expanded student body (from approximately 22,000 to 32,000 students) and urban footprint. This transformation involved creating a School of Engineering; enlarging the student body; undertaking a seemingly endless set of construction projects, such as the Siegel Center basketball arena on Broad Street; and, most significantly, launching a downtown BioTech Park north of Broad Street. The rebranded VCU Health Systems (formerly Medical College of Virginia) became one of the largest employers in the region (over 9,000 employees by 2015). To this day, it is difficult to imagine the Richmond downtown region, or neighborhoods such as Carver and The Fan, without VCU—the university is interwoven into the city's fabric, by design.

Trani also sought to raise the school's status by taking leadership roles in Richmond's major business organizations. Throughout his tenure as president, Trani was deeply involved in the Greater Richmond Chamber of Commerce and Richmond Renaissance. He also heightened VCU's academic and economic footprint by forging relationships with elected and nonelected officials in the commonwealth's General Assembly, located just east of the university itself. Yet, most of Trani's plans did not require extensive collaboration with city government beyond obtaining necessary zoning and permitting approvals. At the beginning of Trani's tenure as president, he was careful not to antagonize neighborhoods on or around the campus, namely Oregon Hill (a predominantly white working- and middle-class neighborhood notorious with the city's African Americans for its history of entrenched racism). He also, by and large, steered comfortably clear of the dynamics and drama of city hall. In doing so, Trani transformed VCU into the largest public university in Virginia, as well as arguably the most powerful single organization in the city of Richmond—perhaps even more powerful than local government itself.[41]

From the standpoint of economic development, the BioTech Park symbolized Trani's vision to convert VCU and downtown Richmond into an intellectual and research center. He succeeded. In essence, as white Richmonders turned their backs on the city by relocating to the suburbs, Trani committed a predominantly white institution to building a better Richmond. And he did it in largely poor white and African American enclaves—initially, and remarkably, without much controversy. The assembling of the "Park" in 1993 was instrumental in this process. Located north of Broad Street near Richmond's Jackson Ward District, Trani beat back skepticism by soliciting help from America's first elected Black governor, L. Douglas Wilder (who was in office at the time), and Richmond's city manager Robert Bobb.[42] The concept sought to cluster biotechnology firms and research-oriented institutions in the core of the city.

Trani continued to build and was instrumental in the creation of VCU's School of Engineering. The school was to focus on biomedical engineering and would help develop technical talent for the region, bolstering longer-term economic development. By the mid-2010s, the BioTech Park was home to over sixty research firms or entities, employing some 2,400 people, including scientists, researchers, and engineers. A 2016 report estimated that VCU, including the BioTech Park, had an annual economic impact of $4 billion on the Richmond metropolitan area, including sustaining 47,000 jobs, with a regional economic multiplier of 3.7 (every $1 spent by VCU generated $3.70 in total economic impact).[43] These efforts were instrumental in reviving a city that had all but hollowed out.

Modernity is often costly, and VCUs' expansion eventually gave rise to detractors. Like other colleges and universities located in cities, VCU's relationship with Richmond was complex, offering both the promise of job and knowledge creation, health care for low-income residents, real estate and economic development, and increasing numbers of community-engaged students and faculty fanning out to nonprofits across the city. At the same time, as scholar Davarian Baldwin and others demonstrate, higher education in the last decades of the twentieth century came under intensifying criticism for self-interested overexpansion, real estate tax exemption, and local research projects based on "'surveying local residents constantly'— often Black and Brown people living in lower-income communities—without producing results that benefited those surveyed."[44] Richmond leaders were so desperate for outside expansion that they helped facilitate VCU's growth without much input from vulnerable communities around the school. This was not surprising insofar as the city during Trani's presidency lacked a clear poverty-fighting plan, a clear concept of how an entity like VCU might contribute to such a plan, or the institutional muscle to persuade or compel VCU (or others) to participate if they had such a plan.⁴⁵ Indeed, during this time period, most city leaders were grateful for VCU's presence and were inclined (with occasional exception) to grant the university wide latitude to execute its plans. VCU's expansion, as Trani recognized, contributed to a more basic goal: sustaining the economic viability of the city.⁴⁶

Rebooting Retail: The Case of Stony Point Fashion Park

Eventually, Richmond resolved to take another chance on retail, despite the resounding failure of the 6th Street Marketplace—this time, in a more affluent area. In fact, retail eventually helped to revitalize Richmond, but in a manner that had class and racial implications. Despite declines in manufacturing employment, especially in tobacco, downtown employment at state government, financial institutions, and major employers like Dominion Resources (energy) remained relatively stable—although most of these jobs were not held by city residents (let alone low-income city residents).⁴⁷ Growing employment in health and education driven by VCU improved the employment base, and the BioTech Center helped attract new high-value companies to the city. But these developments did relatively little to impact Richmond's perceived and actual ongoing fiscal crisis (VCU did not pay taxes to the City of Richmond) or to address the city's poverty rate. Consequently, local elected officials sought to increase the city's tax base by further facilitating private investments and employment opportunities.

As Richmond sought to use retail to regenerate itself, the city struggled to compete with its suburban counterparts. By the late 1990s, retail became a highly contested battleground, a zero-sum competition with neighboring localities. Many city residents, particularly affluent residents in the First District, routinely shopped at suburban outlets such as Henrico's Willow Lawn, located just across the city's westernmost boundary line on Broad Street. Tax revenues from that retail economic activity buffered the coffers of the counties, not Richmond. The vast network of freeways and expressways built in the metropolitan area, rather than serving as the backbone of a revitalized central city, became an avenue for draining economic activity out of the city center. Suburban residents working downtown proved to be little interested in returning downtown to shop on the weekends, especially with the easy availability of ever-expanding suburban commercial spaces.⁴⁸ The decline and collapse of legacy downtown retailers as well as the 6th Street Marketplace meant Richmond shoppers who might have preferred to shop in the city had relatively few options. Henrico's aggressive plans for the development of the Short Pump shopping center in the late 1990s added increased urgency to Richmond's effort to revive its retail sector.

The saga of Stony Point Fashion Park illustrates how Richmond's economic development worked in practice during the 1990s and the next decade—when it went well. In 1995, a respected national developer, Taubman Centers, announced plans to build an upscale mall in South Richmond, on the city's western edge just off the Chippenham Parkway, a major commuter road connecting Richmond and Chesterfield County. City manager Robert Bobb expressed strong enthusiasm for the project, and the concept quickly won approval from the Planning Commission. Taubman reported receiving unsolicited letters from Richmond residents imploring the company to build the project. Taubman sought no subsidy for the project and initially projected the mall could be constructed and opened in time for the holiday season of 1998.[49]

The only holdup, initially, was the challenge of landing two anchor department stores to make the mall viable, and 1996 came and went without Taubman able to land a commitment from a major high-end national chain. In 1997, Taubman secured a commitment from Dillard's to become an anchor, but another two years passed without a second chain following suit. The reticence of the chains had less to do with the Richmond market as such—analysts and project champions generally agreed that Richmond could sustain at least one "slightly upscale" retail outlet. Rather, there was hesitancy about *where* in Richmond upscale retail should go—at Stony Point in the Richmond city limits, or at the ambitious Short Pump Town Center project in Henrico County, a massive effort championed by county manager Virgil Hazelett to make Henrico the commercial center of the region. Some analysts judged that one but not both of these projects would be viable.[50]

With progress seemingly stalled on the Stony Point development, in 1999 Mayor Tim Kaine and the city council sought to grease the wheels by offering a subsidy to the project. Figures upwards of $20 million were floated.[51] Ultimately the city council authorized a $13.5 million subsidy package to the project, with Taubman Centers obligated to repay the subsidy with interest if the project did not generate at least $13.5 million of new revenue for the city within five years.[52] Taubman Centers continued to battle feverishly with Short Pump to land retailers and filed two unsuccessful lawsuits in an effort to block the Short Pump project. At the same time, Taubman scaled back original plans for an enclosed Stony Point and converted the project into an open-air complex.[53]

Both the Short Pump (1.2 million square feet) and Stony Point (690,000 square feet) retail centers ultimately opened in September 2003. Saks Fifth Avenue and Dillard's served as the primary anchors for Stony Point and brought numerous additional chains to the Richmond market for the first time. City leaders praised the project for giving city (and suburban) shoppers an opportunity to spend money within the city limits and contribute to city coffers through sales taxes. (Despite Stony Point, Richmond's retail base continued to be underdeveloped for years.)[54] They also praised the injection of about 2,000 new employment opportunities at Stony Point and projected $3.8 million in annual new revenue. The primary effort made to ensure that city residents would benefit from the new Stony Point employment opportunities was a two-day recruiting fair held at the Convention Center downtown in August 2003.[55]

Local leaders lined up to champion Stony Point's success and demonstration of possibility: Mayor Rudy McCollum, city manager Calvin Jamison, and former mayor Tim Kaine, among many others, touted the development. On its own terms, the mall was well-regarded by shoppers and appreciated for its outdoor water fountains and dog-friendly policies.[56] Stony Point was relatively successful over the next decade but was dwarfed in scale and growth by Short Pump Town Center. In recent years, it has experienced a downturn, with about one-third of storefronts vacant. Indeed, the mall was put up for sale in late 2021.[57]

Like VCU's expansion, Stony Point had class-based implications. First, the project was intended to meet (or induce) the demand of high-end, wealthy consumers for high-end products. Second, the project was not a substantial source of new living-wage jobs for previously underemployed Richmond residents, let alone those located miles away in Richmond's concentrated pockets of poverty. In fact, from the beginning, contractors, elected officials, and others branded Stony Point Fashion Park as an affluent space. The area was not located near Richmond's vulnerable communities and was not easily accessible by bus for residents of those communities, whether for work or leisure.[58] Nonetheless city leaders, thirsty for new developments, lauded the project because of its economic and revenue benefits.

Performing Arts Center

Redeveloping Richmond was not limited to retail and research—the arts too were essential to reimagining the city. Richmond, like many segregated southern cities, had two cultural centers: one white, the other Black; one vastly more resourced, in fact, than the other. For most of the twentieth century, the city's African American and white artistic communities were deeply segregated by race. Museums and art galleries were segregated. Boards and administrations at these institutions were not effectively integrated until the twilight of the twentieth century. Jackson Ward, the heart of Black arts in Richmond and the center of the city's Black entertainment district, had all but dissolved by the 1970s. Jackson Ward's dissolution typified Richmond's enduring legacy of systemic disinvestment. Performing arts in the white community, however, was often a reflection not just of resources but of philanthropy. From Monument Avenue to what is now Arthur Ashe Boulevard, arts and culture reflected white resources.

Redevelopment in Richmond often exacerbated class and race tensions, as people brought their biases to bear on who should orchestrate redeveloping downtown. Richmond's historical legacy of unresolved racial antipathy often meant that new projects were criticized on racial terms. The arts were no exception. Some African Americans perceived the Performing Arts Center project, a major initiative of the business community in the first decade of the twenty-first century, as centered on white elites' tastes and a white cultural vision for what downtown Richmond could and should be. The original proposal aimed to secure a cluster of performance spaces located downtown, just blocks from city hall, that would bring together various performing arts groups into one hub. Business leader Jim Ukrop, whose family made its fortune in the grocery business, organized a robust business coalition in favor of the concept, conceived of as a public-private partnership in which public tax dollars would be matched by privately raised funds to support construction. These plans appeared set to move forward smoothly when the city council in 2003 adopted a one-penny increase in the meals tax (from $.05/$1.00 to $.06/$1.00) to raise funds for the project.[59]

Upon taking office, Mayor Doug Wilder sharply criticized the original scope of the project, portraying it as an example of (predominantly) white elites using their political muscle to milk the public purse. He pushed to renegotiate the deal and to redirect the enhanced meals tax revenues going forward to the broader City of the Future building plan (see chapter 3). Wilder's criticisms led to the project being scaled down to include renovation of the 1,800-seat Carpenter Theatre concert hall (originally built in 1928 as a theater); two smaller performance stages; and rehearsal, classroom, and office space, including a digital music lab; plans for an additional music hall on Broad Street were scrapped. The total cost of the project, finalized in

2007, was nearly $74 million, with the city contributing $25 million to the renovation.[60] The complex, dubbed Richmond CenterStage, opened in the fall of 2009.[61] The city then allocated funds for the renovation (and rebranding) of the Altria Theater adjacent to Monroe Park on VCU's main campus, a historic 3,600-seat venue dating to 1927 (originally named "The Mosque"). The renovated, restored, and renamed theater reopened in 2014.[62]

The downtown performing arts initiative did in fact help revitalize Richmond as a regional destination for musical performances and Broadway productions. CenterStage hosted the Richmond Symphony, the Richmond Ballet, the Virginia Opera, and numerous local and youth arts organizations. In this way it contributed to the general livability and attractiveness of the city, providing a wide range of arts and cultural performances year-round and adding to the vitality of Richmond. In conjunction with these venues, in 2012 the city designated an "Arts and Culture District" of several blocks in proximity to CenterStage, offering permitting assistance and other support for venues and businesses in the area.[63] A "First Fridays" art exhibit walk (first launched in 2001) grew in impact and popularity, and numerous new restaurants on Grace Street near the Performing Arts Center and art galleries began to dot the landscape of an area that had all but been abandoned years prior.[64] These projects, particularly considering Richmond's hollowing out during the late twentieth century, were qualified successes. Ten years after its opening, Jim Ukrop reflected with satisfaction that Richmond CenterStage (subsequently renamed as the Dominion Energy Center) had in fact led to the revitalization of downtown and the immediately surrounding area and had created a viable regional asset.[65] Arguably, these projects helped the city and the Richmond region attract and retain new business activity, contributing to the city's overall resurgence. But there has been little evidence of heightened downtown activity spilling over into meaningful new investment in Richmond's most impoverished neighborhoods.

Targeted Development Policies: Neighborhoods in Bloom and Real Estate Tax Exemption

Initiatives aimed at catering to high-end tastes or reflecting the priorities of elite actors hardly exhausted the totality of Richmond's development efforts in the late 1990s and into the next decade. Standing alongside the rather traditional model of "economic development," defined by subsidies to new or existing employers or by various types of public-private partnerships largely focused on downtown development, was the somewhat competing paradigm of "community development." Community development in Richmond's context meant a focus on improving the quality of life—safety, amenities, overall development level—of Richmond's neighborhoods, many of which by the 1990s visibly suffered from blight and disinvestment. Here city government had leverage to act through the use of federally provided dollars (principally Community Development Block Grants) and planning policies aimed at stimulating reinvestments in aging neighborhoods. Like other U.S. cities, Richmond sought to use these federal dollars to offset decades of systemic disinvestment and revitalize neglected, typically Black and Brown neighborhoods.[66]

The most innovative and significant effort to maximize the impact of Richmond's community development dollars was the Neighborhoods in Bloom initiative launched in July 1999 during the mayoral tenure of Tim Kaine. The initiative concentrated use of Community Development Block Grants and other federal funds, previously spread citywide, in six discrete neighborhoods: Blackwell (Southside), Carver and Newtowne West (adjacent to VCU's northwest boundary), Church Hill Central (East End), Highland Park–Southern Tip (Northside), Jackson Ward (adjacent to downtown), and Southern Barton Heights (Northside). A seventh area, Oregon Hill (just south of the VCU main campus), also received some investments. These neighborhoods, all judged to be in varying levels of blight in the 1990s, received a total of nearly $14 million in public investment over a five-year period, with a further $4.5 million in investment coming from the Richmond branch of the Local Initiatives Support Corporation. The neighborhoods also were prioritized for city services related to redevelopment, including code enforcement and resale of derelict properties. The operative theory was that concentrated public investment in specific places could make neighborhoods sufficiently viable so as to catalyze follow-on private investment by businesses and real estate investors, helping to bring struggling neighborhoods back to life.[67]

A 2005 Federal Reserve study led by John Accordino of VCU and George Galster of Wayne State University found that the impacts of Neighborhoods in Bloom had proved effective. The study noted that across the neighborhoods, home values rose at a faster pace than citywide over the five years of the program. The Federal Reserve study even identified a threshold level at which public investment became effective: neighborhoods that received investment exceeding $20,100 per block showed much stronger effects than areas with lower investment. The study also praised the competence of the city officials responsible for the program, citing their commitment to taking a data-driven approach. Neighborhoods in Bloom was hailed by the federal Department of Housing and Urban Development as a national model.[68]

This initiative emerged from an agreement among city council members to focus investments so as to have more impact; the original program expired in 2005 as Richmond converted to its new governance system, although the designation continued to be used in planning documents. A follow-up study in 2017 found that over the next ten years covering Doug Wilder's term as mayor and Dwight Jones's first six years as mayor, 41 percent of Richmond's federal funds were invested in these same neighborhoods. The study also found that the initial catalyzing effects from Neighborhoods in Bloom proper had led to sustained revitalization, albeit not dramatic impacts on the neighborhoods' socioeconomic profiles or poverty rates.[69]

While Neighborhoods in Bloom targeted specific areas, Richmond also employed a generous tax abatement program to encourage improvement and rehabilitation of older buildings. In combination with state and federal tax credits for investments in historic buildings, Richmond's tax abatement program provided powerful incentives for investors to acquire, renovate, and bring to resale aging housing and commercial properties. First established in 1979, the abatement initially allowed individuals making rehabilitation investments in buildings at least twenty years old to receive a tax credit on the value of the improved building for up to five years following the improvement. In 1995, the city council extended the abatement to fifteen years per property, and use of the program exploded. By 2007, after the abatement had been reduced back to ten years per property, an estimated $1.135 billion of real estate was abated, at an annual cost to the city of $14.6 million in uncollected revenues; over 80 percent of the nearly 4,700 properties in the program were residential.[70] In time, these policies changed Richmond's landscape.

Popular for obvious reasons in the real estate development community, the tax abatements were widely considered a citywide policy success through the aughts. By the end of that decade, critical questions began to be raised concerning the substantial amount of revenues forgone by the city and whether the tool still remained appropriate. Critics worried that the generous abatement accelerated gentrification to the benefit largely of white newcomers and also observed that many of the rehabilitation projects were taking place not on dilapidated blocks but in relatively affluent neighborhoods.[71]

People also pointed out that Richmond's subsidies had no explicit provisions to protect or enhance housing affordability and came in the context of a weak citywide approach to housing more generally (see chapter 6). In the wake of news stories about a particularly egregious case of a prominent developer getting up to $2.4 million in tax rebates for preserving a tiny piece of an older building in a new apartment complex, the city council in 2014 took action to prevent abuses of the program, but the program remained intact, with improvements on buildings twenty years old or older eligible for abatements for up to ten years.[72] A 2019 VCU study deemed the program a net positive for the city but also recommended several alterations to increase the impact of the policy on "disinvested neighborhoods" and to promote the production of more units of affordable housing.[73]

Blocked Mobility: The Stalled Quest for Regional Transit

In addition to attracting and stimulating new economic activity in the city, Richmond policymakers also sought to expand access for city residents to suburban economic opportunities via mass transit. Standing in the proverbial doorway of those efforts was lingering NIMBYism, applied to public transportation. Half a century before the Montgomery bus boycott, Black residents in Richmond resisted racial segregation of the city's early twentieth-century trolley system.[74] The long struggle to desegregate public transportation was followed by white exit from the use of public transit, facilitated by the ongoing suburbanization of American metropolitan areas.[75] As white Americans (literally) got off the bus, they came to associate busing and train transit with Black commuters and (by the same racist logic) criminality.[76]

That mentality impeded efforts to expand transit in Richmond—for decades. As early as the mid-1980s, business leaders in Richmond identified the need for improved public transit as a requirement of a more functional region. In the mid-1990s, Richmond grassroots and elected leaders campaigned, to expand bus service from the City of Richmond into Chesterfield and Henrico Counties. They met almost complete failure. White discomfort and resistance to busing across county lines all but ensured that public transportation in the Richmond metro region remained one of America's worst systems.[77]

The roots of the failure lay in part in the peculiar organization of Richmond's transit provider, the Greater Richmond Transit Company (GRTC). The GRTC was reorganized in 1989 as a joint venture of the City of Richmond and Chesterfield County, with each locality having three seats on the board of directors. Henrico County opted out of the arrangement entirely, although it utilized GRTC services on a contract basis. Richmond City Council agreed to sell 50 percent control in the GRTC to Chesterfield for $50,000, an arrangement championed by city council member (and former city manager) William Leidinger. Leidinger argued that the move would lead over time to greater regional cooperation (including participation of Henrico and Hanover Counties) and allow the region to better compete for state funding. Black council members Chuck Richardson and Walter Kenney expressed concerns about the deal but voted to support it anyway.[78] While Richmond leaders hoped the agreement was a step toward regional transit, many believed the motivation for Chesterfield County's participation on the board was to control, minimize, and block plans for substantial expansion of public transit in the county and region.[79]

Chesterfield County's refusal to allow bus service to its Cloverleaf Mall, located just west of the city, was a flashpoint in the mid-1990s. In fact, then-councilman Tim Kaine stated that the opposition appeared racially motivated; service to the mall finally began in 1996.[80] In 1998, the Greater Richmond Chamber of Commerce issued a report calling for a $12.5 million investment to extend bus lines from Richmond into the surrounding counties. Robert Grey Jr., vice president of law firm LeClair Ryan, championed the effort, stating, "If the region is to prosper, we must have better ways of connecting residents with jobs." The chairman of Reynolds Metal Company, Jeremiah Sheehan, added, "Expansion of bus service is essential if we want to expand economic opportunity and avoid the gridlock that blights other metropolitan areas."[81] A bipartisan effort to implement that plan, led by state senators Henry L. Marsh and John Watkins in the 1998 General Assembly session, stalled when elected Chesterfield supervisors conveyed opposition to state legislators.[82]

A year later, city leaders tried again. In an April 1999 editorial, Mayor Tim Kaine remarked, "We are rare among thriving metropolitan areas for our lack of meaningful regional public transportation. Our bus routes should be planned based on current and future citizen need rather than limited by stereotypes or artificial boundaries."[83] That spring Marsh and Watkins succeeded in getting $5.1 million into the state budget for regional transit initiatives, although Chesterfield again balked at implementation.[84] Finally, in early 2000, Chesterfield leadership expressed support for establishing service—using vans rather than full-size buses. This concept won board approval in the summer of 2000, and service on the Chesterfield LINK connecting downtown Richmond to Chesterfield via two express and four local routes, finally began in June 2001, as the start of a two-year pilot program.[85]

The transit initiative died at the altar of anti-urbanism. Chesterfield residents enthusiastically welcomed the van service at first, and it received positive media coverage, but this initial success proved short-lived. In the spring of 2003, with the pilot set to expire, the Chesterfield board opted to spend $100,000 to maintain partial service past June 2003, for one additional year. But the uncertainty around the service led ridership to plummet, and the LINK service shut down in 2004.[86] In 2005 Chesterfield added two new expressway routes into the county on a pilot basis—again only to be put in doubt several years later when grant funding expired.[87]

Chesterfield's slow-walk approach to transit meant that truly meaningful progress toward a proper regional transit system would not be possible in the 1990s or the next decade.[88] Public explanations for the reluctance became subtler, shifting from racial frames to fiscal concerns. Suburban conversations on transit rarely questioned the norms of car ownership or extensive public subsidies and support to private automobile travels. Cars were viewed as the default; public transit was a luxury item to be indulged in only if scarce finances allowed (or if the state was willing to fund outright). Yet in the end there can be little doubt that the positions taken by the county supervisors reflected a widespread desire among county residents not to become too intertwined or too connected with the City of Richmond. Express service to make commutes downtown for suburban residents faster might be acceptable, but transit service based on a principle of allowing all residents of the metropolis to access all employment, commercial, civic, and cultural locations in the metropolis via public transit would certainly not. The conservatism of county residents—and the extent to which the attraction of county life was precisely in limiting contact with the city—for many years proved a more potent political force than the recommendations of either business or political leaders in Greater Richmond.[89] In the meantime, the Brookings Institution published a study in 2011 designating Richmond as 92nd out of the nation's top 100 metropolitan areas in transit access, measured by overall transit coverage and access to employment via public transit.[90]

Confronting the Great Recession: The Jones Administration and Beyond

The mechanisms perpetuating racial inequality in Richmond were born in the crucible of Jim Crow segregation's kleptocratic oligarchy.[91] The residual implications? Deeply entrenched poverty, residential segregation, and wealth disparity still remained even as Richmond began to emerge from the shadow of segregation in the late twentieth century.[92] Yet by the late aughts, the City of Richmond, by several measures, began to rebound: crime remained down from its mid-1990s peak, population slowly began to climb again, schools (despite much drama) had shown tangible progress, and there was evidence of increased business activity and investment. Then the Great Recession of 2008–9 would, for a time, flatten the city's progress, devastating the city's employment figures and sending the poverty rate spiraling to unprecedented levels.

This was the historical context that informed Dwight C. Jones's tenure as mayor. From the beginning, Jones expressed a desire to tackle poverty and make the city work to the benefit of those historically left behind—including Black people in general, but especially poor and working-class Black citizens in Richmond. It took considerable time to establish what this might mean in practice. Within his first year, Jones's reorganized the city's economic and community development functions, placing them together under his newly hired economic development chief, Peter H. Chapman.[93] The Jones administration also moved in its first two years to complete a revised Comprehensive Economic Development Strategy mapping out the city's economic strengths and weaknesses and outlining over a dozen specific opportunities for growth and investment.[94]

Those ideas took time to develop, and they eventually fused with a separate stream of policy recommendations generated by the Mayor's Anti-Poverty Commission. In the first two years of the Jones administration, however, some of the most visible progress—and conflict—carried over from the efforts of an influential holdover from the Wilder administration: Rachel Flynn, the city's charismatic director of planning, who had mobilized considerable civic support for a revised downtown master plan, including a remarkably bold and progressive approach to developing the James River as a major community asset.

Revving up the Riverfront: Rachel Flynn and the Downtown Master Plan

While many urban policymakers focus on attracting new investment to spur development, some focus on maximizing the use of natural and historical assets already present in the city. There has been, demonstrated in the epic showdowns in New York City between Jane Jacobs and Robert Moses, an ongoing battle over the types of development that modern cities require to thrive.[95] Richmond has not been immune to these dynamics. Indeed, Monument Avenue itself, we know now, was a naked real estate deal under the guise of a City Beautiful initiative.[96] These well-worn battles remerged in Richmond during the late aughts.

In the spring of 2006, the Wilder administration hired an experienced urban planner, Rachel Flynn, to direct the city's planning department. Flynn brought cutting-edge civic engagement techniques to Richmond and applied them to two central questions: first, how best to redevelop downtown, and second, how to take better advantage of Richmond's natural resources, namely using the James River as a civic and economic resource.[97] Well into the first decade of the twenty-first century, Richmond's downtown was over-asphalted. Large portions of the downtown area consisted of privately owned parking lots. The relative waste of this space appalled Flynn.[98] Yet, underutilized parking lots, most often owned by absentee speculators, were not the only wasteful remnants of a downtown region that had paved parking lots for the convenience of downtown workers during the mid-twentieth century. The tattered remains of the 6th Street Marketplace and general decline of the Coliseum area were reminders of building projects from the 1970s forward. Indeed, Flynn recognized that Richmond had essentially reorganized its downtown to attract non-Richmonders who failed to show up for anything other than work. Flynn turned inward. She envisioned a more walkable, transit-oriented, and greener downtown and, like an increasing number of city residents, was skeptical of using "big projects" (as opposed to incremental evolution) to reinvigorate Richmond's continued development. Further, Richmond—unlike other cities with rivers running through downtown (such as the frequently cited San Antonio)—had not adopted a systematic plan to provide public access to the river and establish the riverfront as a central hub for commercial and recreational activity. Flynn aimed to tackle both of these issues with the development of a new downtown master plan, animated by the following principle: the best downtown and riverfront land should be claimed for public use.[99]

Repurposing downtown Richmond in the name of public use and pedestrian culture motivated Flynn's master plan. Richmond's long-held deference to private property, as well as the material fact that much of the best riverfront property was occupied by the headquarters of Dominion Energy, flew in the face of Flynn's vision. She sought to dial back on the "automobilization" of downtown Richmond—she envisioned two-way streets, slower traffic patterns, more and safer pedestrian usage, burying parking lots underground, improving infrastructure, and providing ample access to green spaces. Central to the plan was the natural beauty of the James River itself. Flynn emphasized the waterway as Richmond's principal attraction, Richmond's answer to Central Park. Indeed, the James River might be not only a recreational area but a historical attraction as well.[100] The river, the plan held, was an underutilized public good that historically Richmonders failed to see as anything other than an industrial source of power; specifically, the plan envisioned using public funds to acquire crucial property near the river for use as "waterfront park land," with a goal of establishing continuous public access to the river.[101]

To execute these ideas, Flynn quickly established relationships with emerging local planning organizations. She began with organizations such as the Partnership for Smarter Growth to build public support. The master plan came to public attention through a series of large public meetings that were followed by extended charettes (participatory planning sessions). The idea? To build civic participation, something that Richmonders were unaccustomed to during the Jim Crow era—reimagining the city with broad public input. The process of gathering and organizing public input was, in many ways, still new to Richmond in the early aughts. Though criticized by the *Richmond Free Press* and others for being excessively tilted to white Richmond residents—one headline about the launch of the process read "Sea of Whiteness"—the efforts garnered considerable public input over time, including from Black residents.[102]

The Echo Harbour development proposal put these ideas to the test. It turned out to be a battle between business-as-usual and fidelity to the downtown plan. The Echo Harbour proposal aimed to place 100 high-end condominium units directly on the waterfront. The height of the proposed building would have obstructed the iconic view of the James River from Libby Hill Park in Church Hill; the bend in the river visible from that vantage point lent the city its name in 1737: it had reminded William Byrd II, Richmond's colonial founder, of the view of the River Thames in London at Richmond Hill.[103] The project's developers requested a special-use permit from the Planning Commission followed by the city council, promising that the project would bring jobs and revenue to the city. But Flynn and community allies believed that the project not only ruined a historic view but compromised the spirit and letter of the downtown master plan. Equally important, they held that the Echo Harbour proposal would continue the trend of privatizing significant stretches of waterfront property. In an April 2009 planning commission meeting, Flynn drew a line in the sand by rejecting a suggestion that the city continue to negotiate an acceptable agreement with the developer.[104] The pointed exchange—illustrating Flynn's refusal to compromise basic principles—led to calls from several council members for

Flynn's resignation (calls Jones ignored).[105] Eventually the council refuted efforts to weaken the downtown master plan and make it easier for private actors to secure a special-use permit at variance with the plan's "character area designations."[106] The Echo Harbour project, which was never built, died at the table of democracy.[107]

Flynn's bold stand on Echo Harbour proved to be one of her last ones in Richmond. The full ambitions of the downtown master plan, particularly regarding riverfront access, were only partly realized prior to Flynn's departure in the spring of 2011. Flynn's exit resulted in part from dissatisfaction with the reshuffling of the administration that weakened her role in the municipal hierarchy; but it also reflected genuine philosophical differences between Flynn and the Jones team. In a valedictory column for the *Richmond Times-Dispatch*—part love letter, part parting shot—Flynn recommended that Richmond focus on dramatically improving public transportation, improving access to and amenities along the James River, adding more trees and better landscaping throughout the city to make it more attractive, and deconcentrating poverty, starting with the redevelopment of Gilpin Court, the city's largest and oldest public housing community.[108] She, in effect, laid out a plan for the future that charted a new course emphasizing natural and human resources and public participation in planning processes.

Jones's subsequent emphasis on big-growth projects belied Flynn's emphasis on organic development, greening the city, and extensive community participation. To be sure, Jones supported deconcentrating poverty, expanding public transportation, and revitalizing the riverfront.[109] However, he also believed that Richmond needed bigger development projects to revive downtown, reverse decades of private disinvestment, and help combat poverty.

In the first two years following his reelection in 2012, Jones pursued three high-profile projects, all of which involved public subsidies to private entities. The search for investments and additional resources continued to characterize long-standing economic pragmatism at city hall. This manifested as a three-way deal with the Washington NFL franchise, Bon Secours Health, and the city; a proposed minor league baseball stadium for Shockoe Bottom, in close vicinity to historic former slave markets; and a combined state-local partnership to bring privately held Stone Brewing to Richmond. Two of these proposals passed in the council, though not without controversy; the Shockoe Bottom baseball proposal inspired staunch public opposition and was withdrawn. During Jones's tenure as mayor, Richmond struggled to develop a model of economic development that could both achieve stated policy goals and win broad community support.

Blocked Kick: The Washington NFL Team Training Camp Deal

Nothing better exemplified Richmond's timeworn commitment to big-ticket items and the city's failure to deliver on promises of prosperity than the Washington NFL team training facility. As mayor, Jones frequently stated his goal was to make Richmond a "Tier One" city on par with leading national cities.[110] But Jones's favoring of big-ticket items and public-private partnerships did not always produce the intended result. Indeed, the reality of Richmond's distinctly second-tier status was illustrated by another high-profile deal, in which the city was used essentially as a pawn in a larger state-level play to attract a major brand and franchise to Virginia. In the summer of 2012, Virginia governor Bob McDonnell (R) announced a deal with the then Washington Redskins NFL franchise. The proposal aimed to keep the team's training center in Loudon County, Virginia, and to continue its summer preseason camp in state, preferably in Richmond. McDonnell, whose wife had been a cheerleader for the team, had longer-range hopes of inducing the team to build a new stadium in northern Virginia. Washington's general manager, Bruce Allen, was the brother of former Virginia governor and senator George F. Allen, another Republican; both Allens were sons of George H. Allen, the legendary Washington coach of the 1970s "Over the Hill Gang" that reached the Super Bowl in 1972–73. The Washington franchise was widely supported in central Virginia, and Richmond mayor Jones signed on to the proposal without hesitation. Jones seemed to believe that the plan might generate tourist revenue and increase Richmond's national profile.[111]

The triumvirate of Richmond, the NFL, and Bon Secours completed a three-way trade as complex as any player transaction. The city agreed to spend $10 million to build a complete football training center, including office space, indoor training, locker rooms, and medical facilities, along with two side-by-side outdoor football fields, on leased state property adjacent to the Science Museum of Virginia on Broad Street, only blocks from the central Boulevard (now Arthur Ashe Boulevard) artery. Bon Secours Health System would become sponsor of the training center and contribute $3.3 million payable to Richmond's Economic Development Authority, with up to an additional $3.1 million in revenue for the city to be generated by the health system leasing the building. In exchange, the city provided Bon Secours a long-term (sixty-year) lease on the former Westhampton School facility in the city's West End, where the health system planned to house a school of nursing and a school of imaging. Bon Secours also pledged to expand its community hospital in the city's East End, blocks from Creighton Court and other public housing communities. The Washington football team then committed to hold its summer training camp in Richmond for eight years. In a provision that eventually attracted public scorn, the city also agreed to provide the Washington franchise, one of the most valuable in professional sports, with $500,000 annually in cash or in-kind services for each year of the camp. Among the final provisions included was a stipulation that Bon Secours pay $100,000 annually for ten years to support school projects as a form of compensation for using the former RPS facility at Westhampton.[112]

Once the deal was finalized in late November, the city moved with remarkable speed to construct the facility to be ready for the 2013 preseason, although there was public blowback after a contractor clear-cut a popular wooded walking trail on the property in haste to move construction forward.[113] The camp opened as scheduled in July 2013 and generated significant attendance (over 165,000 visitors, including over 40,000 unique persons) and media attention, much of it centered on Washington's second-year quarterback Robert Griffin III, coming off his NFL Rookie of the Year season.[114] But local food vendors complained that they were not able to turn a profit from the training camp (Washington used its national vendors inside the camp), and there was limited evidence that visitors significantly stimulated local business activity.[115] Nonetheless, the first year in public perception was a qualified success, as the camp had gone smoothly, the city had welcomed the team, and many residents at least appreciated the novelty of having a widely supported NFL team in town.[116]

The popularity of the arrangement waned, however, for several reasons. First, the training camp never generated significant add-on economic stimulus for local businesses; in the second year, local vendors reported a worse situation than in the first year due in part to schedule changes that meant the team would no longer practice at lunchtime (often the hottest part of a sweltering summer day in Richmond).[117] Second, attendance at the camp, which remained strong in 2014, dropped off markedly in 2015 and in the following years. Whereas over 167,000 fans had visited the camp in 2014, in 2016 the figure was just 45,000.[118] Third, many Richmonders did not perceive the Washington team as a generous or particularly committed community partner, especially in insisting on the $500,000 annual payment and on using volunteers rather than paid locals to staff the camp.[119] Fourth, the city had difficulty leasing the center to private tenants other than Bon Secours in the offseason, meaning the modern, impressive building sat partly unused most of the year rather than generating additional lease revenue. The playing fields also sat empty for months at a time. As the Washington team did not intend to share the field with RPS athletic teams—many of which were practicing and playing in neglected facilities—the manicured fields served no community benefit the three seasons of the year the Washington team was absent.

Fifth, and most significantly from a development perspective, Bon Secours did not follow through with its development commitments in a timely way. After acquiring the Westhampton property lease, Bon Secours at the end of 2016 abandoned its plans to locate a nursing school on the site, outraging several members of the city council who had voted for the deal. Instead, Bon Secours turned the Westhampton site into a mixed-use development containing office space and some 128 apartments in a $53 million project, breaking ground in 2019.[120] On the other end of town in the East End, Bon Secours did not fulfill its commitment to expand the Richmond Community Hospital in the 2010s, completing the new medical office building nearby the hospital only in early 2023, just before its contractual deadline.[121]

The Jones administration sought to counter early skepticism of the deal in 2013 by noting that in addition to economic impact during the camp, the agreement as a whole would lead to a further $40 million in investment in the city by Bon Secours.[122] Jones's defense of the deal was partly vindicated by a 2019 assessment by VCU's Center for Urban and Regional Analysis that found the training camp alone had generated over $47 million in economic activity. The study concluded that while the project created a net fiscal loss for the city over the 2013–20 period of $4 million, the deal as a whole was projected to generate significant new revenue for the city in the 2020s from the Westhampton development, with expected net fiscal benefits over the entire 2013–33 period totaling $14.2 million.[123]

By 2016, however, the deal with the Washington franchise had few defenders; an August poll showed that some three-quarters of residents did not think the city had gotten a good return on its investment and opposed continuing to pay the $500,000 annual subsidy.[124] More substantively, the deal left the city with little leverage other than public criticism and shaming to get Bon Secours to follow through in a timely manner on its 2012 stated commitments to the East End. This point is telling, insofar as the promised East End investment was the one component of the training camp deal that promised to directly benefit low-income Richmond communities. Many Richmond residents took from this sequence of events the lesson that economic development claims are often overblown and the city's most powerful institutions are not necessarily trustworthy. The deal also came to represent the city's recurring penchant for being taken advantage of by private entities in large-scale economic development deals.

Swing and a Miss: The Shockoe Bottom Baseball Proposal

The apparent early success of the NFL training camp deal in the summer of 2013 fueled Mayor Jones's confidence that the city was ready to swing for the proverbial fences. That fall, Jones unveiled a far more ambitious plan: a multipronged $200 million project anchored by a new minor league baseball stadium in Shockoe Bottom, to be located just nine blocks east of city hall, in close proximity to the interstate highways running through the city's core. The Shockoe Bottom plan sought to accomplish several things at once: provide Richmond with a new minor league stadium to replace the aging Diamond facility on the Boulevard; ensure that the popular Richmond Flying Squirrels AA franchise (replacement for the AAA Richmond Braves, the team that had departed in 2008 for a new stadium in suburban Atlanta) would have a new and permanent home; fund a heritage site in close proximity to the stadium focused on the history of slavery in America and Virginia's role in it; bring a new hotel, grocery store, and apartment complex downtown, serviced by a new parking deck; and finally, clear away the old stadium from the Boulevard to allow for lucrative new retail development to come to the site (also located in close proximity to an interstate interchange). The baseball stadium component of the project would be paid for by a tax increment financing zone in the project area.[125]

Venture Richmond, the successor to Richmond Renaissance and the primary booster of business development in downtown Richmond, immediately announced its support. The organization, headed by former deputy city manager (and future mayoral candidate) Jack Berry, remained one of the most vocal and influential lobbyists for the project over the next nine months. Businesses in the immediate Shockoe area announced their support, as did the Flying Squirrels. Establishment Black politicians, such as delegate Delores McQuinn, also backed the plan as the best way to raise funds for a slavery memorial. Jones himself tied his personal story as a Virginia Union graduate into the project pitch—Virginia Union University had its origins as a seminary for Black students established just after the Civil War on the site formerly housing the infamous Lumpkin's Jail, a notorious jail for enslaved people. In Jones's narrative, the development proposal represented a similar transformation of a painful historical location into a site of both economic progress and the memorialization of slavery.[126]

Jones's ballpark plan sent city hall headlong into another battle between determined development interests and equally determined project opponents who rejected the project narrative. As both sides recognized, Richmond had invested millions of dollars into Confederate memorialization but had done, at that point, very little to financially support African American history and the legacy of slavery. Richmond was the second largest slave-trading city in the slave South, but visitors to the city might never know that based on the sparse memorialization downtown to enslaved people.

The ghosts of Richmond's unresolved history reawakened. From the beginning, the most consistent and vociferous opposition to the plan came from community activists holding a very different view of Lumpkin's Jail and the entire Shockoe Bottom area. Lumpkin's Jail (also known as the Devil's Half-Acre) had been used as a holding facility for enslaved persons prior to sale; its proprietor, Robert Lumpkin, had a reputation for cruelty and violence, and the facility maintained overcrowded, inhumane conditions.[127] Shockoe Bottom itself was the site of Richmond's slave markets, widely considered as one of the epicenters of the slave trade in America. Two preexisting organizations, the Sacred Ground Historical Reclamation Project and the Defenders for Freedom, Justice, and Equality, led by the interracial married couple Ana Edwards and Phil Wilayto, loudly and immediately protested the Shockoe baseball plan as a desecration of what they termed "sacred ground" that "would forever diminish the enormity of what happened here."[128] Edwards and Wilayto called for an alternative plan involving a memorial park dedicated to the memory of the enslaved persons who suffered in Shockoe Bottom.[129] Edwards and Wilayto's stance gained traction in the activist community and beyond, including with *Richmond Times-Dispatch*'s sole Black columnist, Michael Paul Williams, who wrote a favorable column focused on Edwards's views, offering this conclusion: "Building a stadium in Shockoe would be history repeating itself in the worst way."[130]

Principled militancy collided headlong with the politics of pragmatism. The Jones administration was well aware of activist opposition before announcing the project, and supporters sought to emphasize that the project as a whole offered the most realistic avenue for funding a proper slavery memorial. They also pointed to economic benefits for Black residents and the city's coffers as a result of the project. In one contentious council meeting, Ninth District councilwoman Michelle Mosby, a project supporter, stated,

"Your [protest] signs don't put up [the memorial]. Money is what is going to put the heritage site up."[131] Others quietly questioned whether it was reasonable to designate just one part of the city as "sacred ground" given that the crimes and injustices associated with slavery involved the entire city (and state). But most progressive activists in the city believed project opponents, not the city administration, were on the moral high ground. In an April 2014 rally (one of many demonstrations against the project), descendants of Solomon Northup, the New York man kidnapped into slavery depicted in the 2013 film *12 Years a Slave* (based on Northup's memoir), arrived in Richmond to protest the project; after being kidnapped, Northup had spent time in Richmond, probably in or near Shockoe Bottom, before being taken farther south to New Orleans.[132]

Nonetheless, the project seemed to be on course for approval. In February 2014, the council voted by a 6–3 margin to authorize the administration to continue negotiations on the project, rejecting a series of amendments offered by its president, Charles Samuels (including a requirement for an archaeological dig on the site prior to construction, a new Shockoe traffic study, and completion of a development plan for the Boulevard prior to the Shockoe plan moving forward). Council members Michelle Mosby, Cynthia Newbille, and Ellen Robertson—Black women representing three of the four poorest districts in the city—supported the project, along with Fourth District representative Kathy Graziano, a reliable supporter of economic development proposals. Reva Trammell, Parker Agelasto and Samuels opposed the project (opposition that hardened when the council defeated Samuels's amendments). That left Jonathan Baliles and Chris Hilbert of the First and Third Districts as the decisive swing votes. Hilbert supported the Samuels amendments but still voted for the overall resolution after the amendments failed. He hoped that the administration would address the issues named by Samuels. Baliles offered an amendment, unanimously adopted, intended to limit the financial risk to the city if the project went badly and then voted for the overall resolution.[133]

Momentum stalled, however, when the administration could not meet a deadline to bring back to the council a completed deal by the end of March. Then in a dramatic turn of events in late May, Samuels and Baliles released a public statement saying they opposed the Shockoe stadium, days before the scheduled final vote.[134] That statement, along with Hilbert's announcement that month that he too would be voting no, signaled the end. Jones in fact withdrew the proposal before it could be voted down at a May 27 council meeting.[135] The administration initially contended it would bring the proposal back in time, but the sudden, forced resignation of chief administrative officer Byron C. Marshall in September 2014 in effect ended any prospects for the project being revived, as Marshall had played a lead role in assembling and negotiating the deal.[136]

Within months, Jones's economic development team had moved on to a less problematic and less complicated project it could place in the win column. Backed by state support, the city moved quickly to assemble a financial package to support San Diego–based Stone Brewing's location of a major new production facility in the Fulton neighborhood, creating 288 jobs.[137] Nonetheless, the collapse of the Shockoe stadium deal surprised many Richmonders who assumed that strong support from the business community combined with strong support from elected mayoral leadership and most of the city's Black politicians would be enough to push a major deal through. Not for the last time, the city's elites underestimated the capacity of grassroots activism to turn public opinion on a development question, as well as the independence of the city council under the mayor-council form of government.

From Economic Development to Community Wealth Building: Small Steps toward a New Paradigm

Just days after the demise of the Shockoe plan, a new entity promising a different paradigm for both economic development and human services delivery launched in city hall: the Office of Community Wealth Building (OCWB), a new division charged with coordinating implementation of a multipronged attack on poverty that had been years in the making. By the end of his tenure, the OCWB had become a permanent agency, a defining feature of Jones's own legacy, and a marker of hope that city government could in fact act in meaningful ways on behalf of the one-quarter of the city struggling below the poverty line. Jones in 2015 established the policy goal of cutting the poverty rate for children from 40 percent to 20 percent and for residents overall from 25 percent to 15 percent by the year 2030. That same year saw the council unanimously approve Jones's proposal to make the OCWB a permanent agency, reporting directly to the chief administrative officer. In his February 2015 State of the City address, Jones summarized what was at stake:

> Right now, one part of town is vibrant, prosperous and forward-looking. And then when you cross the Martin Luther King Bridge,

you find another Richmond—one that has largely been ignored, overlooked and shunned.

The old Richmond allowed a generation of Richmonders to believe that they don't have a chance to succeed.... We'll reach our full potential only when we move beyond the tale of two cities.[138]

While Jones both originated and remained the lead champion of the initiative, the substance of Richmond's anti-poverty initiative was largely hatched outside traditional bureaucratic channels. Drawing on an idea originally proposed by Councilwoman Ellen Robertson, Jones in May 2011 announced the formation of the Mayor's Anti-Poverty Commission, composed of over forty community members across multiple sectors, to be chaired by Robertson and by Jones's deputy chief administrative officer for human services, Dr. Carolyn N. Graham.[139] The commission formed committees looking at education, housing, workforce and economic development, transportation, health, and policy and over the next twelve months developed an extensive list of action proposals. Significantly, the administration included a wide variety of voices in the process, including those of community members who disagreed with some of the administration's positions.[140] To garner wider input, the proposals were vetted in a series of public meetings in the late spring and early summer of 2012. That summer, Dr. Thad Williamson of the University of Richmond, who had chaired the Policy Committee, was tapped to draft the commission report, drawing on the copious materials produced by each of the committees, the public feedback, and additional research. Dr. John Moeser, a retired VCU professor then affiliated with the Bonner Center for Civic Engagement at the University of Richmond, contributed to the report's historical section.

The commission released the final report January 2013, shortly after Jones was sworn in for his second term as mayor. The 144-page report presented a detailed, statistical look at poverty in the City of Richmond, including trends over time, its correlation with race and gender, and the geographic distribution of poverty across the city; a historical section noting major decision points leading to the concentration of poverty in Richmond; and then summaries of the research, findings, and policy proposals of each committee. The report identified five high-level policy priorities: (1) improving the city's educational system by encompassing early childhood, K–12 education, and transition into college or workforce training; (2) strengthening workforce development opportunities for city residents in ways tailored to their needs; (3) creating or attracting more living-wage jobs to the city, including one or more major employers; (4) developing a citywide strategy to expand affordable housing while pursuing redevelopment of public housing with a commitment to one-for-one replacement of public housing units and the creation of a housing navigators program; and (5) developing a regional transportation system. The report also included a range of second-tier recommendations and a brief set of recommendations for the Jones administration regarding implementation.[141]

The report made headline news, but it would be an additional year before the commission framework significantly impacted policy and programmatic commitments. Councilwoman Robertson and Professor Williamson, with support from the mayor's office, cochaired an additional year of planning, dubbed the Maggie L. Walker Initiative for Expanding Opportunity and Fighting Poverty. That effort included seven additional task forces, involving numerous city employees and community members, tasked with identifying specific action steps to be undertaken by city government, consistent with the framework of the Anti-Poverty Commission report. The initiative also established the Maggie L. Walker Citizens Advisory Board, consisting primarily of residents living in poverty or in low-income neighborhoods, to vet all proposals; that board included outspoken community activists Duron Chavis and Lillie A. Estes (herself a frequent critic of Jones on other issues).[142] Amid the planning effort, the *New York Times* published a profile of Mayor Jones focused on the anti-poverty effort, in which he starkly declared, "If this is something we can't do, we don't deserve to be here."[143]

Jones put his money where his mouth was. Drawing on a detailed plan developed by the Maggie L. Walker Initiative, in March 2014 Jones introduced a budget proposal with $3.4 million dedicated to poverty-fighting initiatives. This included $1 million of initial capitalization for the city's Affordable Housing Trust Fund, previously established but not funded; a local match on a federal application to establish a Broad Street Bus Rapid Transit line to connect the breadth of the city east to west; funding to expand the city's pilot workforce development program, the Center for Workforce Innovation; funds for economic development, including a social enterprise initiative; and funds for afterschool programming for middle school students, an initiative to connect high school students to college opportunities, and early childhood education. The proposal also established a new entity within city hall, initially termed the "Mayor's Office of Community Wealth Building," charged with coordinating implementation of the initiatives, communicating the overall plan to stakeholders in and outside of government, and providing ongoing policy and strategic guidance on poverty reduction efforts to the mayor. The adoption of the term "community wealth building" was a deliberate shift out of concern that "anti-poverty" might be heard as "anti–poor people" and to signal an emphasis on a holistic approach to community and human development. The city council approved these plans during the budget process, and Thad Williamson was announced as the inaugural director of the Office of Community Wealth Building effective June 1, 2014.[144]

The initiative aimed to create economic pathways forward for Richmond's most vulnerable communities. Much of the initial work of the OCWB consisted of programmatic initiatives involving collaboration with Richmond Public Schools as well as with the Richmond Redevelopment and Housing Authority (see chapter 6). Notably, in June 2015 the OCWB and Mayor Jones announced formally their goal of cutting overall poverty in the City of Richmond by 40 percent and child poverty by 50 percent by the year 2030. In practice, achieving this would mean lifting about 1,000 *additional* Richmond adults a year above the poverty line for at least ten consecutive years. (In any given year, some households would rise above the poverty line, but others would fall below it; the goal thus would be to create interventions and initiatives that could lift a further 1,000 people out of poverty annually compared with the status quo.)[145]

The city chose the fledgling Center for Workforce Innovation to spearhead progress. Launched in 2010 as a partnership between the Department of Economic and Community Development and the Department of Social Services under the leadership of Jamison Manion, the city's workforce administrator, the program represented a sustained effort to tackle poverty by connecting underemployed city residents to jobs with local employers while also providing classes, training, and individualized support to participants. In 2014–15, the new funding also permitted establishment of a holistic, family-based program, eventually titled Building Lives of Independence and Self-Sufficiency—or BLISS—which sought to engage public housing residents with not only workforce development support but also a wide variety of supports aimed at identifying and removing barriers to progress, with the ultimate goal of helping residents obtain secure employment and improved housing. The program used a comprehensive matrix tracking eighteen areas of family well-being, from "crisis" to "thriving," following progress for each family in each category on a quarterly basis.[146] In December 2015, both BLISS and the overall Center for Workforce Innovation were formally transferred to the Office of Community Wealth Building upon the OCWB's establishment as a permanent city agency. By 2016, the center was helping over 200 residents a year find employment, a figure that would rise to 600 by

2019 after the OCWB received a five-year matching grant from the Virginia Department of Social Services to expand capacity starting in 2017.[147]

The strategy also aimed to help young people access further education and positive career trajectories. The OCWB launched a fruitful collaboration with Richmond Public Schools in 2014 concentrated on providing focused support to help the city's graduating seniors apply for college and financial aid or connect to other career development opportunities.[148] The long-term goal was to create a citywide scholarship program to allow all RPS graduates to attend college.[149] Funding for five fully staffed "Future Centers" to provide hands-on support to students in the city's comprehensive high schools was included in the FY 2016 budget, allowing the program to launch during the 2015–16 school year.[150]

Richmond's community wealth-building plan received another boost in September 2014 when the city received a federal Transportation Investment Generating Economic Recovery (TIGER) grant from the U.S. Department of Transportation. The grant provided nearly $25 million in federal funding for a Bus Rapid Transit (BRT) line, from Willow Lawn at the Henrico-Richmond border to the west to Rocketts Landing on the eastern edge of the city.[151] Existing city bus service had frequent stops, making longer journeys slow and cumbersome, especially for workers. The BRT was designed to travel at a higher average speed with fewer stops, making journeys of several miles faster for working-class riders and more appealing to potential new customers. The new BRT route in Richmond on Broad Street would include a dedicated lane over much of the route, priority traffic signaling for buses to accelerate travel, and new dedicated vehicles. It was envisioned that the Broad Street line would be the first arm of a truly regional BRT system and that the GRTC would add additional feeder lines to give residents of Church Hill and other neighborhoods connecting access to the BRT. After an extensive review process and some modifications to the initial plan, the project was completed and the GRTC Pulse began offering service in June 2018.[152]

By the mid-2010s, economic revitalization in Richmond following the Great Recession seemed to be on the upswing.[153] Yet as Jones transitioned out of office, there was still no guarantee that Richmond's least-advantaged residents would significantly benefit from the growth. As we demonstrate in the next chapter, the burgeoning growth brought heightened concerns about gentrification and its impact on longtime residents, especially long-term Black residents with limited or fixed incomes. The most ambitious idea the OCWB pursued to affect this dynamic and directly impact the distribution of wealth and income, beyond workforce development efforts, was a "social enterprise" initiative formally started in 2015. Modeled on the pioneering Evergreen Cooperatives in Cleveland, the concept entailed large employers such as health systems, VCU, larger corporations, and where possible government itself offering a percentage of contracts and subcontracts to firms specifically committed to employing residents from Richmond's poorest neighborhoods. Those firms in turn would be organized as cooperatives committed to paying living wages, providing full benefits, and offering additional supports to employees.[154] The 2016 Richmond Social Enterprise Study, based on extensive conversations with anchor institutions in Richmond, identified two possible niche spaces where startup social enterprises might be successful—one in health care involving outpatient outreach and the other in public housing building and plant maintenance. The study recommended that a nonprofit organization parallel to the Office of Community Wealth Building be established to operate as the fiscal agent for the initiative.[155]

Taken together, the community wealth-building strategy in Richmond aimed to provide support to residents in obtaining living-wage jobs via trainings, certifications, and additional supports; to expand geographical access to existing employment opportunities regionally through better public (and bike) transit; to expand the number of living-wage jobs in the city itself; to partner with the school system to help parents prepare young children for school and help graduates prepare for life after high school; and to attempt to support and expand smaller businesses, especially Black-owned businesses, while working toward development of a social enterprise sector. The intent was to build linkages and connections between Richmond's deep pockets of concentrated wealth and its deep pockets of concentrated poverty, so that subsequent growth might actually lead to tangible reductions in poverty.[156] At the same time, this employment-based strategy would be matched with longer-term strategies to improve educational outcomes and housing as well as advocacy for policy changes at both the local and state level. Yet progress on employment continued as the leading strategy, insofar as it provided the most immediate means of getting cash to residents, helping to stabilize families and thereby enhance learning and educational progress for children and making it easier for families to obtain quality housing (and for the city and its partners to pursue redevelopment or revitalization of existing public housing).

Richmond's community wealth-building initiative thus aimed at providing not just additional services or resources but also sufficient support to allow individuals and households to substantially improve their economic circumstances and eventually transition from "getting by" to thriving and accumulating wealth. That aspiration, in a sense, stood athwart not only Richmond's history but years of state and federal policy and decades of growing economic inequality and insecurity at the national level. As important as the policy details was the act of institutionalizing the office, requiring the mayor to provide an annual update on its progress, and establishing wealth building as a permanent function of city government. While many Richmond residents were not affected by or even aware of this shift, within city government the priority of fighting poverty was well known and frequently articulated: year after year, the city's budget director would tell agency directors not to ask for new funds unless it was a contractual commitment or legal obligation, a matter of health or safety, or related to fighting poverty. In that sense, Jones, with the support of the city council, used the power of his office to alter the DNA of city government, in law and in practice, in ways it would take deliberate effort for future mayors and councils to undo.

Moreover, the initiative showed that bringing grassroots Richmond, including activist voices, to the policymaking table not only could be done but could yield more credibility and sustainable success than the standard formula of tapping into the business community and other elite networks to help develop policy. In the eyes of many in activist Richmond (and beyond), no one lent more credibility to Richmond's community wealth-building initiative than one of the mayor's toughest critics, Lillie A. Estes, the Gilpin Court resident and tenant activist who served on both the Mayor's Anti-Poverty Commission and the Maggie L. Walker Citizens Advisory Board. Estes proudly (but not uncritically) championed the mission and work of the office:

> We didn't want to keep using the term "poverty," so we intentionally changed it to how we build wealth in the community, because wealth connotes the ability to determine where the resources go, how they go. They were receptive to that, so we created a community wealth-building office that has grown nationally....
>
> We even had [*The Nation*] magazine come interview me and some other people and talk about, "How do we take the capital of the Confederacy, and move it into dealing with—how do you really build wealth in a neighborhood or a city that has intentionally had separation and segregation?" ... So they fast-tracked it, and I think it's a very good beginning.[157]

Even with these initial strides to develop equity-centered policies and programs, it remained an open question whether Richmond's leaders would continue to commit the resources, energy, and attention needed to realize the boldest aims of the city's community wealth-building initiatives, or would remain content with milder initiatives that helped people but failed to change systems.[158] Among the most entrenched of those systems was the city's housing market and long-standing patterns of racial segregation and deeply concentrated poverty. Richmond's efforts to meet its housing needs (and its uneven track record) are the focus of the following chapter.

6

The Persistence of Segregation

Housing Richmond, 1988–2016

The days of large public housing projects are over.

RICHARD C. GENTRY, RICHMOND REDEVELOPMENT AND HOUSING
AUTHORITY CHIEF EXECUTIVE OFFICER, OCTOBER 1990

I can't afford to get out. . . . Sometimes, I'm like, my next check, I'll live anywhere, you know? I'll live on someone's couch just to claim a good address and put my kid in a good school. [If nothing changes] my 10-year-old will go to a failing school and get a poor education that will result in him living back in the poor community that I raised him up in, just because I know my address is still 2218 Walcott Place.

CHIMERE MILES, CREIGHTON COURT RESIDENT, JULY 2016

Concentrations of poverty and wealth characterize the landscape of modern Richmond. There remains no starker example of the contrast than the gulf between the East End, where public housing communities are made up almost exclusively of poor African Americans, and the spacious, manicured, and overwhelmingly white West End neighborhoods composing some of wealthiest enclaves in the Commonwealth of Virginia (not merely the city). The vast divide between these neighborhoods, including shocking, racialized disparities in wealth, health, and quality of life, is a defining characteristic of Richmond politics and public policy. For decades, that same divide also distorted civic life in the capital city. Tellingly, when critics lambaste the continuity of racial segregation in Richmond, attention almost always focuses on entrenched, concentrated Black poverty. The equally entrenched reality of affluent, nearly all-white neighborhoods is rarely discussed. Likewise, many well-off Richmonders have not been willing to confront the fact that, in the end, the persistence of segregation and concentrated poverty in the city largely reflects their own policy preferences and unexamined assumptions about where different people belong.

This chapter, in its focus on public housing in Richmond and the broader crisis of affordable housing, illuminates the communities and people most harmed by Richmond's historic patterns of segregation.[1] Between 1988 and 2016, Richmond largely failed to transform the city's most economically challenged neighborhoods, especially its public housing communities. The failure was not for want of trying—city leaders designated concentrated poverty a priority to be addressed over three decades ago. Indeed, the compression of impoverished African American communities into substandard, isolated public housing communities proved to be one of the most destructive urban initiatives of the twentieth century—not just in Richmond but nationally. Yet, responsibility for the failure of public housing lies not only with city hall and its policymakers; it is also rooted in the fact that many white Richmonders came to regard the racialized geography of the city as normal (or even natural) and showed little interest in inviting meaningful changes to *their* neighborhoods. At the turn of the twenty-first century (as table 6.1 demonstrates), over half of the city's census tracts were either 80 percent Black or 80 percent white, and numerous neighborhoods were almost completely homogeneous. Segregationist proclivities in Richmond survived the era of formal segregation.

Any consideration of the politics of public and affordable housing in Richmond requires an understanding of the historical forces and policy decisions that created, reinforced, and reproduced racial segregation after

TABLE 6.1. Race and residential patterns by census tract in City of Richmond, 2000

Race/ethnicity composition	Number of census tracts (out of 65)
Black population > 95%	12
Black population > 80%	24
(Non-Hispanic) white population > 90%	7
(Non-Hispanic) white population > 80%	14
Black population > 30% *and* (non-Hispanic) white population > 30%	13

Source: 2000 U.S. Census via Social Explorer.
Note: Citywide population in 2000 = 56.9% Black and 37.7% (non-Hispanic) white

the 1970s. This chapter analyzes the history of public housing in Richmond and the prehistory of stark racial segregation. First, however, we take a brief detour into democratic theory to state clearly the normative issues at stake in housing policy. We see cities as potential sites for enacting democracy and social justice. Likewise, we see housing, which involves both where and how people live, not simply as an economic commodity but as a building block of neighborhoods, communities, and democracy.

Housing Justice: What We Mean

In the most fundamental sense, cities are constituted of people living and working together—coexisting. Because people must live in particular places and because they typically seek both private comforts and public goods in the places they live, housing and housing patterns are the root structure of any city. All residents desire safe living conditions in buildings that provide adequate shelter and in neighborhoods that are generally safe and have access to essential goods such as food, transportation, and education. Residents with higher incomes seek (and are in position to obtain) more than this; they look for more comfortable private living spaces but also (depending on preference) either immediate access to valued urban goods (such as culture and entertainment) or calm and quiet. Households generally cluster with other households with similar income levels and similar preferences, but neither economic nor racial segregation need be total in urban environments. According to many accounts of the "just city," urban social justice involves people of different economic means as well as different races and ethnicities

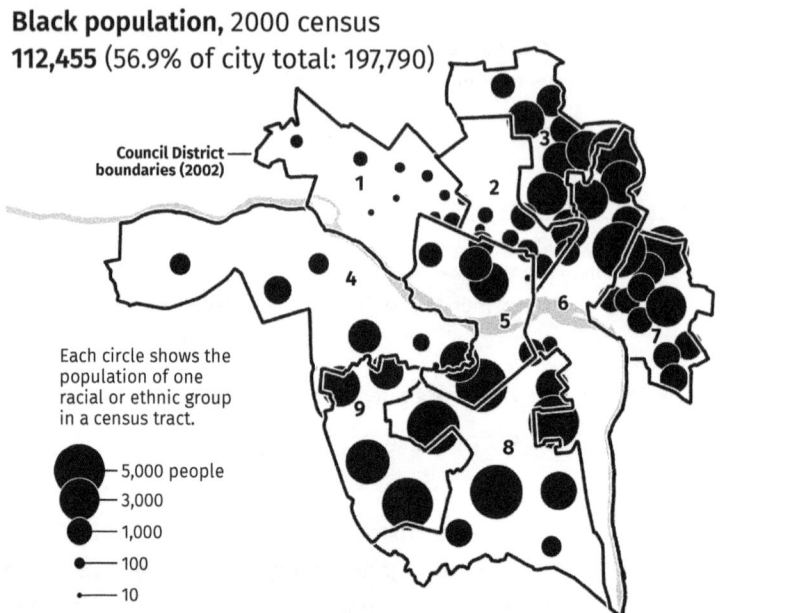

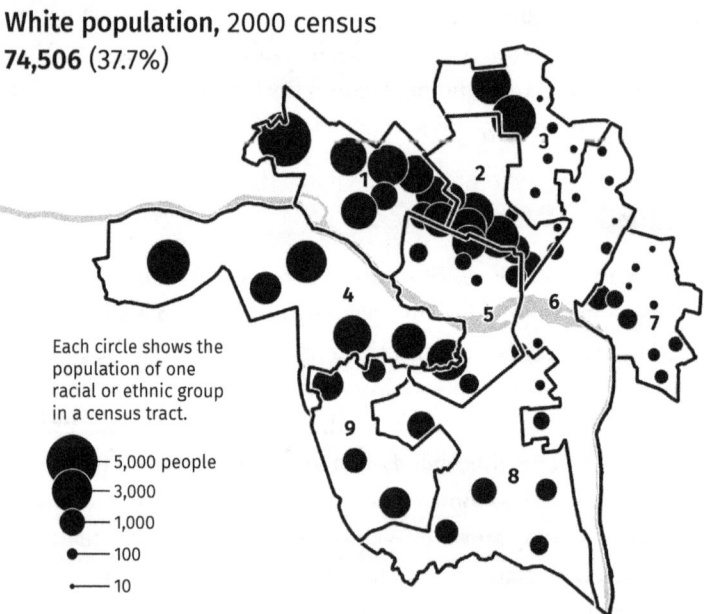

Map 6.1 Black and white populations by council district, 2000.
Map by Riley D. Champine of the University of Richmond Digital Scholarship Lab, based on data from the City of Richmond and IPUMS NHGIS (University of Minnesota, www.nhgis.org).

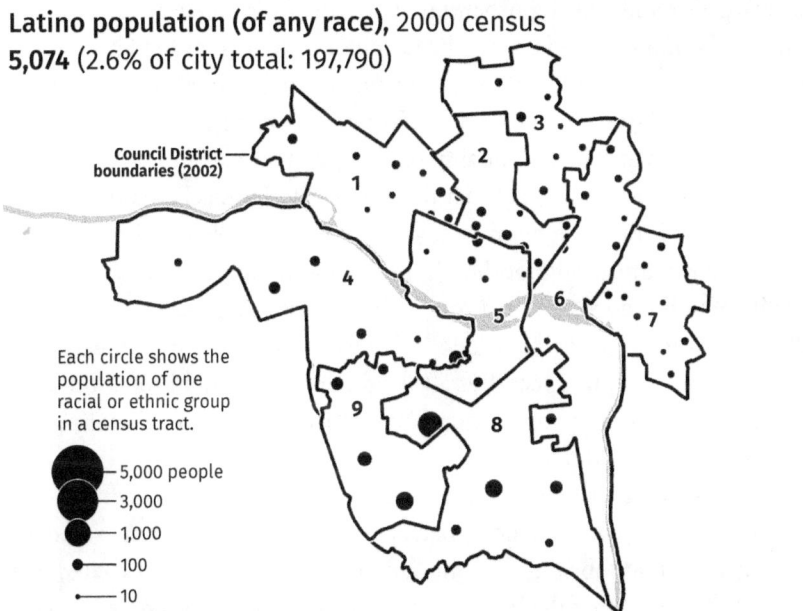

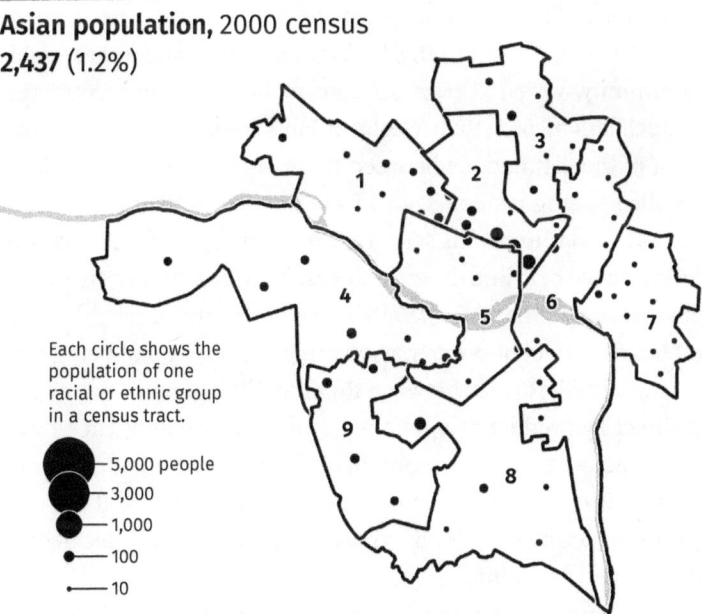

Map 6.2. Latino and Asian populations by council district, 2000. Map by Riley D. Champine of the University of Richmond Digital Scholarship Lab, based on data from the City of Richmond and IPUMS NHGIS (University of Minnesota, www.nhgis.org).

living together and sharing urban public goods, from safety to recreation to public education.² In this view, clustering of residents on the basis of race or ethnicity is consistent with social justice so long as it is voluntary and so long as such clustering does not confer privileges or disadvantages on any group in terms of access to quality public goods and services.³ In short, in a racially diverse city, the fact that there are majority-Black, majority-white, and majority-Latino neighborhoods need not be a problem in itself; what is a problem is if those neighborhoods differ substantially in quality of life and quality of public goods or are a result of unfair housing practices. Likewise, all neighborhoods need not be identical or equal in, say, average housing size as measured by square feet; but all neighborhoods should meet the basic needs of residents and provide good-quality access to essential public goods and especially education.

Housing patterns in Richmond, and their associated socioeconomic, racial, and political consequences, persistently violated these basic standards of justice, in both obvious and more subtle ways. A frequently cited 2015 VCU study found that the life expectancy of Richmond residents in majority-white Westover Hills was twenty years longer than life expectancy for residents in and around Gilpin Court, Richmond's oldest and largest public housing community, which is over 90 percent Black.⁴ Gilpin Court residents have much less income than Westover Hills residents, but this is only the beginning of the distinctions between these enclaves. Gilpin residents, like most public housing residents, also have less access to green space, to affordable quality food, to health services, and to public safety, while they face greater incidence of crime, homelessness, litter, and public disorder in their neighborhood. In this way, the environment in such a neighborhood often multiplies the effect of poverty, worsening the impacts of being poor. The stark, racialized disparities between Richmond neighborhoods evident today are a direct by-product of public policy decisions dating back nearly a century: both active policy decisions that concentrated and "contained" impoverished African Americans in certain parts of the city, and the city's refusal or inability to take sufficiently robust policy steps to reverse decades of segregationist policymaking.⁵

Racialized housing segregation affected more than where people lived—it affected how they lived as well. By the late twentieth century, concentrated poverty gave rise to even starker differences between affluent whites in the West End and their poorer counterparts in the East End and on the Southside. Gaping economic distinctions meant that people in the same municipality might have little in common and little if any community with persons on the other side of the economic divide. Majority-white neighborhoods were spatially, economically, and perhaps psychologically separate from poorer Black enclaves (and increasingly, Latino enclaves as well) in the East End and on the Southside. But at certain points in the city, the worlds of white and non-white, rich and poor, touched and even collided. Collisions of this nature became more likely as patterns of gentrification deepened. The economic incentives to move into areas once exclusively inhabited by people of color finally eclipsed the fear of these spaces.

From a metropolitan-wide perspective, the even deeper structural divide persisted between Richmond and its surrounding counties. In the mid-1980s, this divide broke down in straightforward racial terms: the contrast between the majority-Black city and the overwhelmingly white suburbs. In the decades following Massive Resistance, Richmond's suburban neighbors refused to be connected by transit to the city and avoided building the kinds of public housing found there. By the mid-2010s, in Richmond as elsewhere, the picture became more complex: racial and socioeconomic diversity in the counties, especially Henrico County, increased markedly, and poverty rates in the counties rose slightly as well (from a low baseline). But the basic picture of concentrated, primarily Black poverty located in one corner of the region—the eastern third of the City of Richmond, both north and south of the James River, including four public housing communities concentrated in one square mile—remained remarkably unchanged over the decades examined in this book.

Over time, Richmond leaders undertook efforts to change, and even transform, living conditions in the city's public housing communities. They did so with no meaningful support from neighboring local governments and with sporadic, uneven support from the state and federal government. Often, the stated goals of those efforts were to improve neighborhood conditions *and* the well-being of residents most impacted by public housing redevelopment plans. Indeed, in the 2010s local policy and practice evolved significantly in the direction of strengthening protections and public commitments to residents affected by redevelopment, especially after the perceived shortcomings of the earlier, federally funded redevelopment of the Blackwell public housing community on the Southside in the late 1990s and early aughts.[6] But it was still unclear whether Richmond had the moral and political will either to undertake a process of massive transformation of long-standing public housing communities or to implement it in a way that delivered on promises made to low-income residents and neighborhoods. Indeed, some activists and observers began questioning whether such transformation was a desirable goal at all; others strongly supported the goal but doubted Richmond's capacity to achieve it.

By the mid-2010s, Richmond also grappled with accelerated processes of gentrification, resulting from the city's population growth since 2005. Gentrification led to rapidly rising housing values due to increased demand, creating burdens for both renters and property owners on fixed incomes (due to higher tax bills). But in Richmond (as in some other places) the process also had a starker implication as a proxy for racial change. As shown below, starting in the mid-aughts, whites began returning to the city in larger and larger numbers, reversing over three decades of "white flight" and setting Richmond on a path to no longer being a majority-Black city. The City of Richmond and its partners established important tools aimed at expanding the supply of affordable housing and offsetting the costs of gentrification, particularly the Affordable Housing Trust Fund and the Maggie Walker Community Land Trust. But over the period of this study, the city did not invest in these or related tools at the scale needed to meaningfully dent the city's worsening affordable housing crisis.

By the 2010s, Richmond leaders struggled to devise viable strategies to address older, decaying public housing communities. They also grappled with the challenges associated with rapid growth. Both ordinary residents and policy practitioners sensed Richmond was in a race against the clock. The city needed to take meaningful action to address both problems *before* a feared future of resumed majority-white political control of the city, in which the interest and political will to address the housing needs of low-income residents of color (and redress poverty more generally) might weaken.[7]

Segregating Richmond

By the 1970s, Richmond leaders had inherited a deeply segregated city but not the policy tools, financial resources, or political will required to seriously address those patterns. The clustering of Black people into certain parts of the city (such as Shockoe Valley and Jackson Ward) began immediately after the Civil War. De facto segregation coupled with profoundly powerful social norms delineated certain neighborhoods as white or Black in the Reconstruction decades. Then in 1911, Richmond became the second city in the United States, behind Baltimore, to enact racial zoning laws. While the U.S. Supreme Court struck down explicitly racialized zoning ordinances in 1917, Richmond (like other southern cities) adopted alternative tactics over the coming decades to maintain the color line.[8]

Segregationists redlined Richmond in the 1930s. Redlining, the practice of deliberately withholding private (and in turn public) investment from specific neighborhoods on the basis of race, impacted not just Richmond but most American cities with sizable ethnic and minority populations.[9] Maps of Richmond drawn in the 1930s, sponsored by the federal Home Owners' Loan Corporation and factored into federal lending, divided the city according to the racial composition of its neighborhoods, with Black neighborhoods deemed not creditworthy.[10] As noted by Julian Maxwell Hayter, during the appraisal process, the Federal Housing Administration "ordered local lenders to use its color-coded Residential Security Maps." Those maps specified that

> green and blue areas, populated by whites, were in good standing, but lenders considered yellow and red areas—often made up of Jews, immigrants, white laborers, and African Americans—high risk. Local lenders eventually designated all of Richmond's African American neighborhoods red regardless of their socioeconomic status. This process of denying loans to or jacking up interest rates on potential African American borrowers became known as "redlining." These policies eventually allowed a handful of whites to invest in their own communities, strengthen patterns of residential segregation, and systematically ignore the development of black neighborhoods.[11]

These maps allowed local lenders and politicians not merely to use race to assess financial risk in homeownership but to construct and perpetuate racially homogeneous communities. African American communities, which were given red designations, were systematically disinvested in. Residents of redlined communities often failed to receive fair market value for their homes, signed loans with extremely high interest rates, or were forced into a practice known as contract buying whereby white speculators bought property in Black enclaves and forced residents into coercive leases that made it virtually impossible for residents to make the payments. (The process would begin anew when residents defaulted on payment.) While white homeowners in the mid-twentieth century used their home equity to build or sustain generational wealth, race-based redlining, local government disinvestment in Black neighborhoods, and racist real estate practices stymied real estate wealth building for many Black people in Richmond and nationwide.[12]

Notably, Black Richmonders in the early twentieth century had in fact developed an alternative model of neighborhood and economic development, within the constraints of segregation. In 1903, Maggie L. Walker led the development of banking and credit institutions for the explicit purposes of helping Black Richmonders save and build wealth and generating capital to invest in Black-owned businesses and in housing. While Walker's goal was "uplift" of Black Richmonders, she also maintained strategic relationships with white individuals and institutions, both to advance her efforts and to protect Black people from hostile forces (either in state government or white-owned competitors).[13] In the first half of the twentieth century, Jackson Ward stood as a model of the level of commercial and cultural development possible when Black neighborhoods were provided meaningful access to credit and capital. Tragically but not surprisingly, given the biased decision-making at local, state, and federal levels, Jackson Ward was bisected by the Richmond-Petersburg Turnpike in the 1950s.[14]

The Great Depression and decades of Jim Crow–era neglect had already undermined the viability of Richmond's Black communities by the 1940s. Even Jackson Ward (a redlined district), famed for its redbrick Greek Revival rowhouses, and the acknowledged economic, political, and social epicenter of Black Richmond during the mid-twentieth century, had suffered from years of systemic neglect. Segregationists often failed to distribute services equitably throughout Richmond's white and Black neighborhoods, and by the 1930s areas such as Jackson Ward and Navy Hill struggled to keep pace with their white counterparts. Despite the district being commonly referred to as the "Wall Street of the South," residents of Jackson Ward suffered from high death rates, crime, delinquency, and tuberculosis. Representative of their lack of regard for Black Richmond, city officials also placed several municipal dumps in Black neighborhoods.[15]

Policymakers used public housing as a new tool to meet the challenges of the affordable housing crisis exacerbated by the Great Depression and then World War II.[16] In 1940, the city established the Richmond Redevelopment and Housing Authority (RRHA) to address the problem of providing housing for Richmonders (primarily Black) of limited income, utilizing newly available federal dollars.[17] The RRHA's aggressive program of public housing construction, combined with the bisection or outright decimation of existing Black neighborhoods by highway construction, confined low-income Blacks to certain parts of the city, out of sight (and mind) of the white residents who at the time constituted the majority of the city population.

Richmond's embrace of public housing was not without controversy.[18] When the Virginia General Assembly passed enabling legislation for public housing authorities in 1939, cities such as Alexandria and Newport News moved quickly to take advantage of federal funds to eliminate slums and develop public housing. In Richmond, the prospect of federally subsidized public housing sparked both ideological opposition and concern about its long-term impact. Mayor J. Fulmer Bright, who had been in office since 1924, argued that creating a housing authority "violates every principle of sound business, democracy, Americanism, individualism, and other fine traits." Bright worried about the long-term impact of public housing: "I believe that these very Federal housing projects, now being constructed to relieve the ills of which we complain, will in themselves constitute the slums of the next generation, twenty years hence."[19] Fearful that public housing would push out families who could not afford the rent payments and would create a "preferred class of citizens," Bright vetoed the city council's narrow vote to form a public housing authority. Bright's noninterventionist approach to development cost him the 1940 election, held in April. Gordon B. Ambler, a supporter of slum clearance, public housing, and annexation, took office as mayor and became integral to the creation of the RRHA that October.[20]

Backed by over $3 million in federal funds, the new authority moved briskly to erect the city's first public housing community: in 1941, the city razed nearly 200 homes in Apostle Town, an area on the north side of Jackson Ward, and broke ground on the new community called Gilpin Court, containing some 297 public housing units.[21] In the following decades, Gilpin became the largest public housing development between Baltimore and Atlanta, with 783 units. Then in July 1949, the federal government allocated additional construction funding through the Housing Act of 1949. In 1951, the city council approved RRHA plans for the construction of 504 units in the East End for Black families (Creighton Court) and 402 units for white families on the Southside (Hillside Court).[22] Richmond public housing would remain formally segregated by race until the mid-1960s.[23]

The development of Gilpin, Creighton, and Hillside Courts paralleled the implementation of aggressively segregationist urban renewal policies that leveled, refurbished, displaced, or marginalized most of Richmond's Black neighborhoods. Between 1955 and 1957, Virginia and the City of Richmond displaced more than 7,000 people—10 percent of the city's Black population—during the construction of the Richmond-Petersburg Turnpike (now I-95 and I-64) and the Belvidere Street Extension (which cuts through the heart of mid-Richmond). At the same time, the city built large-scale public housing to help offset the lost housing units.[24] The RRHA extended Gilpin Court in 1957 by 338 units and effectively severed the area from the rest of Jackson Ward during the construction of the Richmond-Petersburg Turnpike in the 1950s. Toward the end of that decade, Richmond also proceeded with "slum clearance" of some forty blocks in Shockoe Valley—site of the city's oldest Black communities dating back to the antebellum era. The RRHA then constructed three additional public housing developments in the East End, all in close proximity to 504-unit Creighton Court: Whitcomb Court (1958, 447 units), Fairfield Court (1958, 447 units), and Mosby Court (1962, 458 units). These initiatives altogether constructed roughly 1,850 public housing units largely for African Americans families within an area of approximately one square mile.[25]

Richmond's last major clearance effort, of the Fulton neighborhood in east Richmond, took place in the early 1970s. The 2,800 residents displaced received relocation payments and other assistance in accordance with federal regulations, but the scars on the neighborhood persisted for decades.[26] By this time, however, public housing policy nationally began to turn away from construction of large-scale communities and toward community-based planning, neighborhood revitalization and historical conservation. As the national stigma against public housing intensified and the federal government cut funding to housing programs, the RRHA shifted its focus to senior housing and scattered-site urban redevelopment for low-income families. In an important development, after the downtown expressway bisected the historic Randolph neighborhood (named for early twentieth-century Black educator Virginia Randolph) in the 1970s, the RRHA shelved initial plans to build another large cluster of public housing akin to the "courts" built in the 1950s and 1960s. Instead, with a push from young RRHA staffer T. K. Somanath, who urged the authority to listen to residents' ideas, Randolph was rebuilt as a mixed-income neighborhood anchored by a park and community center, with scattered public housing units.[27] Randolph would remain a mixed-income neighborhood containing low-income, working-class, and middle-class households for decades and stood as an example of how the housing needs of low-income Richmonders might be accommodated in a less isolated neighborhood setting than those offered by the large-scale public housing communities.

By 1980, four decades of local housing policy had acted to entrench, not relieve, the racial segregation of housing in Richmond. The racialized geography that continues to define twenty-first-century Richmond was almost entirely constructed under white-led political regimes. Federal funding for public housing declined in the 1980s, at the same time public stigma against "the projects" intensified. Black political leadership stopped digging the proverbial hole of racial segregation but struggled with the dual challenges of, first, mitigating the consequences of residential segregation, and second, taking proactive steps to overcome it (without causing yet further harm). This struggle, as we will see, was in part a result of leadership and governance challenges as well as a consequence of the general predicament of governing a resource-starved city with overwhelming needs. The struggle was also because of embedded racial segregation. Indeed, for much of the time under study, many officials and citizens believed that Richmond's deep segregation was simply a condition of life and part of the natural order rather than the result of deliberate policy choices that at least in theory might be undone by deliberate and sustained countervailing policies and practices.

Grappling with the Segregated City, 1988–2008

Forty-five years after its opening, the newness, attendant hope, and promise of Gilpin Court had long faded. The national stigmatization of public housing as "warehouses for the poor" coupled with declining federal fiscal support for maintaining and upgrading buildings placed residents in aging infrastructure with little public buy-in for the housing program. Some Richmond leaders in the 1980s (and beyond) pushed back against the dominant Reagan-era narratives about public housing residents, as well as the decade's very specific cuts to public housing budgets and urban programs more generally.[28] But the federal cuts of the 1980s slammed the door shut on the New Deal dream of publicly funded, decent, non-stigmatized public housing. Already challenged communities like Gilpin Court bore the full brunt of this decisive shift in national policy.

Public housing residents, though, had their own opinions about the state of subsidized housing. "Living in Gilpin Court is like being tied to an albatross: It carries a weight that is both uncommon and troublesome." So began a three-part profile of Gilpin Court residents published in the *Richmond Times-Dispatch* in December 1985 by journalist Bonnie Winston (later managing editor for the *Richmond Free Press*). Winston offered this testimony from a longtime Gilpin resident to support that statement:

> Inez Hill recalled the time she was summoned for jury duty, and after a long night of deciding someone's fate, a fellow juror offered her a ride home. "No," she said, declining the offer, knowing in the back of her mind the stigma attached to the housing development where she has lived for 14 years. She'd lost dates before when they found out where she lived.

But the man insisted, saying it was late and that a woman shouldn't be left alone at night to find her way home.

Again she said no, and yet he insisted.

"Finally, I told him OK," Mrs. Hill said. "Then he asked me where I lived and when I said Gilpin Court, he said, 'Oh, ma'am. I'm sorry. I can't take you there.'"[29]

Winston went on to share testimony concerning how the stigma associated with Gilpin Court was easily transferred from parents to children:

> [The parents] all want more for their children, if they have to punish them, beat them or bargain with them to stay off the streets and in school. They want their children to have, to achieve, to grow up to live somewhere else besides Gilpin Court.
>
> They don't want their children to be branded as they believe they have. And yet some already have fallen into the pattern. In school, many have been labeled emotionally disturbed, learning disabled and handicapped.
>
> One woman said her son, who has been placed in that category, was chastised by the teacher in front of the other pupils in his grade-school class about being lazy "like his mother who lives in Gilpin Court and just wants to sit around and collect welfare."
>
> "The teacher doesn't know me," said the woman, who holds a job and collects some child support from her former husband for his children and welfare for the others. "She has no right to say that to my son in front of the class. She admitted she said it, but tried to brush it off by saying she was just playing with him. She has no right to play with him like that."[30]

Winston's account detailed the interlocking realities of poverty, crime, single-parent homes, and the intense social stigma of living in public housing. Roland Turpin, the CEO of the RRHA, situated Gilpin's problems within a wider context: "We can't deal with the crime problem in a constructive way unless we deal with the socio-economic and value system," said Turpin. "We are reaping the negatives from a forgotten group who have lost hope because they have missed out on the educational system, the economic system and certain family and social values. We cannot successfully eradicate the problem of crime until we are willing to address these kinds of issues."[31]

Turpin and other leaders stressed the decency of most public housing residents. In fact, they emphasized that crime was largely caused by outsiders and spoke with empathy about the ways in which public housing residents were often both stigmatized and taken advantage of by outsiders. They also stressed the imperative of providing supportive services to residents and the fact that success stories were possible. But not all residents Winston interviewed believed change was on the horizon anytime soon. As one underemployed man told the journalist, "Nothing will change. Not the face lifts on the buildings or anything can change the way things are. The face lifts will affect the view from outside in, but not the view from inside out."[32] That blunt street-level assessment proved to be largely prophetic over the coming decades.

Harrowing testimonies about life in Gilpin Court and other public housing communities would appear periodically, remarkably unchanged from the 1980s to the 2010s. So too would recurring observations about the vast inequalities between Richmond neighborhoods and the equally vast social gulf between the Richmond of Gilpin Court and the Richmond of the wealthy West End enclave Windsor Farms. Homicides in the "courts" were treated as a routine, unremarkable story by local media. In 2020, longtime Creighton Court resident and Richmond Tenants Organization leader Marilyn Olds described the reality she knew intimately across many decades but that many Richmonders ignored: "Could you imagine being afraid to get out of your car to go into your house at night? Look out the window. Do you hear the sounds of gunshots echoing in your home? Do you put your children in the bathtub? Sleep on the floor? Walk under the window because of the shootings where you live?"[33]

The violence and fear associated with Richmond public housing scarred generations of residents and children; a 2014 survey of Creighton Court residents found that 41 percent "never" felt safe in their community at night.[34] Even so, these powerful accounts told only part of the larger story: for many Richmond residents, life in public housing was a significant step up, from either homelessness or private rental housing in dilapidated conditions, often with negligent landlords. For others, friendships and networks of support with fellow public housing residents provided affective support even within challenging circumstances.[35] Applicants for Richmond public housing often had to wait at least six months to get a unit, while the waiting list for a Section 8 voucher normally numbered thousands of people.[36] Public housing offered the city's poorest residents a baseline of stability in units that normally met building safety codes and in neighborhoods that (alongside crime, debris, and despair) offered services and, for some, a sense of community.

To be sure, Richmond leaders, Black and white, routinely voiced the need for, and devoted considerable effort to, transformation of Richmond's public housing. They sought to provide better neighborhood environments and a better life for low-income Richmonders. But the predicament of public housing was part of a larger problem: the availability, or lack thereof, of affordable housing in Richmond.[37] That crisis was a function of both poverty (too little income) and an insufficient supply of decent, code-compliant housing plausibly affordable to low-income families surviving on low-wage, often sporadic work. Pressure from community leaders and advocates to assure that redevelopment of public housing avoided exacerbating the affordable housing crisis (by reducing the number of affordable housing units available to the very poor) complicated the ability of city leaders to make good on their frequent proclamations of change.

Ultimately, Richmond failed to summon the political will or the financial muscle necessary to transform public housing. Whereas Richmond officials had expressed hope in the late 1990s that the city might emulate Atlanta by obtaining newly available federal redevelopment grants, Richmond received only one such grant over a three-decade period. Those funds went to redevelop public housing in Blackwell on the Southside. An initial effort in the late aughts to redevelop Gilpin Court stalled in the wake of resident opposition and leadership changes in the housing authority. A subsequent effort in the second term of Mayor Dwight C. Jones's tenure to redevelop Creighton Court also failed to win federal support, although the redevelopment project proceeded anyway, at a much slower rate and without much of the concerted community plan that had been envisioned to support residents. Indeed, to compare what had actually taken place by 2016 with what had been envisioned by city leadership as early as 1990 is to take the measure of Richmond's collective inability to tackle its deepest and most vexing challenge.

By the mid-1980s, the Richmond Redevelopment and Housing Authority was one of the most consequential entities in the City of Richmond. It acted as landlord for some 4,500 public housing households, and it provided federal Section 8 housing vouchers to some 2,500 recipients, allowing them to rent in the private market.[38] All told, the RRHA provided housing for nearly 10 percent of the city population; it also offered services to thousands of residents, either directly or in partnership with city and nonprofit agencies. Further, the RRHA owned large amounts of property in addition to actively occupied housing units. It was also a central and necessary player in many neighborhood development and redevelopment projects. Any meaningful change to public housing required the RRHA: from full-scale redevelopment of public housing to improving conditions and services in the existing units.

Despite its critical importance for the city, the authority's governance structure remained opaque, unclear, and frequently contested. The RRHA CEO and staff reported to a local board of commissioners appointed by the city council; but council members did not typically provide clear directives to the board on policy, nor did they get involved in day-to-day operations and personnel matters. At the same time, RRHA leadership had to follow the directives and policies of the federal Department of Housing and Urban Development (HUD), which laid out extensive regulations governing the operations of housing authorities. The RRHA leadership thus needed to navigate federal requirements, the RRHA board, the (sometimes unclear or contradictory) expectations of the city council, and the expectations and demands of its thousands of tenants. In this muddy and often tangled context, establishing a clear strategic direction for the authority and sticking to it for a prolonged period of time proved a challenge.

Indeed, at the end of the 1980s, effective control over the RRHA became an explosive political issue. Between 1950 and 1980, the housing authority had been led by Frederic Fay, who oversaw the construction of new public housing units between 1950 and the early 1970s. In 1980, Roland L. Turpin, a Richmond native, was appointed CEO of the RRHA, with the blessing of then-mayor Henry L. Marsh and the first majority-Black council. Turpin enjoyed the respect and support of prominent tenant leaders during his tenure, and he represented Richmond on national boards such as the National Association of Housing and Redevelopment Officials. As noted above, Turpin saw the mission of the housing authority in terms of equity and justice: the authority was not just a landlord; it had a further responsibility to support the well-being of some of society's most neglected citizens.[39]

In early 1989, Turpin's status changed dramatically. The five-person RRHA Board of Commissioners had commissioned a series of reports on the RRHA's operations and practices from third-party consultants. The reports, which initially were not shared publicly, contained criticisms of the RRHA's staffing and operations. In early February 1989, the board, despite community protest, voted 4–1 to remove Turpin as CEO. The vote provoked an immediate outcry. Tenant leader Alma Barlow, who had a proven record of activism and social justice advocacy, expressed strong support for Turpin and attributed the vote to politics: specifically, that board members appointed by former mayor Roy West and the post-1982 council majority saw an opportunity to remove a key holdover from the Marsh years.[40] Turpin supporters claimed that board chair Louise Toney and board counsel Leroy Hassell (a political ally of West and, at the time, also the school board chair) had collaborated to remove him for political reasons; Turpin echoed the charge, stating, "A lot of good public servants have been, in effect, run out of the city of Richmond in the last several years. Now it has come to me in this room today."[41] Some community members noted that Hassell had also played a pivotal role in the 1988 resignation of Lois Harrison-Jones as Richmond Public Schools superintendent (see chapter 4).[42]

Henry Marsh, still a council member at the time, weighed in. Marsh introduced a motion calling for a city council investigation into the dismissal of Turpin, with support from Chuck Richardson and Walter Kenney, who had already spoken in protest of the RRHA board's actions. The three council members attended a mass gathering in support of Turpin held at 31st Street Baptist Church, and over 300 people signed a community petition demanding Turpin's reinstatement. At the subsequent council meeting, West tabled Marsh's motion and introduced a substitute motion calling for a HUD inquiry into general RRHA operations, with no specific examination of the dismissal of Turpin. That motion passed 6–3, with Marsh, Richardson, and Kenney objecting. Rev. Paul Nichols, the lone RRHA commissioner to stand in support of Turpin, resigned the board in protest.[43]

Following the community pushback, the commissioners sought to justify their decision by citing shortcomings in Turpin's management style and problems in areas such as computer systems, personnel management, and staff accountability. The board released one of the previously private consultant reports, which cited criticism of Turpin's management style in general terms but also offered praise. Indeed, much of the report focused on tension between the board and the administrative staff, as well as general governance problems with the RRHA. The report noted that "a multitude of powerful, interested 'influencers' impact the RRHA management team," citing HUD, the city council, community groups, the city manager, and the board itself. It recommended an extended retreat to come to consensus on the organization's goals and vision (a retreat that never happened).[44]

Release of the consultant reports did little to placate Turpin supporters, and he issued statements defending his management and the achievements of the agency.[45] Indeed, the commissioners who removed Turpin appeared to ignore the very people who were essential to public housing—the residents themselves. Nevertheless, the community protests ultimately proved futile, and Turpin eventually moved on to positions in Washington, DC, and

Dayton.⁴⁶ The board then appointed Richard C. Gentry, previously director of the public housing authority in Austin, Texas, as the new CEO in late 1989. Gentry remained in the role for eight years, providing stability to the organization and helping to garner federal resources for the redevelopment of the Blackwell public housing community in 1997.⁴⁷

Gentry brought a somewhat improbable profile to the job, as a white native North Carolinian and former theology student. He initially took a job in a regional HUD office in North Carolina in 1972 in order to be close to home. Continuing this career trajectory, Gentry went on to lead local housing authorities in Greensboro and Austin. In Richmond, Gentry moved swiftly in his first year to address crime and drug activity, identified as the most urgent issues in RRHA communities. Those steps included erecting hundreds of "No Trespassing" signs to discourage loitering of outsiders, an action meant to prevent nonresidents from using public housing as a site for drug transactions.⁴⁸ (Later in the decade, the authority and the city would privatize a number of streets for the same reason, since police could not legally prevent outsiders from being on public streets within the communities.)⁴⁹ Over the objections of Alma Barlow and the Richmond Tenants Organization, the RRHA moved to tighten lease provisions to make it easier to evict residents for drug activity (including activities undertaken by a tenant's family members and visitors). The authority formed a neighborhood anti-crime team in Gilpin Court, partly in response to a 1990 lawsuit filed by the Richmond Tenants Organization against the RRHA for failing to provide a safe environment. This anti-crime team was credited with a 37 percent drop in violent crime in Gilpin by 1992. The RRHA also received a federal grant to offer drug addiction treatment to residents, the result of a panel discussion in which a resident described being unable to access treatment without going to jail.⁵⁰

Gentry also had vision. In 1990 at an event commemorating the fiftieth anniversary of the RRHA, he starkly forecasted that "the days of large public housing projects are over" and that Gilpin Court could not continue in its present form.⁵¹ Gentry pointed to pilot initiatives to convert housing authority–acquired properties to homeownership in Carver, using a rent-to-own model, as an example for remaking public housing. The goal? To create mixed-income neighborhoods where highly subsidized housing blended in with other housing. At the same time, he sought to maintain and upgrade the existing housing units and supported numerous social services and workforce and economic development efforts aimed at creating more opportunities for residents, from youth programs to a consumer cooperative launched by residents in Gilpin and two other communities. He also encouraged the creation of a resident-owned business providing maintenance services on RRHA units.[52] Gentry frequently cited with pride the RRHA's 99 percent occupancy rate and track record of keeping units code-compliant.[53] Indeed, the RRHA in the mid-1990s was routinely cited by HUD as one of best-run housing authorities in the nation, as measured by its annual compliance scorecard.[54]

Over time Gentry won over a good number of residents and became a significant critic of national housing policies that trapped families in poverty. Gentry criticized HUD rules tying household rent to 30 percent of income on the grounds it created poverty traps (sometimes known as a "cliff effect"): as households went to work and saw incomes rise, they owed more and also incurred more expenses such as transportation and child care, making it in many cases economically irrational to remain in the labor market.[55] Like Turpin before him, Gentry had leadership roles in national organizations representing public housing authorities, which he often used both to protest federal cuts to local agencies and to argue that local authorities should have more flexibility to set their own rules and rent.[56] Gentry, who lived in the West End, also used his proximity to white middle-class Richmonders. He encouraged those on the other side of town to reject "us vs. them" thinking in favor of engaging with public housing residents and the problems of the city more generally.[57]

This track record led Gentry's name to surface as a potential successor to Robert Bobb as city manager following Bobb's departure to Oakland.[58] Instead, Gentry accepted an advocacy position with the Washington, DC, office of the Local Initiatives Support Corporation in early 1998.[59] Before his departure, however, he secured a $27 million Housing Opportunities for People Everywhere (HOPE) VI grant from the federal government to redevelop and transform Blackwell; Richmond announced the grant October 1997.

HOPE VI was a signature urban initiative of the Clinton presidency. The program was based on the premise of tearing down and replacing aging, distressed public housing with mixed-income housing communities. The program aimed to deconcentrate poverty while providing both new housing options and supportive social services for residents (required as part of the grant). Under new rules intended to accelerate the redevelopment process, the federal government lifted a long-standing requirement of one-for-one replacement of public housing units, although housing authorities had to make an intentional effort to find quality housing for all displaced residents.[60] Richmond leaders, including several residents, toured Atlanta, which had moved aggressively with multiple HOPE VI projects that would in effect end traditional public housing in that city, as a potential model for Richmond.[61]

The announcement of the Blackwell award was met with considerable though not universal enthusiasm. Some long-term residents welcomed the chance to rid the area of long-standing crime problems and create a more livable neighborhood, though others worried that the project would simply move poor people from one low-income area to another. Edward Robinson, a thirty-two-year-old resident who had grown up in Blackwell, expressed hope that "maybe [the grant] will stop the crime and give people a better way to live. They should have done this when they first started building (the public housing units) and maybe it wouldn't be as bad as it is."[62] The initial plan submitted to HUD called for over 800 new units to be created, including 586 apartment units.[63]

Implementation of the project got off to a rocky start. The RRHA was forced to alter and scale back the plan in part due to neighborhood opposition to a planned 150-unit apartment building at the intersection of Cowardin and Semmes Avenues, adjacent to the Blackwell area, causing HUD to reevaluate the project and a delay in the first payments on the grant.[64] The revised project plans ultimately called for replacing the 440 public housing units with a total of 537 units of housing, including 417 units in the Blackwell neighborhood or on Hull Street and 120 single-family homes in other parts of the city. Just over 160 of the replacement units would be multifamily units in Blackwell.[65] In addition to the replacement units, the RRHA offered vouchers to eligible residents and sought to enroll residents in a Blackwell-specific self-sufficiency program offering employment, training, and education support to help residents lift their incomes and transition successfully to new housing.[66]

The resident engagement and support components of the project, however, struggled to win over concerned residents. A twenty-member Self-Sufficiency and Community Building Task Force, formed as an advisory panel to the project, became an adversarial space in which resident members, along with invited nonresident activists Shirley Harvey, Donald Hatcher, and Marty Jewell, harshly criticized RRHA officials. Specific complaints included poor communication with residents and the RRHA's moving forward with razing units and relocating residents without sufficient warning or a clear plan for transitional relocation during construction and remodeling. By September 1999, the RRHA had disbanded the task force; a town hall held by Congressman Bobby Scott for Blackwell residents that month drew over 300 people who aired criticisms of the HOPE VI project and the RRHA staff.[67] Residents wanted more input into processes that could shape their lives.

RRHA staff and the board responded forcefully to the criticism. Ken Johnson, a leading figure in the Black business community and chair of the board of commissioners, pushed the case for dramatic change to Richmond's public housing model: "We've created a system where people think they'll be in public housing for 30 or 40 years. . . . They're mental concentration camps."[68] Tyrone Curtis, a longtime staff member who had succeeded Gentry as the RRHA's CEO, repeatedly emphasized that the value of the initiative was supporting residents in transitioning to self-sufficiency: "Our goal really is to get Blackwell residents qualified, in large numbers, for something other than public housing."[69] As of 2002, 172 families were involved in the self-sufficiency program; a total of 378 Blackwell families received relocation assistance from Blackwell, including up to $1,100 for moving costs.[70]

In August 2001, the RRHA completed the first phase of construction—ninety-nine town houses for low- or moderate-income families who qualified for public housing, of which twenty-five were reserved for returning Blackwell residents.[71] Of the nearly 400 displaced families, a small number returned, including families in the public housing units and two families who purchased homes in Blackwell.[72] A 2007 study found that a large percentage of Blackwell households moved to other distressed neighborhoods, with 45 percent reentering public housing and 37 percent using vouchers to relocate.[73] Blackwell public housing resident Lander Freeman, a staunch opponent of HOPE VI, summed up the results like this: "HOPE VI did nothing for most and did something for a chosen few. For most, it did nothing but displace them."[74]

HOPE VI in Richmond failed to engender goodwill or build public confidence. Against the backdrop of stalled construction and uneven outcomes, RRHA CEO Curtis eventually acknowledged that the HOPE VI process had resulted in "growing pains" and lessons learned, but he continued to defend the project.[75] Blackwell's problems curtailed the RRHA's plans for redevelopment of public housing in other areas of the city. By the spring of 2002, Mosby resident Robin Davis embodied public discontent. She stated, "I hope that revitalization for Gilpin and Mosby Court will not turn into another HOPE VI in Blackwell—residents left without a place to go."[76] When the RRHA pushed forward with filing an application for a HOPE VI grant for Mosby South (the section of the community in closest proximity to downtown) in early 2003, resident activists and the Legal Aid Justice Center filed a forty-four-page statement with HUD charging the RRHA with including inaccurate and incomplete information in its application. The grant was unsuccessful; plans to redevelop Mosby or other public housing communities were, for a time, put on hold.[77]

While the RRHA bore the brunt of resident and activist criticism for the glacial, uneven implementation of HOPE VI in Blackwell, the counties were also implicated. Curtis and other city leaders tried to push the point that housing the region's poorest residents should have been treated as a regional responsibility. They met firm resistance. In 1998 Tim Kaine, drawing on a report by well-known urban analyst David Rusk, pushed the idea of expanding the RRHA into a regional housing authority with the ability to build new low-income housing in the surrounding counties.[78] Chesterfield and Henrico Counties each refused to sign on to the proposal; neither had traditional public housing, and each had only a limited number of voucher-supported subsidized housing units. Henrico County manager Virgil Hazelett stated the counties' position in 2002: "We use what is available to us through the development community.... If a developer comes forward and wants to use [low-income] tax credits, we look at it. It's all market-driven in Henrico."[79] As with public transportation, county leaders washed their hands of any responsibility to meaningfully assist Richmond in addressing its deep problems, and state-level action to compel cooperation was absent.

Tyrone Curtis retired as RRHA CEO in 2003, having stayed an extra year to help the agency address accounting issues identified by a 2001 external audit. He was replaced by Sheila Hill-Christian, a respected, up-and-coming public administrator who had worked in city hall in several roles before becoming COO of the Greater Richmond Transit Company.[80] Hill-Christian focused on improving management and internal processes in her two-year tenure as CEO, strengthening coordination of services for residents, and creating a new strategic plan for the authority. Continuing the direction set by Gentry and Curtis, her strategic plan envisioned redeveloping public housing into mixed-income communities, while also emphasizing commercial development, good management, and improved customer services. The new plan dovetailed with an emphasis on housing announced by Mayor Doug Wilder in early 2006. Observing that the city did not have a coherent vision on land use and housing, Wilder sought to hire a "housing czar" to coordinate housing policy and also launched a taskforce to examine citywide housing needs. Michael Paul Williams editorialized in the *Richmond Times-Dispatch* that "confronting and dismantling Richmond's residential apartheid, which concentrates the region's poor in pockets of urban despair, will be Mayor L. Douglas Wilder's most important undertaking." But Williams also quoted

Virginia Local Initiatives Support Corporation program director Greta Harris, who noted that "the devil is always in the details and implementation" and warned that "the people who have been impacted the most by what is or isn't done very rarely are at the decision-making table."[81]

Leadership instability stalled early momentum. Wilder's appointee to the "housing czar" position left the city after just three months.[82] Sheila Hill-Christian left the RRHA CEO position in 2006 to become executive director of the Virginia Lottery under then-governor Tim Kaine before returning to city hall in late 2007 to become chief administrative officer for the city under Wilder. The reins for leading the RRHA's next development push fell to Anthony Scott, a graduate of Howard and UCLA whose previous experience included leading a community development corporation in Los Angeles and work with the Virginia Department of Housing and Community Development. He was first hired by the RRHA as deputy executive director in 2005 before being named its new CEO in 2007.[83]

Scott reaffirmed the core goals of Hill-Christian's strategic plan and also stressed the imperative of Richmond adapting to new HUD guidelines impacting the authority's operations. The Northside redevelopment of 60 units of public housing (Dove Court) and over 200 units of run-down private housing into a mixed-income community, launched in 2008, was heralded by Scott as a dress rehearsal for the larger, more consequential lift: seeking once again to redevelop Gilpin Court, the largest public housing community.[84] Scott moved proactively to bring residential leadership on board, coauthoring a March 2008 op-ed in the *Richmond Times-Dispatch* with Annie Giles and Delores Robinson, president and vice president of the Richmond Tenants Organization, that declared, "There is a viable plan to improve public housing in Richmond," and "[The] RRHA does not believe the conditions of our public housing communities are acceptable by any measure."[85]

Scott and the RRHA sought to follow up that grim diagnosis with action. In the fall of 2008, the authority formally launched a planning process intended to transform Gilpin Court into a new neighborhood, "North Jackson Ward." The nearly 1,000 units of Gilpin Court and adjoining Fay Towers (senior housing) would be razed, with about 2,000 new units taking their place, 30 percent of which would be public housing equivalent. Not all existing Gilpin residents would be able to stay in the new community; these residents would be offered vouchers or slots in other public housing in Richmond.[86] Over the next two years, a new wave of tenant-led activism waylaid the RRHA's initiative. With the shadow of Blackwell looming large, advocates demanded that the housing authority and the city commit to "one-for-one replacement" of all public housing units eliminated during the redevelopment process.[87] A new tenant organization, independent of the official Richmond Tenants Organization, was launched by longtime residents and activists Lillie A. Estes (Gilpin Court) and Cora Hayes (Randolph), with support from the Legal Aid Justice Center. This new group, Residents of Public Housing in Richmond against Mass Evictions (RePHRAME), pushed for one-for-one replacement as well as broader changes at the housing authority, including appointment of additional residents to the board of commissioners.[88] (The city council, which had in 1999 expanded the RRHA board from five to seven members to include a tenant, did so again in 2010, expanding the board to nine commissioners with two total seats for residents: ordinarily, one public housing resident and one Section 8 recipient.)[89]

The controversy over one-for-one replacement reflected national policy shifts. In the 1990s, Congress suspended the previous one-for-one requirement, and the Clinton administration began allowing communities receiving HOPE VI grants to pursue redevelopment plans that reduced the number of public housing equivalent units in a community. Residents in communities that received HOPE VI funding had the option of returning to the new development (if units were available), moving to other public housing, or receiving a portable Section 8 voucher if they met eligibility requirements, such as being current on their rent and being lease-compliant.[90] Portable vouchers were sometimes framed as a gateway into better neighborhoods, but in a community like Richmond this was rarely the case. Landlords were under no obligation to accept Section 8 vouchers, and few landlords in the surrounding counties were willing to rent to voucher recipients relocating from Richmond public housing.[91] Nor, for that matter, were many landlords in Richmond's prosperous neighborhoods. Indeed, when housing markets got hot, as in the early aughts, RRHA struggled to disburse all its available vouchers: not because of lack of demand for subsidized housing but for lack of landlords willing to accept them.[92]

Consequently, redevelopment proposals for Gilpin Court and other large RRHA communities had a potentially fatal flaw: lateral movement. Rather than deconcentrate poverty, the principal effect might be to move residents from an extremely high-poverty census tract to another area of the city that was *also* high-poverty, and not necessarily in an improved housing unit. In these circumstances, advocates urged that the city and the RRHA jointly adopt a firm commitment to one-for-one housing replacement as an unconditional component of any redevelopment plan.[93] Those demands—as well as the competing impetus from Dwight C. Jones's administration to move forward with redevelopment—were echoed in the housing policy language finally adopted by the Mayor's Anti-Poverty Commission in 2013:

- Redevelopment of current housing stock should be careful to include and not eliminate housing for low-income residents. Specifically, redevelopment should not lead to a net loss of public housing units. . . .
- Crucial to the success of redevelopment is that it *not* simply displace and disperse current residents. Successful redevelopment requires comprehensive holistic human services that enable residents to create the capabilities they need to thrive in the new communities. Residents should be involved from the outset in shaping redevelopment plans and treated as equal partners, and a strong emphasis should be placed on leveraging redevelopment to create expanded job opportunities for residents.
- The work of building trust and collaboration with residents needs to begin *before* redevelopment plans are launched. A focus on redevelopment should not come at the expense of attention to the needs of the remaining public housing communities.[94]

By the time the Anti-Poverty Commission stated these principles (2012–13), Anthony Scott had already moved on from the RRHA and the Gilpin Court project was shelved. But the city and the RRHA under its new CEO, Adrienne Goolsby, were already at work on a new "public housing transformation" initiative focused on the roughly 500 units of public housing at Creighton Court in the East End. Creighton Court, located just off Interstate 64, sat on the city's eastern border and was adjacent to Fairfield Court, another large public housing community. The plan for Creighton Court involved redeveloping at a *higher* density on the Creighton Court site; redeveloping the old Armstrong High School building, located nearby Creighton, into additional housing; and then creating additional housing, including deeply subsidized units, at scattered sites across the city.[95] Mayor Dwight C. Jones lent strong support to the initiative, repeatedly stating that he regarded East End public housing as a vast "monument to poverty" and systemic racism.[96]

Two fundamental shifts in federal policy impacted the specifics of the Creighton Court proposal. In 2009, HUD instituted a new program, Choice Neighborhoods, to replace the HOPE VI program. The Choice Neighborhoods framework responded to frequent criticisms of HOPE VI by seeking to strengthen protections for residents and improve community processes related to the grant. First, Choice reinstituted a one-for-one unit replacement requirement for public housing removed during redevelopment processes.

Replacement units could be either traditional public housing or public housing–equivalent units that would be rented to very low-income residents issued project-based vouchers. Project-based vouchers differed from tenant-based Section 8 vouchers in that they were tied to a specific hard unit that was obliged to be rented to a low-income resident.[97] Second, Choice encouraged a "build-first" process by which housing authorities would commit to build new replacement units *before* demolition of older public housing units so that residents would be assured of a place to go during the redevelopment process.[98]

In addition, the Choice Neighborhoods framework required extensive community collaboration, including resident participation and support and financial and nonfinancial support from community partners. After Adrienne Goolsby, who occupied her CEO position for less than three years, departed in January 2015, former executive director of the nonprofit Better Housing Coalition and RRHA staff member T. K. Somanath was named interim and then permanent CEO.[99] Over the course of 2015 and early 2016, Somanath focused on preparing to apply for a Choice Neighborhoods award, projected at $30 million, to support Creighton Court redevelopment. The RRHA had previously contracted with The Community Builders, a national nonprofit organization with extensive experience in public housing redevelopments nationwide, including in Norfolk, Virginia.[100]

The Office of Community Wealth Building led development of the "People Plan" component of the Choice Neighborhoods application, in close collaboration with the Richmond City Health District. The aim of the People Plan was to assemble community resources focused on school improvement, employment supports for residents, health services, and especially transition support. At the heart of the model was the creation of a "Family Transition Coach" program that sought to engage Creighton residents holistically and develop plans leading to successful transition from public housing to private housing, either in a subsidized unit or the general market.[101] The application also required a "Neighborhood Plan" showing how the redevelopment proposal would leverage revitalization of the surrounding area, as well as the "Housing Plan" proper, spelling out the specific plans for the development of new units and verifying the commitment to one-for-one replacement.

Planners sought to engage and build trust with residents. Extensive resident engagement, including frequent community meetings, creation of a resident leadership team, and engagement with Richmond Tenants Organization president Marilyn Olds yielded qualified (though skeptical) resident support for the application. The People Plan was informed by an extensive survey of Creighton residents conducted in 2014 that documented residents' views of their neighborhood, personal and neighborhood obstacles, and aspirations for the future. In rough terms, the survey found that about 30 percent wished to stay in the Creighton footprint or the immediate area, 35 percent preferred to leave the area, and the remainder were undecided. If they required relocation, a large majority of residents wished to receive a housing voucher, though some also favored homeownership, moving to the private market, or transitioning to another public housing unit or a senior complex.[102] While formal tenant organizational leadership tended to be elderly, longtime residents, the RRHA's own demographic data showed that the majority of residents consisted of families with children; most had lived in Creighton for less than five years, with many parents regarding the community as transitional housing.[103] In the summer of 2015 the Office of Community Wealth Building, with support from The Community Builders and the national firm Urban Strategies, assembled a variety of public agencies, nonprofit organizations, university representatives, and community groups into a service provider network to support the grant. Many of these partners would make either a financial or a service commitment to support residents during the grant. The Community Foundation of Greater Richmond also committed significant support to the plan.[104]

The plan implicated actual people. At stake were the aspirations of parents like Chimere Miles, a highly engaged Creighton resident who told a reporter, "I can't afford to get out. . . . Sometimes, I'm like, my next check, I'll live anywhere, you know? I'll live on someone's couch just to claim a good address and put my kid in a good school." Miles continued, making it clear that if the plan fell apart, "my 10-year-old will go to a failing school and get a poor education that will result in him living back in the poor community that I raised him up in, just because I know my address is still 2218 Walcott Place."[105] Public housing redevelopment simultaneously stoked residents' deepest fears (of displacement) and their deepest aspirations for improved living conditions and upward mobility.

Richmond's Choice application, filed in June 2016, represented a far more intentional effort to bring about the full resources of the community to support a people-focused redevelopment process than previous efforts in Richmond had. A total of $174 million was committed in support of the various parts of the application. In late September, however, HUD informed city leaders that its application would be denied and Richmond would not receive the $30 million grant.[106] It was subsequently revealed that the RRHA had received a score of 1 out of 8, virtually the lowest possible, on the criterion of "Project Leadership Capacity of Lead Applicant."[107] Here the issues with Blackwell, which by 2016 still had not been completely resolved, haunted the city's future efforts. HUD simply did not believe Richmond's housing authority had the capacity to implement a complex redevelopment process successfully.

Somanath and other city leaders expressed determination to push forward with the Creighton redevelopment plan, even without federal support. The family transition coach program envisioned in the People Plan launched in 2016 as a partnership between Richmond Opportunities, Inc., which was an RRHA-affiliated nonprofit, and the Richmond City Health District, focused on supporting Creighton residents.[108] Work started at the old Armstrong High School site in late 2018, and the Armstrong Renaissance Apartments opened in October 2020, with thirty Creighton families initially moving into the new units.[109] A total of 256 units were to be built at the Armstrong site. Demolition of Creighton Court proper, to pave the way for new housing construction on the site, began in June 2022. Still to be demonstrated was whether the city and the RRHA would successfully follow through on their commitments—memorialized in a Creighton "Tenants' Bill of Rights" adopted in April 2020—to ensure that all residents obtained quality housing through the process.[110]

Meanwhile, the RRHA's penchant for turning over leadership continued unabated—no fewer than six people served as RRHA CEO between 2018 and 2022 (including three interim CEOs). The frequent churn in leadership made it nearly impossible for the RRHA to develop, implement, and sustain a comprehensive community redevelopment process. But the instability reflected deeper governance issues that had been identified as early as the 1980s but left largely unresolved. The housing authority board was appointed by the city council but had to work within mandates set by the federal government. The council did not provide clear directives to its appointees on the direction of the housing authority. While for nearly thirty years both council members and RRHA leadership consistently emphasized the imperative of redevelopment, this did not translate into a long-term, well-understood strategic plan that could anchor the city's long-haul approach to its most difficult policy challenge. Instead, as with Richmond Public Schools, there was a tendency to place hope in the arrival of new leaders who might solve the Gordian knot of redevelopment; but those leaders, with increasing speed, tended to fall afoul of Richmond's complex dynamics.

The creation of the elected office of mayor in 2004 offered some hope in this regard. Theoretically, the elected mayor could articulate a bold housing agenda and use both the bully pulpit and the resources of city government to push the RRHA in the desired direction. Douglas Wilder set off on such a course in 2006, but with limited tangible outcomes. Dwight Jones sought to do the same and in his second term gained some traction. RRHA CEO T. K. Somanath, going against the often-insular culture of RRHA staff, sought full partnership and cooperation with the city, including frequent communications and extensive collaboration with the city's Department of Economic and Community Development and Office of Community Wealth Building and with the mayor and chief administrative officer. The perceived close alignment of the city and the RRHA during the Creighton application process made it far easier to bring community partners to the table. But there was no guarantee that philanthropic, nonprofit, and business partners would stay at the table if they did not see the RRHA and city hall working from a unified plan.

The example of the RRHA illustrated how Richmond's elected mayor, in critically important ways, was not in fact a "strong" mayor. Jones and other mayors could seek to influence the appointment of commissioners to the RRHA board through council allies but could not directly pick commissioners. The mayor could request and encourage collaboration with the RRHA but could not give directives to the RRHA CEO or staff. Given the deep problems within the RRHA, there was indeed an incentive for the mayor's office and staff not to get too involved, for fear of being blamed for problems and situations one could not rectify. The structure largely militated against close cooperation and coordination between the city and the RRHA, although individual personalities at times could overcome this, with sufficient motivation.

Consequently, it is difficult to pinpoint responsibility for why Richmond was unable to make a meaningful dent in the concentration of poverty and the condition of public housing over a thirty-year period. Deconcentrating poverty was a stated aim of generations of leaders, and yet public housing in Richmond in 2016 looked much like it had in 1988. Fundamentally, the RRHA was only indirectly accountable to Richmond voters and the wider public. Staff ran the organization, with part-time board commissioners generally unable to keep up with the many details; those board members in turn as a group had little strategic guidance from the council that appointed them. The notion that Richmond's elected leaders should develop a robust, strategic plan for housing, including public housing and redevelopment, and then work to bring the RRHA in line with that plan at times was articulated over the course of this study, including in the mayoral terms of Wilder and Jones, but an institutional divide between the authority and the council persisted. That lack of clear guidance allowed the housing authority to develop an insular internal culture that at its worst treated residents with bureaucratic paternalism.[111] Certainly, by the 2010s it was difficult to imagine RRHA residents showing the level and depth of public support for any leader associated with the housing authority that residents had shown for CEO Roland Turpin in the 1980s. Lack of trust in turn made meaningful progress on a constructive, let alone transformational, agenda nearly impossible.

The sum result was a collective governance failure. That failure was twofold: the organization of the housing authority vis-à-vis city government did not facilitate effective redevelopment within a morally defensible, people-centered framework, and city leaders did not act to alter the organizational framework to make it more functional or clearly delineate responsibility and accountability for action and inaction. Those city leaders included not just the political class but also the business and institutional leaders who largely sat on the sidelines while the various stalled or failed efforts to revitalize public housing in Richmond played out.[112] This neglect had costs: specifically, it created the real risk that public housing at some future point in Richmond would simply be dismantled by brute force rather than through a process that engaged and sought to support and empower residents in a meaningful way.

Another alternative seemed lost on most policymakers altogether: the strategy not of deconcentrating poverty through redevelopment but of directly *reducing* poverty and improving quality of life in and around public housing by concerted effort to connect residents to jobs and wealth-building opportunities as well as by provision of strong public services. Instead of parched, often grassless public space with rundown athletic and playground facilities, one could imagine communities that were green and clean and featured the best-quality facilities the public could possibly provide, including ample community and employment resource centers. Importantly, Richmond *did* in fact make nods in this direction in the 2010s: the Richmond City Health District opened community health centers in each of the large public housing communities; that program eventually merged with an Office of Community Wealth Building initiative to hire resident "community navigators" to assist residents in identifying and accessing needed services and programs. The health centers promoted public health, offered some immediate care and diagnostic services, and provided information and referrals, and each employed a community resident on a full-time basis.[113] A new middle school (Martin Luther King, Jr. Middle School) and adjoining pre-kindergarten center was built adjacent to Mosby Court, opening in 2014, and later Henry L. Marsh Elementary School was built in the East End. Community initiatives too, such as a community garden developed in Gilpin Court and a green pedestrian corridor to connect Hillside Court with Oak Grove–Bellemeade Elementary School, as well as efforts by the Kinfolk Community Empowerment Center near Mosby Court to create community gardens and a "food justice corridor," aimed to improve quality of life for public housing residents.[114]

Yet these initiatives stood side-by-side with long-standing, visible neglect and disinvestment in the communities, perhaps best encapsulated by the extended closure of the Calhoun Center swimming pool near Gilpin Court.[115] Policymakers' persistent prioritization of redevelopment crowded out attention to the immediate needs of the existing communities. In short, financial and political will to implement both parts of the strategy that the Mayor's Anti-Poverty Commission had recommended—pursuing redevelopment through a people-centered process including a commitment to one-for-one replacement *and* taking steps to improve community life in the near term—never materialized in a sustained way over the decades of this study.

The Broader Problem of Affordable Housing

Public housing policy, however critical, was only one part of housing policy in Richmond. The serious dilemmas facing the RRHA and other city leaders derived from the facts of widespread poverty and an insufficient supply of decent, affordable housing. Consequently, while thousands of Richmonders experienced housing instability (either homelessness or the brink of it), *tens* of thousands of Richmonders were cost-burdened by available housing. Rapid population growth after 2005 in turn accelerated patterns of gentrification, making it difficult for long-term residents to remain in their neighborhoods due to rising rents or property tax bills.[116] Runaway gentrification raised profound questions of racial justice: Black residents who had played an instrumental role in helping distressed neighborhoods survive in the 1980s and 1990s might find themselves displaced by (predominantly) white newcomers pouring back into the city.

Beginning in the mid-aughts, both investment capital and whites began flowing into Richmond at extraordinary rates. This trend paralleled similar trends in historically majority-minority cities.[117] Favorable property values,

TABLE 6.2. Housing and demographic trends in City of Richmond, 1990–2020

	1990	2000	2008–12	2016–20
Poverty rate	20.9%	21.4%	26.7%	20.9%
Adults twenty-five and over with educational attainment less than high school diploma	31.9%	24.8%	19.4%	13.1%
Per capita white income	$39,118	$46,485	$45,895	$52,023
Per capita Black income	$16,257	$18,954	$16,910	$19,443
Total population	203,056	197,790	205,348	229,233
Black (non-Latino) population	111,644	112,455	102,038	104,961
White (non-Latino) population	87,222	74,506	80,335	94,400
Latino population	1,898	5,074	12,539	16,220
Percentage renters	53.7%	53.9%	56.0%	56.3%
Median rent	$738	$755	$904	$992
Median rent as percentage of household income	27.5%	27.4%	34.2%	31.8%
Percentage renters cost-burdened	42.4%	41.4%	55.2%	51.3%
Median home value	$117,324	$122,132	$207,852	$226,391
Median year housing built	1953	1955	1954	1957
Total housing units	94,141	92,282	98,318	100,930
Vacant housing units	8,804	7,733	14,543	9,925

Source: U.S. Census 1990, 2000; and American Community Survey Five-Year Estimates (2008–12 and 2016–20), accessed via Social Explorer.
Note: All dollar values expressed as 2016 dollars. Per capita white income in 1990 includes Latino whites; per capita white income refers to non-Latino whites all other years.

historic tax credits, and tax abatements for property rehabilitation fueled inward migration.[118] Between 2000 and 2020, the non-Hispanic white population in the City of Richmond increased by more than 25 percent, while the Latino population tripled over the same time (see table 6.2).

As table 6.2 shows, the influx of new residents predictably led to higher rents and home values (that is, gentrification). Median rent, holding inflation constant, increased by over 30 percent between 2000 and 2016–20 in Richmond, while the median value of homeowner-occupied homes nearly doubled. The number of Richmond renters classified as rent-burdened increased from 41.4 percent to 51.3 percent between 2000 and 2016–20, and median percentage of household income in rent also went up significantly over the

TABLE 6.3. Demographic changes by census tract in City of Richmond, 2000 and 2015–2019

Race/ethnicity composition	2000 (number of census tracts out of 65)	2015–19 (number of census tracts out of 66)
Black population > 90%	16	4
(Non-Hispanic) white population > 90%	7	5
Two race/ethnicities with population > 30%	13	15

Source: U.S. Census, 2000; and American Community Survey Five-Year Estimates (2015–19), via Social Explorer (using 2010 census tract definitions).

Note: Citywide population in 2015–19 = 40.8% white (non-Hispanic), 46.6% Black, and 6.9% Latino

same time period (from 27.4 percent to 31.8 percent). In short, the city became a more expensive place to live. Whereas city population increased 15.9 percent between 2000 and 2016–20, the supply of housing as measured by total housing units increased by just 9.4 percent.

By the late 2010s, substantial and in some cases dramatic demographic changes were evident in many—but not all—Richmond neighborhoods. Between 2000 and 2015–19, numerous historically all-Black Richmond neighborhoods—from Church Hill to Byrd Park, Northside to Southside—saw a substantial decrease in the proportion of Black residents, with corresponding increases for white and Latino residents (see table 6.3). The changes sharply reduced the number of nearly all-Black neighborhoods and led to a slight increase in the number of substantially integrated Richmond neighborhoods (defined as neighborhoods in which at least two racial/ethnic groups have at least a 30 percent share of the population). Yet while whites did move into some previously nearly all-Black neighborhoods on the Northside and in Church Hill, census tracts containing public housing remained overwhelmingly Black. The social and racial isolation of public housing residents remained largely unaffected by the city's changing currents.

Experts had anticipated the gentrification wave of the 2010s for nearly two decades. In 1993, the city's Department of Community Development and the RRHA jointly developed a five-year housing plan. The plan called for investing $183 million to build or rehabilitate some 3,000 units in a five-year period, with the city putting up just under $20 million of the total. (Federal grants and loans would also be used, with public money leveraging private investment.)[119] Later in the 1990s, Richmond launched the Neighborhoods in Bloom initiative (discussed in chapter 5), which also included area-specific plans for each of the neighborhoods involved. In 2001, the city adopted a ten-year master plan (not actually updated until 2020) that focused on neighborhood revitalization as a citywide strategy. The plan noted the sharp increase in vacant and abandoned structures (over 2,500) and observed that the city had "high levels of vacant, abandoned, deteriorated and poorly maintained housing," that demolishing substandard housing could threaten historic architecture, and that the city had a large number of tax-delinquent properties. It also reported that "social and physical conditions within public housing projects often have negative impacts both for public housing residents and for residents in the surrounding neighborhoods."[120] The plan called for development of 2,000 new units to accommodate population growth, including through higher-density development, and for providing incentives and resources to facilitate renovating dilapidated structures and preserving units with architectural value. The plan also called for engaging the counties on affordable housing while working to develop more affordable housing in the city. It did not, however, identify a specific mechanism or funding source to promote those goals.[121]

In 2006, Mayor Wilder formed a task force focused on housing, led by Laura Lafayette, an executive of the Richmond Association of Realtors and an influential affordable housing advocate. The task force promoted new zoning policies to promote mixed-use development, an affordable dwelling unit ordinance, an affordable housing trust fund, and a demonstration project in which the RRHA would partner with nonprofit developers.[122] The affordable housing ordinance brought forward in 2007 by city council members Kathy Graziano and Ellen Robertson focused on incentives rather than mandates to encourage affordable housing production. As they explained in an editorial, "The simplest overview of the program is that it creates specific incentives for the private sector to build more affordable housing, both for sale and for rent (within a market rate development)." Graziano and Robertson further detailed that "the program would be voluntary; no builder will be forced to do anything. But if a developer/builder wishes to use the powers of the ordinance, he may be able to get permission for greater density on his property; put simply, he may be able to put more units on a specific piece of property than ordinary zoning would permit, so long as some of the additional units are 'affordable,' according to an income-based schedule."[123]

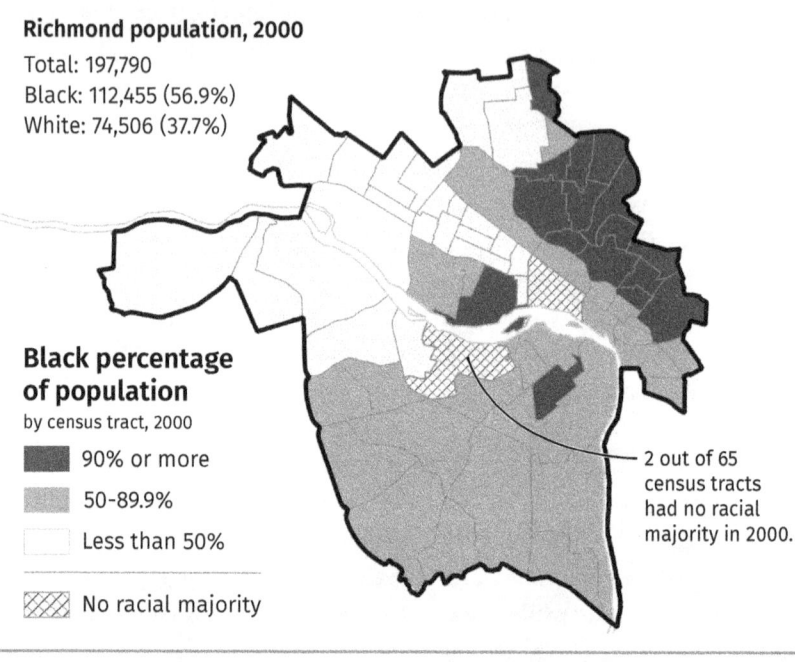

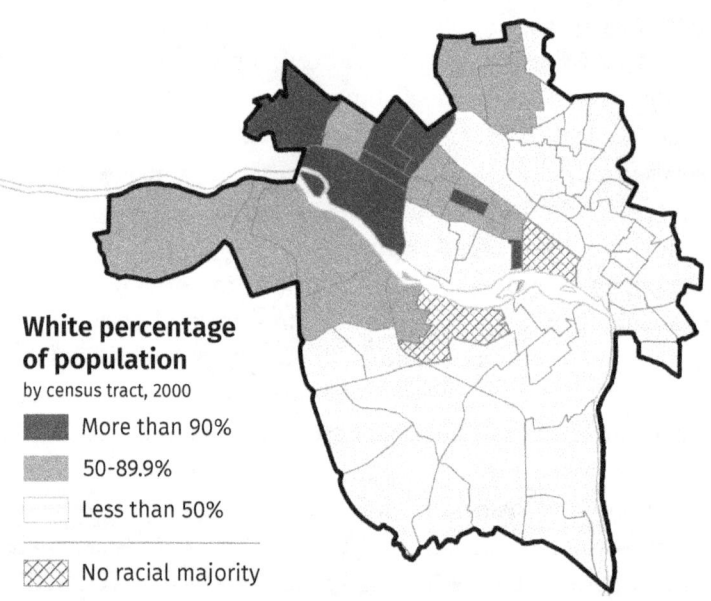

Map 6.3. Black and white populations by census tract, 2000.
Map by Riley D. Champine of the University of Richmond Digital Scholarship Lab, based on data from the City of Richmond and IPUMS NHGIS (University of Minnesota, www.nhgis.org).

Richmond population, 2019 (2015–2019 American Community Survey)
Total: 226,622
Black: 105,557 (46.6%)
White: 92,454 (40.8%)

Black percentage of population
by census tract, 2019

- 90% or more
- 50–89.9%
- Less than 50%
- No racial majority

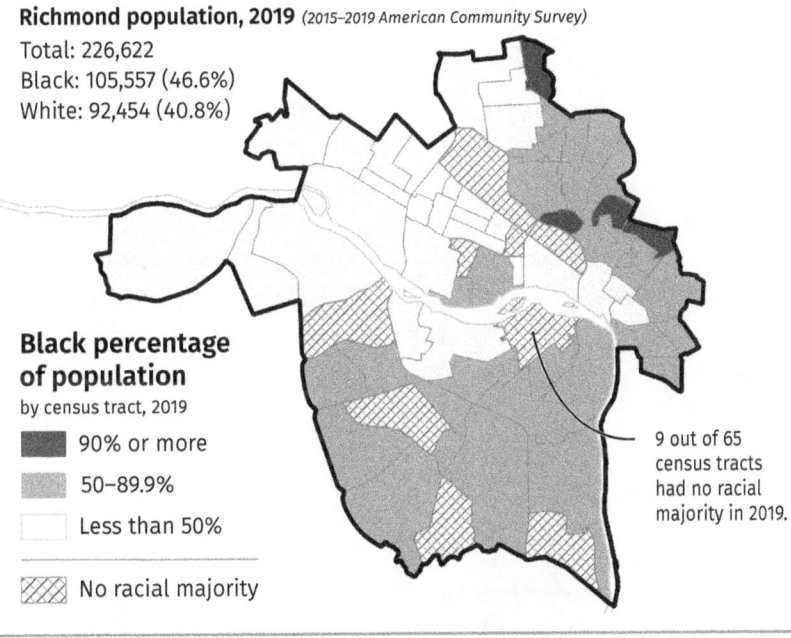

9 out of 65 census tracts had no racial majority in 2019.

White percentage of population
by census tract, 2019

- 90% or more
- 50–89.9%
- Less than 50%
- No racial majority

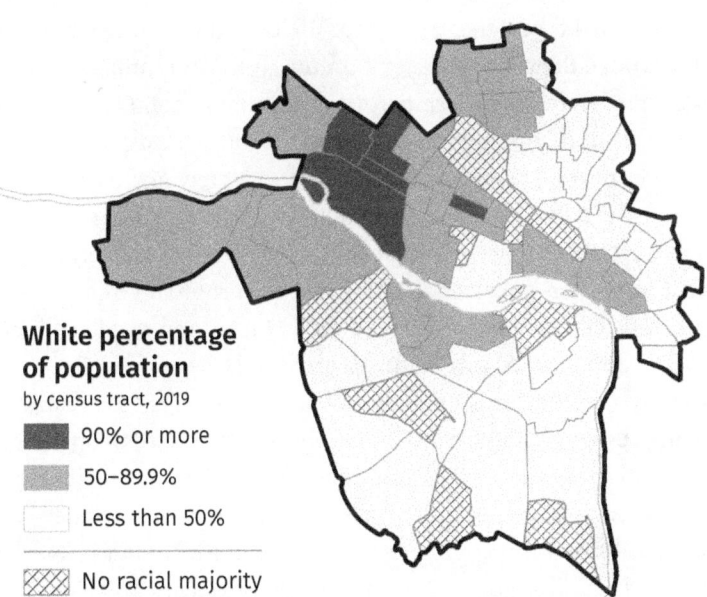

Map 6.4. Black and white populations by census tract, 2015–2019.
Map by Riley D. Champine of the University of Richmond Digital Scholarship Lab, based on data from the City of Richmond and IPUMS NHGIS (University of Minnesota, www.nhgis.org).

The city council adopted the Graziano-Robertson ordinance in 2007.[124] In 2008, the council also created an Affordable Housing Trust Fund but did not allocate significant funds to it for several years.[125] In 2014, as part of the larger anti-poverty agenda, Mayor Jones proposed an initial capitalization of the fund for $1 million. Initial projects funded by the trust fund were unveiled in November 2015. Over the fund's first two years (FY 2015–16), nearly $2.2 million in awards went to seventeen projects, leading to the creation of over 460 units and nearly $50 million in total economic impact.[126] Finally, in 2016 housing advocates formed the Maggie Walker Community Land Trust, creating a promising new tool to address the city's affordable housing needs going forward.[127] Still unclear was whether the city could utilize these various tools (and others) at sufficient scale to meet both its long-standing and its fast-emerging housing challenges.

Two generations on from Bonnie Winston's profile of life in Gilpin Court in the mid-1980s, thousands of children have continued to grow up in the same environments. A 2015 study by the Equality of Opportunity Project (now Opportunity Insights) found that the City of Richmond was the 48th worst locality in the United States (out of 2,478 county equivalent units) in which to grow up poor, in terms of fostering upward economic mobility. Growing up poor in the City of Richmond was estimated to reduce the expected adult annual income by nearly $3,900 a year compared with growing up poor in an "average" county.[128] As we have seen throughout this book, school "failure" was linked inextricably to entrenched poverty, which was inextricably linked to segregated and often substandard housing, in a mutually reinforcing iron triangle of racialized inequality. Yet even as Richmond residents bore that brunt of institutionalized inequality, Henrico and Chesterfield Counties exhibited upward mobility for poor children roughly equivalent to (Henrico) or higher than (Chesterfield) the national average. In other words, conditions and arrangements in the City of Richmond specifically *worsened* the life prospects of poor kids, above and beyond the *general* impact of poverty. Statewide, regional, and local structures combined to ensure that Richmond's patterns of poverty reproduced from one generation to the next, with policymakers as yet still unable to act at sufficient scale to break the cycle.

The inability of governance structures to meaningfully address known problems naturally calls the legitimacy and future of those structures into doubt. In the final chapter, after briefly recapping major themes of this study, we turn from describing and analyzing Richmond's urban governance structure to consideration of alternative possibilities for the future. Richmond and Virginia residents still have the possibility of creating a twenty-first-century Richmond that is more than a long extension of the epochal decisions of the past and the entrenched patterns of racialized inequality those decisions locked into place.

7

Toward a Just Twenty-First-Century Richmond

Over the three decades examined in this book, Richmonders wrestled with the profound material legacies of Jim Crow racism: concentrated poverty, inadequate housing, inadequate schools, high underemployment, extraordinary racial and economic inequality, and corrosive distrust of public institutions, all punctuated by high levels of crime and violence. In this context, some people believed that calls to de-monumentalize Richmond were an unhelpful diversion, expending energy that might be better spent dealing with other relics of the Jim Crow system. Responsible political and civic leadership meant making concrete improvements in the daily lives of Richmond residents, especially economically and racially excluded groups, not wasting time and energy on symbolic battles likely to end in defeat.[1] For politicians such as Henry Marsh and his twentieth-century political lineage, there were deeper concerns: namely, a fight over monuments could heighten Richmond's racial polarization, making it more difficult to cooperate with and extract resources from Richmond's white-dominated business community. Political responsibility, including serving constituents effectively, required eschewing direct confrontation with Confederate iconography as a matter of political course.[2]

Indeed, for many of these leaders, raising the issue of the monuments was an indication that one was not actually serious about tackling the on-the-ground facts of racial inequality in Richmond. The real legacy of the Confederacy was evident not merely in public space but also in public institutions. Mayor Dwight C. Jones once stated he wished to tear down the lasting vestige of white supremacy: "the monument to poverty that is public housing in this city's East End."[3] He was not alone. The city's leaders spent the better portion of the late twentieth century performing political triage—seeking to topple not Confederate monuments but the remnants of Jim Crow segregation. As poverty deepened in African American communities in the twilight of the twentieth century, Black Richmonders and their elected officials prioritized present-day needs over historical memory.

Jim Crow cast a long shadow over Richmond well into the twenty-first century, embodied in the continuity of structural racism.[4] Attitudes toward the Confederate monuments changed rapidly after the August 2017 events in Charlottesville, when it became clear that Confederate statuary in the South had become vivid symbols of a vicious modern-day politics of white supremacy, inextricably linked to the politics of Donald Trump's White House. Many older Black leaders, including Jones, applauded when Mayor Levar Stoney dramatically ordered the takedown of Stonewall Jackson from the intersection of Monument Avenue and Arthur Ashe Boulevard on July 1, 2020.[5] Nonetheless, it is instructive to remember *why* for so many years a good number of the city's Black political leaders declined to name the monuments as an urgent problem—not out of fear but as a prudential exercise of political responsibility. Richmond's problems were so acute that policymakers and elected officials had to react to the most pressing priority in front of them rather than waste political capital tilting at proverbial windmills.

Richmond politics and governance over the past generation belies simplistic narratives and stock expectations. The governance of the city cannot be understood as simply a function of zero-sum racial conflict, inept municipal government, corporate capture of local government, southern conservatism, liberal social engineering run amok, or other familiar tropes. Richmond politics at times has exhibited some of these features and has seen its fair share of opportunists, flamboyant characters, and political careerists. But the city also has had at its core fundamentally decent people, motivated by laudable aims of securing a greater measure of racial and social justice, who have sought to address extremely serious, entrenched problems using the resources and tools available to them, often in the face of indifference or opposition from other levels of government, neighboring localities, and powerful interests within Richmond itself.

Black politicians paved the road to Richmond's resurgence. Even so, they have received scant praise for laying the building blocks that allowed contemporary Richmond to turn a corner. Our evidence shows that their efforts succeeded, by and large, in shaping Richmond as a viable, livable, and interesting city, increasingly attractive to middle- and upper-class newcomers. These victories were hard-earned, and the fundamental viability of Richmond creates the possibility for yet deeper change in the near future. Majority-Black political leadership—often with scant resources— shepherded the city through its most challenging hours and did in fact lay the groundwork for the city's recent renaissance (along with its accompanying problems and possibilities).

Indeed, contemporary discussions about gentrification reflect the relative success of Black political leadership in Richmond (and, perhaps, similarly situated cities with sizable minority populations). Confronted with the triple challenge of segregated schools, deep poverty, and housing segregation, leaders from Marsh to Jones actively sought both new in-migration and new investment to shore up tax bases and create new opportunities. Put more frankly, Black leaders, and their attempts to lure tax dollars back into Richmond, helped create the conditions necessary for gentrification, preferring to deal with the complications it brought rather than being stuck in a cycle of decline. Yet, history demonstrates that Richmond, especially between 1990 and 2010, largely failed to narrow racial inequality, to reduce poverty in a sustained way, or to improve the long-term life prospects of children, especially low-income children of color—even though virtually every prominent city leader marked those concerns as a priority (and to varying degrees took action on them). From this perspective, Richmond over the past generation has been both a qualified functional success and a social justice failure, albeit punctuated by periodic bright spots over the years, as well as by promising recent initiatives.

In closing, we draw on our research and community engagement experience—along with many ideas and initiatives generated by fellow community members—to share possible pathways for Richmond to become a more just city. Our fundamental assessment is that Richmond's ongoing, institutionalized inequities reflect the continuity of fundamentally racist public policy decisions made in the early and mid-twentieth century *and* that most current residents and leaders aspire to a more equitable city and region and have taken some meaningful steps to come to terms with the legacy of racial apartheid. These steps remain small relative to the scale of the task. Over three decades have passed since city manager Robert Bobb declared that the city needed a "Marshall Plan" (see chapter 2). Today, the city still needs a Marshall Plan equivalent to meet the needs of Richmond's most disadvantaged residents. The fear that Richmond might fail to rise to the historic moment by not matching ambitious language with political and organizational will remains palpable among many Richmond residents. The continuity of poverty is a constant reminder in cities with sizable Black and Brown populations that the promises of the civil rights revolution remain unfulfilled. At stake is whether Richmond might yet make good on the long promise of nearly half a century of majority-Black political control of city government to build a substantially more just city.

Reimagining Richmond's future requires altitudinal reforms at the state and local levels. This conclusion outlines a roadmap to change, as follows: First, we address the substance of a policy agenda that meaningfully redresses the deep challenges described in this book, with a primary focus on education, economic development, and housing. Second, we briefly consider possible alterations to the city charter—that is, to the structure of city government—ranging from modest tweaks to major overhauls, and ask how these potential changes might impact the ability of the city to implement an ambitious policy agenda. Third, we consider crucial elements of statewide policy that might impact Richmond (and other similarly situated cities). While our discussion of each of these pathways is necessarily brief, we hope it helps illuminate future possibilities not only for Richmond but for urban America more broadly. Importantly, almost all the ideas have already emerged in one form or another in Richmond, both through formal initiatives (such as the Mayor's Anti-Poverty Commission) and community advocacy. In this sense, the agenda presented below reflects some Richmonders' own highest hopes and ideas for the future of their city. At the same time, it reflects our best judgment drawn from decades of study, research, and teaching in our respective fields, as well as our extensive public service both within and adjacent to city hall.

Policy Pathway I: Education

The COVID-19 pandemic disrupted implementation of the Richmond Public Schools' 2019 strategic plan with its five focal areas, "Exciting and Rigorous

Teaching and Learning," "Skilled and Supported Staff," "Safe and Loving School Cultures," "Deep Partnerships with Families and Community," and "Modern Systems and Infrastructure," and exacerbated many of the poverty-related challenges facing RPS students. It is difficult to see how Richmond schools can overcome the array of obstacles to their success without a massive infusion of resources to students and families, invested inside and outside of schools. For purposes of illustration, we focus here on five major needs that could be the core of sustained investment: offsetting the impact of poverty on student learning; state-of-the-art recruitment and retention of school leadership and teacher staff; pro-integration zoning policies; rapid facilities modernization; and adoption of staggered school board terms.[6]

Offsetting the Impact of Poverty

In recent years, over 25 percent of RPS kindergarteners have arrived at school without basic preliteracy skills, including the ability to recognize letters and numbers, name colors, or demonstrate other basic skills, as measured by the state Phonological Awareness Literacy Screening test.[7] Investment in enhanced early childhood education, including but not limited to universal preschool for three- and four-year-olds, would mitigate that challenge. As a second step, the schools might identify children who enter school already behind and target intensive resource support to these children, including holistic engagement with a child's entire family. The BLISS (Building Lives of Independence and Self-Sufficiency) program launched by the city's Office of Community Wealth Building in 2014–15 offers a model of holistic family engagement focused on helping parents obtain sufficiently well-paying employment to exit poverty while also addressing specific pitfalls and challenges that may hold a family back.[8] If Richmond had the resources to provide intensive, timely support to each child known to be behind academically from an earlier age, it might be able to sharply improve the number of students reading by third grade and on grade level at the higher levels.[9]

Likewise, inadequate summer and after-school programming and support has been a major challenge in Richmond for years. While considerable progress has been made toward ensuring that RPS students have access to after-school programming and enrichment activities at all elementary and middle schools, access to quality summertime programs remains uneven and a source of inequity.[10] There is also room for greater investment in allowing all kids to access the city's assets, including the James River, local colleges and universities, cultural museums, and historic sites, in an ongoing way. Last, there are large inequities between the Parent-Teacher Association resources provided to students at favored schools and to those at majority-Black, high-poverty schools, including some with no functional PTA at all. A citywide fund to provide minimum funding to all school PTAs along with operational support could help establish a minimum baseline of parent and community engagement in all schools. The aim of these efforts is to offset the pronounced inequality between the resources (time, money) that middle-class parents and poorer parents are able to provide for their children outside of school days.

School-Based Leadership and Teacher Recruitment, Redevelopment, and Retention

David Kirp's insightful 2013 book, *Improbable Scholars*, about public school success in Union City, New Jersey, emphasizes the strong investment made in professional development of both principals and teachers as a key factor in Union City's success as a relatively high-performing, high-poverty district.[11] Real-time tracking data on student learning were used in a developmental, rather than a punitive, fashion, both to identify students needing additional work and to allow teachers time to adjust both content and teaching style as needed to help students learn. Providing RPS personnel strong front-end professional development support to understand the context of the City of Richmond, its inequities, and the history of RPS itself, as well as asset-based and trauma-informed approaches to teaching children in poverty, would benefit both teachers and students. From a broader perspective, a systemic commitment to treat teachers as knowledgeable professionals due consistent professional respect in and outside of school (and support for lifelong learning), as well as substantially better pay, might also positively impact both teacher morale and the quality of instruction.

Equally important, and perhaps more manageable in short order, is a dedicated focus on recruitment and development of building-level leadership—principals and assistant principals. As with any system, there is a crucial balancing act required between giving principals flexibility to deal with specific situations and assuring that system-wide norms and regulations are followed. Principals play a critical role in establishing school cultures; in some school buildings, maintaining order has historically been the prime directive, a goal that is also inherently in tension with RPS's recent "Lead with Love" mantra. The job of being an urban school principal especially in a challenged school is perhaps one of the most difficult and significant roles in the entire community; Richmond needs to prioritize attracting, training and retaining the strongest possible people to these important positions.

RPS's human resources efforts, and internal organization generally, also have been hampered by long-outdated technology and systems. Investment in better systems, better training, and better internal processes remains a critical need for both Richmond Public Schools and the city itself: "It takes forever to do anything" is a common refrain for employees within both systems. Part of that upgrade may include merging duplicative functions within RPS and the city, such as procurement and auditing.[12]

Pro-Integration Zoning and Enrollment Policies

We emphasized in chapter 4 that Richmond city schools remain substantially segregated. Several schools are nearly 100 percent Black, and several others are nearly 100 percent Black and Latino. While white enrollment in city schools has grown since 2010, over 60 percent of white (non-Hispanic) elementary students in the district attend just four schools (out of twenty-six elementary schools citywide). Missing has been both a commitment to deliberately fostering racially integrated schools and a plausible strategy for doing so.

A major obstacle to change is the fact that the majority of middle- and upper-class white parents in the system have been willing to send their children only to a select number of schools. These include William Fox, Mary Munford, Linwood Holton, and Patrick Henry Elementary Schools, Albert Hill and Binford (now Dogwood) Middle Schools, and at the high school level the specialty schools Community High, Open High, CodeRVA, and the Appomattox and Maggie L. Walker Governor's Schools. A few other schools have been regarded by middle-class families as acceptable if not necessarily desirable schools, including John B. Cary (now Lois Harrison-Jones), J. B. Fisher, and Westover Hills Elementary Schools and Huguenot and Thomas Jefferson High Schools. The small number of secondary schools deemed to be acceptable has created a common pattern where white families send their kids to a favored elementary school and then leave the system. In 2017, a community organization called STAY RVA formed, consisting primarily of middle-class parents, with the aim of encouraging parents to break this pattern and commit to staying in the system until graduation.[13]

Elementary schools are zoned as neighborhood schools, meaning their enrollment inevitably tracks underlying patterns of housing segregation, at least in part. Moreover, the fundamental fact that fewer than 12 percent of RPS students are non-Hispanic white ensures that many schools will continue to consist almost entirely of students of color for years to come. However, there are possibilities for encouraging integration even within neighborhood-based schools. For instance, William Fox, where whites are the largest demographic group, is zoned adjacent to Carver Elementary School, which had a total of thirteen white students in 2021–22. Two racially diverse schools could be created in this footprint directly by rezoning, or by "pairing" elementary schools to create larger zones, and having students attend kindergarten through second grade in one building and third through fifth grade in the other. That was the concept explored but not adopted by the school board in 2019.

At the secondary school level, Richmond's 2019 strategic plan called for turning each middle and high school into a "specialty" school focused on a specific theme, such as math/science, the arts, or history/social science. The schools might be zoned not solely on the basis of neighborhood but by using an open enrollment model with a weighted lottery system to allow students citywide access to schools with a favored theme. Binford (now Dogwood) Middle School, at one point considered a candidate for closure, dramatically revived following adoption of an arts theme in 2015, seeing its enrollment grow from 214 to 451 students between 2014–15 and 2020–21; the number of white students attending Binford grew from 12 to 128 over that same time period.[14] While this is just one example, the Binford case demonstrates the possibility of fairly dramatic demographic shifts in specific schools in response to perceived and actual improvements in school curriculum and climate.

RPS might also stand to benefit by reforming its current open enrollment system—which requires families to provide their own transportation to schools attended out-of-zone—to mitigate segregation by race and socioeconomic class. The policy makes it possible for middle-class parents with means to use open enrollment while others cannot. Basic fairness dictates that the open enrollment system should be extended to all families by providing transportation to students attending a school out-of-zone (an admittedly costly proposition) while giving priority to families receiving subsidized housing or seeking moves that would increase school integration. Without such critical adjustments, fairness and integration would be better served by ending the practice entirely.

If these policies succeeded and more schools were in fact deemed "acceptable" by more people over time, one could imagine significantly greater numbers of white, Latino, and Black middle-class families enrolling and staying in RPS, which in turn would make it far easier to meaningfully achieve racial and class integration systemwide. Here Richmond leaders carry a moral obligation, all too rarely embraced, to forcefully make the case for racially and socioeconomically integrated education. The case is not that Black or Brown kids "need" to be around white kids to succeed. Rather, the case is, first, that in a multicultural, multiracial society, learning to interact, work, and play with people across established lines of difference is both a civic skill and a life skill. Segregated schools cannot incubate inclusive, multicultural democracy. Second, so long as there are significant differences in political and civic influence tracking race and class, having privileged parents from all backgrounds invested in *more* schools is likely to increase advocacy and activism on behalf of improving schools and school conditions, not only in more school buildings but across the school system as a whole.

Modernizing Facilities

Perhaps the most vexing challenge facing RPS, and the most glaring evidence of Virginia's long neglect of its capital city, is the condition of the city school buildings. A large majority of schools are decades old, in varying states of disrepair, and in need of either renovation or complete rebuilds. In 2020, Richmond acted to replace some of the most glaring examples of unfit buildings, including opening three new schools with funding from the enhanced meals tax proposed by Mayor Levar Stoney and passed by the city council in 2018. Richmond City Council has shown a willingness to fund new school construction and even to raise already-high taxes to do so when confronted with a sense of urgency. The primary obstacle is lack of debt capacity to move forward more rapidly with multiple projects simultaneously. At the current rate of change, Richmond schools will not have modernized facilities for decades to come. Dedicated additional local revenue (that is, taxes) is one possible pathway to accelerate the process; selling off unused school and city property for the explicit purpose of generating capital funds for new school construction is another. Yet another is considering public-private funding models in at least some cases, such as a proposed rebuild of Richmond Technical Center at the former Altria warehouse in Southside (donated to the school system in 2017), which local employers plausibly might have a strong interest in helping fund. Finally, and perhaps most plausibly in the near term, the Commonwealth of Virginia could provide substantial school construction funds to Richmond, as reparations for years of neglect and insufficient school funding. This possibility is explored in more depth below.

Staggered School Board Terms

Creating and sustaining a long-term strategy to promote racial and class integration, as well as other long-term strategic goals, would be made more tractable by introduction of staggered terms for school board members, a common practice in other Virginia localities. Staggered terms—in which one part of the board stands for election at the same time as the quadrennial presidential election, and the other part stands for election during midterm congressional elections—are widely believed to promote policy stability and to support the maintenance of institutional knowledge. Consider a typical four-year school board term: often, an incoming board moves to replace administrative leadership, a process that takes up the first year; the second year is used to define a strategic plan; the third year is initial implementation of the plan; and in the middle of the fourth year an election takes place with voters having little real evidence as to whether there has been progress. Depending on the election results, the process may reset to step one in the new term. Staggered terms, in contrast, would mean no single election could reverse the direction of the system or force yet another reset.[15]

Policy Path II: Economic Development and Community Wealth Building

School success is profoundly linked to the success of equitable economic development and community wealth-building strategies in two major ways. First, meeting the urgent funding needs of RPS will be easier to accomplish with a growing local tax base. Second, significantly reducing the child poverty rate in Richmond would make the work of teachers and principals considerably more manageable. When large proportions of children in a classroom bring major unmet needs to school, academics and learning inevitably take a back seat at least some of the time to dealing with immediate needs while maintaining a sense of stability. Reduced poverty might help minimize the level of trauma that individual students experience, as well as the high incidence of student homelessness or transience; and it would provide parents more stability and capacity to be involved in supporting their children's academic growth. An original aspiration of the Education Compact adopted in 2017 was to create a comprehensive citywide plan to support families and children inside and outside of the classroom, as a partnership between RPS, the various city agencies serving the system's families outside the classroom, and community organizations. In practice the compact generally had a more limited role in simply establishing a space for dialogue between the city council, the school board, and the mayor's office, but the potential to use the framework to support a more comprehensive vision remains.

But what can Richmond do to actually reduce the poverty rate? The poverty rate in Richmond, after peaking in the years after the Great Recession at well over 25 percent, receded to less than 20 percent by 2019—about the same level as in 2000. The primary operational focus of the Office of Community Wealth Building since 2017 has been expanding and maintaining an intensive workforce development program tailored to the needs and common challenges facing individuals and families in poverty. The program provides intensive workforce development services to nearly 1,000 residents a year in three locations, and in the last year of normal operations prior to the pandemic (FY 2019), it helped 600 residents secure employment. The OCWB also launched Virginia's first local Living Wage Certification program in 2018, recognizing local employers for providing strong wages and benefits to employees.[16]

Yet bolder approaches might further mitigate local poverty, especially when paired with workforce development efforts. In 2020, Richmond began piloting a basic income program for a select number of households engaged in OCWB workforce programming. These families received an additional cash supplement of $500 a month for two years to meet household needs, over and above earned wages and tax credits. Basic income programs have been embraced by numerous cities since 2020; in Richmond's case, the program was a response to the OCWB's finding that low-level wages are often far too low to meet a household's true needs. A single parent supporting two young children and hence in need of childcare would (in 2020) require at least a thirty-dollars-an-hour job to meet childcare and other expenses—far more than the ten-dollars-an-hour jobs common at the low end of the labor market.[17] Expanding the basic income model on a citywide basis, especially if combined with state-level changes (to make the state Earned Income Tax Credit refundable, implemented partially in 2022) and federal-level changes (renewing the Child Tax Credit implemented in 2021 and then withdrawn), could create a more viable path to long-term economic stability for thousands of families. An initiative to support 3,000 Richmond households a year with a monthly $500 supplement would cost $18 million annually to implement: a significant cost, but still just under 2 percent of the city's current annual budget. While important details would need to be worked through, this direct, cash-based approach would immediately improve prospects for helping Richmond residents more easily overcome the "cliff effect" (falling public benefits as wages rise) that has long held back Richmond residents working to escape poverty.

Richmond's focus on specifically targeted workforce development as a complement to federally funded regional workforce programs will likely remain critically important. But the community wealth-building vision as launched under Dwight C. Jones was broader and embraced a more ambitious goal: *not* just "anti-poverty" in the sense of helping an individual or household cross an arbitrary income threshold but *building wealth* in ways that allow individuals or households to develop a sense of security and to effectively plan for the future. The two goals are related insofar as many people just *above* the federal poverty line inevitably fall below it over the course of several years when adverse events happen, especially if they are not cushioned by offsetting assets. Moving from "getting by" to "economically secure"—that is, helping people who are just above the poverty line to stay there over the long term, is as important to reducing overall poverty as immediate assistance to individuals who at a given moment in time are in dire need.

Three strategies to build wealth articulated in Richmond by the Office of Community Wealth Building but not fully realized by 2023 include institution-based social enterprise development; Promise Scholarships; and support for homeownership. We noted in chapter 5 that Richmond in 2016 conducted a social enterprise feasibility study that recommended the eventual launch of a network of new cooperatives modeled on the Evergreen Cooperatives initiative in Cleveland, Ohio. In Cleveland, hospitals, universities, and other large "anchors" (permanent, rooted major institutions) committed to using a cooperative laundry as a supplier and then extended the approach to locally grown food and solar installations. The cooperatives pay living wages and generous benefits and give employees the opportunity to build wealth through owning a share of the companies in which they work. Anchor institutions benefit directly from services provided and indirectly as the firms work to strengthen the surrounding neighborhoods by increasing localized employment.[18] The initial effort in Richmond stalled in the face of organizational and legal hurdles, but the basic idea remains viable if there is sufficient political support from city leadership and crucial anchor institutions, such as VCU, VCU Health, Bon Secours, the Commonwealth of Virginia, and others. Enabling state legislation could help overcome procurement concerns, and the city and philanthropic partners could establish a new nonprofit entity to incubate the cooperatives.[19]

"Promise Scholarships" refers to local initiatives to provide guaranteed college scholarship support to students in a given public school system.

Several dozen such initiatives exist nationally; the first and still one of the most ambitious is in Kalamazoo, Michigan, which has been credited with helping thousands of high school graduates attend and graduate from a two- or four-year college.[20] In Richmond, the OCWB, RPS, and the RPS Education Foundation partnered to create the RVA Future Centers initiative in 2015, consisting of fully staffed, dedicated college and career advising spaces within each of the city's five large comprehensive high schools.[21] The original intent was to add scholarship support for all graduating RPS students to facilitate successful enrollment in a postsecondary college or training program, but this has yet to take place. Legislation in 2021 in Virginia making community college tuition free for low- and middle-income students entering high-demand fields makes such an initiative more feasible; if total assistance of up to $16,000 ($4,000 per year) were offered to 1,000 RPS graduates a year, the total cost at full build-out would be $16 million a year.[22] The value of such an investment could help RPS graduates jump from high school to an educational and employment track with a much higher likelihood of obtaining economic security. The presence of meaningful scholarship support might also reinforce RPS's efforts to build stronger cultures of school success.[23]

Finally, assisted homeownership provides another path to help residents move from economic precarity to genuine stability. The Equitable Affordable Housing Plan published in 2022 by the city's Housing and Community Development department laid out a detailed plan to bolster housing security, including support for sustainable, affordable homeownership. That plan emphasized collaborating with residents already engaged in OCWB programs to provide transition support and specific assistance to households, as well as building homeownership opportunities for public housing residents as part of future public housing redevelopment. The plan also called for a tax rebate for the development of housing units affordable for residents earning between 40 percent and 80 percent of area median income. Other potential ideas included creating a program to build small houses quickly on currently vacant lots, utilizing a social enterprise that employed low-income city residents; launching an "anti-displacement grant program" to assist low-income homeowners impacted by rising property taxes; and creating a "workforce housing" program to provide subsidies to lower-income city employees to obtain housing in the city.[24]

Taken together, these strategies aim to create pathways by which residents could potentially move from poverty to employment, and then from employment to economic security, business ownership, and homeownership, while also increasing opportunities for young people to move to higher tiers on the economic ladder through support for postsecondary education. These ideas are hardly a comprehensive account of the programmatic interventions that could potentially occur to support wealth building in Richmond. They differ from existing initiatives less in intent than in scale. Getting to scale comes with a hefty price tag, however: fully implementing all the initiatives noted above would likely require at least $50 million a year, on top of investments in education and housing development.

That observation again raises the question of economic development within the city, understood as attracting, retaining, and enhancing public and private investment so as to expand the city's employment and tax base. As we have shown, Richmond has a long history with elite-driven initiatives that either succeeded legislatively but failed in practice or were defeated before they could be enacted. In 2022, the City of Richmond released and adopted a new economic development framework, the Strategic Plan for Equitable Economic Development (or SPEED), intended to redress past failures and link economic development processes more clearly to equity concerns, including poverty reduction. The plan acknowledged past difficulties, such as the rejected Navy Hill/Coliseum proposal of 2019–20, and called for a "more collaborative approach" involving more stakeholders on bigger projects.[25] The document insisted that big projects were critically important to the city's future, however, and that "'organic' development alone" could not bring about new investment on the required scale.[26] City officials held hope that the "Diamond District" initiative to build a new minor league baseball stadium alongside new housing and mixed-used development, adopted unanimously by the city council in September 2022, might provide a successful model of both economic success and equitable inclusion. Even so, it remained to be seen whether elite actors would be willing to move from embracing the language of equity to equity-minded practices and actions. Doing so would require sharing power and embracing more voices. Failure to do so would likely doom those same elite actors' boldest ambitions for economic development in the city, no matter how well intended.

Policy Path III: Housing

Many of the policy tools available to meet the city's housing needs have been developed since 2010 but have yet to be taken to scale: the Affordable Housing Trust Fund, the Maggie Walker Community Land Trust (which also serves as the city's land bank), and processes to move vacant properties back on the market so as to expand supply. The city's Richmond 300 Master Plan established a framework for balancing projected population growth with steps to offset gentrification and foster inclusive, diverse neighborhoods.[27] Nonetheless, the failure of the city to develop and sustain a widely supported, people-centered strategy to address its aging public housing communities, combined with the general lack of resources committed to deeply affordable housing, calls into serious question whether Richmond's development in coming decades will produce a more equitable city.

For Richmond to become a more just city, it will need high-quality housing across the spectrum of affordability—from public housing to workforce housing, serving residents who earn less than 30 percent of the area median income to those who earn between 60 and 80 percent. Our focus here is on an affordable housing policy in Richmond that would both improve the quality of life in deeply segregated, aging public housing communities, including working to remove the stigma associated with residence in public housing through thoughtful mixed-income development, and increase substantially the supply of deeply affordable housing in the city and region. While achieving this aim likely requires the redevelopment of existing public housing communities, the goal should not simply be to ensure that all current public housing residents have good options for replacement housing or to ensure that the total supply of deeply subsidized units does not decrease as a result of redevelopment. Instead, the aim should be to increase the availability of deeply subsidized units over time, within Richmond and the surrounding area, so as to better meet actual need and to do so in a way that—with other supports—reduces poverty rather than reconcentrates it in new places and in new forms.

Here we see potential for bold and creative thinking to link the public housing question to existing counter-gentrification mechanisms such as the Maggie Walker Community Land Trust and Land Bank. Prior to or in conjunction with the redevelopment of the remaining five large public housing communities (Fairfield Court, Gilpin Court, Hillside Court, Mosby Court, and Whitcomb Court), Richmond could make a concerted effort both to transfer long-term tax-delinquent and surplus properties to the community land trust, with the expectation that the properties would be rehabbed or rebuilt as affordable housing across the housing affordability spectrum.[28] Equally or even more important, the land bank could be capitalized to directly buy and return to productive use vacant buildings (more than 750 in mid-2023) or vacant parcels, with the ultimate aim of creating affordable housing.[29] Finally, the city could accelerate new affordable housing production through other tools such as the Affordable Housing Trust Fund and bond financing, with the long-term goal of creating thousands of new affordable housing units in the next decade.[30] A substantial portion of those new units (perhaps 30 percent) could be designated as public housing equivalent, meaning they would be deeply subsidized via a project-based voucher. Those units would then be offered first to residents of current public housing in advance of redevelopment moving forward.

This approach amounts to a more aggressive version of the "build first" strategy partly realized in the Creighton Court redevelopment. Instead of partially building first in a staged process (as in Creighton), the aim is to make full one-for-one replacement of deeply subsidized housing, as well as strong social supports, available before redevelopment of a particular community takes place. (For instance, 780 new subsidized units would be created and made available to Gilpin Court residents prior to its redevelopment.) Then, additional deeply subsidized units would be part of the redeveloped new neighborhood built on the current Gilpin Court site, equivalent to about 25–30 percent of units (as per current redevelopment plans promoted by the Richmond Redevelopment and Housing Authority). The net result would be a transparent, publicly understandable commitment to make a quality housing option available to Gilpin residents prior to redevelopment; setting aside units in the rebuilt neighborhood for those Gilpin residents who may want to remain in the redeveloped neighborhood; and actually *increasing* the number of deeply subsidized units available. Throughout this process, residents would receive strong support in developing a transition plan to connect not only to quality housing but also to workforce development and educational, health, childcare, and other needed services.

We believe a bold approach and commitment on this scale is needed to overcome deep-seated resident and public distrust of both the RRHA and city government on redevelopment issues. The staged process of redevelopment at Creighton Court, while a clear improvement on Blackwell in terms of protections for residents, was not well understood by many city residents. A commitment to *increase* the availability of subsidized units would also address the underlying demand for subsidized housing, evidenced by long waiting lists for public housing and Section 8 vouchers. The proposed strategy would increase deeply subsidized units from about 2,500 to about 3,500 units, including both deeply subsidized units in the rebuilt, mixed-income communities and new units in other locations. Along with these interventions, additional public and private resources dedicated to creating more affordable housing options across different price points to rent and buy are critical.

Richmond will need help from its neighbors in addressing its housing needs—there are limits to this strategy if pursued simply within city boundaries. Creating new units on currently tax-delinquent or vacant property in significant numbers would take years to accomplish, even if the goal were given top priority. The strategy might also raise concerns about reconcentrating poverty in a new form, depending on the location of the units. Expanding the strategy to include new subsidized units in the counties (private rental housing tied to accepting project-based vouchers) would alleviate that concern. Accomplishing that, however, would require buy-in from the counties as well as expansion of public transportation.

Finally, while we believe the traditional focus on ensuring that hard units of deeply subsidized public housing remain available is critically important, this can be complemented by other approaches. Expanded housing vouchers, whether locally or federally funded, can also help more families find affordable housing: families are responsible for paying approximately 30 percent of gross income for rent and utilities, with the voucher covering fair market rent payments beyond that threshold. Prominent housing scholar Matthew Desmond argues for expansion of voucher programs federally as the core basis of an anti-eviction, anti-homelessness initiative; preliminary discussion has taken place in Richmond about establishing a local voucher program to support families directly with housing costs.[31]

Clearly, both the broad plan to redevelop existing public housing while *expanding* the availability of subsidized housing sketched above and the broader investments needed to meet housing needs in Richmond (including essential services for residents) would require large-scale resources, beyond what the city currently has. Nonetheless, dedicating either specific existing revenue or a portion of future revenue streams could allow Richmond to move in this direction, while at the same time advocating for dramatically enhanced support from state and federal sources.

You Can Imagine It, but Can You Do It? Reconsidering Richmond's Form of Government

The agenda sketched above might be ambitious, but with political will and the means to follow through on that will, it is also plausible. Many of the ideas noted above have already been introduced or considered in Richmond in some form in the last decade. The harder question is whether city government and its associated agencies have the capacity to execute an agenda of this scale. Or, to be more precise, can Richmond city government really implement a transformative set of reforms at the same time it provides essential city services—from public safety to garbage collection to permitting to providing water and gas—at a high level of effectiveness? Asking that question raises the issue not only of the city bureaucracy per se but of the larger system of governance that Richmond adopted in 2004.

The 2022–23 City Charter Review Commission established by Richmond City Council laid out a series of recommendations intended to recast the mayor-council system as a more balanced partnership between the mayor and the council. The commission recommended, for instance, that both the mayor and the council have a substantial role in the hiring and dismissal of both the chief administrative officer and the city attorney, that the council be given more oversight power in the budget development and amendment process, and that the mayor be required to present monthly public updates to (and receive questions from) council members.[32]

The commission, however, also developed for consideration a more dramatic alternative: shifting to a seven-person council, consisting of six districted representatives and an elected mayor to be elected at-large via a ranked-choice voting procedure. The council in turn would appoint a professional city manager to oversee daily operations, while the elected mayor would serve as leader (and a voting member) of the council. The commission noted that this structure (common in many American cities) might reduce conflict and increase transparency in the policy process. The overall reduction in council size might permit better compensation of both officials and their aides and also make it easier for the council to reach consensus. Fewer seats would also increase political competition, presumably increasing the quality of elected candidates over time. Increased compensation would make it possible for council members to devote more time to the role, commensurate with additional responsibilities. Finally, an elected mayor leading a seven-person body would have significant opportunity to lead on policy matters while being free from the burden of responsibility for administering the city's complex organizational structure.[33]

Our judgment is that maintaining some version of the elected mayor system gives Richmond the best opportunity to take decisive action of the type outlined in the first section of this chapter, to redress long-standing inequities in education, housing, and economic opportunity with bold strategies that address those challenges at the scale they exist. Policy leadership powers, a citywide perspective, and the credibility of having been elected by voters citywide are still necessary ingredients in establishing a clear direction for city government. Clear leadership from an elected mayor can also usefully align the actions and activities of other prominent community actors, such as philanthropists, the universities, and the business community, with the city's policy priorities. At its best moments, such as the downtown master planning process under Doug Wilder and the poverty-fighting efforts under Dwight Jones, mayoral leadership has also invited grassroots community voices and ordinary residents into the policymaking process, creating greater buy-in than plans solely developed by internal professional staff or traditional elite networks.

At the same time, experience has shown that it is a tall order indeed to expect to have on a regular basis a mayor who is strong in both policy and political leadership *and* in administrative oversight. Further, the *type* of political skill the current mayoral position rewards—either brute force or using control of the administrative and budgetary apparatus to win over support from a working majority of council—may not in fact be the most conducive to building a strong policy consensus for sustained changes. An elected mayor who is *part* of the city council would be driven to build consensus among his or her colleagues based on the merits of a given policy or initiative and to become skilled in forging compromises that allow buy-in from as many members as possible. As an alternative to leadership organized around primarily one individual, one can—perhaps for the first time in Richmond's history—imagine a city council in the future that, with a prod from an elected mayor, is able to reach consensus on fairly bold, equity-based initiatives like those sketched above (subject to necessary compromises). The City Charter Review Commission's suggestion of an elected, full-time mayor leading a seven-member council is worthy of serious consideration as one possible method of obtaining both effective political leadership and stronger collective oversight of the city administration.

This leads us to an obvious but critically important point: mayors and city council members are human beings. The cognitive, emotional, political, and even spiritual demands of leading a city with Richmond's severe challenges are high. We believe mayors, council members, and leaders more generally can be more or less skilled, more or less strategic, more or less thoughtful, and more or less persistent in how they approach their work. We do not, however, subscribe to a "hero" theory of urban political leadership. Even if a person of superior qualities in multiple areas could be found and elected to the Richmond mayor's seat, we do not think that would in itself amount to a lasting solution to Richmond's toughest problems.

Lasting progress will require both stronger municipal governance *and* stronger civic organizations that can articulate and sustain comprehensive policy commitments that are bigger than any single person, official, or administration and that can help hold officials accountable for implementation of stated commitments and policies. Such organizations could take a lead role in policy development and in all aspects of the electoral process, from candidate selection to holding elected officials accountable. Robust organizations of this kind can also be a training ground for future formal leadership roles. In this regard, Richmond's civic infrastructure was relatively weak over most of the time period of this study. But in earlier periods of Richmond's history, powerful organizations such as the Richmond Crusade for Voters decisively influenced the trajectory of Richmond politics and hence the city itself.[34] A critically important question going forward is whether multiracial, cross-cutting, citywide organizations capable of proactively shaping a bold policy agenda will emerge, acting not in place of but in concert with organizations representing more specific issues and constituencies.

In short, Richmond's future depends not just on the qualities of who gets elected to office nor on the specific responsibilities of that person's various roles, though these are both critically important. It also depends on how much Richmond residents truly want meaningful change, their willingness to learn about the issues and what it takes to bring change given the city's deep obstacles, and how hard they are willing to work (and organize and advocate) to obtain it.

A Capital City Agenda: The Virginia Rules, Revisited

In turning the corner, state-level politics matter. Stronger internal governance might improve the functioning of Richmond's city government and might deploy existing resources more strategically to better address long-standing problems while meeting ongoing needs. But from a larger perspective, this still amounts to making the most of a bad hand within regional and statewide arrangements that still systematically disadvantage the city. To fully meet demands for equity and inclusion, strong internal governance would need to be connected to significant regional and statewide reforms.

Richmond's poverty rate of approximately 20 percent is significantly higher than most state capitals nationwide. (The poverty rate in the capitals of Virginia's two largest neighbors, Maryland and North Carolina, are 11 percent and 12 percent, respectively.)[35] That poverty rate is inextricably linked to decades of public and private disinvestment in Richmond, especially its East End and Southside, that the state has aided and abetted. Three immediate corrective steps that the Commonwealth of Virginia could enact through General Assembly action are these:

1. Dramatically increasing the annual payment in lieu of taxes that the state pays to the City of Richmond for the larger proportion of city land that is nontaxable state property or part of VCU, as well as for the various services associated with serving the state government. For 2022, the annual payment equaled just $3.7 million; a figure ten times that level both would have been appropriate and would have allowed Richmond to make significant new investments in education and equity without increasing the local tax burden.[36]
2. Altering the "Local Composite Index" formula used to generate base school funding assistance to localities. The current formula calculates local capacity-to-pay based on total wealth while ignoring poverty. Revising this formula, as well as substantially increasing existing "At-Risk Add-On" funding for localities with high poverty, could increase school funding by tens of millions of dollars year-by-year, again without increasing the local tax burden.[37]
3. Dramatically increasing state assistance to Richmond and similar localities to accelerate new school construction. As noted above, Richmond has no realistic possibility of renovating or replacing its many aging school facilities within less than a thirty-year time frame using existing resources. If not addressed, a substantial number of low-income children, primarily children of color, will continue to spend some or all of their K–12 education in substandard facilities that undermine learning and show disrespect for the students and staff in the building. Virginia could rectify this situation at a much faster pace by transferring funds to localities to facilitate school construction or even by taking direct responsibility for financing and building new schools and transferring the buildings to local authorities. While Virginia's School Construction Assistance Program, established in 2022 with initial funding of $450 million, is a good start, it will need to be funded at much larger scale and to prioritize disadvantaged localities to significantly impact the next generation of Richmond students.[38]

These three steps, especially if taken simultaneously, could substantially improve Richmond's fiscal position and allow the city to begin making the kinds of critical investments in housing, workforce development, school infrastructure, and other needs required to build a more equitable city. Virginia could further strengthen Richmond's prospects by requiring that Virginia Commonwealth University enter into a comprehensive partnership agreement with the City of Richmond committing VCU to train and hire local residents for university and health system jobs as well as for ongoing construction projects. The General Assembly could also increase the latitude Richmond has to create a living wage ordinance, strengthen local procurement, employ more targeted tax and tax relief policies, and enable other innovations now effectively barred by the Dillon Rule.[39]

Equally critical are measures to directly tackle regional inequalities—that is, the divide between Richmond and its suburban neighbors, particularly Chesterfield and Henrico Counties. Transportation offers the most promising near-term avenue for genuine regional cooperation of the kind that ties localities together. The 2020 creation of the Central Virginia Transportation Authority, and the related restructuring of the Greater Richmond Transit Company to include Henrico County as a full partner, provides an institutional framework for expansion of Bus Rapid Transit lines throughout the major employment and residential corridors of the region, a goal of Richmond identified by the Mayor's Anti-Poverty Commission Report (2013).[40] The fight now has become less about the general desirability of more bus service in the counties, which county leaders widely accept, and more about the relative level of investment in mass transit as opposed to road maintenance. (More distant possibilities include a light rail system, as well as high-speed rail connectivity of the Richmond region with Washington, DC, and the rest of the I-95 corridor.)

Adopting a regional approach to affordable housing is still a challenging conversation in Richmond, but it is unavoidable if the city is to meet its affordable housing needs without simply reconcentrating poverty within tight parameters in the city limits. Virginia could facilitate this by requiring or incentivizing counties to adopt robust inclusive zoning ordinances to allow faster construction of multifamily housing units in the counties. More specifically, the state could provide funding and support for development of new, deeply subsidized units located near mass transit nodes to serve as quality replacement housing units for current residents of Richmond public housing. (Federal policy requires residents relocated by public housing redevelopment to be offered replacement housing with access to transit and other services.) Related to this, existing poverty-fighting organizations that now focus exclusively or nearly exclusively on city residents could be broadened into regional or quasi-regional entities. For instance, it is possible to imagine Henrico County becoming a partner of Richmond's Office of

Community Wealth Building and the entity expanding to provide workforce development and related services to families at or below the poverty line on a regional basis.

The most challenging conversation of all concerns the possibility of regionalizing Richmond public education in some form. The separation of county and city schools has been foundational to the uneven development of the Richmond metropolitan area over the past half century, and even now the notion of mixing city and county students is seen as threatening to many county residents and elected officials. Here, too, however, we see the possibility of significant movement at the secondary school level. The 2019 Richmond Public Schools strategic plan called for turning the city's five comprehensive high schools into specialty schools organized around themes such arts or science, technology, engineering, and math. If sufficient resources were devoted to creating recognized, top-tier facilities and resources at those schools, they might become attractive to at least some county students. The state board of education could mandate that all high schools in the Richmond region maintain a percentage of seats for cross-jurisdiction open enrollment, allowing Richmond students to access county high schools and opening the doors of city schools to interested county residents. (Transportation would have to be provided to all students, as is already done at regional Governor's Schools.) The investment in the Richmond specialty schools is critical to making this proposition attractive to county residents and hence politically palatable: some county residents already attend high school in the city at the regional Maggie L. Walker Governor's School, and other regional high schools, such as Appomattox Governor's School and CodeRVA, are successful and well established. A plan of this sort may be seen as a stretch goal for RPS given the current condition of most of its high schools, but substantial state backing and support to create top-tier facilities comparable to existing county schools could produce rapid change.

Indeed, a crucial takeaway is that making significant, breakthrough progress on Richmond's intertwined challenges of poverty, education, and housing will require bolder, more resource-intensive efforts, tied to specific goals to be accomplished in a finite amount of time. Richmond cannot keep its long-standing patterns of segregated housing and schools in place and also expect to disrupt the perpetuation of racial and economic inequality. Breaking those patterns will require, at some point, more disruptive change, not simple expansion and continuation of existing efforts.

If anti-urbanism helped shape Richmond from the mid-twentieth century to now, the path forward requires city-county alliances. In that light, at some point in the next generation the Richmond region may have reason to reconsider a foundational decision made over sixty years ago: namely, the rejection (in a 1961 referendum) of a proposal to merge Henrico County and the City of Richmond. On the one hand, there are powerful forces locking the status quo in place: the still-gaping inequalities between the county and the city give county residents powerful, self-interested reasons to refuse any consideration of merging with the city.[41] In addition, many Henrico residents are politically conservative and have little wish to be in the same political boat with Richmond's liberal-leaning polity; conversely, many Richmond residents, Black and white and Latino, have no interest in wrestling with conservative ideologues in local government. Indeed, Richmond residents might well prefer to trust city government, with all its challenges, to better safeguard their interests than a much larger, merged polity in which Black and progressive elected officials play a relatively reduced role.

On the other hand, there has been significant demographic convergence over the past twenty years between Henrico and Richmond, with Henrico growing racially much more diverse (less white) at the same time that Richmond has grown whiter. There has been political convergence to a degree, too, as Henrico since 2008 has regularly voted blue in statewide and national elections, although not by the overwhelming margin seen in the city.[42] Henrico officials are now relatively pro-transit and have at least some interest in promoting affordable housing and stronger services and opportunities for low-income residents. Finally, there are the facts that a combined Richmond-Henrico government could allow collective savings by merging duplicative functions and that a combined Richmond-Henrico, with population close to 600,000 people, would immediately be seen as a major American city and a magnet for continued economic development. In these circumstances, too, Chesterfield County would likely want to get in the picture rather than be left behind, leading potentially to a combined metropolitan city of nearly 1 million people that would be perceived as a powerhouse truly competitive with Atlanta and Charlotte.

This possibility sounds, perhaps shockingly, much like a 1950s boosterism vision for what a Greater Richmond might look like. In that era, city leaders assumed expansion of the city's geography and reach was essential to its economic viability and vitality. And yet it is also perhaps exactly what Richmond might have become, if not held back for so long by central Virginia's overriding twentieth-century commitment to maintaining racial segregation in schools and housing, a commitment that eventually led to a contained, majority-Black city surrounded and locked in by more prosperous, majority-white counties.

While that possibility perhaps sits on the more distant horizon, its time has not yet come. We do not believe Richmond residents will, or should, trade off the possibility of using their control of the tools of local government to push for dramatic change until another concerted push has been made to deliver on the long promise of majority-Black control of city hall. The window for effective control or influence over the levers of local power to pursue an assertive commitment to genuine racial equity may be closing in the wake of population growth and gentrification, but it is not yet closed. We conclude this study in hope and expectation that Richmond leaders and citizens, with the support of state-level officials, will take up bold, comprehensive policy commitments of the kind outlined in this chapter, conscious of but not constrained by the layers of history and complexity previous generations have wrestled to confront and overcome.

There is hardly a moment to lose.

Acknowledgments

The animating question when Amy Howard and I began conceptualizing this project in 2008 and 2009 was, "Why hasn't Richmond's leadership class taken meaningful steps to address the community's most obvious and glaring problem—namely, racial, economic and educational inequity?" Fifteen years later, that's still a good question. It's one that frequently occurs to newcomers to Richmond, or to anyone who tracks local public affairs in this city.

Our work on this project was encouraged, if not instigated, by our dear colleague John V. Moeser. Fortuitously, my arrival at the University of Richmond (UR) in the fall of 2005 coincided with the start of Dr. Moeser's tenure at UR following his retirement from Virginia Commonwealth University, where he had spent more than three decades in teaching, scholarship, and civic advocacy. When Dr. Moeser stated in talks and conversation that the "story of Richmond is the story of America," I initially dismissed the claim as local propaganda. But over time, I began to realize the truth of Dr. Moeser's statement. In earlier work, I characterized the American metropolitan form as an engine of systemic injustice; argued that cities facilitated stronger civic and political participation of the kind suitable to a self-governing republic; and suggested that the best remedy to challenges of urban sprawl would be to improve the conditions of life in central cities.

Richmond, as I came to appreciate, exemplifies the challenges facing American metropolitan areas in general, often in magnified form. So Dr. Howard and I initially imagined a community study at the intersection of our primary disciplines of political science and history that could lay bare the city's civic condition and place it in broader context. To that end, working with UR undergraduate Lucas Hakkenberg, we undertook a series of interviews of Richmond civic, business, and political leaders, and we began archival work to learn more about what happened in Richmond in the 1980s and 1990s in the run-up to the political reform of 2004.

Over the next couple of years, the project changed significantly, in two ways. First, then-UR president Edward L. Ayers sent me a hard copy of the recently completed dissertation by University of Virginia PhD graduate Dr. Julian M. Hayter. The dissertation sat on a chair in my office for several months, waiting for the right time to be opened. When I finally read through the thesis—the basis for Dr. Hayter's subsequent book *The Dream Is Lost*—I knew that the work would powerfully add to the literature on Richmond's development since the 1970s and that Amy and I needed to be in touch with Dr. Hayter. To our good fortune, Julian ended up on the faculty of the University of Richmond in 2012. After publication of *The Dream Is Lost*, he joined our project, strengthening its connection to the broader historiography of the civil rights movement and post–civil rights era.

Second, both Amy Howard and I had the opportunity, in different ways, to actually contribute to policymaking and implementation in Richmond in the early 2010s—in my case, in a full-time role in city government for two years. We each made the decision to prioritize helping Richmond leaders who seemed sincerely interested in actually tackling some of Richmond's toughest problems over completing a book complaining about Richmond's failure to do so. That was a significant professional and personal decision, but it was the only reasonable decision from an ethical point of view. And, it has made for a much better, albeit different, book than what we originally envisioned.

When I first arrived in Richmond in 2005, few people (myself included) would have pegged me as a likely candidate to be invited into city hall to lead a significant municipal initiative. Indeed, I initially assumed that my role in the community would be as a critic who pushed and prodded city leaders while championing just causes. But what I soon found is that whenever I delivered what I considered to be pretty damning critiques of Richmond's status quo, many people—included elected officials—largely agreed with what I was saying. And as I was invited to participate in nascent civic efforts in the first term of Mayor Dwight C. Jones—both the Mayor's Redistricting Advisory Commission (2011) and the Mayor's Anti-Poverty Commission (2011–13)—I came to appreciate that many elected officials in Richmond saw themselves as struggling to advance the cause of racial and social justice, while keeping the city afloat, against difficult odds.

Equally important, through the resultant work (some of which is described in this book), I had the opportunity to forge meaningful relationships with community members across the full spectrum of the city, including leaders in public housing neighborhoods who welcomed allies and strategic support. Among those community members was Lillie A. Estes, a powerful and distinctive personality who mixed understandable rage at the status quo with a theological and philosophical commitment to hope and to building community. We didn't agree on all the policy details, but we connected as people. On the morning of my first day in city hall as director of the newly launched Mayor's Office of Community Wealth Building on June 3, 2014, the first phone call I received came from Ms. Estes. She reached out with encouragement and said that if I kept my integrity, things would go well. True words to live by!

My goal when working for the City of Richmond was to perform the duties that were laid out for me and our team as well as we could. But the doing of the work shaped and reshaped the scholarship presented in this book, confirming or strengthening some of my presumptions about how city government functioned while challenging others. I got to see city government at some of its finest moments, as well as some of its lowest. Overall, I left with stronger belief in the power and capacity of local government to positively impact residents' lives and with greater determination to continue to contribute to Richmond's realizing its potential for transformative change.

In the writing of this book I would like to thank my coauthors, Julian M. Hayter and Amy L. Howard, for their expertise, wisdom, friendship, and good judgment. We have sustained each other in this work, and I am grateful to Amy and Julian both personally and professionally for their unwavering support and commitment to productive collaboration.

My spouse, Adria L. Scharf, also has played a major role in the production of these pages. It was through Adria's extensive network of social justice activists and advocates from her fourteen-year tenure as executive director of the Richmond Peace Education Center that I first met community activists like Lillie A. Estes and Cora Hayes. I rode the coattails of her positive reputation in the community, especially in the early days of the anti-poverty work, and we collaborated on issues ranging from public housing to school funding to school rezoning. We also shared the amazing experience of raising our son, Sahara, in Richmond Public Schools. There were many school-level challenges in Sahara's scholastic journey, but each and every year, from pre-K onward, there was a capable and caring teacher in his classroom. I thank

Adria and Sahara for their love, support, and continued willingness to go on this journey together.

I am also grateful to many friends, university colleagues, city hall colleagues, civic leaders, and collaborators, not all of whom I can name here, for sharing their knowledge of the city and participating in the work of trying to improve it. I thank Beth Almore, Danny Avula, Melody Barnes, Risha Berry, Ram Bhagat, Rev. Yvonne Bibbs, Marland Buckner, Rev. Benjamin Campbell, Carla Childs, Kelly Chopus, Taikein Cooper, Betty Neal Crutcher, Nicholas Feucht, Harold Fitrer, Thomas Fitzpatrick, Tanya Gonzalez, Reggie Gordon, Greta Harris, Crystal Hoyt, Glyn Hughes, Christina Mastroianni, Clarence McGill, Rev. Bo Millner, Rev. Robin Mines, Valaryee Mitchell, Ruth Morrison, Dayshaun Penn, Evette Roots, Andrew Schoeneman, Vilma Seymour, Tom Shields, Genevieve Siegel-Hawley, Andrea Simpson, Errol Somay, Mary Tate, Jim Thompson, Albert Walker, Corey D. B. Walker, and Leah Walker for their insights, collaboration, and friendship.

This project is also informed by a long line of academic mentors in the fields of history, political science, and ethics, mentors who trained, challenged, and prodded my thinking and work. Some have now passed on, but their words and their example live on. Thanks go to Gar Alperovitz, James Cone, Perry Curtis, Wendell Dietrich, Beverly Harrison, William McLoughlin, Christopher Morse, Robert Putnam, Larry Rasmussen, Houston Roberson, and Michael Sandel.

Numerous UR students contributed to this project over the years. Lucas Hakkenberg led or co-led the majority of the structured interviews that took place in the formative phase of the project. Other students have contributed transcriptions, fact-checking, and research, including Christian Herald, Jeffrey Hunt, Alicia Jiggetts, Ben Panko, Eileen Pomeroy, and T. J. Tann.

We also express appreciation to the numerous community leaders who agreed to be interviewed for the project for their time, insight, and candor.

This book owes a large debt to generations of journalists in Richmond who covered the city and its workings in detail, in some cases for decades. The tenacious reporting of Jeremy Lazarus of the *Richmond Free Press* and Michael Paul Williams of the *Richmond Times-Dispatch* over many years and many difficult events deserves particular note. The deep and serious coverage provided by the *Richmond Free Press*, the *Richmond Times-Dispatch*, and *Style Weekly* over the time period of this study not only has been an invaluable research resource but also is a testament to the critical, ongoing importance of robust and varied journalism for the practice of urban democracy. The staff of the Virginia Commonwealth University Rare Books and Periodicals archive at Cabell Library provided generous and courteous access to print copies of the *Richmond Free Press* (subsequently digitized by the Library of Virginia) and *Style Weekly*, which were extremely helpful in the early stages of this research.

I also thank, with deep gratitude, the Jepson School of Leadership Studies and the University of Richmond for sustained and patient support of this project over many years.

We appreciate the support and guidance of editor Lucas Church and acquisitions assistant Thomas Bedenbaugh at the University of North Carolina Press through the publication process. Julie Bush and Mary Carley Caviness handled our final manuscript with thoughtfulness and care in the copyediting and production process: thank you! We also thank our anonymous academic reviewers for their very helpful comments and recommendations. Riley Champine produced excellent maps, which improve this book.

Finally, I wish to thank other members of my immediate family for their examples and their support. My sister, Treeby W. Brown, is a model public servant, and my brother, Dr. George S. Williamson, is a model historian. I like to think that as the youngest child, some of both of them rubbed off on me! I continued to be blessed by the lives of my remarkable parents, Joan A. Williamson and Dr. Samuel R. Williamson Jr., and thank them profoundly for their unstinting love, advice, and encouragement.

— THAD WILLIAMSON

I owe a great debt to Thad Williamson and Amy Howard. Both have devoted themselves not only to the University of Richmond and the City of Richmond but to the history of Richmond. I'd like to thank them for their continued support and for the collaborative work that we've done over the years. These two, more than anyone I know, live their beliefs. This book is a testament to teamwork and our shared commitment to usable scholarship. They are, in the end, just good people.

Special thanks go to Riley Champine for the maps, to the readers, and to everyone at UNC Press.

Ed Ayers, Brian Balogh, Annie Evans, Rob Nelson, Tony Field, New American History, and Bunk History have kept me grounded through the years. Ed and Brian, you have made me a better historian, scholar, and person. Also, thanks go to Claudrena Harold—we need to break bread more often!

Thanks go to Sandra Peart and everyone at the Jepson School of Leadership Studies. You will never be rid of me. Thanks for making work less like work and more like a family (of the non-dysfunctional persuasion).

Thanks also go to my colleagues on the City of Richmond's Monument Avenue Commission. Our work together helped change Richmond's landscape.

A special shout-out goes to Marvin Chiles, Bert Ashe, Ernest McGowan, Corey Walker, Shelby Driskill, Eric and Nicole, Pippa Holloway, and Andrea Simpson. A super-special shout-out goes to Ernesto Semán, Soledad Marambio, and Clarita!

Ted Elmore and the folks at BridgePark RVA have been essential to my understanding not just of Richmond but of how professional relationships can blossom into genuine friendships. Big up to Marc Cheatham—the hippest hip-hop head of heads.

I could not have done any of this without my wife, Cate, and my daughter, Evelyn. You two are the core of my being.

I am eternally grateful for the people in my life outside of the academy. You all keep me going in untold ways. Thanks, Mom! You continue to ask questions that challenge my understanding of life. My father, who passed away in 2016, was instrumental to my love of history. Aunt Tam, Kelley, and Brandon, thanks for keeping what's left of the family alive. Cousin Cynthia too! Hold down the westside, Tez! Keep pressing, Veronica!

In the words of Ice Cube, "I gotta say, what's up?" Once again, it's on—Travis Weaver, Erwin Thomas, Matt Jeter, Courtney Quinn and AQ, Marcus Willis, Danny Gregory, Rick and Cathy Engel, Uncle John, Aunt Hanna, D-Lew, Duck, Steve Graves, Rico Harvey, Alex Isaacson (congrats!), Chris Loomis, Dorothy Frazier, Aaron Nuzum, the Millers, and everyone else I forgot.

I also want to thank hip-hop music for teaching me how to mine sources, read liner notes, respect my parents' music, and love and respect expertise.

Last, I'm forever indebted to the ancestors—my dad, Uncle Barney, Aunt Patty, Big Evelyn, Toots, Gobbles, Aunt Sylvie, Cousin Ika, and Mother and Daddy Green.

—JULIAN M. HAYTER

Thad Williamson and Julian Hayter, thank you for being outstanding colleagues, coauthors, and forces for positive change at the University of Richmond and in Richmond. Each of you has made important contributions toward a more just city. I feel fortunate to work with you and, more so, to have you as trusted, beloved, and admired friends.

Thanks go to Riley Champine for his excellent maps. A shout-out of appreciation goes to Gretchen Schoel for her years of friendship and, separately, for keenly copyediting this book. Props to the many students over the years, referenced by Thad above, for their excellent work moving this project forward.

I wouldn't have even started on this project with Thad over a decade ago if it hadn't been for my Richmond mentor and dear friend, Dr. John Moeser. I remember standing with him and Thad in the Bonner Center for Civic Engagement in 2009 and hearing these words: "You two really need to write a book on Richmond." Gratefully, Julian joined the team after writing his own outstanding book on Richmond, and here we are. John transitioned from life in 2022, but his wisdom, integrity, and fight for a more just city and region live on as we work to uphold the example he set.

I have learned and continue to learn so much from community leaders in Richmond. Chimere Miles, Chanel Bea, Albert Walker, Gwen Corley-Creighton, Laura Lafayette, Greta Harris, Lynn McAteer, Rev. Dr. Ben Campbell, Reggie Gordon, Cathy Howard, Vanessa Diamond, Lynn Pelco, Elaine Summerfield, Lauranett Lee, Dr. Danny Avula, Damon Jiggetts, Tanya Gonzalez, Harold Fitrer, Ryan Rinn, Burt Pinnock, Marland Buckner, Jonathan Zur, and many others have shared their time, experiences, expertise, and friendship with me. Thank you.

Wonderful colleagues at UR, including Sylvia Gale, Glyn Hughes, Blake Stack, Derek Miller, Kim Dean-Anderson, Terry Dolson, Alexandra Byrum, Anthony Crenshaw, Adrienne Piazza, Nicole Maurantonio, Patricia Herrera, Eric Yellin, Nicole Sackley, Melissa Ooten, Andy Gurka, Elizabeth Outka, Shelby Driskill, Tom Shields, Ernest McGowen, Lauren Tilton, Burt Ashe, and Monika Siebert, asked questions, provided support and encouragement, and kept faith in the project and in me along the way. Thank you.

Kevin Pelletier, Kendra Vendetti, Emerson, and Lisette have nourished me and my family with food, friendship, and laughter in Richmond for over fifteen years. Love y'all.

From near and far for over three decades, Ashley Davis, Jean DeMoss, Rachel Dunifon, and Sally Richmond have proved the power of sustained friendship through all-the-things. Here's to the next thirty years.

My extended family—fab parents, Donna and David Howard; awesome sis and crew, Jennie, Tom, and Jackson Joyce and Alyssa and Jordan Wolf; wonderful brother and team, Matt, Carrie, Bryan, and Ben Howard and Torie

Sedimeyer; super-lucky-to-have in-laws, Jeanne O'Brien, Ben and Charlie Nelson, Bob and Kathy Nelson; and chosen family Kim and Ellie Hurst—offered continuous love and support, as always. I appreciate each one of you.

All I do is deeply enriched by my beloveds, the anchor of my life: my partner, Robert Nelson, and our incredible daughter, Meseret. Always—and always.

—AMY L. HOWARD

This book is dedicated, with fondness and with profound hope for the future, to the memory of two very different, unique, and much beloved Richmonders, both animated by a concern for people, an aspiration for Richmond to achieve a greater level of justice, and a willingness to devote themselves to that ongoing work, not for a season, but for a lifetime.

The memories of Lillie A. Estes and John V. Moeser are blessings to us and to the City of Richmond.

Appendix

Oral History Sources

Most interviews were conducted in 2010 and 2011 by Lucas Hakkenberg (University of Richmond undergraduate) and Thad Williamson, with Amy Howard present for some interviews. A limited number of interviews took place in 2012. Affiliations and titles refer to positions held by interviewees at the time of the interview.

Parker Agelasto, Richmond City Council–elect (Fifth District)

Edward Ayers, president, University of Richmond

Stephen Baril, Williams Mullen (law firm)

Kim Bridges, Richmond School Board (First District)

Rev. Ben Campbell, Richmond Hill (ecumenical urban retreat center)

Betsy Carr, Virginia House of Delegates (formerly of the Richmond School Board)

Donald Coleman, Richmond School Board (Seventh District)

Doug Conner, Richmond City Council (Ninth District)

Rob Corcoran, community activist (Hope in the Cities)

Bob Crum, Richmond Regional Planning District Commission

Valena Dixon, Richmond Redevelopment and Housing Authority

Robert Dortch, pastor and community activist (U-Turn Academy)

John Douglass, University of Richmond School of Law

Ana Edwards, community activist (Sacred Ground Historical Reclamation Project)

Lillie A. Estes, community activist (RePHRAME)

Harold Fitrer, Communities in Schools

Rachel Flynn, director of community planning, City of Richmond

Matthew Freeman, diversity consultant

Kimberly Gray, Richmond School Board (Second District)

Kathy Graziano, Richmond City Council (Fourth District)

Antione Green, Richmond Crusade for Voters

Bill Hall, Dominion Energy

Virgil Hazelett, Henrico County manager

Maurice Henderson, Richmond School Board (Fifth District)

Rev. Morris Henderson, pastor, 31st Street Baptist Church

David M. Hicks, senior policy adviser to Mayor Dwight C. Jones

Chris Hilbert, Richmond City Council (Third District)

Susan Horne, Lead Virginia

Alan Hutson, philanthropic consultant

Marty Jewell, Richmond City Council (Fifth District)

Timothy M. Kaine, former governor of Virginia and Richmond mayor

Hugh Keogh, Virginia Chamber of Commerce

Laura Lafayette, Richmond Association of Realtors

James R. Leaman, AFL-CIO

Donald McEachin, Virginia Senate (Ninth District)

John V. Moeser, Bonner Center for Civic Engagement, University of Richmond, and retired professor, Virginia Commonwealth University

Norma Murdoch-Kitt, Richmond School Board (Third District)

Charles Nance, former Richmond School Board member (Second District)

Rev. Tyrone Nelson, pastor, Sixth Mount Zion Baptist Church

Bill Pantele, former city council president (Second District)

Edward Peeples, community activist and retired professor, Virginia Commonwealth University

Silver Persinger, community activist

Trip Pollard, Southern Environment Law Center

Liz Povar, Virginia Economic Development Partnership

Chuck Richardson, former Richmond City Council member (Fifth District)

Ellen Robertson, Richmond City Council (Sixth District)

Charles Samuels, Richmond City Council (Second District)

John Sarvay, community consultant and blogger

Kim Scheeler, Greater Richmond Chamber of Commerce

Andrew Schoeneman, community activist (RePHRAME)

Tom Shields, University of Richmond

Oliver Singleton, Metropolitan Business League

Bob Skunda, Virginia Biotechnology Research Park

Doug Smith, Virginia Interfaith Center for Public Policy

Myra Goodman Smith, Leadership Metro Richmond

T. K. Somanath, Better Housing Coalition

Jay Stegmaier, Chesterfield County administrator

Eugene Trani, president emeritus, Virginia Commonwealth University

James E. Ukrop, First Market Bank

Michel Zajur, Virginia Hispanic Chamber of Commerce

Notes

CHAPTER 1

1. Thessaly La Force, Zoë Lescaze, Nancy Haas, and M. H. Miller, "The 25 Most Influential Works of Protest Art since World War II," *New York Times Style Magazine*, October 15, 2020.

2. "Richmond Protestors Topple Columbus Statue, Throw It in Lake," AP News, June 10, 2020, https://apnews.com/article/e99df0a4ec90e92540a2780d83cee56d; Michael Levenson, "Protesters Topple Statue of Jefferson Davis on Richmond's Monument Avenue," *New York Times*, June 11, 2020; "A Timeline of a Month of Protests in Richmond," Radio IQ/WTVF, July 1, 2020, www.wvtf.org/news/2020-07-01/a-timeline-of-a-month-of-protests-in-richmond.

3. Derrick Bryson Taylor, "George Floyd Protests: A Timeline," *New York Times*, November 5, 2021. For data on Americans shot by police from 2010 to 2016, see Rob Arthur, Taylor Dolven, Keegan Hamilton, Allison McCann, and Carter Sherman, "Shot by Cops and Forgotten," VICE News, December 12, 2017, news.vice.com/en/article/xwvv3a/shot-by-cops.

4. Before the American Civil War, Richmond not only was one of the South's few industrialized cities (and many of the city's enslaved were factory workers) but also was one of the South's most prominent slave-trading centers. See Midori Takagi, *Rearing Wolves to Our Own Destruction: Slavery in Richmond, Virginia, 1782–1865* (Charlottesville: University of Virginia Press, 1999); and Edward E. Baptist, *The Half Has Never Been Told* (New York: Basic Books, 2016).

5. Stephen V. Ash, *Rebel Richmond: Life and Death in the Confederate Capital* (Chapel Hill: University of North Carolina Press, 2019); Margaret Edds, *What the Eyes Can't See: Ralph Northam, Black Resolve, and a Racial Reckoning in Virginia* (Columbia: University of South Carolina Press, 2022).

6. Julian Maxwell Hayter, *The Dream Is Lost: Voting Rights and the Politics of Race in Richmond, Virginia* (Lexington: University Press of Kentucky, 2017), 2; Edmund Morgan, *American Slavery, American Freedom: The Ordeal of Colonial Virginia* (New York: Norton, 1975).

7. For a remarkable study of Reconstruction era Richmond, including the brief emergence of a progressive multiracial coalition, see Peter Rachleff, *Black Labor in Richmond, 1865–1890* (Urbana: University of Illinois Press, 1989).

8. For more on life during the formative stages of Jim Crow segregation in Richmond, see Blair L. M. Kelley, *Right to Ride: Streetcar Boycotts and African American Citizenship in the Era of* Plessy v. Ferguson (Chapel Hill: University of North Carolina Press, 2010); and Raymond Gavins, *The Perils and Prospects of Southern Black Leadership: Gordon Blaine Hancock, 1884–1970* (Durham, NC: Duke University Press, 1977).

9. Interracialism among Virginia's Black and white elites was shaped by the "lingering paternalism" left over from the antebellum period and by what remained of it after the Civil War. For more on interracial cooperation in Richmond and Virginia, see Clayton McClure Brooks, *The Uplift Generation: Cooperation across the Color Line in Early Twentieth-Century Virginia* (Charlottesville: University of Virginia Press, 2017). On eugenics and social control in Virginia, see Elizabeth Catte, *Pure America: Eugenics and the Making of Modern America* (Cleveland: Belt Publishing, 2021); and Pippa Holloway, *Sexuality, Politics, and Social Control in Virginia, 1920–1945* (Chapel Hill: University of North Carolina Press, 2006).

10. Brent Tarter, *The Grandees of Government: The Origins and Persistence of Undemocratic Politics in Virginia* (Charlottesville: University of Virginia Press, 2013), 7.

11. See, for example, John V. Moeser and Rutledge M. Dennis, *The Politics of Annexation: Oligarchic Power in a Southern City* (Cambridge, MA: Schenkman, 1982); Christopher Silver, *Twentieth-Century Richmond: Planning, Politics, and Race* (Knoxville: University of Tennessee Press, 1984); Benjamin Campbell, *Richmond's Unhealed History* (Richmond: Brandylane, 2011); Hayter, *Dream Is Lost*; and Thad Williamson with John V. Moeser, *Mayor's Anti-Poverty Commission Report*, City of Richmond, January 18, 2013, www.rva.gov/sites/default/files/2019-10/Antipovertycommissionfinal1_17_2013c--printready.pdf.

12. The legacy of white paternalism and African American resistance to paternalism outlived the segregated system. Marvin Chiles argues that the road to contemporary Richmond was paved by paternalistic yet misguided intentions. On this account, Richmond's current issues of housing, income, and educational inequality are not the result of malicious planning by white elites and African American political leadership. Rather, they are the result of misguided reforms and the continuity of paternalism in the late twentieth century. For more on racial resistance in Richmond and its relationship to the present, see Marvin T. Chiles, *The Struggle for Change: Race and the Politics of Reconciliation in Modern Richmond* (Charlottesville: University of Virginia Press, 2023).

13. The continuity of American racism has forced scholars to reimagine the legacy of the American civil rights movement, especially its political implications. For more on the political legacy of the movement, see Jesse H. Rhodes, *Ballot Blocked: The Political Erosion of the Voting Rights Act* (Stanford: Stanford University Press, 2017).

14. On Confederate statuary, see Karen L. Cox, *No Common Ground: Confederate Monuments and the Ongoing Fight for Racial Justice* (Chapel Hill: University of North Carolina Press, 2021).

15. For more on the local implications of Jim Crow segregation in the twentieth century, see Thomas W. Hanchett, *Sorting Out the New South City: Race, Class, and Urban Development in Charlotte, 1875–1975* (Chapel Hill: University of North Carolina Press, 1998); Tracy E. K'Meyer, *Civil Rights in the Gateway to the South: Louisville, Kentucky, 1945–1980*

(Lexington: University Press of Kentucky, 2009); Leonard N. Moore, *Black Rage in New Orleans: Police Brutality and African American Activism from World War II to Hurricane Katrina* (Baton Rouge: Louisiana State University Press, 2010); William Graves and Heather A. Smith, *Charlotte, NC: The Global Evolution of a New South City* (Athens: University of Georgia Press, 2010); Steven Estes, *Charleston in Black and White: Race and Power in the South after the Civil Rights Movement* (Chapel Hill: University of North Carolina Press, 2015); and Maurice J. Hobson, *The Legend of the Black Mecca: Politics and Class in the Making of Modern Atlanta* (Chapel Hill: University of North Carolina Press, 2017).

16. For more on what segregation means to the current era, see Paul A. Jargowsky, "The Persistence of Segregation in the 21st Century," *Minnesota Journal of Law and Inequality* 36, no. 2 (July 2018), 207–30.

17. On urban politics and altitudinal implications of segregation, see Lawrence T. Brown, *The Black Butterfly: The Harmful Politics of Race and Space in America* (Baltimore: Johns Hopkins University Press, 2021); and Richard Rothstein, *The Color of Law: A Forgotten History of How Our Government Segregated America* (New York: Liveright, 2017).

18. For review of the epochal legal conflicts following Richmond's 1970 partial annexation of Chesterfield County, culminating in the establishment of single-member council districts and the election of the first majority-Black council in 1977, see City of Richmond v. United States, 422 U.S. 358 (1975), and Moeser and Dennis, *The Politics of Annexation*.

19. This study focuses on the period between 1988, when Roy West, the second Black mayor under the councilmanic system established in 1977, was voted out of the position, and 2016, the end of the second term of Dwight C. Jones, the second mayor under the new system established by the political reform of 2004.

20. David Armitage, "In Defense of Presentism," in *History and Human Flourishing*, ed. Darrin M. McMahon (New York: Oxford University Press, 2020), 44–69, accessed January 19, 2021, https://scholar.harvard.edu/files/armitage/files/in_defence_of_presentism.pdf.

21. In 2021, Richmond formally established an "Equity Agenda" encompassing ten distinct policy areas. See "The Richmond Equity Agenda," City of Richmond website, accessed October 13, 2022, www.rva.gov/rvaequity.

22. Blaming African American representatives for problems created by segregationists was not specific to Richmond. For more on the shadow of segregation and who paid the cost, see H. Paul Friesema, "Black Control of Central Cities: The Hollow Prize," *Journal of the American Institute of Planners* 35, no. 2 (1969), 75–79; Hayter, *Dream Is Lost*, chap. 4; and Clarence N. Stone, *Regime Politics: Governing Atlanta, 1946–1988* (Lawrence: University Press of Kansas, 1989).

23. "Race, Space and Power in Richmond, Virginia," Virginia Commonwealth University Office of Health Equity, accessed June 22, 2023, https://healthequity.vcu.edu/history-and-health-program/learning-modules/race-space-and-power-in-richmond-virginia/.

24. U.S. Census Bureau, County Population Totals, 2010–19, accessed March 19, 2024, www.census.gov/data/datasets/time-series/demo/popest/2010s-counties-total.html; and Metropolitan and Micropolitan Statistical Areas Total, 2010–19, accessed March 19, 2024, www.census.gov/data/tables/time-series/demo/popest/2010s-total-metro-and-micro-statistical-areas.html. Wherever feasible, 2016 data is cited here and elsewhere throughout the book as the cutoff date for this study. We comment on some of the most recent trends in Richmond in chapter 6 (demographic change) and in the conclusion.

25. These localities include the independent cities of Richmond, Petersburg, Hopewell, and Colonial Heights and Amelia, Caroline, Charles City, Chesterfield, Dinwiddie, Goochland, Hanover, Henrico, King William, New Kent, Powhatan, Prince George, and Sussex Counties.

26. U.S. Census Bureau, American Community Survey, 2012–16, five-year estimates for population and poverty rate, accessed March 19, 2024, via Social Explorer, www.socialexplorer.com/tables/ACS2016_5yr.

27. U.S. Census Bureau, American Community Survey, 2012–16, five-year estimates for race, accessed March 19, 2024, via Social Explorer, www.socialexplorer.com/tables/ACS2016_5yr.

28. For more on the inequalities between suburban and urban life in the South, see Matthew D. Lassiter, *The Silent Majority: Suburban Politics in the Sunbelt South* (Princeton, NJ: Princeton University Press, 2006); and Mark H. Rose and Raymond A. Mohl, *Interstate: Highway Politics and Policy since 1939* (Knoxville: University of Tennessee Press, 2012).

29. In Virginia, local governments are limited to the powers specifically granted to them by the General Assembly, an arrangement known as the Dillon Rule. Should cities or counties seek to enact innovative public policies, those policies require statewide approval from the General Assembly. For more on the Dillon Rule, see Tartar, *Grandees of Government*, 386; and Tabler v. Fairfax County, 221 Va. 200 (1980).

30. For more on the process of defining cities and how that process has changed and continues to change over time, see R. Adam Dastrup, *Introduction to Human Geography* (Montreal: Pressbooks, 2019); and "Defining Cities and Urban Centers," accessed June 23, 2023, via Oklahoma State Libraries, https://open.library.okstate.edu/culturalgeography/chapter/6-1/.

31. Commonly referred to as the "hollow prize problem," experts hold that minority mayors assumed political control of cities that were beginning to show the deepening effects of deindustrialization, white flight, declining tax bases, rising blight, and the like. These mayors too struggled to meet these challenges and were often pathologized in local and national media for failing to resolve these (and other) issues. Neil Kraus and Todd Swanstrom, "Minority Mayors and the Hollow Prize Problem," *PS: Political Science and Politics* 34, no. 1 (March 2001): 99–105.

32. The complexities of coming to terms with the continuity of segregation ran well into and beyond the twentieth century. Marvin Chiles argues that because urban revitalization in Richmond was most often profit-driven and shaped by the economic "thinking that created disparate levels of white corporate wealth and black urban poverty, it is bound to exacerbate systemic racism." Marvin T. Chiles, "'Here We Go Again': Race and Redevelopment in Downtown Richmond, Virginia, 1977–Present," *Journal of Urban History* 49, no. 1 (January 2023): 133–59.

33. School board member Maurice Henderson put it this way in 2010, after citing the "bimodal distribution of economic prosperity in the city" as Richmond's biggest challenge: "We have two very separate populations, not separated by race, but by economic acquisition. Or ability to make income, or to hold and retain wealth . . . one with, and one without, just to be very clear here." Maurice Henderson, interview with Lucas Hakkenberg and Thad Williamson, November 11, 2010.

34. U.S. Census Bureau, American Community Survey, 2012–16, five-year estimates for poverty and household income.

35. See Katrin Anacker, ed., *The New American Suburb: Poverty, Race, and the Economic Crisis* (New York: Routledge, 2016); Dylan Gottlieb, "'Closer to Heaven': Race and Diversity in Suburban America," *Journal of Urban History* 41, no. 5 (September 2015): 927–35.

36. The historiography of urban planning and its racist implications is decades old. See, for example, Stone, *Regime Politics*; Friesema, "Black Control of Central Cities"; and Kraus and Swanstrom, "Minority Mayors and the Hollow Prize Problem." See also Brian D. Boyer, *Cities Destroyed for Cash: The FHA Scandal at HUD* (Chicago: Follett, 1973); Brown, *Black Butterfly*; Juliet Gainsborough, *Fenced Off: The Suburbanization of American Politics* (Washington: Georgetown University Press, 2001); Lassiter, *Silent Majority*; Thad Williamson, *Sprawl, Justice, and Citizenship: The Civic Costs of the American Way of Life* (New York: Oxford University Press, 2010); and Keeanga-Yamahtta Taylor, *Race for Profit: How Banks and Real Estate Undermined Black Homeownership* (Chapel Hill: University of North Carolina Press, 2021).

37. Much has been made about Richmond's urban history in light of New Deal housing policies. See Campbell, *Richmond's Unhealed History*; and Hayter, *Dream Is Lost*, chap. 1.

38. The moratorium on city-county lines in Virginia was originally intended to be temporary—policymakers in the commonwealth, who have favored county autonomy over city expansion since the 1970s, have extended the provision every time the moratorium is set to expire. For anti-urbanism in Virginia's General Assembly, see Andrew V. Sorrell and Bruce A. Vlk, "Virginia's Never-Ending Moratorium on City-County Annexations," *Virginia News Letter* 88, no. 1 (2012): 1–9.

39. Ronald L. Heinemann, John G. Kolp, Anthony S. Parent Jr., and William G. Shade, *Old Dominion, New Commonwealth: A History of Virginia, 1607–2007* (Charlottesville: University of Virginia Press, 2007), 365–67.

40. In 2014, Virginia ranked forty-ninth in the amount of cash and food benefits provided through safety net programs, accounting for state differences in cost of living. See "State Safety Net Interactive," Brookings, accessed February 29, 2024, www.brookings.edu/articles/state-safety-net-interactive/. In the legislative sessions of 2020 and 2021, Virginia's General Assembly demonstrated a much more assertive progressivism on a wide range of issues, from criminal justice to voting rights to public sector collective bargaining. Those initiatives did not coalesce into a large-scale plan to dramatically assist Richmond or other cities but showed the possibility of bold state action on a range of issues given favorable political circumstances.

41. Richard Schragger, "The Legal Status of Virginia's Cities and Implications for Policy" (Policy History Conference, Richmond, Virginia, June 6, 2012); Richard Schragger and C. Alex Retzloff, "The Failure of Home Rule Reform in Virginia: Race, Localism, and the Constitution of 1971," Virginia Public Law and Legal Theory Research Paper No. 2020-35, April 13, 2020, https://papers.ssrn.com/sol3/papers.cfm?abstract_id=3574765.

42. See Moeser and Dennis, *Politics of Annexation*.

43. Carmen Francine Foster, "Tension, Resistance, and Transition: School Desegregation in Richmond's North Side, 1960–63" (PhD diss., University of Virginia, 2014).

44. Robbins L. Gates, *The Making of Massive Resistance: Virginia's Politics of Public School Desegregation, 1954–1956* (Chapel Hill: University of North Carolina Press, 1964); Matthew D. Lassiter and Andrew B. Lewis, eds., *The Moderates' Dilemma: Massive Resistance to School Desegregation in Virginia* (Charlottesville: University of Virginia Press, 1998).

45. Robert A. Pratt, *The Color of Their Skin: Education and Race in Richmond, Virginia, 1954–89* (Charlottesville: University of Virginia Press, 1992).

46. Hayter, *Dream Is Lost*, 36; U.S. Census 1950 and 1960, accessed February 29, 2024, via Social Explorer, www.socialexplorer.com/tables/C1950CompDS and www.socialexplorer.com/tables/C1960CountyDS.

47. See Pratt, *Color of Their Skin*, for a detailed account.

48. The Supreme Court issued a 4–4 decision upholding the lower court's judgment. (The ninth justice—Richmond native and former city school board chairman Lewis Powell—recused himself from the case.) The legal reasoning of the court in the Richmond case was upheld in Detroit's *Milliken v. Bradley*; the court majority found that unless suburban school systems were created for the explicit purpose of fostering racial segregation, courts had no civil rights basis for compelling school systems within a metropolitan area to merge. Dissenting justice Thurgood Marshall predicted that the decision would perpetuate a two-tiered system of public education in the United States. Lassiter, *Silent Majority*, chap. 11. See also Milliken v. Bradley, 418 U.S. 717 (1974).

49. Thad Williamson and Amy Howard, "People Power," *Style Weekly*, July 12, 2011.

50. See Hayter, *Dream Is Lost*.

51. See Rob Corcoran, *Trustbuilding: An Honest Conversation on Race, Reconciliation, and Responsibility* (Charlottesville: University of Virginia Press, 2010).

52. Jacqueline Homann, "Get to Know America's Midsize Cities," Metro Ideas Project, February 10, 2016, https://metroideas.org/blog/get-to-know-americas-midsize-cities/.

53. U.S. Census Bureau, Metropolitan and Micropolitan Statistical Areas Population Tables and Components of Change, 2010–19, accessed February 29, 2024, www2.census.gov/programs-surveys/popest/datasets/2010-2019/metro/totals/cbsa-est2019-alldata.csv.

54. See Williamson, *Sprawl, Justice, and Citizenship*.

55. Jack Trammell, *The Richmond Slave Trade: The Economic Backbone of the Old Dominion* (Charleston: History Press, 2012).

56. See Moeser and Dennis, *Politics of Annexation*; Pratt, *Color of Their Skin*; James Ryan, *Five Miles Away, a World Apart: One City, Two Schools, and the Story of Educational Opportunity in Modern America* (New York: Oxford University Press, 2010); and Campbell, *Richmond's Unhealed History*.

57. This account is strongly influenced by John Rawls, *A Theory of Justice* (Cambridge, MA: Harvard University Press, 1971), and is also consonant with the revision of Rawls put forward recently by Danielle Allen, *Justice by Means of Democracy* (Chicago: University of Chicago Press, 2023). For other, related discussions of justice in urban contexts, see Susan Fainstein, *The Just City* (Ithaca: Cornell University Press, 2010); Williamson, *Sprawl, Justice, and Citizenship*; and Clarissa Hayward and Todd Swanstrom, eds., *Justice and the American Metropolis* (Minneapolis: University of Minnesota Press, 2011).

58. On the Lost Cause narrative in Richmond, see, among others, Matthew Mace Barbee, *Race and Masculinity in Southern Memory: History of Richmond, Virginia's Monument Avenue, 1948–1996* (Lanham, MD: Lexington Books, 2013).

CHAPTER 2

1. City of Richmond v. United States, 422 U.S. 358 (1975); for a detailed and authoritative account of these events, see John V. Moeser and Rutledge M. Dennis, *The Politics of Annexation: Oligarchic Power in a Southern City* (Cambridge, MA: Schenkman, 1982). Some 45,700 of the new residents were white. See also Lelia Barghouty, "How the Former

Confederate Capital Slashed Black Voting Power, Overnight," *Washington Post*, July 17, 2023.

2. Moeser and Dennis, *Politics of Annexation*; Julian Maxwell Hayter, *The Dream Is Lost: Voting Rights and the Politics of Race in Richmond, Virginia* (Lexington: University Press of Kentucky, 2017).

3. Maurice J. Hobson, *The Legend of the Black Mecca: Politics and Class in the Making of Modern Atlanta* (Chapel Hill: University of North Carolina Press, 2017); Clarence N. Stone, *Regime Politics: Governing Atlanta, 1946–1988* (Lawrence: University Press of Kansas, 1989).

4. Marvin T. Chiles, *The Struggle for Change: Race and the Politics of Reconciliation in Modern Richmond* (Charlottesville: University of Virginia Press, 2023), chap. 2.

5. See H. Paul Friesema, "Black Control of Central Cities: The Hollow Prize," *Journal of the American Institute of Planners* 35, no. 2 (1969): 75–79, for early use of the term in this context.

6. Moeser and Dennis, *Politics of Annexation*. For more on the dilemma of vote dilution that followed the Voting Rights Act of 1965, see J. Morgan Kousser, *Colorblind Injustice: Minority Voting Rights and the Undoing of the Second Reconstruction* (Chapel Hill: University of North Carolina Press, 1999); and Richard M. Valelly, *The Two Reconstructions: The Struggle for Black Enfranchisement* (Chicago: University of Chicago Press, 2004).

7. Chiles, *Struggle for Change*, chap. 2; and Hayter, *Dream Is Lost*, chap. 3.

8. Hayter, *Dream Is Lost*, chap. 4.

9. Marvin T. Chiles, "'Tough on Conduct': Punitive Leadership in Urban Public Schools; A Case Study of *Angry Principal* Dr. Roy A. West, 1986–1991," *Spectrum: A Journal on Black Men* 8, no. 1 (Fall 2020): 55–85; Hayter, *Dream Is Lost*, chaps. 4 and 5.

10. The Court ruled the contracting set-asides unconstitutional in City of Richmond v. J. A. Croson Co., 488 U.S. 469 (1989). On West's tenure as mayor, see Hayter, *Dream Is Lost*, chap. 5.

11. Robert Goldblum, "Henry Marsh's Unfinished Business," *Style Weekly*, November 1, 1988.

12. See Stone, *Regime Politics*.

13. Peter Hardin, "City's Set-Aside Program Struck Down—Rigid Quotas Held Unjustified," *Richmond Times-Dispatch*, January 23, 1989. See also W. Avon Drake and Robert D. Holsworth, *Affirmative Action and the Stalled Quest for Black Progress* (Urbana: University of Illinois Press, 1996), for detailed discussion.

14. City of Richmond v. J. A. Croson Co., 488 U.S. 469 (1989).

15. Prior to the *Croson* decision, Marsh had remarked, "If cities like Richmond can't have set asides, it means that a critical phase of the civil rights movement will have a big setback. The right to equal opportunity in housing, in education and in voting—all of those are influenced by economics. If you don't have money, you don't have all the opportunities in education, you can't buy a house, you can't elect officials in some cases." Goldblum, "Henry Marsh's Unfinished Business."

16. Arthur Hodges, "Interview: Bill Leidinger Talks about the Tax Issue," *Style Weekly*, March 6, 1990.

17. See table 2.1.

18. See Robert A. Pratt, *The Color of Their Skin: Education and Race in Richmond, Virginia, 1954–89* (Charlottesville: University of Virginia Press, 1992).

19. Jeanne Cummings, "Won't Seek Mayorship, West Says," *Richmond Times-Dispatch*, June 29, 1988. In stepping aside, West also noted that the demands on the job of mayor far exceeded the part-time ceremonial role provided for in the city charter.

20. Jeanne Cummings, "Madame Mayor—Mrs. Williams Pledges to Do What's Best for Richmond," *Richmond Times-Dispatch*, July 2, 1988; Robert Goldblum, "Mayor's Role Downplayed under Williams?," *Style Weekly*, July 19, 1988.

21. Robert Holsworth, "Council Elections: Where Are the Issues?," *Style Weekly*, May 10, 1988.

22. Robert Holsworth, "Toward a Richmond Political Renaissance," *Style Weekly*, August 23, 1988.

23. Goldblum, "Mayor's Role Downplayed under Williams?"

24. Tom Campbell, "New Manager Plans to Make Things Happen in Richmond," *Richmond Times-Dispatch*, July 20, 1986.

25. In assessments provided for reporters one year into Bobb's tenure, Mayor Roy A. West praised Bobb's management as "visionary in nature and deeply rooted in substance"; Fourth District representative Andrew J. Gillespie III stated, "Robert Bobb may be the finest manager in the country"; and Henry L. Marsh III said, "He deserves an excellent rating. His leadership has been creative, energetic, fair and highly professional." Jeanne Cummings, "Attitudes, Not Projects, Have Tested Bobb," *Richmond Times-Dispatch*, July 23, 1987.

26. Gordon Hickey, "Bobb Leaves His Legacy—Departing Manager Still Harbors Big Dreams for Richmond Projects," *Richmond Times-Dispatch*, November 10, 1997.

27. A positive 1994 *Style Weekly* profile of Bobb noted that with Henry Marsh moving on to the Virginia state senate, "Richmond is Bobb's government to lead. He knows the issues, the players and the limits of his office. As Bobb's Chief of Staff Joyce Wilson says, City Hall 'Is his organization.'" John W. Maloney, "Bobb's Drive," *Style Weekly*, June 21, 1994.

28. For further detail on Marsh's extensive career, see Henry L. Marsh III, *The Memoirs of Hon. Henry L. Marsh, III: Civil Rights Champion, Public Servant, Lawyer* (GrantHouse Publishers, 2018).

29. Hayter, *Dream Is Lost*, chap. 4; Goldblum, "Mayor's Role Downplayed under Williams?"

30. Bruce Potter, "Five Issues Critical to the City's Future Will Be Studied," *Richmond Times-Dispatch*, September 13, 1990.

31. Richmond Tomorrow, *Citizen's Report: A Strategic Plan for Richmond's Future* (City of Richmond, June 1991).

32. Richmond Tomorrow, *Citizen's Report*; Michael Paul Williams, "Task Force Offers Vision for the City," *Richmond Times-Dispatch*, June 25, 1991.

33. Williams, "Task Force Offers Vision for the City."

34. Susan Betts, "Robert Bobb: A Mechanic of Government," *Style Weekly*, November 10, 1992.

35. Speaking in 2010, community activist Rob Corcoran, a longtime leader of Hope in the Cities (one of the few multiracial civic organizations in Richmond at the time), contrasted the attitudinal progress in Richmond with respect to race with lack of progress in addressing the structural and policy dimensions of racialized inequality in the Richmond region. "Broadly speaking there is a more mature understanding of race relations than there was twenty years ago. There is no question about that. . . . But in general, if you

take the whole big picture, there has been no significant structural change or significant change, I don't think, in the continuing disparities of race and class and the way our regional school systems are set up." Rob Corcoran, interview with Lucas Hakkenberg and Thad Williamson, July 16, 2010.

36. Robert Goldblum, "In the Eye of the Storm," *Style Weekly*, September 6, 1988. Hassell elaborated his views in a September 1988 interview in the aftermath of a major schools controversy (see chapter 4):

> The position I take offends a lot of people, though there are a lot of blacks who share the same vision I do. But there are a lot of people who feel that because the city is 50 percent black, it's ours to do with what we please. That attitude is not healthy if you care about the city's financial future.... If you view the city as a black city or a white city, you'll never be able to attract business here. But that improves the tax base, which, in turn, improves Council's ability to fund the schools. The best way to improve the plight of poor people, both black and white, is to improve public education.

37. The other member of the original majority-Black council, Claudette McDaniel, controversially defected from the Marsh coalition in the late 1980s. McDaniel would be unseated in the 1990 election. Paul Bradley, "Pair Took Different Paths to Council—They Step Down from Shared Ground," *Richmond Times-Dispatch*, June 25, 1990.

38. *Richmond Free Press*, January 16–18, 1992. Statement by publisher Raymond Boone.

39. Williams subsequently won the Pulitzer Prize in 2021 for coverage of the events of summer 2020 in Richmond. See "The 2021 Pulitzer Prize Winner in Commentary" on the Pulitzer Prizes website, accessed August 24, 2023, www.pulitzer.org/winners/michael-paul-williams-richmond-va-times-dispatch.

40. Sue Miles Nevitt, "The Power and the Politics of Reverend Jones," *Style Weekly*, June 26, 1990.

41. Holsworth, "Toward a Richmond Political Renaissance"; see also Robert D. Holsworth, *Let Your Life Speak: A Study of Politics, Religion, and Antinuclear Weapons Activism* (Madison: University of Wisconsin Press, 1989).

42. Arthur Hodges, "Being There: At the Election of the Mayor," *Style Weekly*, July 10, 1990; Paul Bradley, "New Faces, New Mayor, New Suit Open Council Session—Thompson Shows Flair for Drama," *Richmond Times-Dispatch*, July 3, 1990.

43. "Mayor Kenney?" (staff editorial), *Richmond Times-Dispatch*, June 28, 1990.

44. Lisa Antonelli Bacon, "Councilman John Thompson," *Style Weekly*, December 4, 1990.

45. Sue Robinson, "1990 Richmonder of the Year," *Style Weekly*, January 8, 1991 (profile of Cheek).

46. Rob Corcoran, *Trustbuilding: An Honest Conversation on Race, Reconciliation, and Responsibility* (Charlottesville: University of Virginia Press, 2010).

47. *Mayor's Redistricting Advisory Committee Final Report*, City of Richmond, July 6, 2011, table 2 (listing voter turnout by district and citywide in council elections from 1977 to 2008), https://web.archive.org/web/20151017170042/http://www.richmondgov.com/CommissionAntiPoverty/documents/RedistrictingPresentation070611.pdf.

48. W. Avon Drake, "Challenge to Richmond's Black Leadership: Strategy Urgently Needed to Help the Poor in the Inner City," *Richmond Free Press*, April 30–May 2, 1992.

49. Drake, "Challenge to Richmond's Black Leadership."

50. Drake, "Challenge to Richmond's Black Leadership." See also Drake and Holsworth, *Affirmative Action and the Stalled Quest for Black Progress.*

51. Drake, "Challenge to Richmond's Black Leadership."

52. James A. Crupi, *Back to the Future: Richmond at the Crossroads* (Strategic Leadership Solutions, Inc., 1993), 3.

53. Crupi, *Back to the Future,* 3–5.

54. Crupi, *Back to the Future,* 6–10.

55. Crupi, *Back to the Future,* 9–11.

56. Crupi, *Back to the Future,* 15.

57. Crupi, *Back to the Future,* 18.

58. Crupi, *Back to the Future,* 19–23.

59. Crupi, *Back to the Future,* 23–24.

60. Crupi, *Back to the Future,* 18–19.

61. "Crupi Returns" (staff editorial), *Richmond Free Press,* January 6–8, 1994.

62. Gordon Hickey, "Morrissey Rebuked for Courthouse Brawl," *Richmond Times-Dispatch,* March 3, 1992.

63. "Democratic Primary Set for City Offices," *Richmond Times-Dispatch,* February 17, 1993; Alan Cooper, "Ministers Endorse Hicks as Prosecutor—Conference Backed Morrissey in 1989," *Richmond Times-Dispatch,* March 9, 1993; "Morrissey Counters Hicks Support," *Richmond Free Press,* April 29–May 1, 1993. Hicks had resigned his position in the Commonwealth's Attorney's office the previous summer.

64. David M. Hicks, interview with Amy Howard and Thad Williamson, August 15, 2011.

65. Alan Cooper, "Hicks Wins Primary with 63%—GOP Crossover Vote Said to Help Challenger," *Richmond Times-Dispatch,* June 9, 1993; Mike Allen, "Indictments 'Catastrophic,'" *Richmond Times-Dispatch,* June 9, 1993; "Joe Morrissey Timeline," *Richmond Times-Dispatch,* June 30, 2014.

66. Hazel Trice Edney, "Showdown at City Hall: Bobb v. Council in Power Fight," *Richmond Free Press,* August 20–22, 1992. The meeting took place on September 3, 1992; see Hazel Trice Edney, "What Happened Behind Closed Doors," *Richmond Free Press,* September 10–12, 1992.

67. Edney, "Showdown at City Hall."

68. The editorialists added, "Indeed, in the past, there were questions about whether council was aware that it was Mr. Bobb's boss. Or whether council possessed the ability to lead. This being the case, what young, reasonably bright and ambitious executive wouldn't recognize the leadership void and exploit it to the maximum?" "Showdown" (staff editorial), *Richmond Free Press,* August 20–22, 1992.

69. "The Next Step for City Hall" (staff editorial), *Richmond Free Press,* September 10–12, 1992; "Just Clean It Up" (staff editorial), *Richmond Free Press,* November 12–14, 1992; "City Hall Darling" (staff editorial), *Richmond Free Press,* May 12–14, 1994.

70. Doug Sease, "City Should Give Thanks to Bobb" (letter), *Richmond Free Press,* September 10–12, 1992.

71. Mike Allen, "Contracts Policy Changes Sought—Goal Is to Increase Hiring of Minorities," *Richmond Times-Dispatch,* January 4, 1994.

72. Hazel Trice Edney, "Bobb, at NAACP Forum, Catches It on the Chin Again," *Richmond Free Press*, January 20–22, 1994.

73. "Bobb Wins on Waivers," *Richmond Free Press*, March 17–19, 1994.

74. Hazel Trice Edney, "City Rights Unit: Bobb 'Gutted' Us," *Richmond Free Press*, December 8–10, 1994; Gordon Hickey, "Bias Panel Budget Decried," *Richmond Times-Dispatch*, December 10, 1994.

75. John W. Maloney, "Who's Running and Why You Should Care," *Style Weekly*, April 26, 1994.

76. Maloney, "Who's Running." Added Moeser: "What we desperately need in this city are political coalitions that cut across race, where blacks and whites together support candidates that represent a point of view. . . . That's what makes democracy."

77. "Looking Back and Ahead," interview with Doug Wilder by Raymond Boone, *Richmond Free Press*, March 17–19, 1994.

78. "Crusade Backs Only 1 Incumbent," *Richmond Free Press*, March 24–26, 1994.

79. "Crusade Endorsements" (staff editorial), *Richmond Free Press*, March 31–April 2, 1994. Marty Jewell elaborated on this theme in a subsequent letter. "When one looks at a black majority government, you would think that the paramount aim of the elected officials would be to serve those who put them in office and to end unfair policies. Why else elect them? The great preponderance of African Americans in this city, though, seem to be losing ground." Marty Jewell, "Crusade: Time for a New City Council" (letter), *Richmond Free Press*, April 7–9, 1994.

80. John W. Maloney, "For the Record—Mayor to Amend Campaign Reports, Ukrops Fueled Crusade," *Style Weekly*, September 20, 1994.

81. A. Peter Bailey, "West Knew What Hit Him—but Kenney Didn't," *Richmond Free Press*, May 12–14, 1994.

82. Terone Green, "People Power Elected New Council" (letter), *Richmond Free Press*, May 19–21, 1994.

83. A. Peter Bailey, "The True Political Reality in Richmond," *Richmond Free Press*, May 19–21, 1994.

84. Gordon Hickey, "Moody's Cuts City's Bond Rating—Spending, Decision to Lower Tax Rate Cited," *Richmond Times-Dispatch*, May 27, 1994.

85. Leonidas Young, "Young: No Political Link to Marsh" (letter), *Richmond Free Press*, June 30–July 2, 1994.

86. Jeremy M. Lazarus, "'We Will Respect Citizens,'" *Richmond Free Press*, July 7–9, 1994.

87. "The 2nd District," *Style Weekly*, April 26, 1994 (candidate profiles). Earlier in 1994 Republican state delegate John Watkins of Chesterfield County had floated a proposal to create a regional governance structure focused on sanitation, utilities, and transportation—only to receive immediate pushback from county elected officials. Susan Winiecki, "Watkins Is Surprised by Agitation over Bill," *Richmond Times-Dispatch*, February 7, 1994.

88. "City Council's Principles—We Will Respect Citizens," *Richmond Free Press*, July 14–16, 1994 (reprint of Richmond City Council statement).

89. Shortly after its adoption, *Richmond Free Press* columnist Peter Bailey offered a cogent and prescient rejoinder to the council's statement of principles: "The statement as a whole sounds so good that it makes one's heart beat faster in anticipation, but it is sorely lacking in details. Council should understand that good intentions are simply not enough

and that, as cartoonist Ted Key once wrote, 'Ultimately we are judged by our actions, not our dreams.'" A. Peter Bailey, "City Council Will Be Judged on Actions, Not Dreams," *Richmond Free Press*, July 21–23, 1994.

CHAPTER 3

1. For more on Richmond politics in the 1990s, see Marvin T. Chiles, *The Struggle for Change: Race and the Politics of Reconciliation in Modern Richmond* (Charlottesville: University of Virginia Press, 2023), part 3.

2. Nelson Wikstrom, "Richmond: Implementation of and Experience with Strong-Mayor Form of Government," in *More Than Mayor or Manager: Campaigns to Change Form of Government in America's Large Cities*, ed. James H. Svara and Douglas J. Watson (Washington, DC: Georgetown University Press, 2010), 81–102. The mayor-council system that Richmond adopted in 2004 provided the mayor fewer specific powers than numerous "strong mayor" cities: the mayor's principal formal powers included (1) introducing the budget, (2) hiring (with council consent) and dismissing a chief administrative officer who in turn managed the city's business, and (3) a veto power on legislation, with the council being able to override with six votes (added in 2005).

3. For more on systems of local government, see Kathy Hayes and Semoon Chang, "The Relative Efficiency of City Manager and Mayor-Council Forms of Government," *Southern Economic Journal* 57, no. 1 (July 1990): 167–77; Kimberly L. Nelson and James H. Svara, "Form of Government Still Matters: Fostering Innovation in U.S. Municipal Governments," *American Review of Public Administration* 42, no. 3 (2012): 257–81; and National Civic League, *Model City Charter*, 9th ed. (Denver: National Civic League, 2021), www.nationalcivicleague.org/resources/model-city-charter-9th-edition/.

4. On Young, see Elizabeth A. DeVoss, "Making Richmond Greater: A Study of the Greater Richmond Community Corps" (honors thesis, Jepson School of Leadership Studies, University of Richmond, April 1995), 1; Robert Woodson, "Churches, Faith-Based and Other Neighborhood Groups: Can They Solve Our Social Problems?," *Vital Speeches of the Day: Chicago* 64, no. 22 (September 1998): 679–81; and Joey Matthews, "Pulpit to Politics: Remembering Leonidas B. Young II," *Richmond Free Press*, January 21–23, 2016.

5. Tina Eshelman, "Look Back: 'Murder Capital' No More," *Richmond Magazine*, January 29, 2020.

6. Panel members included Commonwealth's Attorney David Hicks; Rev. Dwight C. Jones (of First Baptist Church); city council members Viola Baskerville, Anthony Jones, and Tim Kaine; city manager Robert Bobb; school board chairman Melvin Law; chief Richmond circuit judge Robert Harris; Richard Gentry, executive director of the Richmond Redevelopment and Housing Authority; Dr. Eugene Trani, president of Virginia Commonwealth University; Dr. Allix James, retired president of Virginia Union University; Randolph McElroy of Nations Bank and Robert Norfleet of Crestar Bank; Rev. Robert Trache (of St. James's Episcopal Church); Robert Taylor (retired pastor, Fourth Baptist Church); Bernice Travers (mother of two homicide victims and president of the Northside Richmond Business Association); Thomas Hall (Virginia State University); Alvin Dyson (Richmond Crusade for Voters); and Blair Nelsen (school board, Second District). The *Richmond Free Press* initially criticized Young and Hicks for not including "ordinary citizens" on the panel. "No Ordinary Citizens from High-Crime Areas on City Crime Panel,"

Richmond Free Press, July 28–30, 1994; "4 New Members Named to City Crime Panel," *Richmond Free Press*, August 4–6, 1994.

7. Amy L. Howard and Thad Williamson, "Reframing Public Housing in Richmond, Virginia: Segregation, Resident Resistance, and the Future of Redevelopment," *Cities* 57 (September 2016): 33–39.

8. Hazel Trice Edney and Jeremy M. Lazarus, "Citizens Cry Out for Help—Bias, Neglect Blamed for Escalating Violence; City Hall Vows Action," *Richmond Free Press*, August 11–13, 1994.

9. Data provided by the Richmond Police Department also showed that 81 percent of "suspected or arrested offenders" in Richmond since 1987 were Black males. "Facts Related to Crime in City," *Richmond Free Press*, August 11–13, 1994.

10. Edney and Lazarus, "Citizens Cry Out for Help."

11. Hazel Trice Edney, "'Full Alert' against City Crime," *Richmond Free Press*, September 15–17, 1994.

12. Edney, "'Full Alert' against City Crime."

13. Jean E. Morris, "Drug Smuggling: The Source of Neighborhood Killings," *Richmond Free Press*, August 18–20, 1994; Gordon Hickey, "'Full Alert' Sounded for Troubled Areas," *Richmond Times-Dispatch*, August 11, 1994.

14. Jeremy M. Lazarus, "Brake on City Crime," *Richmond Free Press*, September 29–October 1, 1994.

15. "Police Officers Told to Reach Out," *Richmond Free Press*, July 21–23, 1994; Frank Green, "Reno Visits Gilpin Court—Weed and Seed Program Praised for Lowering Crime Levels," *Richmond Times-Dispatch*, July 18, 1994.

16. Goins v. Commonwealth, 470 S.E.2d 114 (1996); "The Manhunt," *Richmond Free Press*, October 20–22, 1994; Alan Cooper, "Tamika Jones Describes Killings—Key Witness Takes the Stand at Goins Trial," *Richmond Times-Dispatch*, June 13, 1995; Alan Cooper, "Jury: Death to Goins—Recommendation to Be Considered in Sentence," *Richmond Times-Dispatch*, June 15, 1995.

17. Hazel Trice Edney, "Fear Grips Gilpin," *Richmond Free Press*, November 17–19, 1994.

18. Jeremy M. Lazarus, "Tight Security for Tamika," *Richmond Free Press*, October 27–29, 1994.

19. Edney, "Fear Grips Gilpin." Quotations are Edney's paraphrase of Andrews's statement.

20. Edney, "Fear Grips Gilpin." Direct quotation of Andrews.

21. Wesley Byrd Carter, MD, "Love, Protect Our Children," *Richmond Free Press*, October 27–29, 1994.

22. "3,000 Say Goodbye to 6 Gilpin Court Victims," *Richmond Free Press*, October 27–29, 1994.

23. Jeremy M. Lazarus, "City Judge: Jobs the Key to Ending the Violence," *Richmond Free Press*, August 11–13, 1994.

24. Lazarus, "City Judge." Quotation is a paraphrase of Judge Alton's comments by reporter Jeremy Lazarus.

25. For more on Richardson, see Chuck Richardson, *Cease Fire! Cease Fire! Councilman Chuck, a Hero(in) Addiction* (Richmond: Chuck Richardson, 2021).

26. Gordon Hickey, "Richardson Seeks Help for Drug Use," *Richmond Times-Dispatch*, July 7, 1994.

27. Jeremy M. Lazarus, "New Group's Aim: To Oust Richardson," *Richmond Free Press*, July 21–23, 1994; "Our Political Culture" (staff editorial), *Richmond Free Press*, July 21–23, 1994; Gordon Hickey, "Richardson Keeps Office—Jury Won't Remove Him from Council," *Richmond Times-Dispatch*, September 24, 1994.

28. Gordon Hickey, "Richardson Resigns after Arrest; 18 Year Tenure on Council Comes to an End," *Richmond Times-Dispatch*, September 19, 1995; Mark Bowes and Deborah Kelly, "Richardson Resigns after Arrest—Videotape Shows Alleged Drug Deal, Case Sources Say," *Richmond Times-Dispatch*, September 19, 1995.

29. James Forman Jr., *Locking Up Our Own: Crime and Punishment in Black America* (New York: Farrar, Straus and Giroux, 2017).

30. Gordon Hickey, "Mayor Backs No-Parole Plan," *Richmond Times-Dispatch*, September 3, 1994.

31. Gordon Hickey, "City Plans to Put More Police on the Street," *Richmond Times-Dispatch*, September 13, 1994.

32. Hazel Trice Edney, "Yes to At-Large Mayor; No to Four-Year Terms," *Richmond Free Press*, November 9–11, 1995; Gordon Hickey, "Council Majority, Citizens Group for At-Large Mayor," *Richmond Times-Dispatch*, November 5, 1995. The at-large mayor proposal won support from nearly two-thirds of voters.

33. Jeff E. Schapiro and Gordon Hickey, "Governor Intervenes on Mayor—His Bill Calls for At-Large Vote in November," *Richmond Times-Dispatch*, February 17, 1996.

34. E. Martin Jewell, "At-Large Proposal Aims to Turn Back the Clock" (letter to the editor), *Richmond Free Press*, February 8–10, 1996.

35. The February 15–17, 1996, edition of the *Richmond Free Press* included a staff editorial as well as separate columns by L. Douglas Wilder and Roy West opposing the mayor proposal. Ironically, in light of subsequent developments, Wilder (in an apparent shot at Leonidas Young) called for an "end [to] the delusions of comparisons to a modern day 'Moses' sent to lead us from the 'wilderness.'" Wilder also stated that "care must be taken to ensure that the council-manager form of government, which has worked well for the city since its adoption, is not compromised or that a truly 'strong mayor' form of government is formed." Within a few years, Wilder adopted a very different position on that question. L. Douglas Wilder, "There's War within Our Ranks," *Richmond Free Press*, February 15–17, 1996.

36. Gordon Hickey, "Young Issues Challenge to Political Foes—He'll Withdraw If They Back At-Large Mayor Effort," *Richmond Times-Dispatch*, January 23, 1996; "Mayor Young Jumps Bad," *Richmond Free Press*, January 25–27, 1996.

37. "Amateur Hour" (editorial), *Richmond Free Press*, January 25–27, 1996.

38. Jeremy M. Lazarus, "At-Large Election Out for '96," *Richmond Free Press*, February 29–March 2, 1996; "At-Large Panel Named," *Richmond Free Press*, March 7–9, 1996.

39. Jeremy M. Lazarus, "Mayor's Campaign Falling Apart?," *Richmond Free Press*, April 25–27, 1996; "We Endorse 7 for a Winning City" (editorial), *Richmond Free Press*, May 2–4, 1996.

40. "We had so many people against him outside the community that we had to send a message from inside the community," stated the Reverend Alonzo Anderson, a Young ally. Commented another supporter, "Nobody runs Church Hill, but Church Hill." Hazel Trice Edney, "Mayor in Seventh Heaven," *Richmond Free Press*, May 9–11, 1996; Jeremy M. Lazarus, "The Results," *Richmond Free Press*, May 9–11, 1996.

41. "Baskerville, Kaine, Young Want Mayor's Job," *Richmond Free Press*, June 20–22, 1996; Tom Campbell, "Chavis to Be Next Mayor? He's Now Emerging as Compromise Choice," *Richmond Times-Dispatch*, June 30, 1996; Hazel Trice Edney, "Young's Exit from Mayor's Office," *Richmond Free Press*, July 3–5, 1996.

42. Jeremy M. Lazarus, "Mayor Chavis Tells Plans for City," *Richmond Free Press*, July 3–6, 1996. A 1994 *Times-Dispatch* editorial went so far as to describe Chavis as the council's "outstanding member," stating that Chavis had "the rare quality that defines true leadership—he never lets his ego interfere with the city's business." "Council Elections," *Richmond Times-Dispatch*, April 25, 1994. In 1993 Chavis called for a merger of city and county governments, winning praise from *Times-Dispatch* editorialists. "Insight and Guts" (staff editorial), *Richmond Times-Dispatch*, June 25, 1993.

43. Jeremy M. Lazarus, "Chavis Acknowledges Personal Challenges," *Richmond Free Press*, July 3–6, 1996; "Chavis Firm Reorganizing," *Richmond Times-Dispatch*, February 6, 1998.

44. Gordon Hickey, "Richmond's Mayor Won't Seek Re-election to Council—Chavis Cites Time, Money in Decision," *Richmond Times-Dispatch*, February 13, 1998. See also Gordon Hickey, "Three-Way Race for Mayor Deadlocked—Behind the Scenes Negotiating On for July 1," *Richmond Times-Dispatch*, June 21, 1998. Before stepping down, Chavis had a few parting words about the state of city hall. Provoked by the unwillingness of the regional Airport Commission to make a firm commitment to minority participation on contracts resulting from a $156 million expansion of the regional airport, Chavis claimed that the city had failed to make racial progress and, in some respects, had gone backward. Hazel Trice Edney, "Economic Bias in Area Saddens Mayor Chavis," *Richmond Free Press*, February 5–7, 1998; Hazel Trice Edney, "Mayor's Comments Spark Lively Debate on Economic Justice," *Richmond Free Press*, February 12–14, 1998.

45. Tom Campbell, "Joel Harris Gets 30 Months, $10,000 Fine—Offers Apology for Pain He Caused," *Richmond Times-Dispatch*, February 20, 1998; Tom Campbell, "Joel Harris, Wife Plead Guilty," *Richmond Times-Dispatch*, September 10, 1997.

46. Tom Campbell, "Young Enters Plea of Guilty—Councilman Resigns, Faces Sentencing May 4," *Richmond Times-Dispatch*, February 2, 1999. Young had been indicted in the fall of 1998 on a total of nineteen counts, including racketeering and money laundering; after Young pleaded guilty to four counts, the remaining charges were dropped.

47. Larry O'Dell, "Ex-Richmond Mayor Gets Two Years," AP Wire story, May 15, 1999.

48. Ned Oliver, "Leonidas B. Young II, Pastor and Former Richmond Mayor, Dies at 62," *Richmond Times-Dispatch*, January 21, 2016.

49. Hazel Trice Edney, "City Council's Broken Promises," *Richmond Free Press*, June 27–29, 1996, 7.

50. "27 Hopefuls Tell Why They Are Running," *Richmond Free Press*, April 30–May 2, 1998.

51. "27 Hopefuls Tell Why They Are Running."

52. "27 Hopefuls Tell Why They Are Running."

53. "27 Hopefuls Tell Why They Are Running."

54. Michael Paul Williams, "Voters Don't Buy All Big Spenders," *Richmond Times-Dispatch*, May 6, 1998. Commenting on results of the 1998 council elections, *Richmond Free Press* editorialists praised voters, noting that "they placed the quality of the candidate over race. That was underscored in the 8th, where Reva Trammell was elected the district's

first white representative. This is encouraging." "The Elections" (staff editorial), *Richmond Free Press*, May 7–9, 1998.

55. Jeremy M. Lazarus, "A Hot Issue: Race of Mayor," *Richmond Free Press*, June 25–27, 1998; Jeremy M. Lazarus, "Kaine, McCollum Team Up for City's Top Posts," *Richmond Free Press*, June 18–20, 1998.

56. "Kaine, McCollum for City's Top Spots" (staff editorial), *Richmond Free Press*, June 25–27, 1998.

57. Jeremy M. Lazarus, "Kaine, McCollum in Top Spots," *Richmond Free Press*, July 2–4, 1998.

58. The accounts in this chapter of the mayoral terms of Tim Kaine, L. Douglas Wilder, and Dwight C. Jones draw in part from Thad Williamson, "The Tangled Relationship of Democracy, Leadership, and Justice in Urban America: A View from Richmond," in *Good Democratic Leadership: On Prudence and Judgment in Modern Democracies*, ed. John Kane and Haig Patapan (New York: Oxford University Press, 2014), 32–50.

59. Jeremy M. Lazarus and Dorothy Rowley, "Council Interviews Jamison," *Richmond Free Press*, October 8–10, 1998.

60. Jeremy M. Lazarus, "Jamison Candidacy under Council Scrutiny," *Richmond Free Press*, October 15–17, 1998.

61. Jeremy M. Lazarus, "'Excited' Jamison Ready to Go—Controversial Candidate Wins 8–1 Vote," *Richmond Free Press*, November 25–28, 1998.

62. Gordon Hickey, "City Net Didn't Come Up Brimming—Leaks, Racial Factor Cited in Manager Search," *Richmond Times-Dispatch*, December 27, 1998. Sources told reporter Gordon Hickey that some potential white candidates had declined to apply on the assumption the council would hire a Black candidate, and Mayor Kaine said some promising candidates feared having their names leaked, jeopardizing their current employment.

63. Indeed, Calvin Jamison's workweek typically started with a 7:30 a.m. meeting with Kaine. Gordon Hickey, "Taking Control: Calvin Jamison Tackles City Manager Job Piece by Piece," *Richmond Times-Dispatch*, October 10, 1999. As Kaine prepared to exit the role in September 2001, former city manager Robert Bobb observed, "Mayor Kaine proved that you didn't have to necessarily change the city charter to effectively have a strong mayor in a council-manager system." Jeremy Redmon, "Leadership on the Line—Jamison Up for a Raise, but Criticisms Also Put Him on the Spot," *Richmond Times-Dispatch*, September 10, 2001. A 2002 article about economic development efforts published emails from Kaine to Jamison and other officials (from 2001) that provided an example of Kaine exerting mayoral authority: Kaine wrote, "Justified or not, we are getting a reputation from some of our key economic stakeholders for not being able to take decisive action on important project proposals. . . . I think that we need to have an internal rule that we will NEVER receive written proposals without establishing a very specific timetable for providing [a] written response and then taking prompt action." Jeremy Redmon, "Advice: Retract Offer to Cordish—Emails Reveal Doubts about Canal Project," *Richmond Times-Dispatch*, August 4, 2002.

64. Gordon Hickey, "Kaine Upbeat on State of City—Downtown Projects, Crime Drop Cited," *Richmond Times-Dispatch*, January 11, 2000. A 2005 assessment amid Kaine's (successful) campaign for governor stressed Kaine's primacy in policymaking, in contrast to the Bobb era, and emphasized that he treated the position as a full-time job. "There was no question that Tim was quarterback," stated Commonwealth's Attorney David Hicks. Melissa Scott Sinclair, "Is Kaine Able?," *Style Weekly*, October 12, 2005.

65. For more on the Richmond Slave Trail Commission, see City of Richmond website, accessed September 30, 2023, www.rva.gov/slave-trail-commission/richmond-city-council-slave-trail-commission. The resolution creating the commission in July 1998 was brought forward by new council member Sa'ad El-Amin and passed unanimously. Gordon Hickey, "Plight of Slaves to Be Memorialized," *Richmond Times-Dispatch*, July 14, 1988.

66. Alan Cooper, "$100 Million Is Awarded in Bias Case—Nationwide Insurance Plans Appeal," *Richmond Times-Dispatch*, October 27, 1998.

67. Alan Cooper, "$17.5 Million to Be Paid in HOME Case—Rates, Bias against Black Homeowners among Issues," *Richmond Times-Dispatch*, April 25, 2000. The Virginia Supreme Court in January 2000 had vacated the jury's $100.5 million award after challenges to HOME's standing to sue, a ruling Kaine and HOME challenged and obtained a rehearing on. That question was still being litigated when the settlement was reached.

68. "The Second District" (candidate profiles), *Style Weekly*, April 26, 1994.

69. Gordon Hickey, "Raising Kaine in the City: New Mayor's Manner Belies His Plans for Change," *Richmond Times-Dispatch*, July 13, 1998.

70. Speaking in 2000 about his proposal for a city council commission to study adopting a directly elected mayor system, Kaine stated, "An elected mayor would have a mandate from the voters. . . . I was elected Councilperson with less than 1,000 votes. You end up with less votes than a student council president." John Toivonen, "Is It Time?," *Style Weekly*, August 29, 2000.

71. Tom Campbell and Gordon Hickey, "Project Targets Drugs, Violence—City, U.S. Team Up for Stiffer Sentences," *Richmond Times-Dispatch*, February 22, 1997.

72. Carrie Johnson, "Number of Killings Down in City—Police Programs Are Being Credited," *Richmond Times-Dispatch*, July 5, 1999.

73. Highland Park civic activist (and future council member) Ellen Robertson praised the impact of the Blitz to Bloom initiative on reducing crime in the neighborhoods but also said, "All we've done is taken care of the crumbs . . . and crumbs have to fall from a loaf of bread. . . . Will the guys be back on the corner? Is there still a loaf of bread? . . . The black community deserves to know what is being done above the black community level to protect us from being victims of the bigger man's game." Likewise, longtime community activist Arthur Burton, another Highland Park resident, asked, "How many people can you take out of a community and still have a community?" Burton added, "I think [the large number of arrests] shows there are a lot of suffering people in our community." Gordon Hickey, "Blitz Puts Bloom Back on Highland Park Rose," *Richmond Times-Dispatch*, October 12, 1999. See also Jim Mason, "Gilpin Court, Jackson Ward Targets—Crime-Fighting Blitz Starts Sunday," *Richmond Times-Dispatch*, October 13, 2000; and Carrie Johnson, "City Council, Police Discuss Concerns," *Richmond Times-Dispatch*, March 15, 2001.

74. Carrie Johnson, "Oliver: Cut Killings Further—Police Chief Wants Another 10% Reduction in City Slayings," *Richmond Times-Dispatch*, March 7, 2000.

75. Jerry Oliver, "Do Police-As-Buddies Go Too Far?," *Richmond Times-Dispatch*, June 25, 2000.

76. "Richmond will miss him sorely, and will have a hard time finding someone of similar caliber and capability to replace him," editorialized the *Times-Dispatch*. "Oliver Departs," *Richmond Times-Dispatch*, January 3, 2002.

77. L. Douglas Wilder, "Richmond Needs Relief from Government Gone Awry," *Richmond Times-Dispatch*, July 7, 2002. Wilder cited the departure of Oliver and the failure to replace him in a timely way as one of several examples of city hall dysfunction necessitating dramatic change.

78. In a 2003 op-ed, McCollum summarized the city's recent accomplishments, citing "restoration of Main Street Station; neighborhood investments; corporate relocations and expansions; opening of the Stony Point retail park; increases in downtown's residential population; a financial reserve that is stronger than it has been in over 20 years; thousands of new jobs; over $2 billion in economic development; and new partnerships, including the business community, that are creating educational improvements and job opportunities." McCollum also expressed concern that "questioning and debate on Richmond's form of government is being shaped by reactions to allegations about certain individuals rather than by successful policy outcomes. While I do not condone unethical or illegal behavior, I regret that these actions have cast shadows on the performance of all local government officials and doubt on our government's ability to respond to the needs of citizens." Rudy McCollum, "Government Structure Isn't Real Issue," *Richmond Times-Dispatch*, October 31, 2003. See also Calvin Jamison's articles in the *Richmond Times-Dispatch*: "City Progresses along the Road from Rhetoric to Results," November 1, 2002; "City's Strength Showed during Isabel," November 1, 2003; "Richmond Records Impressive Gains," March 7, 2004; and "City Can Cite Much Progress," January 16, 2005.

79. Tom Campbell, "El-Amin to Plead Guilty—Councilman Expected to Resign," *Richmond Times-Dispatch*, June 26, 2003; Tom Campbell, "Hedgepeth Charged with Taking Bribe—Councilwoman Accused of Selling Vote," *Richmond Times-Dispatch*, July 25, 2003.

80. Tom Campbell, "Evans Pleads Guilty to Fraud—Former Aide to City Manager Admits Stealing Approximately $500,000 from City Hall," *Richmond Times-Dispatch*, December 31, 2003; Tom Campbell, "Evans Gets Ten Years, Must Pay Back Money He Stole," *Richmond Times-Dispatch*, April 9, 2004; Jeremy Redmon, "A Sordid Past Haunts Richmond's Officials: From Faked Deaths to Scam's Misspelled Clues, Troubles with the Law Are Carefully Documented," *Richmond Times-Dispatch*, March 30, 2004.

81. "Text of U.S. Affidavit Naming Hedgepeth and 'CW,'" affidavit filed by federal agent David P. Hulser, printed in *Richmond Free Press*, July 31–August 2, 2003; Michael Paul Williams, "City Council Reputation Tarnished," *Richmond Times-Dispatch*, July 28, 2003; Ray McAllister, "Richmond Scandals: We May Be Able to Compete Nationally Soon," *Richmond Times-Dispatch*, July 29, 2003. Hedgepeth, who worked as a middle school teacher in Richmond and also served as an associate pastor at a local church, was charged with accepting $500 in connection with the mayor vote (for a candidate who was not in fact nominated) and $2,000 cash in connection with the council seat.

82. Jeremy Redmon, "Hedgepeth Steps Down," *Richmond Times-Dispatch*, April 4, 2004. Developer H. Louis Salomonsky had previously pleaded guilty to conspiring to bribe Hedgepeth ahead of the January 2003 mayoral vote. Salomonsky was vice chair of the city's Industrial Development Authority at the time of his indictment in October 2003. Jeremy Redmon, "Officials Focusing on City Business—Salomonsky Charges 'Unfortunate,'" *Richmond Times-Dispatch*, October 11, 2003; Tom Campbell, "Salomonsky Gets Two Years in Bribery Case—Developer Apologizes for Actions, but Judge Imposes the Maximum Punishment," *Richmond Times-Dispatch*, March 6, 2004.

83. Mayor Rudy McCollum responded to the "cesspool" remark, delivered in a public letter from Wilder released weeks before a citywide advisory referendum on changing the form of government, by calling it "overblown flub," adding, "I really don't see how creating a dictatorship would accomplish the challenges that were outlined" (concerning crime, public education, public health, and taxes). Jeremy Redmon, "Wilder Pushes for Reform in City," *Richmond Times-Dispatch*, October 22, 2003. See also Nelson Wikstrom, "Richmond: Implementation of and Experience with Strong-Mayor Form of Government," in *More Than Mayor or Manager: Campaigns to Change Form of Government in America's Large Cities*, eds. James H. Svara and Douglas J. Watson (Washington, DC: Georgetown University Press, 2010), 81–102.

84. Jeremy Redmon, "Businesses Give to Wilder Panel; $60,000 to Help Study Reform Ideas," *Richmond Times-Dispatch*, January 6, 2003. The twelve businesses making donations, according to a news account, were "BB&T, a North Carolina–based banking company with offices in Richmond"; "Swedish Match North America, a tobacco-products manufacturer that has its headquarters in Richmond"; "Chesapeake Corp., a specialty-packaging company based in Richmond"; "Performance Food Group, a Richmond-based restaurant distributor"; "Markel Corp., a specialty-insurance company with headquarters in Richmond"; "Ukrop's Super Markets Inc., a Richmond-based grocery chain"; "LandAmerica Financial Group Inc., a Richmond-based title insurance and real estate-services company"; "CCA Industries Inc., a company whose businesses include The Jefferson Hotel"; "HCA Richmond Hospitals, a network of hospitals"; "Hunton & Williams, a local law firm"; "SunTrust Banks, an Atlanta-based banking company with offices in Richmond"; and "Capital One Services Inc., a subsidiary of Capital One Financial Corp., a Falls Church–based credit-card company that has offices in the Richmond area."

85. For criticism of Kaine, see L. Douglas Wilder, "City Voters Should Be Able to Elect a Strong Mayor," *Richmond Times-Dispatch*, April 7, 2002. See also Wilder, "Richmond Needs Relief from Government Gone Awry," and L. Douglas Wilder, "Richmonders Have Tolerated Mediocrity Long Enough," *Richmond Times-Dispatch*, June 2, 2002.

86. Wilder, "Richmonders Have Tolerated Mediocrity Long Enough"; Wilder, "City Voters Should Be Able to Elect a Strong Mayor"; Jeremy Redmon, "Wilder, Bliley Join Forces—Goal: Strong Mayor for City by 2005," *Richmond Times-Dispatch*, July 26, 2002. Wilder had also voiced support for fewer council districts with some members elected at-large, but those ideas were not taken up by the Wilder-Bliley Commission.

87. Nelson Wikstrom, "Multiple Alternatives Are Available to Richmond," *Richmond Times-Dispatch*, June 16, 2003. Wikstrom also presented these ideas at an early meeting of the Wilder-Bliley Commission (in additional to a proposal, not adopted, to make Richmond's local races partisan). Jeremy Redmon, "Council Not Included in Panel—Group Studying Mayoral Reform," *Richmond Times-Dispatch*, September 19, 2002.

88. "Charter Commission Releases Its Questions" (staff report), *Richmond Times-Dispatch*, April 9, 2003.

89. Jeremy M. Lazarus, "Wilder, NAACP at Odds on At-Large Issue," *Richmond Free Press*, October 16–18, 2003. In remarks made at the Crusade for Voters forum shortly before the 2003 advisory referendum, Khalfani also asked, "Since when has Tom Bliley had your interests at heart?" For a detailed account of the debate over the 2004 charter reform, see also Wikstrom, "Richmond."

90. Redmon, "Wilder, Bliley Join Forces."

91. U.S. Census Bureau, Decennial Redistricting Data, 2000, accessed July 1, 2023, data.census.gov.

92. Wikstrom, "Richmond."

93. U.S. Census Bureau, Decennial Redistricting Data, 2000.

94. Voters in the Sixth, Seventh, Eighth, and Ninth Districts accounted for 30.8 percent of total votes citywide in November elections over that period. *Mayor's Redistricting Advisory Committee Final Report*, City of Richmond, July 6, 2011, table 3, https://web.archive.org/web/20151017170042/http://www.richmondgov.com/CommissionAntiPoverty/documents/RedistrictingPresentation070611.pdf.

95. Jeremy Redmon, "City Creates Study Panel," *Richmond Times-Dispatch*, October 15, 2002. The council-appointed commission made a single recommendation for change: lengthening council terms from two to four years. The idea was eventually implemented, beginning with the 2008 elections. Bill Wasson, "Commission to Propose 4-Year Terms," *Richmond Times-Dispatch*, June 24, 2003; Wikstrom, "Richmond."

96. Some council members did, however, attend and speak at commission meetings. Redmon, "Council Not Included in Panel."

97. Jeremy Redmon, "Elected Mayor Proposed—Panel Recommends Changes for City," *Richmond Times-Dispatch*, January 29, 2003.

98. Robert Congdon, "City Must Move beyond Racial Scars," *Richmond Times-Dispatch*, May 9, 2003; Michael Byrne, "No One District Gets Disenfranchised," *Richmond Times-Dispatch*, April 25, 2003; Melvin D. Law, "Direct Election of City's Mayor Will Give Voters More Voice," *Richmond Times-Dispatch*, April 11, 2003. See also "The Debate" (staff editorial), *Richmond Times-Dispatch*, February 13, 2003.

99. Wikstrom, "Richmond"; Jeremy Redmon, "Scott Opposes Proposal for At-Large City Mayor," *Richmond Times-Dispatch*, October 29, 2003; McCollum, "Government Structure Isn't Real Issue"; Jeremy M. Lazarus, "Marsh: 'Say No' to Mayor Proposal," *Richmond Free Press*, September 11–13, 2003; Michael Paul Williams, "Group Sounds Alarm on Mayor-At-Large Plan," *Richmond Times-Dispatch*, July 16, 2003. In comments of July 2003 reported by Michael Paul Williams, Marsh argued that the five-of-nine district requirement did not effectively protect Black political power, since a white candidate could carry a majority-Black district if Black votes were divided between two candidates. "Wealth alone would determine who the next mayor would be," Marsh added. "Money wins elections."

100. Longtime activist Marty Jewell, who would be elected to the city council in 2004 in place of ousted mayor and Fifth District council representative Rudy McCollum, elaborated the reasoning for his support of the proposal in comments in 2010. In explaining that he could not support an at-large, directly elected mayor because it would dilute Black voting power but did support the "Plan B" approach of requiring an elected mayor to win five districts, Jewell noted, "The council-manager form of government works fine where there is no Black-white, rich-poor controversy. Where there is, you need a structure like what we've got. One mayor responsible for the well-being of all the people. And you hold him accountable for it. Nine mini-mayors were killing us because everyone thought that they should have primacy." Marty Jewell, interview with Lucas Hakkenberg and Thad Williamson, July 14, 2010.

101. Jeremy M. Lazarus, "It's No Fix for City's Ills," *Richmond Free Press*, October 9–11, 2003.

102. Notably, however, nearly 49 percent of the "yes" votes on the charter amendment were cast by voters in the First and Fourth Districts, the two whitest districts in the city. Virginia Board of Elections, Historical Results, 2003 Richmond Charter Question, Virginia Department of Elections website, accessed July 1, 2023, https://historical.elections.virginia.gov/ballot_questions/view/2515/.

103. Wikstrom, "Richmond." In an op-ed published after the referendum, Wilder spiked the proverbial football by declaring that the vote had "unmasked the pretenders to the throne of leadership in the African-American community. That, in my judgment, could be the unexpected bonus from the Herculean efforts of persons, too numerous to name, to bring people together rather than continue a pattern of division into two cities." Wilder went on to name-check Marsh and other politicians who either opposed or failed to support the measure, warning them not to block passage of charter change in the General Assembly. "We say to [those] who continue to defy the will of 80 percent of the people: If you still don't get it, and through connivance and artifice seek to defeat the measure by substituting your will, don't believe the people are powerless and will forget." L. Douglas Wilder, "Mayor-at-Large Vote Puts City on Path to Racial Progress," *Richmond Times-Dispatch*, November 30, 2003.

104. Pamela Stallsmith and Tyler Whitley, "Strong Mayor Bill Approved," *Richmond Times-Dispatch*, March 13, 2004.

105. Crupi, *Back to the Future*, 17.

106. Associated Press, "Fiscal Restraint Urged by Wilder," *New York Times*, January 16, 1990, A18. The legislator quoted was Joseph B. Benedetti, a Republican state senator from the Tenth District, which at the time included thirty-seven precincts in south and western Richmond and ten precincts from Henrico County. "Republican Wins Willey's Seat," *Washington Post*, August 13, 1986.

107. Will Jones, "Wilder to Run for Mayor of Richmond: Ex-Governor Reverses Stance, Says He'll Seek to Lead His Hometown," *Richmond Times-Dispatch*, May 30, 2004. The U.S. Department of Justice provided final approval to the new structure the following month. "In Brief" (staff editorial), *Richmond Times-Dispatch*, June 22, 2004.

108. Judson L. Jeffries, *Virginia's Native Son: The Election and Administration of Governor Douglas L. Wilder* (West Lafayette, IN: Purdue University Press, 2000).

109. L. Douglas Wilder, *Son of Virginia: A Life in America's Political Arena* (Guilford, CT: Lyons Press, 2015).

110. Jeremy Redmon, "Wilder, Marsh the Best of Foes—Mayoral Reforms Strain Friendship," *Richmond Times-Dispatch*, December 1, 2002.

111. In an admiring preface to journalist Donald Baker's 1989 campaign biography, Jesse Jackson acknowledged Wilder needed to adopt a wider lens beyond "issues that may still be distinctively black" to be competitive: "To ask a man who could be governor to be the state's top civil rights leader all at the same time may be asking a bit too much." Baker quotes Wilder himself as stating, "I have never really lined up permanently in politics, in such a position as to not be able to shift myself, when the occasion demanded it." Donald P. Baker, *Wilder: Hold Fast to Dreams* (Cabin Johns, MD: Seven Locks Press, 1989), xii–xiii, 283.

112. Robert Holsworth, later a Wilder ally, in 1988 wrote in "Doug Wilder: On the Edge of History," *Style Weekly*, July 26, 1988:

> Although I can admire Wilder's political skills, I still have trouble generating enthusiasm about his candidacy. Politics is about getting votes, but at its best it is also concerned with framing issues in innovative ways, identifying potential solutions to social problems and inspiring citizens to act. Doing this might require Doug Wilder to take the kind of risks that he has been unwilling to assume. His reluctance to jeopardize his chances with bold policy proposals is perfectly understandable. But it does lead to the irony that the ultimate promise of a campaign that has the potential to make history is that it will give us more of what we already have.

113. Virginia Public Access Project, 2004 Richmond Mayoral Election Results, vpap.org, accessed June 30, 2023, www.vpap.org/candidates/5323/elections/.

114. David Ress, "4 Power Brokers Help Shape the City's Landscape," *Richmond Times-Dispatch*, August 14, 2005.

115. Ress, "4 Power Brokers Help Shape the City's Landscape."

116. Ress, "4 Power Brokers Help Shape the City's Landscape."

117. An early profile of Wilder's mayoral tenure in *Governing* noted that Wilder had been shocked and alarmed to receive criticism from the leadership of Richmond Renaissance for his public criticism of city hall. "If this was what was supposedly the combination of forces directing the affairs of the city, then we were in bigger trouble than I had thought." Rob Gurwitt, "Wilder's Last Crusade," *Governing*, June 1, 2005.

118. Wilder ally Marty Jewell's assessment, provided to *Governing* magazine in 2005, is worth quoting in full: "You name the category—public health, education, employment, the economy—we were hurting and the leadership had not addressed it. . . . No one was accountable. The mayor was saying, 'Well, under the statute I preside over meetings and cut ribbons'; the manager was not required to respond to any citizen or citizen issue; and the council was in a situation where you couldn't get three council members to agree on what was for lunch, let alone set benchmarks and hold the manager to those benchmarks." Gurwitt, "Wilder's Last Crusade."

119. Early in his term, a confident Wilder predicted, as summarized by *Governing* magazine, that by the end of his term "city hall will be more responsive, more efficient and more accountable, and a less commanding figure will still be able to run things." Gurwitt, "Wilder's Last Crusade."

120. As one columnist wrote in December 2004, in the wake of Wilder's moves to dismiss the city manager and police chief and claim the authority to dismiss the school superintendent, "The former governor's full-scale attack on City Hall is Richmond's greatest slash-and-burn since Grant." Ray McAllister, "Council Rises Up to Face Wilder in the Great Chutzpah Faceoff," *Richmond Times-Dispatch*, December 16, 2004.

121. David Ress, "A Stirring Year: Mayor L. Douglas Wilder Has Shaken Up Richmond; Is the City Moving Ahead?," *Richmond Times-Dispatch*, January 1, 2006.

122. Wilder was responding to a comment Ukrop had made in a published news report stating that while he had supported Wilder's election and "the concept of a mayor-at-large," he "[didn't] know about the personality." Wilder responded that while Ukrop "might own some other people, . . . I owe my election, I owe my strength—and always have owed it—to the people. And he doesn't own, nor will he own or buy me." Jeremy Redmon, "Wilder

Blasts Council, Ukrop; Mayor Hints That the Cuts the Council Dealt His Office May Not Stick," *Richmond Times-Dispatch*, May 25, 2005. For his part, Ukrop acknowledged Wilder's independence in a 2005 interview, telling the *New Republic*, "Doug Wilder sits in no one's pocket. He doesn't represent anyone's interest other than his own and what he considers the best interests of the city." Jason Zengerle, "Best for Last," *New Republic*, August 8, 2005.

123. Marty Jewell put it this way: "[Before Wilder] you had a city government that almost reveled in its mediocrity. You had nine mini-mayors who were cherry-picking whatever they could pick for themselves in their districts. No one was looking out for the greater good and what's best for the city." Jewell interview, July 14, 2010.

124. L. Douglas Wilder, "In Richmond Citizens Want Accountability; New Administration Provides It," *Richmond Times-Dispatch*, September 4, 2005.

125. David Ress, "Tunstall Leaves His Job as Fire Chief—Department Director Is Asked to Step Down from City Government," *Richmond Times-Dispatch*, May 3, 2005; "City Department Head Loses His Job," *Richmond Times-Dispatch*, September 10, 2005.

126. David Ress, "Nice Guy Finishes First in City Race—Praised for His Demeanor, William E. Harrell Is the New Administrative Officer," *Richmond Times-Dispatch*, March 25, 2005. The well-regarded Harrell told reporters he had withdrawn from city manager opportunities to have a chance to be part of history working with Wilder in the new form of government. "I'm very comfortable being No. 2.... My job is being an administrator." David Ress, "'You've Got Old Man's Hands'—City's Top Bureaucrat Says He Has Grown Into the Hands He Was Dealt," *Richmond Times-Dispatch*, February 6, 2005.

127. Regarding his methods of holding city bureaucrats accountable, early in his tenure Wilder told a journalist, "I like to ask them, 'What do you produce?' ... It surprises a lot of people when you ask it that way, they have to do a double-take, and it's not the majority of time that you get a satisfactory answer." Zengerle, "Best for Last."

128. In an interview with Lucas Hakkenberg and Thad Williamson on June 29, 2010, former city council president and mayoral candidate Bill Pantele cited improving the reputation of the city council as his biggest success and credited Wilder for his support in adopting needed procedural changes.

> I would say my greatest success was in transforming city council from a group that had been the object of scorn and ridicule for many years into a group that was more businesslike, more professional, more respected.... We did it by changing the tone of the meetings. We changed the legislative process.... And I remember my first meeting with Doug Wilder after he had been elected mayor but before he was sworn in. I went to see him in his office at VCU, and by that point I had drafted a memorandum outlining some changes to the process—to council's committee structure and to the legislative process—the idea being to make legislation go through more work before it can get to the council floor.... And to his credit— and he and I had plenty of battles later—but to his credit he understood it almost immediately, and he said that he agreed with those changes.... And it really made a big difference.

129. Jeremy Redmon, "Council Wants Money Back in Budget," *Richmond Times-Dispatch*, May 4, 2005; Jeremy Redmon, "Mayor, Council in Accord—Compromise on Budget Reached; Deal Gives More Money to Police, Schools," *Richmond Times-Dispatch*, May 10, 2005; Jeremy Redmon, "Council Likely to Bump Up Wilder's Salary—If the

City Spending Plan Is Adopted Next Week, He Will Get a 20 Percent Raise," *Richmond Times-Dispatch*, May 17, 2005.

130. Jeremy Redmon, "Budget Battle, Round Two," *Richmond Times-Dispatch*, May 21, 2005; Jeremy Redmon, "City Council Delivers Dual Setback to Wilder after Sharp Letter from Wilder, Council Makes Deep Slashes to His Team," *Richmond Times-Dispatch*, May 24, 2005. Among the proposed cuts was the position held by Wilder's influential senior policy adviser Paul Goldman. Goldman eventually left Wilder's administration in February 2006, following controversy regarding paid political consulting work that Goldman performed for Tim Kaine's successful 2005 gubernatorial campaign. Bill Wasson, "Wilder Aide Goldman Resigns—Mayor Offers No Comment on Departure of Senior Policy Adviser, Political Confidant," *Richmond Times-Dispatch*, February 16, 2006.

131. Jeremy Redmon, "Wilder Asserting Supposed Authority," *Richmond Times-Dispatch*, May 26, 2005; Jeremy Redmon, "Council Vote Defies Wilder—Court Fight May Loom as Members Adopt Their Own Budget Plan," *Richmond Times-Dispatch*, June 1, 2005.

132. Will Jones, "Vice Mayor Says No Budgets Valid—City Council's Dispute with Wilder Appears to Be Headed for Court," *Richmond Times-Dispatch*, June 3, 2005.

133. David Ress, "Sides Call Budget Deal Close," *Richmond Times-Dispatch*, June 12, 2005; David Ress and Jeremy Redmon, "Mayor, Council Reach Deal on Budget—Under Compromise That Avoids Suit, Council Members and Wilder Will Honor Most of the Other's Priorities," *Richmond Times-Dispatch*, June 14, 2005. Under the charter, an adopted budget could not be amended until the start of the new fiscal year (on July 1).

134. Redmon, "Wilder Blasts City Council, Ukrop"; Ress and Redmon, "Mayor, Council Reach Deal on Budget"; David Ress and Jeremy Redmon, "Will Wilder, Council End Up in Court? The Mayor and the Panel Battle over the Budget—and over Power in the City," *Richmond Times-Dispatch*, May 29, 2005; Redmon, "Council Vote Defies Wilder"; Jeremy Redmon and David Ress, "Wilder Seeks to End Standoff but Council Appears to Balk at Proposal and Has Hired Its Own Lawyer," *Richmond Times-Dispatch*, June 10, 2005. School board member Carol A. O. Wolf told a reporter, "This city elected a mayor, they did not elect a dictator. We did not elect this man because we wanted nonstop chaos and confusion. We did not elect him because we wanted the rule of one man." David Ress and Jeremy Redmon, "The Budget Battle—Trenches Deepen in War of Words," *Richmond Times-Dispatch*, May 28, 2005.

135. Mark Holmberg, "Not So Fast, Cowboy, Says Council," *Richmond Times-Dispatch*, May 25, 2005.

136. Ress and Redmon, "Will Wilder, Council End Up in Court?"

137. David Ress, "Wilder Offers Five-Year Plan for Richmond—Proposal Would Cost at Least $250 Million and Would Use Credit Line," *Richmond Times-Dispatch*, January 10, 2006.

138. "The Council's Role" (staff editorial), *Richmond Times-Dispatch*, October 28, 2006. The editorial board added: "Much of the tension between the Council and the mayor seems to be that the city's charter does not properly define their roles under this new form of government."

139. Will Jones, "Power Struggle Stresses Richmond City Workers—At Least 53 of 54 Employees Reapply for Their Jobs as Part of Wilder's Spat with Council," *Richmond Times-Dispatch*, April 28, 2007.

140. Michael Martz, "Council Sues over Employees—Suit Filed against Wilder Challenges Mayor's Claim to More Than 50 City Workers," *Richmond Times-Dispatch*, May 11, 2007.

141. Michael Martz, "Judge Rules against Wilder—Says the City Council Holds the Power to Hire and Fire Its Own Staff," *Richmond Times-Dispatch*, November 30, 2007.

142. Council president Pantele explained the decision in stating, "The [city] charter set out a number of specific criteria for significant operations experience. . . . In reviewing his background and experience, we didn't see that he met those requirements." Amy Biegelsen, "Update: City Council to Reject Harry Black," *Style Weekly*, May 16, 2007. After the 6–3 vote against Black, Pantele added, "The CAO position . . . is not a personal staffer for the mayor. It's not a personal staffer of City Council. The CAO position belongs to the people." Michael Martz, "Council Refuses to Confirm Black—Panel Rejects Nomination of Wilder Aide to Be Acting Chief Administrative Officer," *Richmond Times-Dispatch*, May 19, 2007.

143. Flynn believed that the directly elected mayor system allowed for a bolder policy approach than the previous system. Speaking in 2010, Flynn stated, "I think somebody needs to be in charge and the other method with the city manager form—that guy or gal has really seven or nine bosses for the city that she has to please. I think that's a very hard thing to do. I think you need to have that one person who's in charge and who's been elected by the people, who has that mandate, and is going to go forward." Rachel Flynn, interview with Lucas Hakkenberg, Amy Howard, and Thad Williamson, June 7, 2010.

144. Homicide data for 2004, 2007, and 2008, Richmond Police Department—Crime Incidence Center, accessed August 2, 2022, https://apps.richmondgov.com/applications/CrimeInfo. Councilman Chris Hilbert, who expressed severe disappointment with Wilder's tenure as mayor overall, also believed Wilder deserved specific credit for the crime drop. "Even if there had been no other accomplishment . . . than public safety, that was huge. To me, he did give the city some confidence in itself in that it could do *that* right. . . . He had the gravitas and the street cred . . . to go out and talk about that issue, and people would listen to him. Somebody else might have come out with the same policies, but I'm not sure people would have believed the way they believed him." Chris Hilbert, interview with Lucas Hakkenberg and Thad Williamson, July 1, 2010.

145. Kiran Krishnamurthy, "Wilder Believes You're Better Off: Mayor Cites Reduction in Crime and Other Gains in Annual Address," *Richmond Times-Dispatch*, January 27, 2008.

146. Jim Nolan, "Monroe Accepts Charlotte Job," *Richmond Times-Dispatch*, May 16, 2008.

147. Michael Martz and Will Jones, "Wilder Will Not Run for Re-election," *Richmond Times-Dispatch*, May 17, 2008. First District council member Bruce Tyler summed up the views of many who had welcomed the new form of government in stating, "I'm very appreciative of the fact that he came in and brought a new form of government. I'm also appreciative of the fact that he decided not to run again. . . . It's time to find an individual who can bring people together instead of breaking them apart."

148. Councilman Chris Hilbert of the Third District put it this way in an interview with the national media: "People had tremendous hopes for this mayor. . . . This is someone of tremendous stature, a national figure. He has squandered his mandate on petty infighting that doesn't amount to anything. He is interested in consolidating power for its own sake.

There doesn't even seem to be an agenda." Lisa A. Bacon, "Famous Mayor under Fire in Virginia," *New York Times*, October 21, 2007.

149. Michael Martz, "Support Drops for Wilder—Less Than 40% Would Vote to Re-elect Richmond's Mayor," *Richmond Times-Dispatch*, October 28, 2007. The poll showed that just 39 percent of Black Richmonders and 31 percent of white Richmonders supported a potential Wilder reelection bid and that 66 percent of respondents believed Wilder had overstepped his authority in attempting to evict the school board from city hall in September 2007. In a follow-up article focused on reaction to the stunning poll, former commonwealth's attorney David Hicks quipped that "people thought they were voting for Colin Powell. I think what we ended up with was Dick Cheney." Michael Martz, "Wilder's Woes Inspire Contenders—Poll Results Give Hope to Possible Candidates for Richmond Mayor's Race," *Richmond Times-Dispatch*, October 30, 2007.

150. Wilder declined to make an endorsement in the race, instead publishing an op-ed disparaging the three leading candidates. L. Douglas Wilder, "Would-Be Successors Just Don't Make the Grade," *Richmond Times-Dispatch*, October 19, 2008.

151. Will Jones, "Wilder Supporters Back Grey for Richmond Mayor," *Richmond Times-Dispatch*, September 21, 2008.

152. Will Jones, "Goldman Backs Jones for Mayor," *Richmond Times-Dispatch*, October 22, 2008.

153. Will Jones, "5th District Vote Could Determine Mayor's Race; Diverse Area Closely Matches the City's Racial Mix," *Richmond Times-Dispatch*, October 31, 2008.

154. 2008 Richmond Mayor's Race Results, Virginia Department of Elections website, accessed June 30, 2023, https://historical.elections.virginia.gov/elections/search/year_from:2008/year_to:2008/office_id:73/district_id:33220. See also Richmond Voter Registrar, "November 4, 2008, General Election Canvassed Results," accessed February 4, 2024, https://web.archive.org/web/20150908162949/http://www.richmondgov.com/Registrar/documents/CanvassedResults110408.pdf.

155. In 2001, Jones earned a doctorate from United Theological Seminary in Dayton while continuing to serve his pastorate in Richmond. See biographical information at Virginia Union University website, accessed September 30, 2023, www.vuu.edu/wyatt-tee-walker-social-justice-society-of-preachers-prophetic-witnesses/dr-dwight-c-jones.

156. Early in Jones's second term, former Wilder adviser Paul Goldman neatly encapsulated the differences between Wilder's and Jones's governance styles, stating, "Jones' best insight, to me, is that he realized: 'The mayor is big enough and strong enough. . . . It's a small pond. I don't have to act like the Loch Ness monster to rule. I just have to swim around and everybody steps back.'" Robert C. Zullo, "Dwight C. Jones's Journey to Power in Richmond," *Richmond Times-Dispatch*, April 21, 2013. For related discussion, see Williamson, "Tangled Relationship of Democracy, Leadership, and Justice in Urban America."

157. In an interview with Amy Howard and Thad Williamson on August 15, 2011, Jones's influential senior policy adviser David Hicks emphasized the challenge of rebuilding and sustaining an experienced administrative team:

> One of the things that happened in this first iteration of this new form of government was they decimated the agency head level for better or for worse, and even the level one or two below that. . . . In 2016 we need to figure out, OK, what the

heck is this form of government going to mean for the institutional level of knowledge that you have to have to make the city run.... If it's going to be a full housecleaning every two or eight years, I don't think you can be competitive in a region that has a stable team.

158. Will Jones, "Jones Introduces Marshall; City Council Will Consider Mayor's Pick at July 1 Meeting," *Richmond Times-Dispatch*, June 23, 2009.

159. Speaking in 2010, councilwoman Ellen Robertson stressed the lack of administrative stability in city agencies that Jones inherited and then went on to praise Jones's early efforts: "The budget process that he put together this year was absolutely the best that has ever been done in the City of Richmond. Hands down, the best. We went into that budget cycle thinking, based on assessment values and book values for the land, we were facing a $30 million deficit, minimum. He balanced the budget and did not lay off a soul. He closed the gap through efficiencies [with] a new staff that had walked in and had been here six months." Ellen Robertson, interview with Lucas Hakkenberg and Thad Williamson, June 3, 2010.

160. The new facility opened in July 2014. Joe Macenkar, "New City Jail Opens with Beds to Spare," *Richmond Times-Dispatch*, July 29, 2014. Jones also took proactive steps to address problems in the city's Department of Justice Services, shutting down temporarily the city's youth detention center and deploying his top adviser, David Hicks, to clean up the department as acting director. Michael Martz, "City's Juvenile Services Director Resigns," *Richmond Times-Dispatch*, April 28, 2012.

161. Full disclosure: Thad Williamson served on the Mayor's Anti-Poverty Commission from 2011 to 2013 and was principal author of its final report. He also served, while on leave from the University of Richmond, as the inaugural director of the Office of Community Wealth Building, a new city agency established to coordinate implementation of the Anti-Poverty Commission's recommendations, from June 2014 to May 2016. He then served as a policy adviser to candidate Levar M. Stoney during the 2016 municipal election, then as transition director for Stoney after his election, and finally as a part-time senior policy adviser for Stoney from January 2017 to June 2018 (while teaching full-time at the University of Richmond).

162. Zachary Reid, "Mayor Disbands School Reform Task Force," *Richmond Times-Dispatch*, May 23, 2013.

163. 2012 General Election Results, Virginia Department of Elections website, accessed June 30, 2023, https://historical.elections.virginia.gov/elections/search/year_from:2012/year_to:2012/office_id:73/district_id:33220.

164. Cuffee-Glenn was well-known in Richmond, having previously worked for seventeen years for the city as a neighborhood planner and for another four years as director of planning and community development for the Richmond Redevelopment and Housing Authority. K. Burnell Evans, "Suffolk Manager to Head Jones Administration," *Richmond Times-Dispatch*, April 16, 2015; Jeremy M. Lazarus, "City's New CAO," *Richmond Free Press*, April 17, 2015.

165. For a detailed account of the problems with implementation of the city's RAPIDS software system and the related delay in filing annual financial reports, see Peter Galuszka, "The Frustrating, Depressing, Embarrassing Story behind Richmond City Hall's Mind-Numbing Financial Mayhem," *Style Weekly*, December 1, 2015.

166. The director in question had used time during city business hours to participate in conference calls regarding the church project and also sent emails about the project from his city email account, but he had given up vacation time owed by the city to compensate for the time spent on the church project. Following extensive review of church and city records, as well as interviews, the investigation concluded that there was no evidence that the director (or other city officials) acted illegally in connection with the project. Separately, the investigation, examined concerns related to the fact that six of the top fifty-eight officials in Jones's administration belonged to the church he pastored. The report said the overlap between the church and the city administration "smack[ed] of cronyism" but that no law had been broken. In public remarks accompanying the release of the report, Commonwealth's Attorney Michael Herring called for more transparency in hiring and procurement decisions in which public officials have a prior relationship with a job candidate or contractor. Ned Oliver and K. Burnell Evans, "No Charges in Inquiry," *Richmond Times-Dispatch*, December 1, 2016; Commonwealth's Attorney's Office, *Investigative Report on Alleged Improprieties and Use of City of Richmond Resources at the First Baptist Church Iron Bridge Road Construction Project*, November 2016, accessed September 30, 2023, https://chpn.net/wp-content/uploads/2016/11/JONES-REPORT.pdf.

167. Dwight C. Jones, "Moving Richmond Forward—We Have Accomplished So Much," *Richmond Times-Dispatch*, December 18, 2016.

CHAPTER 4

1. A typical assessment in our interviews is that of Hugh Keogh, speaking in 2010 as CEO of the Virginia Chamber of Commerce: "As a rule, middle-aged white families living in Richmond suburbs are not convinced that they can move back downtown regardless of the attractiveness of the residential opportunities and get the education for their kids and cultural environment for their kids that they really want." Hugh Keogh, interview with Lucas Hakkenberg and Thad Williamson, June 7, 2010.

2. See the appendix for school leaders interviewed for this project.

3. For an account of the national No Child Left Behind policy, see William Hayes, *No Child Left Behind: Past, Present and Future* (Lanham: R&L Education, 2008).

4. When Richmond Public Schools opened in the fall of 1970 under a temporary desegregation plan developed in response to Merhige's order, only 16,429 white students enrolled, compared with the expected total of 21,139. Merhige in early 1971 issued an additional order extending busing citywide and mandating that "the ratio of black to white [students] in each school would be approximately the same as it was in the entire school system." Robert A. Pratt, *The Color of Their Skin: Education and Race in Richmond, Virginia, 1954–89* (Charlottesville: University of Virginia Press, 1992), 48–54.

5. Charles Cox, "Area School Merger Plan Is Killed by Supreme Court in 4–4 Decision," *Richmond Times-Dispatch*, May 22, 1973; "Richmond Accepts School Decision," *New York Times*, October 14, 1973.

6. Milliken v. Bradley, 418 U.S. 717 (1974).

7. For detailed accounts of these decisions and further historical context, see Pratt, *Color of Their Skin*; Matthew Lassiter, *The Silent Majority: Suburban Politics in the Sunbelt South* (Princeton, NJ: Princeton University Press, 2006); and James Ryan, *Five Miles Away,*

a World Apart: One City, Two Schools, and the Story of Educational Opportunity in Modern America (New York: Oxford University Press, 2010).

8. The most detailed assessment of Richmond Public Schools in the first part of the time frame discussed in this chapter is Joshua Cole, "Richmond Public Schools: Post–Court Mandated School Desegregation (1986–2006)" (PhD diss., Virginia Commonwealth University, 2009). We follow Cole's treatment of Merhige's 1986 court decisions (pp. 72–77) as a useful starting point for assessing the condition of RPS during this time period.

9. Randolph Goode, "Judge Merhige Approves City Schools Pupil Plan," *Richmond Times-Dispatch*, April 18, 1986.

10. Cole, "Richmond Public Schools," 94–100.

11. After the return of the neighborhood school concept in 1986, white families gradually began returning to Munford; by the early 2000s, the school once again was a majority-white school.

12. The "model school" concept in Richmond originated in 1969 with the establishment of John B. Cary Elementary School. See Cole, "Richmond Public Schools," 70–72 and 93–110, for detailed discussion of RPS enrollment policies in the late 1980s and 1990s. Whereas early "model schools" like John B. Cary and Bellevue were citywide schools accessible via an application process, after 1992 "model schools" were obliged to first serve neighborhood children, with extra classroom seats made available to out-of-zone student applicants. See Cole, "Richmond Public Schools," 109.

13. Genevieve Siegel-Hawley, Kim Bridges, Thomas Shields, John Moeser, and Renee Hill, "Increasing Diversity in the City Schools: Unexplored Paths of Opportunity" (Policy Memorandum, University of Richmond "Looking Backward, Moving Forward" conference, 2013), appendix, figure 1.

14. Tom Campbell, "Join Ranks on Suit, Marsh Says," *Richmond Times-Dispatch*, March 24, 1984. The school board, then chaired by Rev. Dwight C. Jones, had voted 7–0 to file the suit, which was also backed by Superintendent Richard C. Hunter. Henry L. Marsh sought but failed to get the city council to make a statement in support of the lawsuit. Tom Campbell, "Marsh, Leidinger Resolutions of Lawsuit Support Are Shelved," *Richmond Times-Dispatch*, March 28, 1984. See also Cole, "Richmond Public Schools," 73–74.

15. Bradley v. Baliles, 639 F. Supp. 680 (E.D. Va. 1986) at 690; see also Ryan, *Five Miles Away*, 109–10.

16. Bradley v. Baliles, at 692–93.

17. Bradley v. Baliles, at 695.

18. Bradley v. Baliles, at 696–97.

19. Bradley v. Baliles, at 698.

20. Bradley v. Baliles, at 698.

21. Bradley v. Baliles, at 699.

22. Bradley v. Baliles, at 700–701.

23. Bradley v. Baliles, at 702.

24. Randolph Goode and Chuck Epes, "School Officials to Decide Whether to Appeal Ruling," *Richmond Times-Dispatch*, July 11, 1986, cited in Cole, "Richmond Public Schools," 75.

25. Chuck Epes, "Merhige Was Wrong, Schools Say," *Richmond Times-Dispatch*, December 24, 1986.

26. For instance, in 2011–12, 78 percent and 54 percent of economically disadvantaged Richmond students passed the third grade Standards of Learning test for reading and math, respectively, compared with 77 percent and 48 percent of economically disadvantaged students statewide. See 2011–2 Virginia Standards of Learning results, Virginia Department of Education website, accessed March 11, 2024 www.doe.virginia.gov/data-policy-funding/data-reports/statistics-reports/sol-test-pass-rates-other-results. Much wider gaps between Richmond and statewide performance became evident starting with middle school.

27. Richmond school boards in the period of this study were often criticized for *not* moving fast enough to close school buildings in response to enrollment declines.

28. Cole, "Richmond Public Schools," 124–25. A widely cited 2000 study of more than 1,700 superintendents nationwide found average tenure was seven years, across all districts nationally. Evidence from the Council of the Great City Schools regarding superintendents of larger urban systems found shorter tenure in the same time period (just under three years). See Bruce S. Cooper, Lance D. Fusarelli, and Vincent Carella, "Career Crisis in the School Superintendency? The Results of a National Survey," ERIC, 2000, https://eric.ed.gov/?id=ED443167; see also Council of the Great City Schools, "Urban School Superintendents: Characteristics, Tenure, and Salary; Sixth Survey and Report," *Urban Indicator*, Winter 2008/2009, https://files.eric.ed.gov/fulltext/ED508236.pdf.

29. Michael Paul Williams, "Harrison-Jones to Give Up City School Superintendency," *Richmond Times-Dispatch*, July 6, 1988; "Change of Superintendents" (staff editorial), *Richmond Times-Dispatch*, July 8, 1988.

30. Mike Allen, "Couldn't Stay Silent, West Says," *Richmond Times-Dispatch*, August 23, 1987; Monte R. Young, "City Groups Show Continued Support for Superintendent," *Richmond Times-Dispatch*, September 16, 1987.

31. Tom Campbell, "Pupils Win West Case Judgment," *Richmond Times-Dispatch*, April 5, 1988. The plaintiffs were awarded legal fees but not punitive or compensatory damages. The two ordered searches found to be unconstitutional were for portable radios in one case and marijuana in the other.

32. Monte Young, "The 80's Is Roy West Time," *Richmond Times-Dispatch*, August 25, 1985. Hassell had supported West in the 1987 reassignment controversy (while acknowledging Harrison-Jones's authority to make the transfer). Mike Allen, "Atlanta Considering Harrison-Jones," *Richmond Times-Dispatch*, October 16, 1987.

33. Michael Paul Williams, "Report Points Out School Ills," *Richmond Times-Dispatch*, June 21, 1988.

34. Harrison-Jones told a reporter, "I don't know if I've ever heard that kind of retort.... Getting into those types of verbal battles with your immediate supervisor is something I would never do." Michael Paul Williams, "Superintendent Couldn't Win Fight with Board, She Thought," *Richmond Times-Dispatch*, July 11, 1988. City manager Bobb recommended a cut of $7.5 million from the school board's initial $117 million request from the city for FY 1989, and the council then cut an additional $3.7 million. Chuck Epes, "School Plan Cut to $142 Million," *Richmond Times-Dispatch*, June 23, 1988.

35. Williams, "Superintendent Couldn't Win Fight with Board, She Thought."

36. Sa'ad El-Amin of the Crusade for Voters termed Harrison-Jones's departure an "atrocity." Jeanne Cummings, "Crusade Plan Urges 'Civil Disobedience,'" *Richmond Times-Dispatch*, July 20, 1988; Virginia Churn, "Law Says Hassell Solely Responsible for

Schools' Crisis," *Richmond Times-Dispatch*, July 20, 1988; Michael Paul Williams, "Black Groups Ask Hassell to Quit," *Richmond Times-Dispatch*, August 3, 1988. The Ad Hoc Committee on Public Education, consisting of fourteen Black organizations, charged West and Hassell with seeking to push Harrison-Jones out. Robin Farmer, "Harrison-Jones Says She'll Take City Spirit, Philosophy with Her," *Richmond Times-Dispatch*, October 26, 1988. Hassell responded to critics in a lengthy interview with the *Richmond Times-Dispatch* in September. While he acknowledged that he believed Harrison-Jones's departure was a positive development, he argued that the real concern of the school board's critics was not education but power: "I have had conversations with numerous black clergymen in this town, some who are supportive of [former Mayor, now Councilman Henry] Marsh and the Ad Hoc Committee and others who are not supportive, and persons on both sides of the aisle have tried to convince me that the issue is not . . . 'an anti-Hassell' issue, but rather who will control the destiny of the city of Richmond." Edward Grimsley, Robert G. Holland, Beth Barber, and Kenneth Smith, "School Division—Board Chairman Leroy Hassell on Richmond Schools and Critics," *Richmond Times-Dispatch*, September 11, 1988. In a response, W. Avon Drake of the Ad Hoc Committee on Public Education wrote, "It is in all of our interest that the school division operates effectively. Because 87 percent of its students are black and a significant percentage are from lower-income or single-parent homes, middle-class blacks have a special opportunity to illustrate their civic responsibility. I strongly urge them to enter this dialogue. To the extent that Mr. Hassell's leadership is responsible and effective, we must be supportive. But if he continues on the path of acrimony and partisanship, stronger and more organized opposition will likely develop. This will not be good for Richmond." W. Avon Drake, "Disagrees with Chairman of City's School Board," *Richmond Times-Dispatch*, September 18, 1988.

37. Chuck Epes, "City School Chief Search Continues Despite Protests," *Richmond Times-Dispatch*, July 30, 1988.

38. See Council of the Great City Schools, "Review of the Finance and Business Operations of the Richmond Public Schools," June 5, 2018, www.cgcs.org/cms/lib/DC00001581/Centricity/domain/35/publication%20docs/Richmond%20Finance%20 and%20Operations%20Review.pdf; and Richmond Office of the City Auditor, *Audit of Richmond Public Schools Payroll*, October 28, 2013, Report 2014-02, https://rva.gov/sites/default/files/Auditor/documents/2014/14-02_RichmondPublicSchools_Payroll.pdf, for detailed critiques of Richmond Public Schools' organizational practices and culture during the early and mid-2010s. Critiques of the school system were commonplace in the period of this study; for a particularly poignant example from the early period of this study, see W. Avon Drake, "Education Solutions Begin at Home," *Richmond Times-Dispatch*, November 8, 1993.

39. Daniel L. Duke, *The School That Refused to Die: Continuity and Change at Thomas Jefferson High School* (New York: State University of New York Press, 1995), 170–77, 190–92.

40. Robin Farmer, "School Board Transfers West to New Position," *Richmond Times-Dispatch*, August 31, 1989. The transfer followed a grievance filed by Paul Fleisher, a teacher who had complained about the chain-locked rear doors at Mosby and was subsequently transferred out of the school by West.

41. Ray McAllister, "A Charge Card over the Limit," *Richmond Times-Dispatch*, March 11, 1991; Mark Johnson, "Jones's Job Is Again the Topic of Talks—Use of Credit Card Resurfaces as Issue," *Richmond Times-Dispatch*, June 25, 1991.

42. Robin Farmer, "New Superintendent in Fast Start," *Richmond Times-Dispatch*, September 1, 1991; Paul Bradley, "Jones's Tenure Ends in Doubt—Lost Credibility Cited in Firing of School Board," *Richmond Times-Dispatch*, June 27, 1991. Prior to the school board's termination of Jones's contract, three members of the council—William I. Golding, Charles R. Perkins, and Roy A. West—planned to sue the board (as individuals) for not terminating Jones over the consulting arrangement, which according to the city attorney violated state law. Robin Farmer, "3 to Sue School Board on Ruling," *Richmond Times-Dispatch*, June 8, 1991.

43. Cole, "Richmond Public Schools," 111, table 6, adapted from Robin Farmer, "Judge Holds Up Pupil Shifts at Bellevue—Board Must Hold Public Hearing First," *Richmond Times-Dispatch*, February 7, 1993.

44. Robin Farmer, "Grouping by Race Is Alleged—Bellevue Parent Seeks School Board Probe," *Richmond Times-Dispatch*, December 3, 1992. The following account is informed by the extended discussion of the clustering controversy found in Cole, "Richmond Public Schools," 110–21.

45. School board chair Clarence L. Townes Jr. responded to the initial reports of clustering and to Richardson's additional assertion that clustering was consistent with school board policy by stating, "I unequivocally know nothing about such policy.... I would not serve on the board of education if such policies exist. If I find out there are such policies, they must be amended immediately or I will not serve anymore." Superintendent Brown added, "There is no policy in Richmond public schools nor any administrative procedures that support the segregation of students." Farmer, "Grouping by Race Is Alleged."

46. Cole, "Richmond Public Schools," 118; Robin Farmer, "School Clustering Issue Raises Passions," *Richmond Times-Dispatch*, February 20, 1993. For more on Oliver Hill, see Margaret Edds, *We Face the Dawn: Oliver Hill, Spotswood Robinson, and the Legal Team That Dismantled Jim Crow* (Charlottesville: University of Virginia Press, 2018).

47. Robin Farmer, "Probe of Racial Grouping to End Today," *Richmond Times-Dispatch*, December 4, 1992.

48. Robin Farmer, "'Clustering' Seen at School; Officials Probing Ginter Park Practice," *Richmond Times-Dispatch*, December 10, 1992; Robin Farmer, "School Board Extends Probe into Grouping of White Pupils," *Richmond Times-Dispatch*, December 11, 1992; Robin Farmer, "2nd School May Forgo Grouping—White 'Clustering' Involves Ginter Park," *Richmond Times-Dispatch*, December 19, 1992.

49. Final approval of the reassignment plan followed a charged public hearing in February at which over seventy persons spoke. The court-ordered hearing followed legal action by a group of parents who successfully argued the board was required to hold a public hearing prior to reassigning a significant number of students midyear. Farmer, "Judge Holds Up Pupil Shifts at Bellevue"; Farmer, "School Clustering Issue Raises Passions"; Robin Farmer, "Board Votes to End Clustering; Pupil Reassignments Could Begin Today," *Richmond Times-Dispatch*, February 24, 1993. The school board approved reassignment of up to seventy-six students at Bellevue, as well as reassignment of up to thirty-two students at Ginter Park.

50. Robin Farmer, "City Pupils Are Reacting to Proposals—Parents Say Midyear Changes Disruptive," *Richmond Times-Dispatch*, February 6, 1993; Robin Farmer, "Bellevue Parents Plead Reassignment Case to Public—Plans to Move Clustered Pupils Spark Protest," *Richmond Times-Dispatch*, February 18, 1993; Robin Farmer, "Bellevue: Tears Flow as

Pupils Regroup," *Richmond Times-Dispatch*, February 25, 1993; Robin Farmer, "'Clustering' to Bring U.S. Investigators Here," *Richmond Times-Dispatch*, March 2, 1993.

51. "A Ragged Ending" (editorial), *Richmond Times-Dispatch*, February 25, 1993.

52. Robin Farmer, "5 Richmond School Principals Reassigned," *Richmond Times-Dispatch*, June 19, 1993; Gary Robertson, "Bellevue PTA President Criticizes Superintendent," *Richmond Times-Dispatch*, June 26, 1993. At a July board meeting, the head of the Bellevue PTA stated that 78 percent of Black families surveyed supported Richardson remaining as principal at the school. Peter Bacque, "City Schools to Use Metal Detectors," *Richmond Times-Dispatch*, July 7, 1993.

53. Robin Farmer, "U.S. Says City Schools Violated, Fixed Bias Problem," *Richmond Times-Dispatch*, July 9, 1993.

54. Cole, "Richmond Public Schools," 111, 134; Robin Farmer, "Bellevue Parents Pushing for Whitlock as Principal," *Richmond Times-Dispatch*, June 6, 1995.

55. Janet Caggiano, "Elected School Board Issue Passes the Test—Measure Is Favored Overwhelmingly," *Richmond Times-Dispatch*, November 3, 1993; "City Voters Approve Elected School Board," *Richmond Free Press*, November 4–6, 1993.

56. "Coalition Pushing Elected School Board," *Richmond Times-Dispatch*, October 20, 1993; Robin Farmer, "REA Wins Drive for Vote on Elected School Board," *Richmond Times-Dispatch*, June 18, 1993.

57. REA president Lola V. McDowell stated in March, "We've been getting so many complaints from members about things going on in the schools and not getting any support. . . . The school system is not getting any better, it's just deteriorating." Robin Farmer, "REA Loses Confidence in Board," *Richmond Times-Dispatch*, March 3, 1993; Farmer, "REA Wins Drive for Vote on Elected School Board."

58. Michael Paul Williams, "NAACP Rejects Proposal at Issue: Elections for School Board," *Richmond Times-Dispatch*, October 27, 1993.

59. Farmer, "REA Wins Drive for Vote on Elected School Board."

60. Bill Wasson, "School Board Election Cleared," *Richmond Times-Dispatch*, April 7, 1994; Robin Farmer, "Most School Board Candidates Agree on Hot Topics: They Favor Prayer, School Security, Sex Education," *Richmond Times-Dispatch*, May 1, 1994. Previously the school board had seven members. Richmond's city charter (20.01), as amended in 1994, provides for school board members to be elected from the same districts as council members. For text of the city charter, see LIS, Virginia Law, accessed March 11, 2024, https://law.lis.virginia.gov/charters/richmond.

61. Robin Farmer, "Richmonders Boot Two Incumbents from School Board—Laws, Brown Lose as Panel Elected for First Time," *Richmond Times-Dispatch*, May 4, 1994. The nine members of Richmond's first elected school board were Blair Nelsen (First District), Mark Emblidge (Second District), Melvin Law (Third District), Alexina Fagan (Fourth District), McEva Bowser (Fifth District), Frank Clark (Sixth District), Delores McQuinn (Seventh District), Linda Freeman (Eighth District), and Eugene Mason (Ninth District).

62. The official recorded vote to hire Conn was unanimous. Robin Farmer, "Split School Board Unites behind Conn," *Richmond Times-Dispatch*, March 8, 1995.

63. School board minutes (1995, p. 419), quoted by Cole, "Richmond Public Schools," 136; "Pro Conn" (staff editorial), *Richmond Times-Dispatch*, September 8, 1995.

64. School board minutes (1995, p. 439), quoted by Cole, "Richmond Public Schools," 137–38.

65. "Conn to Teachers: Miss Class for Fun and Pay the Price," *Richmond Free Press*, February 29–March 2, 1996.

66. *Times-Dispatch* editorialists marked the REA's stance on the issue as "inane" and asked, "Are certain teachers unaware that Wednesday, Thursday, and Friday are schooldays?" "Don't Con Conn" (staff editorial), *Richmond Times-Dispatch*, February 23, 1996.

67. Robin Farmer, "City Teachers Ask Built-In Tourney Holiday," *Richmond Times-Dispatch*, February 23, 1996; Michael Paul Williams, "Teacher Calls Foul on CIAA Tournament Rule," *Richmond Times-Dispatch*, March 4, 1996.

68. Williams, "Teacher Calls Foul on CIAA Tournament Rule"; Jeremy M. Lazarus, "Superintendent's Stand Draws Fire," *Richmond Free Press*, March 14–16, 1996.

69. Robin Farmer, "Conn Withdraws Teacher Restrictions—A Mass Grievance Was Filed by 900," *Richmond Times-Dispatch*, June 14, 1996.

70. Lazarus, "Superintendent's Stand Draws Fire." Conn, using information prepared by the human resources director, had initially stated that close to 500 teachers had left for the CIAA in 1995; in April, school board chair Melvin D. Law stated that the number was at most 119 and that the initial information was faulty. "Grievance on Conn's Desk," *Richmond Free Press*, April 11–13, 1996.

71. The school board also approved a 1996–97 academic calendar making the Friday of the CIAA tournament a teacher workday. Robin Farmer, "Conn Withdraws Teacher Restrictions—A Mass Grievance Was Filed by 900," *Richmond Times-Dispatch*, June 14, 1996.

72. "Teachers 1, Students 0" (staff editorial), *Richmond Times-Dispatch*, June 19, 1996.

73. Robin Farmer, "School Board Fires Conn on 5–4 Vote—Superintendent on Leave until Job Ends June 1," *Richmond Times-Dispatch*, March 2, 1997.

74. Robin Farmer, "Conn Letter Said to List Misdeeds—Insubordination Said to Cause Suspension," *Richmond Times-Dispatch*, January 20, 1997. In February, Conn provided the board a detailed written response to the thirteen allegations. See Robin Farmer, "Conn Spells Out Denials to Board Allegations," *Richmond Times-Dispatch*, February 9, 1997.

75. Robin Farmer, "Schools Chief under Fire—Conn Trying to Lead While Board, Employees Question Her Credibility," *Richmond Times-Dispatch*, December 8, 1996; Robin Farmer, "Conn Is Suspended Up to 45 Days; Sources Say School Chief May Be Fired," *Richmond Times-Dispatch*, January 18, 1997.

76. Robin Farmer, "Conn Firing Denounced—Citizens Group Criticizes Board," *Richmond Times-Dispatch*, March 4, 1997.

77. As one teacher put it regarding the CIAA controversy, "Everybody is extremely angry about being painted as a bunch of people who want to run off to an athletic event and don't care about the children." Williams, "Teacher Calls Foul on CIAA Tournament Rule."

78. Indeed, the Crusade for Voters, which had vigorously protested on behalf of Lois Harrison-Jones in 1988, supported the school board's dismissal of Conn. Michael Paul Williams, "Crusade Supports Firing of Conn," *Richmond Times-Dispatch*, March 19, 1997.

79. Robin Farmer, "Va. Beach Educator Selected—Dr. Williams Unanimous Pick to Head City Schools," *Richmond Times-Dispatch*, September 18, 1997.

80. Robin Farmer, "Thinking of Performance—Incoming City School Chief Pledges to Work Closely with the REA," *Richmond Times-Dispatch*, September 19, 1997.

81. Michael Paul Williams, "Richmond Schools Chief Issues a Call to Action," *Richmond Times-Dispatch*, April 23, 1998.

82. Robin Farmer, "Emblidge Heads School Board," *Richmond Time-Dispatch*, July 2, 1998.

83. School-by-School SOL Results for 1998–2002, Virginia Department of Education website, accessed September 30, 2023, www.doe.virginia.gov/data-policy-funding/data-reports/statistics-reports/archived-reports.

84. Robin Farmer, "Richmond Will Strive to Improve SOL Scores," *Richmond Times-Dispatch*, November 1, 1998.

85. For an early account recognizing the impact of poverty, see Robin Farmer, "Summer Study May Boost Test Scores—Some in City Short of Goal," *Richmond Times-Dispatch*, October 9, 1998.

86. For instance, despite a modest improvement in RPS test scores, the 20-point gap in third-grade English pass rates between city schools and the statewide average (35 to 55 percent) in 1998 actually widened to a 25-point gap by 2001 (40 percent to 65 percent). School-by-School SOL Results for 1998–2002.

87. Jason Wermers, "School Chief to Accept Offer," *Richmond Times-Dispatch*, March 7, 2001.

88. Jason Wermers and Paige Akin, "40% of Schools 'Fully Accredited,'" *Richmond Times-Dispatch*, October 17, 2001.

89. Jason Wermers, "City School Chief Plans to Retire," *Richmond Times-Dispatch*, January 8, 2002; Jeremy M. Lazarus, "School Superintendent Drops Bombshell," *Richmond Free Press*, January 10–12, 2002; "Williams Departs" (staff editorial), *Richmond Times-Dispatch*, January 18, 2002.

90. Jason Wermers, "New City Schools Chief Search Is Continuing," *Richmond Times-Dispatch*, June 5, 2002; Jason Wermers, "City Picks New Leaders; School Division's No. 2 Official Is Promoted to Superintendent," *Richmond Times-Dispatch*, July 2, 2002; "Good Luck" (staff editorial), *Richmond Times-Dispatch*, July 3, 2002.

91. Jason Wermers, "Superintendent's Job Tied to SOL Scores," *Richmond Times-Dispatch*, August 1, 2002.

92. Jason Wermers, "SOL Results—64% of Schools Hit Mark—Full Accreditation List Makes Biggest Leap Yet," *Richmond Times-Dispatch*, November 8, 2002.

93. Quoted in Daniel L. Duke, *Leadership for Low-Performing Schools: A Step-by-Step Guide to the School Turnaround Process* (Latham, MD: Rowman and Littlefield, 2015), 193–94.

94. Jewell-Sherman quoted in Kristy Cooper, Laura Kelly, Leslie Boozer, and Aaliyah El-Amin, "Deborah Jewell-Sherman, Richmond Public Schools: Getting to the Heart of the Work," in *Every Child, Every Classroom, Every Day: School Leaders Who Are Making Equity a Reality*, ed. Robert S. Peterkin, Deborah Jewell-Sherman, Laura Kelley, and Leslie Boozer (San Francisco: Jossey-Bass, 2011), 95. See also Duke, *Leadership for Low-Performing Schools*; Daniel L. Duke and Michael Salmonowicz, "Deborah Jewell-Sherman and the Richmond Public Schools: A Promising Start Is Just the Beginning," University of Virginia Partnership for Leaders in Education, unpublished case study, 2005; and Deborah Jewell-Sherman, "City Schools Want to Make Back-to-Class Exciting," *Richmond Times-Dispatch*, August 22, 2004.

95. The Council of the Great City Schools is a national organization providing research and technical support to the nation's largest urban school systems. School systems for cities with populations larger than 250,000 and student enrollment exceeding 35,000

or school districts located in the largest city in their state are eligible to participate; in 2008 there were sixty-six member systems. See Council of the Great City Schools website, accessed September 30, 2023, www.cgcs.org/Page/623; and Council of the Great City Schools, "Urban School Superintendents: Characteristics, Tenure, and Salary; Sixth Survey and Report," *Urban Indicator*, Winter 2008/2009, https://files.eric.ed.gov/fulltext/ED508236.pdf.

96. Council of the Great City Schools, *Charting a New Course for Richmond Public Schools, Report of the Strategic Support Team of the Council of the Great City Schools to Richmond Public Schools*, December 2003, 10–15, http://files.eric.ed.gov/fulltext/ED498857.pdf.

97. Duke and Salmonowicz, "Deborah Jewell-Sherman and the Richmond Public Schools."

98. *Charting a New Course for Richmond Public Schools*, 26–27.

99. The report's enumeration of the district's problems in developing a culture of accountability is quoted below (see *Charting a New Course for Richmond Public Schools*, 29):

- Staff evaluations lack any accountability for performance.
- The district has no mechanism for holding staff, principals, and teachers accountable for student achievement.
- There is no accountability for student performance beyond the SOL results or state accreditation standards. No one is held accountable for course-taking patterns, dropout or discipline rates, SAT scores, or the like.
- Priority is being placed on state accreditation rather than student performance more broadly. The focus on accreditation has a dampening effect on staff expectations about student performance.
- The district's staff takes little personal ownership of student achievement or their department's effectiveness.
- The district operates in silos with little sense of teamwork or shared responsibility for student achievement.

100. *Charting a New Course for Richmond Public Schools*, 75.

101. *Charting a New Course for Richmond Public Schools*, 85.

102. *Charting a New Course for Richmond Public Schools*, 86.

103. Implementation of the report's recommendations later became the basis of a memorandum of understanding between Richmond Public Schools and the Virginia Department of Education, approved in March 2005. Lindsay Kastner, "Plan to Improve City Schools Is Made Official," *Richmond Times-Dispatch*, March 23, 2005.

104. Jason Wermers, "City Urged to Overhaul Special Education—State Calls for 'Immediate Attention,'" *Richmond Times-Dispatch*, March 2, 2003; Jason Wermers, "School Official Resigning," *Richmond Times-Dispatch*, March 13, 2003.

105. Duke and Salmonowicz, "Deborah Jewell-Sherman and the Richmond Public Schools"; Jason Wermers, "Board Supports Jewell-Sherman—7 of 9 Members Vote to Express Confidence in the Superintendent," *Richmond Times-Dispatch*, October 21, 2003.

106. Jason Wermers, "Va. Students Improve Performance on SOLs—City Superintendent Pleased with Progress," *Richmond Times-Dispatch*, November 11, 2003.

107. School-by-School SOL Results for 1998–2002 and 2003–5, Virginia Department of Education website, accessed September 30, 2023, www.doe.virginia.gov/data-policy-funding/data-reports/statistics-reports/archived-reports. In 2003, just 7 of 31 RPS elementary

schools had English pass rates for third graders above 70 percent, below Jewell-Sherman's contract target of 16, with an additional 5 schools achieving at least a 65 percent pass rate.

108. Jason Wermers, "School Chief: Get on Same Page—Jewell-Sherman Says Opponents on School Board and Elsewhere Hamper Progress on SOL Scores," *Richmond Times-Dispatch*, November 19, 2003.

109. See Deborah Jewell-Sherman, "Community Has a Stake in Making Public Schools Work," *Richmond Times-Dispatch*, February 22, 2004, for the debut column in the yearlong series.

110. Olympia Meola, "A Scorecard for City Schools—The School System Institutes Strategies and Benchmarks to Monitor and Obtain Goals," *Richmond Times-Dispatch*, September 14, 2005.

111. Lindsay Kastner, "City Board Rescinds Extension—Timing of Contract for Superintendent Violated State Law," *Richmond Times-Dispatch*, December 9, 2004; Lindsay Kastner, "Schools Chief Signs $152,250 Contract; Board to Determine the Criteria She Must Meet Each Year to Get Bonus," *Richmond Times-Dispatch*, March 10, 2005.

112. Lauren Shepherd, "Group Wants to Help City's Future Leaders—Wilder and Bliley Are Forming a Panel to Outline Some Issues That Need to Be Addressed," *Richmond Times-Dispatch*, December 30, 2003.

113. Lindsay Kastner, "More Powers for New Mayor?," *Richmond Times-Dispatch*, November 20, 2004.

114. Lindsay Kastner, "Wilder Suggests City School Reforms," *Richmond Times-Dispatch*, December 4, 2004.

115. Lindsay Kastner, "Wilder, Howell Target Truancy," *Richmond Times-Dispatch*, February 2, 2005; Lindsay Kastner, "Offices of the Richmond School System to Move—The Administrative Offices Are Going to the East End to the Armstrong High School Site," *Richmond Times-Dispatch*, February 15, 2005; Lindsay Kastner, "School Board to Vote on Budget Proposal in Richmond," *Richmond Times-Dispatch*, March 19, 2005; Lindsay Kastner, "Spellings Backs Charter Schools," *Richmond Times-Dispatch*, March 18, 2005.

116. Lindsay Kastner, "Chief Will Stay On—Jewell-Sherman Had Been Finalist for Job in Norfolk and St. Louis—She Says There's No Place Like Home," *Richmond Times-Dispatch*, March 2, 2005; Kastner, "Schools Chief Signs $152,250 Contract."

117. Gil Klein, "Urban Schools Show Progress," *Richmond Times-Dispatch*, March 29, 2005.

118. Lindsay Kastner and Olympia Meola, "Answers on SOL Do Not Match—Teachers Filled in Students' Choices, but Discrepancies Are Noticed after Review," *Richmond Times-Dispatch*, June 30, 2005.

119. Lindsay Kastner, "Ex-Principal at Oak Grove Fired over SOL Testing," *Richmond Times-Dispatch*, October 7, 2005.

120. David Ress and Lindsay Kastner, "Wilder Creates Watchdog Panel for City Schools," *Richmond Times-Dispatch*, July 20, 2005; Lindsay Kastner, "School Chief Quits Panel—Chesterfield's Cannaday: Wilder Didn't Say Members Would Oversee City Schools," *Richmond Times-Dispatch*, July 27, 2005.

121. Ress and Kastner, "Wilder Creates Watchdog Panel for City Schools."

122. Michael Paul Williams, "Does Board Need Hall Monitors?," *Richmond Times-Dispatch*, July 22, 2005.

123. James Schroeder, "Task Force Insults Richmond's Schools" (letter to the editor), *Richmond Times-Dispatch*, August 6, 2005; Ress and Kastner, "Wilder Creates Watchdog Panel for City Schools."

124. Ress and Kastner, "Wilder Creates Watchdog Panel for City Schools."

125. Lindsay Kastner, "Advisory Panel Questions City's Per-Pupil Spending," *Richmond Times-Dispatch*, April 20, 2006.

126. Lindsay Kastner, "School, City Officials at It Again—Feud in Richmond Involves Who Decides What Schools Are Built," *Richmond Times-Dispatch*, October 2, 2006.

127. Lindsay Kastner, "Wilder Quiet on Schools Elections—Those Familiar with School Board Races Say the Mayor Is Working behind the Scenes," *Richmond Times-Dispatch*, October 9, 2006; Lindsay Kastner, "Wolf, Mimms Re-elected to School Board," *Richmond Times-Dispatch*, November 8, 2006; Lindsay Kastner, "Braxton to Lead School Board," *Richmond Times-Dispatch*, January 3, 2007.

128. Lindsay Kastner, "Audit Identifies School Savings—Richmond System Could Save $19.8 Million; Overstaffing, Poor Record Keeping Cited," *Richmond Times-Dispatch*, February 8, 2007; Michael Martz, "Wilder Sets New Audit of Schools—City Negotiating Price with D.C. Firm; School Board Hasn't Decided Whether to Cooperate," *Richmond Times-Dispatch*, March 9, 2007.

129. Lindsay Kastner and Michael Martz, "School Board Sues City," *Richmond Times-Dispatch*, March 22, 2007.

130. Michael Martz, "Schools Agree to New City Audit," *Richmond Times-Dispatch*, April 6, 2007; Michael Martz, "Next Phase in City-Schools Fight—Court Ruling in Hand, Officials Hope to Find Common Ground," *Richmond Times-Dispatch*, April 8, 2007. The Richmond Circuit Court sided with Wilder on the school board suit, stating that the board had not shown that the delays in payment had caused "irreparable harm." Lindsay Kastner, "Wilder Wins Schools Dispute—Judge: Richmond Doesn't Have to Release Funds Now; School Leaders Mull Appeal," *Richmond Times-Dispatch*, April 7, 2007.

131. Amid the auditing controversy, Wilder pointedly declined an invitation to travel with Jewell-Sherman and board chair Braxton on a Chamber of Commerce regional trip to Oklahoma City, telling Greater Richmond Chamber of Commerce CEO James Dunn in a January letter, "I could not and cannot, in good conscience recommend that any joint venture on a regional basis take place relative to education with the dysfunctional system of responsibility and fiscal accounting now taking place in Richmond Public Schools." Michael Paul Williams, "For Wilder, Isolation Is Not Leading," *Richmond Times-Dispatch*, April 25, 2007. Williams then added his own observation: "All the squabbling shows how utterly unprepared we were to move to this new form of government. More than two years later, we're still working out the kinks."

132. Lindsay Kastner and Michael Martz, "Wilder Criticizes Schools Chief," *Richmond Times-Dispatch*, July 3, 2007.

133. Michael Martz, "City Schools' Eviction Leads to Showdown—Wilder's Ultimatum Prompts Richmond Council to Step In," *Richmond Times-Dispatch*, June 26, 2007. Prior to the explosive events of August and September 2007, former mayor and RPS principal Roy West reemerged in a July 2007 interview with *Style Weekly* offering this public warning concerning Wilder's plans for RPS: "I would say that the mayor's attitude towards public education is similar to his attitude towards everything else. It's egotistically driven. If

he can't control it, he will destroy it. And that's what's happening in public education in Richmond today." Amy Biegelsen, "Wild West," *Style Weekly*, July 11, 2007.

134. Letter of August 3, 2007, reprinted as "Business Leaders Pledge to Help Improve City Schools," *Richmond Times-Dispatch*, August 8, 2007.

135. Jane Martin, "Do Leaders Send Own Kids to City Schools?" (letter to the editor) *Richmond Times-Dispatch*, August 19, 2007. See also Olympia Meola and David Ress, "Many Lean Towards Elected School Boards," *Richmond Times-Dispatch*, September 12, 2007.

136. Michael Martz, "School Critics Explain—Business Leaders Urging Changes in Richmond Schools Give Their Takes," *Richmond Times-Dispatch*, September 10, 2007. While several letter signers said Wilder did not know about the letter in advance, Wilder's reported reaction to its arrival was positive; the mayor stated, "The next step is for the people of the city of Richmond to determine what kind of school system they want and what kind of representation they want." Michael Martz, "Business Leaders Seek School Changes—They Tell Wilder They Want School Board Members Appointed," *Richmond Times-Dispatch*, August 7, 2007. In an effort to reunify community leaders, school board members Betsy Carr and Lisa Dawson reached out to letter signers Robert J. Grey Jr. and William Goodwin to propose forming a new blue-ribbon commission focused on the schools' needs—a proposal quickly rejected by Wilder. Martz, "School Critics Explain."

137. James A. Crupi, *Putting the Future Together*, 2007, 29, https://lmrcommunity.files.wordpress.com/2007/11/putting_the_future_together_final.pdf. The 2007 Crupi Report was supported by some forty business leaders, its release coordinated with the Greater Richmond Chamber of Commerce. Michael Martz, "Leaders Brace for Report's Candor—Consultant Takes Frank Look at Richmond Region after Doing Same in 1993," *Richmond Times-Dispatch*, November 18, 2007. The second report garnered notice but lacked the explosive impact of the 1993 report, with some critics saying that its findings either were obvious or reflected an elite perspective. David Ress, "Report's Critics Cite Lack of Depth—Critique of Richmond Area Obvious and Not Inclusive, They Say," *Richmond Times-Dispatch*, November 21, 2007.

138. Cordel L. Faulk, "Subject: The Richmond School Board," *Richmond Times-Dispatch*, September 23, 2007.

139. Eugene Hickok, "Time for a Long Overdue Talk about Schools," *Richmond Times-Dispatch*, August 19, 2007.

140. Columnist Michael Paul Williams branded the proposal "hubris on steroids." Michael Paul Williams, "School Board Idea Is Out of Left Field," *Richmond Times-Dispatch*, August 8, 2007. In an open response to the letter signers, Rev. Benjamin P. Campbell, pastoral director of Richmond Hill and spouse of an RPS teacher, asked, "Why the attack? ... Our primary problem is not incompetence or waste, nor is it an elected School Board. We have too many distressed children and too few resources. Everybody knows that's the truth." Benjamin P. Campbell, "Here is How We Can Better Richmond's Schools," *Richmond Times-Dispatch*, September 10, 2007.

141. The request for the injunction was filed by Henry L. Marsh, who was retained by the school board in an emergency meeting held while the attempted eviction was ongoing. Michael Martz, "Chaos Erupts at City Hall—Pantele PC Linked to Porn; Council Aides Must Do Interviews," *Richmond Times-Dispatch*, September 22, 2007; "City 'Steadfast'

Wilder Had Authority to Evict School Offices," *Richmond Times-Dispatch*, September 22, 2007; Olympia Meola, "School Board Offices a Mess—Eviction Aftermath Astounds Employees—Confidential Papers Left in Open at City Hall—Richmond Schools Are in Session Today," *Richmond Times-Dispatch*, September 24, 2007. Subsequent investigation found no evidence of criminal activity on any city computer but did find that over eighty employees in numerous departments had visited pornographic sites at least fifty times in violation of city policy, including two who had accessed such sites over 12,000 times in two months. The decision to name Pantele, whose open-access city hall computer was found to have a single hit on an inappropriate site, was widely interpreted as a political ploy to distract from the school board evictions, and he was soon cleared in the matter. Jeremy M. Lazarus, "Pandemonium," *Richmond Free Press*, September 27–29, 2007; Bill Wasson, "City Workers Could Be Fired over Web Porn," *Richmond Times-Dispatch*, September 30, 2007; Michael Martz, "2 Expected to Be Fired over Web Porn—Pantele Says He Has Been Cleared in Probe into Use of Richmond Computers," *Richmond Times-Dispatch*, October 9, 2007.

142. "City 'Steadfast' Wilder Had Authority to Evict School Offices"; Meola, "School Board Offices a Mess."

143. City council member Chris Hilbert provided this extended comment on the events of September 21, 2007, in a July 1, 2010, interview by Lucas Hakkenberg and Thad Williamson:

> It was a classic divide-and-conquer strategy. . . . [Wilder] planned this pretty well. . . . I think the miscalculation that he made was that council and the school board would acquiesce to this. I don't think that he was wrong in his calculation that if he got them out of the building, they would never return. I'm glad that people were resolute in saying this is outside of the law and we took an oath to uphold the law and we're not going to stand for this. Otherwise, if we'd even hesitated on this, Judge Spencer would not [have ruled as she did]. Everybody got together and said this isn't right. If we'd had a lag time, it would have happened.

144. Lazarus, "Pandemonium"; Michael Martz and David Ress, "Council Joins Schools' Suit—It Blasts Wilder for City Hall Eviction Chaos," *Richmond Times-Dispatch*, September 25, 2007.

145. David Ress and Michael Martz, "Schools Audit Sparks Calls for Change—Richmond Officials Pledge to Tighten Purchasing Controls," *Richmond Times-Dispatch*, April 4, 2008.

146. Zachary Reid, "Richmond Schools Chief Will Call It Quits—Jewell-Sherman Says Recent Critical Audit Was Not Factor in Timing of Her Decision," *Richmond Times-Dispatch*, April 8, 2008.

147. Zachary Reid, "Richmond School Superintendent Is Honored," *Richmond Times-Dispatch*, May 7, 2008; Zachary Reid, "Richmond Schools Chief Leaving for Harvard Job—She'll Depart in July; Interim Leader Could Come from City Ranks," *Richmond Times-Dispatch*, June 4, 2008.

148. "Resignation" (staff editorial), *Richmond Times-Dispatch*, April 8, 2008.

149. School-by-School SOL results, 2001–8, Virginia Department of Education website, accessed February 17, 2024, www.doe.virginia.gov/data-policy-funding/data-reports/statistics-reports/sol-test-pass-rates-other-results; Reid, "Richmond School Superintendent Is Honored."

150. Cooper et al., "Deborah Jewell-Sherman, Richmond Public Schools," 96. School board member Kim Bridges (2007–12) offered these reflections on Deborah Jewell-Sherman's tenure and departure in a May 24, 2011, interview with Thad Williamson and Lucas Hakkenberg: "I think she was under enormous pressure from the city administration at that time. . . . Being a superintendent would be an incredibly stressful job. You add the urban component to it and you've increased the level of stress. You add a city administration that was just plain out hostile to the school system, and actually working against efforts the schools had underway, [and] who could blame you for taking a job in higher ed?"

151. Zachary Reid, "Brandon Becomes Chief of Richmond Schools," *Richmond Times-Dispatch*, January 28, 2009.

152. Zachary Reid, "Selling the Schools—A New Marketing Plan Urges Residents to Reconsider Urban Education," *Richmond Times-Dispatch*, May 3, 2009.

153. Michael Martz, "Parents Object to Preschool Consolidation," *Richmond Times-Dispatch*, May 18, 2010.

154. Katrina Comissiong-Williams, a Maymont Elementary parent who favored the proposal, noted the lengths that administrative leaders went to reassure Fox and Munford parents that the Maymont building would be fine and cited this as evidence of continuing inequity within RPS: "Maymont Elementary has heating, cooling, and pest problems. None of them mattered to the School Board members before the strong reaction Superintendent Brandon received to the regional preschool proposal. They were perfectly content to let our children attend elementary school in an aging, poorly maintained building." Katrina Comissiong-Williams, "City School Leaders Favor Students from the Fan," *Richmond Times-Dispatch*, May 30, 2010. See also "Good Move" (staff editorial), *Richmond Times-Dispatch*, June 12, 2010.

155. Michael Martz, "Richmond School Board Votes for Consolidated Preschool Location," *Richmond Times-Dispatch*, June 7, 2010; "Good Move"; Anne Dreyfuss, "Consolidating Kids," *Richmond Magazine*, February 17, 2011.

156. Nick Dutton, "NAACP Blasts Mayor for RPS 'Mediocrity' Statements," WTVR news report, February 15, 2012; Michael Martz, "Mayor Lays Out Priorities for Richmond," *Richmond Times-Dispatch*, February 1, 2012.

157. 2007–8 and 2010–11 SOL Results and Graduation Rates, Virginia Department of Education website, accessed September 30, 2023, www.doe.virginia.gov/data-policy-funding/data-reports/statistics. City accreditation levels fell sharply in 2012, to thirty-two schools of forty-six, after the introduction of a more rigorous math SOL that year. Zachary Reid, "School Accreditation Down after Math Standards Increased," *Richmond Times-Dispatch*, September 27, 2012.

158. Michael Martz, "School Board Has Put a $147.5 Million Budget Request before Mayor Dwight C. Jones," *Richmond Times-Dispatch*, February 17, 2012.

159. Michael Martz, "Jones Forms Task Force to Cut Richmond Schools Budget," *Richmond Times-Dispatch*, March 6, 2012.

160. Robert Bobb Group, *Final Report to the Mayor's School Accountability and Efficiency Task Force*, April 16, 2012 (in Thad Williamson's possession); "Major Recommendations, Projected Savings for Richmond Schools" (staff report), *Richmond Times-Dispatch*, April 11, 2012. The initial recommendations were headlined by a proposal to privatize bus operations, which were projected to save $6 million, and an additional $7.3 million in savings or cuts, including implementing a three-day furlough; cutting twenty teaching positions

(exempting K–3); cutting the custodial staff, security staff, and classroom aides (sixty-three positions in all); cutting eight to twelve central office staff; and reducing the contract length of some personnel.

161. Robert Zullo, "Richmond Schools Likely to Get $5.5m Extra from City Council," *Richmond Times-Dispatch*, April 26, 2012.

162. Robert Zullo, "School Board Critics Say Panel Faces Same Problems Next Year," *Richmond Times-Dispatch*, June 5, 2012.

163. Robert Zullo, "Residents Ask Richmond City Council to Give Schools More Funds," *Richmond Times-Dispatch*, April 11, 2012. Three former school board members, Dave Ballard, Lisa Dawson, and Larry Olanrewaju, published a piece defending the school board and criticizing the "posturing" from the mayor's office. Ballard, Dawson, and Olanrewaju, "Why So Much Contention around Richmond's City Schools?," *Richmond Times-Dispatch*, June 17, 2012.

164. Zachary Reid, "Richmond School Board Being Bypassed after Dispute," *Richmond Times-Dispatch*, June 6, 2012.

165. Michael Paul Williams, "Richmond Elections Could Mean New Dynamic at City Hall," *Richmond Times-Dispatch*, November 7, 2012; Jeremy M. Lazarus, "City Democrats Seek to Oust Critics of Mayor," *Richmond Free Press*, October 4, 2012.

166. Michael Paul Williams, "There Looks to Be a Power behind the School Board," *Richmond Times-Dispatch*, January 4, 2013.

167. "Richmond Schools Superintendent Yvonne Brandon to Step Down," *Richmond Times-Dispatch*, April 16, 2013; Michael Martz, "Departure Called 'Mutual Decision,'" *Richmond Times-Dispatch*, April 16, 2013.

168. Siegel-Hawley et al., "Increasing Diversity in the City Schools," appendix, figure 1.

169. 2011–12 Fall Membership Report, Virginia Department of Education website, accessed September 30, 2023, https://p1pe.doe.virginia.gov/buildatable/fallmembership.

170. Siegel-Hawley et al., "Increasing Diversity in the City Schools," table 4; Olympia Meola, "Bus Doesn't Stop for All—Richmond Parents Whose Kids Attend Schools outside Their Zone Face Tough Choice," *Richmond Times-Dispatch*, September 17, 2007.

171. In 2011, over 60 percent of students at both Cary and Bellevue came from out-of-zone. Siegel-Hawley et al., "Increasing Diversity in the City Schools," table 4.

172. Michael Paul Williams, "Cary Flap Poor Model for the Future," *Richmond Times-Dispatch*, July 18, 2007.

173. Siegel-Hawley et al., "Increasing Diversity in the City Schools," table 4.

174. Cropper Analytics, "Richmond Public Schools 2011–2012 Rezoning Process: Background Report," October 25, 2011, www.croppermap.com/documents/RPSBackgroundReportFull111023.pdf.

175. Zachary Reid, "Redistricting Plan Could Close Three Elementary Schools," *Richmond Times-Dispatch*, February 15, 2012; Michael Paul Williams, "Closing John B. Cary Would Be Tragic," *Richmond Times-Dispatch*, February 17, 2012; Zachary Reid, "Richmond School Board Puts Off Vote on School Closures," *Richmond Times-Dispatch*, June 16, 2012.

176. Zachary Reid, "Session on Richmond School Rezoning Draws Large Crowd," *Richmond Times-Dispatch*, February 16, 2012; Zachary Reid, "City School Board Finds Way to Keep Fisher Elementary Open," *Richmond Times-Dispatch*, July 17, 2012; Zachary Reid, "Richmond School Board Silences 2 Members," *Richmond Times-Dispatch*, August 21, 2012.

177. Zachary Reid, "Cary, Fisher Adding Sixth-Grade Classes Next Year," *Richmond Times-Dispatch*, December 4, 2012.

178. Zachary Reid, "K–6 Idea at Cary, Fisher Elementary Schools on Hold," *Richmond Times-Dispatch*, January 24, 2013.

179. Zachary Reid, "Richmond School Board Approves Budget Plan," *Richmond Times-Dispatch*, February 27, 2013.

180. 2012–13 Fall Membership Report, Virginia Department of Education website, accessed September 30, 2023, https://p1pe.doe.virginia.gov/buildatable/fallmembership.

181. Minutes of April 8, 2013, 7 p.m., Richmond School Board meeting, Richmond Public Schools Board Docs, https://go.boarddocs.com/vsba/richmond/Board.nsf/Public; 2011–12 SOL Test data, Virginia Department of Education website, accessed September 30, 2023, www.doe.virginia.gov/data-policy-funding/data-reports/statistics-reports/sol-test-pass-rates-other-results.

182. Zachary Reid, "Richmond School Board Votes against Closing Schools," *Richmond Times-Dispatch*, April 22, 2013.

183. "A Petition to Rezone the Museum District to William Fox and/or Mary Munford," *RVA News*, April 2, 2013, https://rvanews.com/etc/a-petition-to-rezone-the-museum-district-to-william-fox-andor-mary-munford/89124.

184. The eventually approved proposal reduced the percentage of white children in grades 1–8 in the Blackwell zone from 28.5 percent to zero while increasing in the Westover Hills zone from 13.5 percent to 55.9 percent. Siegel-Hawley et al., "Increasing Diversity in the City Schools," tables 1–2.

185. Zachary Reid, "Richmond School Board Resuscitates School Closures Plan," *Richmond Times-Dispatch*, May 13, 2013. Mamie Taylor responded to the successful motion by introducing an alternative motion to close Fox, J. B. Fisher, Ginter Park, and Carver Elementary Schools. That motion was defeated 5–3. Minutes of the May 13, 2013, Richmond School Board work session, Richmond Public Schools Board Docs, https://go.boarddocs.com/vsba/richmond/Board.nsf/Public. A map of the original Option C rezoning plan presented on May 13, 2013, is in Thad Williamson's possession, obtained May 16, 2013, via the Richmond Public Schools Clerk.

186. Minutes of the May 28, 2013, and June 3, 2013, Richmond School Board work sessions, Richmond Public Schools Board Docs, https://go.boarddocs.com/vsba/richmond/Board.nsf/Public. See also Thad Williamson and Adria Scharf, "50 Questions for the School Board," *RVA News*, May 28, 2013, https://rvanews.com/news/50-questions-for-the-rps-school-board/94318.

187. Thad Williamson, "Twilight Zoning," *Style Weekly*, May 28, 2013; minutes of the May 20, 2013, Richmond School Board meeting, Richmond Public Schools Board Docs, https://go.boarddocs.com/vsba/richmond/Board.nsf/Public.

188. "Richmond Public Schools VA Elementary Rezoning Options," Cropper GIS, May 2013, in Thad Williamson's possession. These projections largely held up in practice after the rezoning. The percentage of white students at John B. Cary fell from 21 percent in 2012–13 to 9 percent in 2013–14, and the percentage of Latino students fell from 7 percent to 1 percent over the same time period. The percentage of Black students increased from 69 percent to 86 percent. Meanwhile, the percentage of Black students at William Fox declined from 23 percent in 2012–13 to 21 percent in 2013–14. By 2015–16, the close of this study, the percentage of Black students at Fox had declined to 17 percent. 2012–13, 2013–14,

and 2015–16 Fall Membership Reports, Virginal Department of Education website, accessed September 30, 2023, https://p1pe.doe.virginia.gov/buildatable/fallmembership. For a related analysis of the 2013 rezoning, see Siegel-Hawley et al., "Increasing Diversity in the City Schools." See also Genevieve Siegel-Hawley, Kimberly Bridges and Thomas J. Shields, "Solidifying Segregation or Promoting Diversity? School Closure and Rezoning in an Urban District," *Education Administration Quarterly* 53 (2017): 107–41.

189. Williamson, "Twilight Zoning."

190. Zachary Reid, "City School Board Votes to Close Three Schools," *Richmond Times-Dispatch*, June 4, 2013.

191. The adjustments kept streets north of the I-195 expressway but south of Cary Street, in close proximity to the school, in the J. B. Cary Elementary zone. See minutes of June 3, 2013, Richmond School Board meeting, Richmond Public Schools Board Docs, https://go.boarddocs.com/vsba/richmond/Board.nsf/Public.

192. "Closure" (staff editorial), *Richmond Times-Dispatch*, May 23, 2013. See also Jeff Bourne and Kim B. Gray, "Should These Richmond Schools Stay Open? No—Under-Enrolled Facilities Are Inefficient, Unsustainable," *Richmond Times-Dispatch*, June 3, 2013.

193. For an overview of the vast research on linkages between concentrated poverty and student achievement, see Rosyln Arlin Mickelson, "Is There Systematic Meaningful Evidence of School Poverty Thresholds?," National Coalition for School Diversity, Research Brief 14, September 2018, www.school-diversity.org/. Mickelson concludes that "educational decision makers should focus on reducing concentrations of school-level poverty to as low a level as is feasible given the available demographic mix." On racial integration and democracy, see Elizabeth Anderson, *The Imperative of Integration* (Princeton, NJ: Princeton University Press, 2010).

194. Minutes of the June 3, 2013, Richmond School Board meeting; Reid, "City School Board Votes to Close Three Schools." See also Donald J. Coleman, "Should These Richmond Schools Stay Open? Yes—Changes Would Undermine Crucial Diversity Potential," *Richmond Times-Dispatch*, June 3, 2013.

195. In the immediate aftermath of the school closing decisions, a grassroots effort called the Richmond Coalition for Quality Education, anchored in the Clark Springs and Randolph communities and supported by a variety of former public officials, community leaders, and concerned academics, formed to seek to reverse the decision as well as pursue legal challenges. A July motion to reverse the closures again failed on a 5–4 vote, and legal challenges ultimately proved unsuccessful. Graham Moomaw, "Push to Revisit School Closures Fails to Sway School Board," *Richmond Times-Dispatch*, July 15, 2013; K. Burnell Evans, "Judge Dismisses Rezoning Lawsuit against Richmond School Board," *Richmond Times-Dispatch*, January 8, 2016.

196. In 2019, the Fox-Cary zoning issue would be revisited as the school board considered but ultimately rejected Superintendent Jason Kamras's proposal to "pair" the two schools, with one building serving K–2 students and the other third–fifth graders. The board did act, however, to reverse much of the 2013 zoning, with the projected effect of reducing the percentage of Black students at Cary from 86 percent to 57 percent and increasing it at Fox from 22 percent to 37 percent. Justin Mattingly, "'It Was Shameful': After Months of Debate, Richmond School Board Changes Little in School Zones," *Richmond Times-Dispatch*, December 18, 2019.

197. Zachary Reid, "Bedden Stays with Richmond Public Schools," *Richmond Times-Dispatch*, March 4, 2015; Graham Moomaw, "$9 M Boost Set for City Schools," *Richmond Times-Dispatch*, May 3, 2015.

198. The initially proposed $1.5 million increase was to be funded from allowing RPS to carry over projected savings from 2015–16 into the new fiscal year. City of Richmond, *Proposed Amendments to the Biennial Fiscal Plan for Fiscal Year 2017*, March 4, 2016, https://rva.gov/sites/default/files/2019-04/2017_ProposedBiennialFiscalPlan.pdf; Michael Paul Williams, "City Can't Afford Not to Invest in Schools," *Richmond Times-Dispatch*, April 1, 2016.

199. Ned Oliver, "Official: City Hopes to Avoid School Closures," *Richmond Times-Dispatch*, May 5, 2016.

200. K. Burnell Evans, "Richmond Schools, City Seek Unity," *Richmond Times-Dispatch*, April 7, 2017; Mark Robinson, "Mayor's Education Compact Gets OK—Richmond's City Council, School Board Sign Off on Mayor Stoney's Education Compact," *Richmond Times-Dispatch*, August 22, 2017. Disclosure: In his capacity as transition director and the senior policy adviser to Stoney in 2016 and 2017, Thad Williamson played a lead role in developing the Education Compact, soliciting community feedback, revising the proposal, and ultimately securing its adoption by the school board and the city council.

201. The board provided no substantive explanation for its decision and signed a separation agreement barring the board from public criticism of Bedden. K. Burnell Evans, "Criticism of Bedden Forbidden under Joint Agreement—Richmond School Board Forfeits Right to Criticize Bedden, Sets $114/Hr Consulting Rate in Separation Agreement," *Richmond Times-Dispatch*, May 4, 2017.

202. K. Burnell Evans, "Richmond School Leaders Vow to Make Improvements—State, Richmond Public Schools Move toward Agreement on Implementing Corrective Actions," *Richmond Times-Dispatch*, June 23, 2017.

203. K. Burnell Evans, "Richmond Public Schools Gets Low Marks in State Review," *Richmond Times-Dispatch*, June 19, 2017.

204. See John Charles Boger and Gary Orfield, eds., *School Resegregation: Must the South Turn Back?* (Chapel Hill: University of North Carolina Press, 2005). See also Sonya Ramsey, "The Troubled History of American Education after the *Brown* Decision," Organization of American Historians, February 2017, www.oah.org/tah/february-3/the-troubled-history-of-american-education-after-the-brown-decision/.

CHAPTER 5

1. For more on the American civil rights movement and anti-poverty, see Sylvie Laurent, *King and the Other America: The Poor People's Campaign and the Quest for Economic Equality* (Berkeley: University of California Press, 2019); and Wesley G. Phelps, *A People's War on Poverty* (Athens: University of Georgia Press, 2014).

2. Bayard Rustin, "From Protest to Politics: The Future of the Civil Rights Movement," *Commentary* 39, no. 2 (1965), 25–31.

3. Julian Maxwell Hayter, *The Dream Is Lost: Voting Rights and the Politics of Race in Richmond, Virginia* (Lexington: University Press of Kentucky, 2017), chap. 4.

4. U.S. Census 1990, Tables SE T93, T94, T101, accessed, June 30, 2023, via Social Explorer, www.socialexplorer.com/tables/C1990. Based on 1989 incomes.

5. U.S. Census 1990, Tables SE T22, SE T43, SE T73, and SE T97, accessed June 30, 2023, via Social Explorer, www.socialexplorer.com/tables/C1990.

6. A 1999 Brookings Institution study found that a college, university, or medical system was a top-ten employer in each of the nation's twenty largest cities. Ira Harkavy and Harmon Zuckerman, "Meds and Eds: Cities' Hidden Assets," Brookings, September 1, 1999, www.brookings.edu/articles/eds-and-meds-cities-hidden-assets/.

7. Hayter, *Dream Is Lost*, 159–64.

8. Hayter, *Dream Is Lost*, 149–50.

9. John V. Moeser and Rutledge M. Dennis, *The Politics of Annexation: Oligarchic Power in a Southern City* (Cambridge, MA: Schenkman, 1982), 183.

10. Andrew V. Sorrell and Bruce A. Vlk, "Virginia's Never-Ending Moratorium on City-Council Annexations," *Virginia News-Letter* 88, no. 1 (2012): 1–2; Stephen J. Hoffman, *Race, Class and Power in the Building of Richmond, 1880–1920* (Jefferson, NC: McFarland, 2004).

11. Christopher Silver, *Twentieth-Century Richmond: Planning, Politics, and Race* (Knoxville: University of Tennessee Press, 1984), chap. 8; Moeser and Dennis, *Politics of Annexation*, chap. 3.

12. While estimates for earlier periods are not readily available, a 2021 analysis estimated that Richmond had $7.4 billion in tax-exempt property located on over 3,200 parcels and that the $88.6 million in forgone taxes from these exemptions (including $15 million from state-owned parcels) were equivalent to 26 percent of property tax revenues. In contrast, the Commonwealth of Virginia issued an annual payment in lieu of taxes to the city amounting to $3.7 million as compensation for its use of city service and infrastructure; Virginia Commonwealth University did not pay one at all. "Tax Exemption in Richmond," September 29, 2021, Center for Tax Property Reform, Princeton, NJ, accessed February 5, 2024, https://web.archive.org/web/20211001194/12/https://centerforpropertytaxreform.org/2021/09/29/tax-exemption-in-richmond/.

13. Fifty percent of the formula is based on total property value, 40 percent is based on total adjusted gross income, and 10 percent is based on taxable retail sales. See Virginia Department of Education website, accessed September 30, 2023, www.doe.virginia.gov/data-policy-funding/school-finance/budget-grants-management/composite-index-of-local-ability-to-pay.

14. Claude Burrows, "City Real Estate Tax to Rise Two 1/2 Cents," *Richmond Times-Dispatch*, March 15, 1988; Will Jones, "Council Okays Cut in Real Estate Tax Rate," *Richmond Times-Dispatch*, April 15, 2008; Jess Nocera, "Henrico Plans to Lower Its Real Estate Tax Rate by 2 Cents for the Coming Year—Real Estate Tax Relief for Henrico County Residents in 2022—Plus a Rebate Check Coming in the Mail," *Richmond Times-Dispatch*, December 10, 2021.

15. Hayter, *Dream Is Lost*, chaps. 4 and 5.

16. For more on the local implications of the civil rights movement in the late twentieth century, see Thomas W. Hanchett, *Sorting Out the New South City: Race, Class, and Urban Development in Charlotte, 1875–1975* (Chapel Hill: University of North Carolina Press, 1998); Tracy E. K'Meyer, *Civil Rights in the Gateway to the South: Louisville, Kentucky, 1945–1980* (Lexington: University Press of Kentucky, 2009); Leonard N. Moore, *Black Rage in New Orleans: Police Brutality and African American Activism from World War II to Hurricane Katrina* (Baton Rouge: Louisiana State University Press, 2011); William Graves

and Heather A. Smith, *Charlotte, NC: The Global Evolution of a New South City* (Athens: University of Georgia Press, 2012); Steven Estes, *Charleston in Black and White: Race and Power in the South after the Civil Rights Movement* (Chapel Hill: University of North Carolina Press, 2015); and Maurice J. Hobson, *The Legend of the Black Mecca: Politics and Class in the Making of Modern Atlanta* (Chapel Hill: University of North Carolina Press, 2017).

17. Timothy J. Bartik, "Local Economic Development Policies," Upjohn Institute Working Paper No. 03-91 (W. E. Upjohn Institute for Employment Research, Kalamazoo, MI, 2003), https://doi.org/10.17848/wp03-91. Bartik cites a 1994 National League of Cities study stating that over 86 percent of local elected officials nationwide believed "'bringing about economic development' is a major responsibility of local governments."

18. For a summary of these critiques, see Thad Williamson, David Imbroscio, and Gar Alperovitz, *Making a Place for Community: Local Democracy in a Global Era* (London: Routledge, 2002).

19. See John P. Blair and Michael C. Carroll, *Local Economic Development: Analysis, Practices, and Globalization* (Los Angeles: SAGE, 2008), esp. 133–54, for a balanced discussion of the policy issues related to local economic development subsidies.

20. Mayor Dwight C. Jones made the connection explicit in remarks delivered at an Aspen Institute policy forum in early 2016. "All economic development does not accrue to the development of poor people," Jones stated. "We have got to be intentional about making sure that economic development accrues to the benefit, not only [to] the city, but particularly to the poor community." Mary Catherine Bitter, "There's a New Way to Build Jobs: Start Local," Aspen Institute, February 3, 2016, www.aspeninstitute.org/blog-posts/community-wealth-building-viable-form-economic-development/.

21. We begin this review of trends in 1980 to document the rapid changes in the region's economy, changes that both materially impacted Richmond and reveal how Richmond leaders interpreted the task before them in the late 1980s: to forestall, shore up, or otherwise mitigate changes that were on balance devastating to the city's economic base.

22. Bureau of Economic Analysis (SIC series, 1980–2000; NAIC 2010–15), accessed June 30, 2023, www.bea.gov/data/employment/employment-county-metro-and-other-areas.

23. Virgil Hazelett, interview with Lucas Hakkenberg, Thad Williamson, and Amy Howard, June 30, 2010.

24. John Reid Blackwell, "Cigarette Making Still Going Strong in South Richmond," *Richmond Times-Dispatch*, August 30, 2013.

25. Bureau of Economic Analysis, based on SIC industry classification; 1980 and 1985 figures based on 1972 classification; 1990 and subsequent figures based on 1987 classification, accessed June 30, 2023, www.bea.gov/data/employment/employment-county-metro-and-other-areas.

26. Jeff E. Schapiro, "Bleak Days for State Workers," *Richmond Times-Dispatch*, January 5, 2003.

27. St. Louis Federal Reserve Branch, "Real Gross Domestic Product: All Industries in Richmond, Virginia," accessed September 20, 2023, https://fred.stlouisfed.org/series/REALGDPALL51760.

28. The 2000 census reported that 29,907 of the city's 40,185 residents below the poverty line (74.4 percent) were Black. U.S. Census 2000, T183 and T187, accessed June 30, 2023, via Social Explorer, www.socialexplorer.com/tables/C2000. For year-by-year poverty estimates in Richmond from 1989 to 2022, see St. Louis Federal Reserve Branch,

"Estimated Percent of People of All Ages in Poverty for Richmond City, VA," Economic Research, Federal Reserve Bank of St. Louis, website, accessed February 18, 2024, https://fred.stlouisfed.org/series/PPAAVA51760A156NCEN.

29. Independent cities in Virginia, because they do not overlap with counties, are treated as county equivalents by the U.S. Census and other data sources.

30. Estelle Sommeiller and Mark Price, "The New Gilded Age: Income Inequality, in the U.S. by State, Metropolitan Area, and County," appendix tables B2 and B11, Economic Policy Institute, July 19, 2018, www.epi.org/publication/the-new-gilded-age-income-inequality-in-the-u-s-by-state-metropolitan-area-and-county/#epi-toc-14area-and-county/#epi-toc-14. Richmond was not shown to be the most unequal locality in Virginia; that distinction went to Charlottesville, found by this measure to be the fifteenth most unequal county unit equivalent in the United States.

31. Sommeiller and Price, "New Gilded Age," table B11.

32. John Logan and Harvey Molotch, *Urban Fortunes: The Political Economy of Place* (Berkeley: University of California Press, 1987).

33. See Lawrence T. Brown, *The Black Butterfly: The Harmful Politics of Race and Space in America* (Baltimore: Johns Hopkins University Press, 2021).

34. Marvin T. Chiles, "'Here We Go Again': Race and Redevelopment in Downtown Richmond, Virginia, 1977–Present," *Journal of Urban History* 49, no. 1 (January 2023): 133–59. Optimism about the 6th Street Marketplace project at the time was widely held. A 1986 analysis by VCU professor John V. Moeser of Richmond politics since 1946 went so far as to describe the period after 1982 as the "Sixth Street" era, marked by an alliance between whites less tied to the old, West End–dominated Richmond ("Main Street") and Blacks less tied to civil rights activism ("Broad Street"). John V. Moeser, "City Politics Since '48: Three Distinct Eras," *Richmond Times-Dispatch*, April 6, 1986.

35. Amy Biegelsen, "Requiem for a Dream: The Last Days of 6th Street Marketplace," *Style Weekly*, June 27, 2007.

36. Biegelsen, "Requiem."

37. John T. Kneebone and Eugene P. Trani, *Fulfilling the Promise: Virginia Commonwealth University and the City of Richmond, 1968–2009* (Charlottesville: University of Virginia Press, 2020).

38. Kneebone and Trani, *Fulfilling the Promise*, chaps. 4 and 5.

39. While VCU was properly recognized for its investments in downtown, like virtually every other predominantly white institution in the city it had a troubling racial history. Since its creation in 1838, the Medical College of Virginia (MCV) had maintained a fractured relationship with Richmond's Black community. The story of MCV stealing bodies of recently deceased slaves in Richmond is increasingly well known. Before the American Civil War, it was common for medical instructors at MCV to rob graves for Black cadavers. In 1994, construction workers unearthed the remains of bodies—along with medical tools and clothes—in a pit near the Kontos Medical Sciences Building at MCV. The practice of exploiting Black bodies continued into the twentieth century. The Racial Integrity Act of 1924 and companion Eugenical Sterilization Act of 1924 not only banned interracial marriages but also forced the sterilization of thousands of the commonwealth's residents (Black and white alike). MCV operated under the shadow of segregation and racist medical care for most of the twentieth century. MCV's hospitals did not fully integrate until 1965.

Chris Wood, "Stolen Corpses: Inside MCV's History with Racist Medicine," *Commonwealth Times*, February 6, 2019. See also Brendan Wolfe, "Racial Integrity Laws (1924–1930)," Encyclopedia Virginia online, December 7, 2020, https://encyclopediavirginia.org/entries/racial-integrity-laws-1924-1930; and Elizabeth Catte "Eugenic Sterilization in Virginia," Encyclopedia Virginia online, July 25, 2023, https://encyclopedia.virginia.org/entries/eugenic-sterilization-in-virginia.

40. Hayter, *Dream Is Lost*, 243.

41. "VCU State's Largest Four-Year Institution," January 19, 2007, VCU news release, www.news.vcu.edu/article/vcu_states_largest_fouryear_public_institution; Kneebone and Trani, *Fulfilling the Promise*, chap. 7 and following. VCU was subsequently overtaken in total enrollment by George Mason University.

42. Kneebone and Trani, *Fulfilling the Promise*, 205.

43. "VCU's Impact on the Region: Talent, Innovation, and Collaboration," Center for Urban and Regional Analysis, L. Douglas Wilder School of Government and Public Policy, VCU, December 2016, https://cura.vcu.edu/media/cura/pdfs/cura-documents/TheImpactofVCUontheRichmondRegion.pdf.

44. Robin F. Bachin and Amy L. Howard, eds., *Engaging Place, Engaging Practices: Urban History and Campus-Community Partnerships* (Philadelphia: Temple University Press, 2023), 6. For a critical examination of urban universities in their host cities, see Davarian Baldwin, *In the Shadow of the Ivory Tower: How Universities Are Plundering Our Cities* (New York: Bold Type Books, 2021).

45. Kneebone and Trani note that shortly after Trani arrived at VCU, a 1990 prospectus for the city's "Richmond Tomorrow" strategic planning process made no reference to VCU at all. Kneebone and Trani, *Fulfilling the Promise*, 181.

46. VCU's expansion in the 1990s and aughts was augmented by various state and federal projects intended to bolster downtown, including the construction of the $43 million Library of Virginia on Broad Street, just a block away from city hall, in 1997, and the construction of a $102 million courthouse building for the U.S. District Court (Eastern District of Virginia) in 2008, just two blocks away from city hall. Gary Robertson, "State Library Opens Today—Governor Calls New Downtown Building a 'Museum for the Mind,'" *Richmond Times-Dispatch*, January 3, 1997; Frank Green, "Federal Court's New Home Opening," *Richmond Times-Dispatch*, September 2, 2008.

47. In 2000, approximately 87,500 residents of Chesterfield, Henrico, and Hanover Counties (combined) worked in the City of Richmond, compared to approximately 52,000 Richmond residents. U.S. Census Bureau, 2000 U.S. Decennial Census, Summary File 3, table PCT053, accessed February 19, 2024, https://data.census.gov.

48. The same freeway system that allowed whites to massively migrate to suburbs in the mid-twentieth century might, city planners nationwide mistakenly believed, be used to entice suburban retail dollars back into the city. Eric Avila, *The Folklore of the Freeway: Race and Revolt in the Modernist City* (Minneapolis: University of Minnesota Press, 2014). In Richmond, planners built a system of expressways and parkways in and around Richmond during the mid-twentieth century—decimating the Black neighborhoods of Jackson Ward (1950s) and then Randolph (1970s) in the process. See Edwin Slipek Jr., "The Lost Neighborhood," *Style Weekly*, November 8, 2006; and Harry Kollatz Jr. and Tina Eshelman, "The Distressway," *Richmond Magazine*, December 16, 2016.

49. Gregory J. Gilligan, "Planners Approve Stony Point Mall Project—Council Plans Public Hearing on Proposal," *Richmond Times-Dispatch*, July 11, 1995; Gregory J. Gilligan, "Is Richmond Ready for Upscale Stores?," *Richmond Times-Dispatch*, June 19, 1995.

50. Gregory J. Gilligan, "Patience: Upscale-Mall Builder Waits for Richmond's 'Window' to Open," *Richmond Times-Dispatch*, March 21, 1999; Gilligan, "Is Richmond Ready for Upscale Stores?"

51. Gregory J. Gilligan, "City Trying to Make Mall a Reality—May Offer Millions to Lure Nordstrom to Stony Point," *Richmond Times-Dispatch*, July 2, 1999.

52. Jeremy Redmon, "Incentive Plan Gets 2nd Look—$13.5 Million Deal Questioned," *Richmond Times-Dispatch*, October 30, 2001.

53. Gregory J. Gilligan, "Stony Point Mall Ground Broken—'A Long-Awaited Day,' Says Ex-Mayor Kaine," *Richmond Times-Dispatch*, March 1, 2002; Gregory J. Gilligan, "Mall vs. Mall—Rival Shopping Centers Taking Shape," *Richmond Times-Dispatch*, August 18, 2002.

54. TIP Strategies and Hill-Christian Consulting Group, "City of Richmond, VA—Comprehensive Economic Development Strategy," November 2010, 22, https://tipstrategies.com/portfolio-project/city-of-richmond-va-comprehensive-economic-development-strategy/.

55. Elizabeth Esfahani, "Job Seekers Crowd the Fair—Stony Point, Short Pump Have 6,000 Spots to Fill," *Richmond Times-Dispatch*, August 2, 2003; "Virginia Malls, by Size," *Richmond Times-Dispatch*, September 17, 2003; Jeremy Redmon, "Residents See Pluses for Area, City," *Richmond Times-Dispatch*, September 17, 2003.

56. Gregory J. Gilligan, "Center Will Be Cordial to Four-Legged Friends," *Richmond Times-Dispatch*, September 17, 2003; Rudy McCollum, "Government Structure Isn't Real Issue," *Richmond Times-Dispatch*, October 31, 2003.

57. Jack Jacobs, "Stony Point Fashion Park Up for Sale for Undisclosed Price," *Richmond BizSense*, September 10, 2021, https://richmondbizsense.com/2021/09/10/stony-point-fashion-park-up-for-sale-to-select-investors-for-undisclosed-price/. In the spring of 2022, a Florida firm bought the property for $15 million. Mike Platania, "Stony Point Fashion Park Sold to Florida Firm for $15M," *Richmond BizSense*, April 6, 2022, https://richmondbizsense.com/2022/04/06/breaking-news-stony-point-fashion-park-sold-to-florida-firm/.

58. In 2023, MapQuest estimated that on a weekday it would take 1 hour and 18 minutes to travel by bus and foot from Hillside Court to Stony Point Fashion Park, a total distance of 9.8 miles. The trip would involve two bus routes (and a transfer between them), some forty-five bus stops, and then walking the final mile on foot. MapQuest search, August 15, 2023.

59. Jeremy Redmon, "City Increases Meals Tax; Group's Attention Turns to Lodging Tax," *Richmond Times-Dispatch*, July 29, 2003.

60. $7.6 million from the enhanced meals tax adopted in 2003 was disbursed to the project prior to the start of Wilder's term and used for preconstruction work. Wilder moved to block further payments and then redirected the revenue going forward to the City of the Future Capital Improvement Program, which in turned funded the additional $25 million in city support for the Carpenter Center renovation (including $2.3 million in fiscal year 2007 and $22.7 million in subsequent years). See City of Richmond Ordinance 2007-235-201, adopted September 10, 2007, City of Richmond website, https://richmondva.legistar.com/Legislation.aspx; and City of Richmond Adopted Capital Improvement Plan, 2008–12, https://rva.gov/sites/default/files/2019-04/2008-2012_CompleteCapitalImprovementPlan.pdf.

See also Will Jones, "New Plan Offered for Arts Center Group to End Use of City Funds, Seek to Reopen the Carpenter Center," *Richmond Times-Dispatch*, October 13, 2005; Dena Sloan and Dave Ress, "Wilder Plan Gets Mixed Reviews," *Richmond Times-Dispatch*, January 11, 2006; Will Jones, "Wilder Endorses New Arts Proposal," *Richmond Times-Dispatch*, January 10, 2007; Will Jones and Dave Ress, "Richmond Performing Arts Center," *Richmond Times-Dispatch*, September 9, 2007; and Will Jones and Michael Martz, "Richmond Council Approves Arts Center," *Richmond Times-Dispatch*, September 11, 2007.

61. Melissa Ruggieri, "Richmond CenterStage Opens Its Doors Saturday," *Richmond Times-Dispatch*, September 9, 2009. The opening inevitably drew comparisons to the 6th Street Marketplace debacle. "CenterStage, which opens to a full slate of events, is set to fill seats," wrote columnist Michael Paul Williams. "But if downtown Richmond's latest savior is to erase memories of its failed Sixth Street predecessor, the next act must fill storefronts." Williams, "CenterStage Must Spark Growth to Be Called Success," *Richmond Times-Dispatch*, September 12, 2009.

62. Peter Bacque, "Historic Altria Theater to Re-open Sunday after Extensive Renovation," *Richmond Times-Dispatch*, November 1, 2014; Altria Theater History, accessed September 30, 2023, www.altriatheater.com/about-us/history.

63. See City of Richmond Ordinance 2012-83-75, adopted May 29, 2012, City of Richmond website, https://richmondva.legistar.com/Legislation.aspx.

64. Cynthia McMullen, "First Fridays Art Event Still Growing," *Richmond Times-Dispatch*, October 5, 2007.

65. James Ukrop and John Bates, "The Dominion Energy Center for the Performing Arts 10 Years Later," *Richmond Times-Dispatch*, August 29, 2019.

66. Martha Biondi, *To Stand and Fight: The Struggle for Civil Rights in Postwar New York City* (Cambridge, MA: Harvard University Press, 2003); Matthew J. Countryman, *Up South: Civil Rights and Black Power in Philadelphia* (Philadelphia: University of Pennsylvania Press, 2006); Guian A. McKee, *The Problem of Jobs: Liberalism, Race, and Deindustrialization in Philadelphia* (Chicago: University of Chicago Press, 2008). For more on the urban dilemma of the late twentieth century, see also Howard Gillette Jr., *Between Justice and Beauty: Race, Planning, and the Failure of Urban Policy in Washington, D.C.* (Philadelphia: University of Pennsylvania Press, 2006); Hanchett, *Sorting Out the New South City*; and Arnold R. Hirsch, *Making the Second Ghetto: Race and Housing in Chicago, 1940–1960* (Chicago: University of Chicago Press, 1998).

67. *Neighborhoods in Bloom: Neighborhood Profiles, 2017*, Federal Reserve Bank of Richmond, accessed February 5, 2024, www.richmondfed.org/-/media/RichmondFedOrg/publications/community_development/neighborhoods_in_bloom/2017/neighborhoods_in_bloom_profiles_2017.pdf; John Accordino, George Galster, and Peter Tatian, *The Impacts of Targeted Public and Nonprofit Investment on Neighborhood Development*, 2005, tables 2A and 3A, Federal Reserve Bank of Richmond, accessed February 5, 2024, www.richmondfed.org/-/media/RichmondFedOrg/publications/community_development/neighborhoods_in_bloom/nib_research.pdf. The Local Initiatives Support Corporation invested an additional $2.1 million in projects citywide during this period.

68. Accordino, Galster, and Tatian, *Impacts of Targeted Public and Nonprofit Investment*, iii–iv; Michael Martz, "Richmond Neighborhood Projects Win Award—Federal Housing Agency Recognizes the City's Work in Revitalizing Six Communities," *Richmond Times-Dispatch*, May 27, 2006.

69. *Neighborhoods in Bloom: Neighborhood Profiles.*

70. Scott Bass and Chris Dovi, "There Goes the 'Hood," *Style Weekly*, April 11, 2007.

71. Rob Walker, "Developers Give Bulk of Credit to Tax Abatements," *Richmond Times-Dispatch*, September 13, 1999; Bass and Dovi, "There Goes the 'Hood."

72. Scott Bass, "Free and Clear," *Style Weekly*, May 7, 2013; Ned Oliver, "Developer Abuse? City Reviews Tax Incentive Program," *Style Weekly*, October 1, 2013; Ned Oliver, "Luxury Apartments Get Tax Breaks," *Richmond Times-Dispatch*, December 6, 2015.

73. VCU Center for Urban and Regional Analysis, *Rehabilitation Tax Abatement; A Comprehensive Assessment of Richmond's Rehabilitation Tax Abatement Policy*, February 2019, accessed February 5, 2024, https://cura.vcu.edu/media/cura/pdfs/cura-documents/RVARehabTaxAbatement(FINALE).pdf.

74. Blair L. M. Kelley, *Right to Ride: Streetcar Boycotts and African American Citizenship in the Era of* Plessy v. Ferguson (Chapel Hill: University of North Carolina Press, 2010), 117–38.

75. Heather McGhee, *The Sum of Us: How Racism Costs Everyone and How We Can Prosper Together* (New York: Random House, 2021); see also Robert Bullard, Glenn Johnson, and Angel Torres, eds., *Highway Robbery: Transportation Racism and New Routes to Equity* (Cambridge, MA: South End Press, 2004).

76. Christof Spieler, "Racism Has Shaped Public Transit and It's Riddled with Inequities," Rice University Kinder Institute for Urban Research, August 24, 2020, https://kinder.rice.edu/urbanedge/racism-has-shaped-public-transit-and-its-riddled-inequities.

77. Frank Green, "Leaders Discuss Need for Bus Lines," *Richmond Times-Dispatch*, September 15, 1986; Will Jones, "Protest by Area Clergy Serves as Symbolic Protest," *Richmond Times-Dispatch*, February 16, 1999.

78. Michael Paul Williams, "City Council Approves Taking Chesterfield as GRTC Partner," *Richmond Times-Dispatch*, April 25, 1989.

79. Randolph P. Smith, "Chesterfield Joins City in Transit System," *Richmond Times-Dispatch*, July 6, 1989.

80. In 1996, Kaine stated, "It has been proven to all of us beyond any doubt that a factor in the county's unwillingness to allow public transportation into the counties to a significant degree is their perception about race. . . . That is behind, to some large degree, the decision in Chesterfield County to not allow the buses to run to Cloverleaf Mall." Kaine added there was concern about the "kinds of jobs that people might get if they're African-American, about the kinds of things they might do if they're African-American. . . . Chesterfield officials have told me as much off the record that race is a factor." See Hazel Trice Edney, "Racism, Boycott Talk in Bus Line Fight," *Richmond Free Press*, March 28–30, 1996. Service to the mall launched in April 1996. Gordon Hickey and Susan Winiecki, "Bus Service Moves beyond Magic Line—Stops at Two Chesterfield Malls to Begin," *Richmond Times-Dispatch*, April 18, 1996.

81. Fred North, "Chamber: Extend GRTC Routes from City to Jobs," *Richmond Free Press*, February 26–28, 1998.

82. "Marsh: Groundwork Laid for Buses-to-Jobs Plan" (staff report), *Richmond Free Press*, March 26–28, 1998. Chesterfield County manager Lane Ramsey subsequently explained that the county was opposed to any measure that would create a long-term fiscal obligation for Chesterfield. Will Jones, "Funding Stymies Area Mass Transit—Local

Officials Are Wary of Short-Term State Role When Regional Needs Require Long-Term Support," *Richmond Times-Dispatch*, September 16, 1998.

83. Tim Kaine, "Transporting Richmonders into New Century, Together," *Richmond Times-Dispatch*, April 17, 1999.

84. Will Jones, "Assembly Offers $5.1 Million for Expansion of Bus Service," *Richmond Times-Dispatch*, March 1, 1999; Gordon Hickey, "GRTC Seeks Bus Routes Study—Operation of Lines into Chesterfield to Be Examined," *Richmond Times-Dispatch*, April 27, 1999.

85. Meredith Fischer, "A New Link to Downtown—Van Service Runs in Chesterfield," *Richmond Times-Dispatch*, June 5, 2001.

86. Meredith Fischer and Will Jones, "LINK Service to Continue—Chesterfield Approves Two Routes," *Richmond Times-Dispatch*, June 19, 2003; Meredith Fischer, "LINK Use Dwindles—Fewer Riders Reported for Chesterfield Service," *Richmond Times-Dispatch*, June 25, 2003; Julian Walker, "Way to Go—Chesterfield County Unveils a Post-LINK Transportation Plan," *Richmond Times-Dispatch*, January 7, 2005.

87. Julian Walker, "Chesterfield Undecided on Future Service," *Richmond Times-Dispatch*, August 16, 2007. The express service was eventually extended with support from state and federal grants—only, yet again, for its viability to be placed in question once those funds were spent. In short, Chesterfield County was unwilling to commit to ongoing funding of bus service in this time period as a general government function. See Michael Martz, "Chesterfield Asks for Funds to Continue Express Bus Routes," *Richmond Times-Dispatch*, February 4, 2012.

88. An analysis published by the Southern Environmental Law Center in 2003 found that the GRTC had "33 percent less miles than similarly sized metropolitan areas." Meredith Fischer and Nicole Johnson, "Routes May Go by the Wayside—The State of Public Transit Appears Grim in Chesterfield and Henrico Counties," *Richmond Times-Dispatch*, April 13, 2004.

89. In 1999, a group called "Citizens Against Busing" urged that Chesterfield resist public transportation connecting the county to the city, claiming it would be the first step in a process of municipal annexation. Chesterfield Board of Supervisors chair Harry G. Daniel told a reporter he had never heard of the group but that its name reflected "practically every doggone phone call I get." Jones, "Assembly Offers $5.1 Million for Expansion of Bus Service." For further discussion see Thad Williamson, "Mobility and Its Opponents: Why Richmond, Virginia Has No Mass Transit" (paper given at Urban Affairs Association Meetings, San Francisco, California, April 2013), in the author's possession.

90. Alan Berube, Elizabeth Kneebone, Robert Puentes, and Adie Tomer, "Missed Opportunity: Transit and Jobs in Metropolitan America," appendix 2, Brookings, May 12, 2011, www.brookings.edu/articles/missed-opportunity-transit-and-jobs-in-metropolitan-america/.

91. Brent Tarter, *The Grandees of Government: The Origins and Persistence of Undemocratic Politics in Virginia* (Charlottesville: University of Virginia Press, 2013), chap. 11.

92. Chiles, "Here We Go Again"; Hayter, *Dream Is Lost*, chaps. 4 and 5.

93. Will Jones, "Richmond Mayor Consolidates Economic, Community Development Departments," *Richmond Times-Dispatch*, September 24, 2009.

94. TIP Strategies and Hill-Christian Consulting Group, "City of Richmond, VA—Comprehensive Economic Development Strategy."

95. Anthony Flint, *Wrestling with Moses: How Jane Jacobs Took On New York's Master Builder and Transformed the American City* (New York: Random House, 2009).

96. On Monument Avenue, see Monument Avenue: A Select Reading List, accessed February 5, 2024, https://onmonumentave.com/resources; see also Matthew Mace Barbee, *Race and Masculinity in Southern Memory: History of Richmond, Virginia's Monument Avenue, 1948–1996* (Lanham, MD: Lexington Books, 2013).

97. Flynn believed in, and was willing to fight for, a green city oriented around people rather than around cars and parking lots. In her previous role in Lynchburg, Virginia, Flynn had clashed with Rev. Jerry Falwell on planning issues, leading Falwell to attack her by name from the pulpit. Amy Biegelsen, "In Like Flynn," *Style Weekly*, January 16, 2008.

98. Reed Williams, "Richmond Revitalization and Development Explored—About 160 People Take a Bus Tour about Growth-Related Issues," *Richmond Times-Dispatch*, September 22, 2008.

99. Mayor Wilder articulated many of these themes in a 2008 editorial strongly endorsing Flynn's efforts; see L. Douglas Wilder, "Our Citizens Want a Vibrant Downtown," *Richmond Times-Dispatch*, April 27, 2008.

100. See Thad Williamson, "Justice, the Public Sector, and Cities: Re-legitimating the Activist State," in *Justice and the American Metropolis*, ed. Clarissa Hayward and Todd Swanstrom (Minneapolis: University of Minnesota Press, 2011), 177–197, for more detailed discussion and analysis of Flynn's tenure in Richmond.

101. City of Richmond, Downtown Master Plan, July 2009, 3–15, https://rva.gov/planning-development-review/downtown-plan; this account of Flynn's vision draws on Thad Williamson, "Echo Chamber," *Style Weekly*, April 29, 2009.

102. Bonnie V. Winston, "Sea of Whiteness—That's What Hits Eyes Hard at City Master Plan Meeting," *Richmond Free Press*, July 26–28, 2007. For a detailed, positive appraisal of the completed process, see John Sarvay, "Anatomy of a Highly Public Plan," *Richmond Times-Dispatch*, October 5, 2008.

103. Marie Tyler-McGraw, *At the Falls: Richmond, Virginia, and Its People* (Chapel Hill: University of North Carolina Press), 1994, 43–45.

104. Will Jones, "Condo Debate Hits Flashpoint," *Richmond Times-Dispatch*, April 21, 2009.

105. Amy Biegelsen, "Flynn's Last Stand?," *Style Weekly*, May 6, 2009.

106. Luz Lazo, "Richmond Council Approves Downtown Master Plan," *Richmond Times-Dispatch*, July 28, 2009; Williamson, "Justice, the Public Sector, and Cities," 189–90; minutes of the July 13 and 27, 2009, Richmond City Council meetings, City of Richmond website, https://richmondva.legistar.com/Calendar.aspx.

107. Williamson, "Echo Chamber." In 2023, The Conservation Fund, Capital Region Land Conservancy, and the city leveraged conservation grants to purchase the land previously held by Echo Harbour LLC for $4.2 million. Karri Peifer, "City Buys Vacant Waterfront Land for a New Public Park," Axios, July 11, 2023, www.axios.com/local/richmond/2023/07/11/dock-street-park-richmond-waterfront-river.

108. Rachel Flynn, "Moving Richmond Forward: Plan Action," *Richmond Times-Dispatch*, May 22, 2011.

109. Dwight C. Jones, "Redefine the City through the Riverfront," *Richmond Times-Dispatch*, April 29, 2012; see also Robert A. Crum Jr., "River Brings Life to the Region," *Richmond Times-Dispatch*, April 29, 2012. Jones included $5 million (total) to fund the plan

in the FY 2013 and FY 2014 capital budget but received some criticism for not including new money in the FY 2015 budget. Columnist Michael Paul Williams argued that the riverfront plan was "not being treated like the game-changer it will be." Michael Paul Williams, "James Project Needs Mayor's Full Support," *Richmond Times-Dispatch*, March 21, 2014.

110. The most concrete definition attached to "Tier One" status during the Jones administration was achievement of a AAA bond rating from Wall Street rating agencies. See, for instance, City of Richmond, *Proposed Amendments to FY 2010-2011 Biennial Fiscal Plan*, March 22, 2010, www.rva.gov/sites/default/files/2019-04/2011_ProposedAmendments BiennialFiscalPlan.pdf Fiscal Year 2011 Budget.

111. Olympia Meola, "8-Year Commitment for Redskins Camp in Richmond, Governor Says," *Richmond Times-Dispatch*, June 6, 2012; Michael Phillips, "Governor Visits Skins Camp, Discusses Future Va. Stadium," *Richmond Times-Dispatch*, August 16, 2013.

112. Robert Zullo, "Redskins Deal Passes after Last-Minute Negotiations," *Richmond Times-Dispatch*, November 27, 2012; Robert Zullo, "Richmond Council Takes Final Steps Toward Redskins Training Camp," *Richmond Times-Dispatch*, December 27, 2012; Tammie Smith, "West End School to Get New Life," *Richmond Times-Dispatch*, December 13, 2013. For a description of the project agreements, see VCU Center for Urban and Regional Analysis, "Bon Secours Redskins," revised March 2019, 12–14, https://cura.vcu.edu/media/cura/pdfs/cura-documents/BSHS-Redskins_FINALE_(MARCH).pdf.

113. Robert Zullo, "Richmond Leaders Angered by Tree Clearing at Redskins Site," *Richmond Times-Dispatch*, January 15, 2013.

114. See "Bon Secours Redskins," tables 2.7 and 2.8, for camp attendance figures.

115. Jacob Geiger, "Businesses Hoping for Redskins Boost Finding Location Is Key to Results," *Richmond Times-Dispatch*, August 4, 2013.

116. A gushing *Times-Dispatch* editorial just after the camp closed referenced the team's colors in declaring, "Central Virginia bleeds burgundy and gold." "Wrap-Up" (staff editorial), *Richmond Times-Dispatch*, August 17, 2013.

117. Jacob Geiger, "Redskins Crowds Bypassed Local Food Truck Court," *Richmond Times-Dispatch*, August 12, 2014.

118. "Bon Secours Redskins," tables 2–7.

119. In 2014, sports columnist Paul Woody called attention to the incongruence between the city's poverty rate and its subsidy payment to the Washington NFL franchise and called on the team to contribute to alleviating poverty in Richmond by "[hiring] people, young, middle-aged and older, from some of the city's most disadvantaged neighborhoods to work at training camp. This would provide real economic impact. These jobs could help students pay for their education and help young mothers and fathers, as well as older mothers and fathers, support their families." Paul Woody, "Redskins and Richmond Can Do Something about Poverty," *Richmond Times-Dispatch*, August 16, 2014.

120. Ned Oliver, "Bon Secours Plan Widely Opposed," *Richmond Times-Dispatch*, December 16, 2016; Mark Robinson, "Bon Secours Breaks Ground on New Mixed-Use Development at Westhampton Property," *Richmond Times-Dispatch*, May 22, 2019.

121. Eric Kolenich and Luca Powell, "Bon Secours Opens East End Medical Building Ten Years after Promising It to the City," *Richmond Times-Dispatch*, January 10, 2023. Philanthropist and business investor Steve Markel, the driving force behind the 2019 opening of the 25th Street Market (grocery store) in the East End, called attention in a blistering editorial to Bon Secours's unfulfilled promises and the inequity of moving investment in

the wealthy West End forward while neglecting the East End. Steve Markel, "Bon Secours Must Keep Its Commitment to Richmond," *Richmond Times-Dispatch*, July 20, 2021. The East End lacked a full-scale grocery store prior to the opening of the 25th Street Market in 2019, with investment from Markel and additional support from the City of Richmond. A year later, a *New York Times* investigative report detailed disinvestment by Bon Secours in Richmond Community Hospital, including significant cutbacks in service, at the same time the chain expanded investments in suburban, more affluent Richmond. The *Times* report quoted former mayor Jones as saying that after leadership changes at Bon Secours and its merger in 2018 with Ohio-based Mercy Health, "there was a major shift from being mission-oriented to being unashamedly, unabashedly profit-oriented." Katie Thomas and Jessica Silver-Greenberg, "How a Hospital Chain Used a Poor Neighborhood to Turn Huge Profits," *New York Times*, September 24, 2022.

122. Robert Zullo, "Ground Officially Broken at Site of Training Camp," *Richmond Times-Dispatch*, February 14, 2013; Michael Martz, "Richmond Makes Last-Minute Preparations for Redskins," *Richmond Times-Dispatch*, July 20, 2013.

123. "Bon Secours Redskins," table 2.25.

124. Louis Llovio, "Football Partnership Remains Controversial," *Richmond Times-Dispatch*, August 9, 2016.

125. Graham Moomaw and Michael Martz, "Mayor Jones's Shockoe Bottom Plan Is More Than a Baseball Stadium," *Richmond Times-Dispatch*, November 11, 2013.

126. Moomaw and Martz, "Mayor Jones's Shockoe Bottom Plan"; Graham Moomaw and Michael Martz, "Council Receives Stadium Plan," *Richmond Times-Dispatch*, November 12, 2013.

127. For more on Lumpkin's Jail, see Kristen Green, *The Devil's Half-Acre: The Untold Story of How One Woman Liberated the South's Most Notorious Slave Jail* (New York: Seal Press, 2022).

128. Edwards quoted in Michael Paul Williams, "Shockoe Ballpark: Unforced Error," *Richmond Times-Dispatch*, October 15, 2013. The Sacred Ground Historical Reclamation Project was initiated by the Defenders, best-known for its quarterly free publication, the *Richmond Defender*, edited by Phil Wilayto, which highlighted progressive and radical activism in Richmond.

129. See Ana Edwards and Phil Wilayto, "The Significance of Richmond's Shockoe Bottom: Why It's the Wrong Place for a Baseball Stadium," *African Diaspora Archaeology Newsletter* 15, no. 1 (2015): article 3. "Richmond's Shockoe Bottom has the potential to become an educational center of international significance," wrote Edwards and Wilayto. "Properly preserved, this small area that once held such cold, commercial brutality could become a life-affirming place of study, reflection and meditation."

130. Williams, "Shockoe Ballpark: Unforced Error."

131. Graham Moomaw, "Shockoe Baseball Stadium Plan Wins Initial Backing, 6–3," *Richmond Times-Dispatch*, February 24, 2014.

132. Graham Moomaw, "Shockoe Stadium Opponents Rally," *Richmond Times-Dispatch*, April 4, 2014.

133. Moomaw, "Shockoe Baseball Stadium Plan Wins Initial Backing, 6–3."

134. In a joint statement, Samuels and Baliles each faulted the administration for failing to provide a complete plan while saying they would be open-minded to reconsidering the

proposal at a future point. Graham Moomaw, "Shockoe Plan in Peril as 5 Council Members Oppose," *Richmond Times-Dispatch*, May 23, 2014.

135. Ned Oliver, "Ballpark Plan Unravels," *Style Weekly*, May 23, 2014; Graham Moomaw, "Mayor Withdraws Shockoe Proposal," *Richmond Times-Dispatch*, May 28, 2014.

136. On Marshall's role in the deal, see, for instance, Graham Moomaw, "As Deadline Comes, Shockoe Deals Still Unfinished," *Richmond Times-Dispatch*, March 27, 2014; and Graham Moomaw, "Council Panel Sees Latest Version of Shockoe Plan," *Richmond Times-Dispatch*, May 15, 2014.

137. The Stone deal, involving support from both the state and the city, was first announced in October 2014; after council approval in 2015, Stone Brewing opened its facilities in Richmond in 2016. The most controversial aspect of the agreement was $8 million in city support for a restaurant attached to the brewery. See Graham Moomaw, "Council Votes Unanimously to Keep Brewery Deal Alive," *Richmond Times-Dispatch*, March 2, 2015. For a defense of the overall deal from a prominent developer, see David White, "A Good Deal for Richmond? Absolutely," *Richmond Times-Dispatch*, July 15, 2016.

138. Joey Matthews, "Mayor Touts Anti-poverty Efforts in City Address," *Richmond Free Press*, February 5–7, 2015.

139. Thad Williamson chaired the Policy Committee of the Anti-Poverty Commission and was lead author of its final report. Amy L. Howard chaired the Housing Task Force of the subsequent Maggie L. Walker Initiative for Expanding Opportunity and Fighting Poverty (cochaired by Williamson and councilwoman Ellen Robertson).

140. In the midst of the Mayor's Anti-Poverty Commission in the spring of 2012, two commission committee chairs, Rev. Ben Campbell and Thad Williamson, publicly lobbied for more school funding and criticized the mayor's task force on school efficiencies (see previous chapter). The influential community activist Lillie A. Estes publicly opposed Jones on numerous issues, including the Shockoe stadium plan, while remaining a member in good standing of both the Mayor's Anti-Poverty Commission and the subsequent Maggie L. Walker Citizens Advisory Board.

141. Thad Williamson with John V. Moeser, *Mayor's Anti-Poverty Commission Report*, City of Richmond, January 18, 2013, www.rva.gov/sites/default/files/2019-10/Antipovertycommissionfinal1_17_2013c--printready.pdf.

142. Tina Griego, "Reality Check," *Style Weekly*, March 18, 2014.

143. Timothy Williams, "Richmond Awaits a Bold Anti-poverty Plan," *New York Times*, October 14, 2013.

144. City of Richmond, *Proposed Amendments to the Biennial Fiscal Plan for Fiscal Year 2015*, March 23, 2014, https://rva.gov/sites/default/files/2019-09/2015_ProposedAmendedBiennialFiscalPlan.pdf.

145. City of Richmond Ordinance 2015-240-236, adopted December 14, 2015, to establish the Office of Community Wealth Building, contains a memorandum detailing the agency's overall strategy. City of Richmond website, https://richmondva.legistar.com/Legislation.aspx.

146. See Michael Martz, "Getting People out of Poverty, into the Work Force Is Focus of State Budget Proposal," *Richmond Times-Dispatch*, February 14, 2016, for an account of the BLISS program, in the context of initial efforts to secure state matching funds for the OCWB.

147. Ned Oliver, "$1.9 Million Grant Will Help Richmond Provide Job Training for Poor Residents," *Richmond Times-Dispatch*, June 30, 2017; Office of Community Wealth Building Annual Reports to City Council 2017 and 2020, accessed February 5, 2024, https://rva.gov/sites/default/files/2021-03/Mayors_Annual_Report_on_Poverty_Reduction_2017.pdf and https://rva.gov/sites/default/files/2021-03/2019-Annual-Performance-Report.pdf.

148. The OCWB also partnered with RPS beginning in 2014 on early childhood issues, leading to a $300,000 grant from the W. K. Kellogg Foundation in 2015, and with NextUp, an after-school initiative aimed at middle school students. See chapter 7 for related discussion.

149. Tina Griego, "Hope and a Promise," *Style Weekly*, March 24, 2015.

150. "RVA Future Centers Open in City's Five High Schools," *Richmond Times-Dispatch*, December 13, 2015. Reaching hundreds of students annually, the Future Centers operated for five years with primary funding from the city, under the aegis of the Richmond Public Schools Education Foundation, before being fully incorporated into Richmond Public Schools in the 2020–21 academic year.

151. Laura Kebede and Graham Moomaw, "Grant Brings $24.9M for Bus Rapid Transit," *Richmond Times-Dispatch*, September 10, 2014.

152. Mark Robinson, "Local, State Leaders Celebrate Launch of Pulse," *Richmond Times-Dispatch*, June 26, 2018. In another significant infrastructure-related development with implications for the city's poverty-fighting plan, in September 2015 the city council approved a lease agreement negotiated by the Jones administration to allow the Port of Virginia to operate the Port of Richmond barge terminal for a forty-year period. The Port of Virginia then moved to invest in infrastructure improvements to the port in order to accommodate anticipated increases in traffic over the following decades. The Jones team believed a revitalized port could help bring a cluster of logistic employers to the Southside, offering good jobs in close proximity to Hillside Court and other low income neighborhoods. Greater Richmond Partnership, "Council OKs 40-Year Lease for Port of Richmond," Greater Richmond Partnership, September 15, 2015, www.grpva.com/news/council-oks-40-year-lease-for-port-of-richmond/.

153. For instance, near the end of Jones's second term, the city negotiated the arrival of CoStar, a burgeoning real estate information company that would become one of Richmond's major employers. CoStar committed to opening a downtown research center with 732 employees (with plans to hire some employees through the Office of Community Wealth Building workforce program). In subsequent years, CoStar's footprint downtown would only expand; at the time of the October 2016 announcement, the CoStar deal was the largest new employer to arrive in Richmond in more than a decade. Carol Hazard, "CoStar to Bring 730 New Jobs in HQ in Richmond," *Richmond Times-Dispatch*, October 25, 2016.

154. For more on the Evergreen Cooperatives, see Brandon Duong, "Despite a Rocky Start, Cleveland Model for Worker Co-ops Stands Test of Time," *Shelterforce*, March 9, 2021.

155. City of Richmond, Office of Community Wealth Building, *Social Enterprise Report*, June 2016, www.rva.gov/sites/default/files/2019-10/SocialEnterprise_6-16.pdf.

156. Tina Griego, "Can Concentrated Wealth Relieve Concentrated Poverty?," *Washington Post*, November 7, 2014 (interview with Thad Williamson).

157. Lillie A. Estes, interview with Center for Global Policy Solutions, YouTube, January 11, 2017, www.youtube.com/watch?v=Ou9SyfuNOqs. See also Sasha Abramsky, "Is the Former Capital of the Confederacy Finally Ready to Confront Its Poverty—and Its Past?,"

The Nation, March 31, 2015. Estes told Abramsky, "I wouldn't be involved if I didn't think this opportunity could reach down to the least of us. It's an opportunity to correct policy that was done discriminatorily [both] economically and politically over decades." She added, "Will it change the city? Of course. How quick or how long, that's the task at hand."

158. For further discussion of both Richmond's initial experiences and the broader concept of community wealth building as a policy paradigm, see Melody C. Barnes and Thad Williamson, "Becoming the American Community We Should Be—but Never Have Been," in *Community Wealth Building and the Reconstruction of American Democracy: Can We Make American Democracy Work?*, ed. Melody C. Barnes, Corey D. B. Walker, and Thad Williamson (Northampton, MA: Elgar, 2020), 10–36.

CHAPTER 6

1. For a broader discussion on public housing in America, see Alex F. Schwartz, *Housing Policy in the United States* (New York: Routledge, 2021).

2. See Susan Fainstein, *The Just City* (Ithaca: Cornell University Press, 2010); Clarissa Hayward and Todd Swanstrom, eds., *Justice and the American Metropolis* (Minneapolis: University of Minnesota Press, 2011); Thad Williamson, *Sprawl, Justice, and Citizenship: The Civic Costs of the American Way of Life* (New York: Oxford University Press, 2010).

3. Iris Marion Young, *Justice and the Politics of Difference* (Princeton, NJ: Princeton University Press, 1990).

4. "Mapping Life Expectancy," VCU Center for Society and Health, November 2015, https://societyhealth.vcu.edu.

5. Christopher Silver, *Twentieth-Century Richmond: Planning, Politics, and Race* (Knoxville: University of Tennessee Press, 1984).

6. See Amy L. Howard and Thad Williamson, "Reframing Public Housing in Richmond, Virginia: Segregation, Resident Resistance, and the Future of Redevelopment," *Cities* 57 (September 2016): 35.

7. Numerous city and community leaders spoke to these themes at a May 2015 public forum, "Why Is Richmond Still Segregated?," sponsored by the *Richmond Times-Dispatch*. Housing Opportunities Made Equal director Heather Mullins Crislip remarked,

> I hope that what you can see is that we still have two systems in place. One where private and stable, inexpensive financing is available to allow middle-class families to create wealth, and one where we developed public housing without the opportunity for wealth creation, and private financing and wealth creation still fall short. Both systems took public investment. But the opportunities that they've created for citizens are vastly different. And the lingering financial and social costs are huge.
> ... The legacy is much lower home ownership rates for African-Americans in the region. The most recent data shows this isn't changing post–housing crisis. In the city of Richmond, where 40 percent of the population is white, whites received 70 percent of the home-purchase and refinanced loans in 2013. The wealth and prosperity of the region depends on creating opportunities for stability and wealth-creation for our families. And for all of our families. And building a housing system that supports that goal is really critical ("Why Is Richmond Still Segregated?," *Richmond Times-Dispatch*, May 3, 2015 [transcript of forum]).

8. Silver, *Twentieth-Century Richmond*, 109–12; Buchanan v. Warley, 245 U.S. 60 (1917).

9. Richard Rothstein, *The Color of Law: A Forgotten History of How Our Government Segregated America* (New York: Liveright Publishing Corporation, 2017). For a comprehensive look at the redlining maps from across the United States, see the Digital Scholarship Lab at the University of Richmond's Mapping Inequality website, accessed February 5, 2024, https://dsl.richmond.edu/panorama/redlining/#loc=5/39.096/-94.57.

10. Some enslaved persons in Richmond, especially those working in tobacco production, often lived apart from their owners. These people often lived near the point of production in what were flood-prone areas in what is now Shockoe Bottom. There were so many of these workers that slave owners often provided "board money" for slave lodging. These communities outlived the slave system, in fact. See Julian Maxwell Hayter, *The Dream Is Lost: Voting Rights and the Politics of Race in Richmond, Virginia* (Lexington: University Press of Kentucky, 2017), 3. See also Midori Takagi, *Rearing Wolves to Our Own Destruction: Slavery in Richmond, Virginia, 1782–1865* (Charlottesville: University of Virginia Press, 1999).

11. Hayter, *Dream Is Lost*, 22.

12. Silver, *Twentieth-Century Richmond*, 142–45.

13. For a detailed analysis of Walker's work to bolster community wealth in Jackson Ward, see Shennette Garrett-Scott, *Banking on Freedom: Black Women in U.S. Finance before the New Deal* (New York: Columbia University Press, 2019).

14. Silver, *Twentieth-Century Richmond*, 184–86. Silver notes that 7,000 Black people, 10 percent of the Black population of Richmond, were displaced by the highway construction.

15. Clayton McClure Brooks, *The Uplift Generation: Cooperation across the Color Line in Early Twentieth-Century Virginia* (Charlottesville: University of Virginia Press, 2017), 42–43, 48; Silver, *Twentieth-Century Richmond*.

16. For an overview of public housing planning and policy, see "American Public Housing at 75: Policy, Planning, and the Public Good," ed. Joseph Heathcott, special issue, *Journal of the American Planning Association* 78, no. 4 (December 2012). For a comparative analysis of public housing development and redevelopment, see Lawrence J. Vale, *After the Projects: Public Housing Redevelopment and the Governance of the Poorest Americans* (New York: Oxford University Press, 2019).

17. Libby Germer, "A Public History of Public Housing: Richmond, Virginia," Yale National Initiative to Strengthen Teaching in Public Schools, accessed June 26, 2023, https://teachers.yale.edu/curriculum/viewer/initiative_15.03.05_u.

18. This historical section draws on material previously published in Howard and Williamson, "Reframing Public Housing in Richmond," 33–39.

19. Quoted in Silver, *Twentieth-Century Richmond*, 147.

20. Silver, *Twentieth-Century Richmond*, 147–50.

21. Silver, *Twentieth-Century Richmond*, 153; Benjamin Campbell, *Richmond's Unhealed History* (Richmond: Brandylane, 2011), 152.

22. "Two Housing Projects Here Are Cleared—Final Word Given by City Council," *Richmond Times-Dispatch*, June 26, 1951.

23. Even after the passage of the 1964 Civil Rights Act banning segregation in public facilities and federal programs after the National Urban League lobbied President Lyndon B. Johnson to order the desegregation of public housing in nine Virginia cities, including Richmond, RRHA leadership resisted immediate change, with chief administrator Frederic Fay stating that existing federal contracts required segregation (though he

acknowledged the new federal law, if upheld as constitutional, might soon require change). "Richmond Housing Agency Plans No Desegregation," *Richmond Times-Dispatch*, August 7, 1964. The first Black families moved into Hillside Court in late 1966 and were targeted by cross burnings. "Cross Burned at Hillside," *Richmond Times-Dispatch*, December 1, 1966.

24. Silver, *Twentieth-Century Richmond*, 185.

25. Hayter, *Dream Is Lost*, 55–56.

26. Silver, *Twentieth-Century Richmond*, 289–303; Howard and Williamson, "Reframing Public Housing in Richmond."

27. Eric Sundquist, "Neighborhood Celebrates Success," *Richmond Times-Dispatch*, October 7, 1990; Michael Paul Williams, "Randolph to Celebrate Years of Work on Rebirth," *Richmond Times-Dispatch*, June 5, 2002; Carol Hazard, "T. K. Somanath: Changing Lives through Affordable Housing," *Richmond Times-Dispatch*, December 10, 2012.

28. Nicholas Dagen Bloom, Fritz Umbach, and Lawrence J. Vale, eds., *Public Housing Myths: Perception, Reality, and Social Policy* (Ithaca: Cornell University Press, 2015).

29. Bonnie V. Winston, "Many in City May Call It a Haven for Crime, but 2,300 Call It Home," *Richmond Times-Dispatch*, December 29, 1985. The stigma of living in public housing was not unique to Richmond. See Amy L. Howard, *More Than Shelter: Activism and Community in San Francisco Public Housing* (Minneapolis: University of Minnesota Press, 2014); and Rhonda Y. Williams, *The Politics of Public Housing: Black Women's Struggles against Urban Inequality* (Oxford: Oxford University Press, 2004).

30. Bonnie V. Winston, "The Life Is One of Big Dreams, Little Money," *Richmond Times-Dispatch*, December 29, 1985.

31. Winston, "Many in City Call It a Haven for Crime, but 2,300 Call It Home."

32. Winston, "Life Is One of Big Dreams, Little Money."

33. "Richmond Residents Move into Affordable Housing," WTVR news, October 27, 2020, www.wtvr.com/news/local-news/richmond-residents-move-into-new-affordable-housing.

34. The Community Builders, "Creighton Court Resident Needs Assessment," on behalf of the Richmond Redevelopment and Housing Authority, 2014, 27 (unpublished internal RRHA document in Thad Williamson's possession).

35. For discussion of affective ties among public housing residents in the San Francisco context, see Howard, *More Than Shelter*.

36. Lauren Shepherd, "Cheap Housing Options—For Those in Need of Affordable Housing, Finding the Right Place to Live Is No Simple Task," *Richmond Times-Dispatch*, December 17, 2003.

37. See table 6.2 for further data and discussion.

38. Richard C. Gentry, "Housing Authority Works to Improve City," *Richmond Times-Dispatch*, June 19, 1994.

39. "Housing Panel Elects Turpin" (staff report), *Richmond Times-Dispatch*, November 8, 1987.

40. Michael Paul Williams, "Backers of Housing Director Say There's Plot Here to Fire Him," *Richmond Times-Dispatch*, February 2, 1989; Michael Paul Williams, "Housing Director Is Fired—Board Refuses to Comment," *Richmond Times-Dispatch*, February 3, 1989; "Rally about Turpin Firing Set," *Richmond Times-Dispatch*, February 10, 1989.

41. Phil Murray, "Turpin Tells of Job's 'War' Zone," *Richmond Times-Dispatch*, February 3, 1989. Hassell, then a partner with the law firm McGuire Woods Battle and Boothe,

worked for the housing authority on a contract basis. See Michael Paul Williams, "Nichols Quits Housing Board," *Richmond Times-Dispatch*, February 9, 1989; and Michael Paul Williams, "Legal Expenses Defended by Housing Authority," *Richmond Times-Dispatch*, July 28, 1989.

42. Williams, "Housing Director Is Fired—Board Refuses to Comment."

43. Murray, "Turpin Tells of Job's 'War' Zone"; Williams, "Nichols Quits Housing Board"; Peter Bacque, "350 Rally in Support of Turpin," *Richmond Times-Dispatch*, February 13, 1989; Michael Paul Williams, "Council Asks HUD to Probe RRHA Affairs," *Richmond Times-Dispatch*, February 14, 1989. Nichols had been initially appointed to the RRHA board in 1981, during Marsh's tenure as mayor.

44. Michael Paul Williams, "Rift between RRHA Board, Turpin Cited in 1987 Report," *Richmond Times-Dispatch*, February 11, 1989; Phil Murray, "RRHA Study Is 'Tainted,' Turpin Says," *Richmond Times-Dispatch*, February 11, 1989.

45. Murray, "RRHA Study Is 'Tainted,' Turpin Says."

46. Phil Murray, "Turpin Named Acting Chief of D.C. Housing Authority," *Richmond Times-Dispatch*, March 3, 1989; "Housing Aide Fired Here Gets Post in Ohio" (staff report), *Richmond Times-Dispatch*, April 30, 1991.

47. Michael Paul Williams, "RRHA Greets Year with Changes—New Director Emphasizes Service Role," *Richmond Times-Dispatch*, February 4, 1990.

48. Brian Kelley, "Gilpin Court Trespassing Signs Go Up," *Richmond Times-Dispatch*, November 9, 1990.

49. For critical discussion, see Don Mitchell, *Mean Streets: Homelessness, Public Spaces, and the Limits of Capital* (Athens: University of Georgia Press, 2020), chap. 6.

50. Michael Paul Williams, "Tenants Oppose Changes," *Richmond Times-Dispatch*; June 15, 1990; Betsy Powell, "Anti-Drug City Lease Is Adopted," *Richmond Times-Dispatch*, July 18, 1990; Gentry, "Housing Authority Works to Improve City"; Frank Green, "Anti-drug Project to Aid Public Housing Residents—RRHA, Hospital, Announce Plans for Unique Program," *Richmond Times-Dispatch*, October 19, 1993; Alan Cooper, "Tenants Sue for Better Security," *Richmond Times-Dispatch*, June 26, 1990.

51. Martin Romjue, "Public Housing Changes Urged," *Richmond Times-Dispatch*, October 2, 1990.

52. Richard C. Gentry, "RRHA Provides Housing—and Services," *Richmond Free Press*, August 13–15, 1992; Michael Paul Williams, "Residents to Care for Property," *Richmond Times-Dispatch*, October 17, 1991; Olivia Winslow, "Housing Authority Program Turning a Profit," *Richmond Times-Dispatch*, March 8, 1993; Gentry, "Housing Authority Works to Improve City"; Gregory J. Gilligan, "Residents Seek Co-op Solution to High Prices—Group Aims to Bring Markets to Projects," *Richmond Times-Dispatch*, July 17, 1994.

53. Gordon Hickey, "Housing Authority Cuts Budget by $1 Million—Reduction in Federal Subsidy Is Expected," *Richmond Times-Dispatch*, February 22, 1996.

54. "U.S. Agency Gives RRHA Perfect Score" (staff report), *Richmond Times-Dispatch*, July 3, 1994; Gordon Hickey, "Housing Spotlight on City as Gentry Takes National Post," *Richmond Times-Dispatch*, October 23, 1995.

55. Richard C. Gentry, "Housing Authority Works to Improve City," *Richmond Times-Dispatch*, June 19, 1994.

56. Hickey, "Housing Spotlight on City as Gentry Takes National Post."

57. Michael Martz, "When Stations in Life Create 'Us' and 'Them': Wealthy Windsor Farms and City Housing Projects Are So Near—and So Far," *Richmond Times-Dispatch*, August 24, 1993.

58. Gordon Hickey, "Housing Chief May Be Interim City Manager—Richard C. Gentry Is Top Candidate," *Richmond Times-Dispatch*, October 15, 1997. Gentry was ruled out from serving in the interim role because the city charter required that an employee appointed by the city manager serve in the role. Tom Campbell, "Manager Discussed," *Richmond Times-Dispatch*, October 17, 1997.

59. Gordon Hickey, "Housing Authority Director Plans Move—Gentry to Leave City Post for Job in Washington," *Richmond Times-Dispatch*, February 24, 1998.

60. For a brief introduction to the voluminous literature on the HOPE VI program, see Susan J. Popkin, "The HOPE VI Program—What about the Residents?," Urban Institute, December 11, 2002, www.urban.org/research/publication/hope-vi-program-what-about-residents. For a more detailed assessment, see Susan J. Popkin, Bruce Katz, Mary K. Cunningham, Karen D. Brown, Jeremy Gustafson, and Margery A. Turner, "A Decade of HOPE VI: Research Findings and Policy Challenges," Urban Institute, May 2004, www.urban.org/sites/default/files/alfresco/publication-pdfs/411002-A-Decade-of-HOPE-VI.PDF.

61. Stacy Hawkins Adams and Carrie Johnson, "From Trash to Trees—Blackwell Residents Expect Grant to Spur Revitalized Neighborhood," *Richmond Times-Dispatch*, October 10, 1997.

62. Adams and Johnson, "From Trash to Trees."

63. Lallen Tyrone Johnson-Hart, "Residential Outcomes of HOPE VI Relocatees in Richmond, Virginia" (master's thesis, Virginia Commonwealth University, 2007), table 4.3.

64. Gordon Hickey, "Blackwell Revitalization Could Commence Soon," *Richmond Times-Dispatch*, November 29, 1998; Gordon Hickey, "First HOPE VI Funds Coming to Richmond," *Richmond Times-Dispatch*, February 5, 1999; Gordon Hickey, "Blackwell Project Delayed 60 Days," *Richmond Times-Dispatch*, November 26, 1999.

65. Richmond Redevelopment and Housing Authority, "Housing Opportunities in Blackwell," 2007, cited in Johnson-Hart, "Residential Outcomes of HOPE VI Relocatees in Richmond, Virginia," table 4.4. See also Hickey, "Blackwell Project Delayed 60 Days." By 2018, a total of 487 units—120 homes outside of Blackwell and 367 units in proximity to Blackwell—had actually been constructed, and the housing authority still planned to transfer vacant land to developers to build another 96 units. Jeremy Lazarus, "Blackwell Development to Continue with 96 Vacant Lots," *Richmond Free Press*, November 15–17, 2018.

66. Lea Setegn, "Fresh Neighborhood, Fresh Start: First Residents Move into Units," *Richmond Times-Dispatch*, August 15, 2001; Lea Setegn, "Help or Hindrance? HOPE VI's History in Blackwell Gives Rise to Questions," *Richmond Times-Dispatch*, May 12, 2002.

67. Gordon Hickey, "Handling of HOPE VI Criticized," *Richmond Times-Dispatch*, September 3, 1999.

68. Lea Setegn, "Where Will They Go? Planned Public Housing Losses Worry Residents," *Richmond Times-Dispatch*, May 13, 2002; Setegn, "Help or Hindrance?"

69. Setegn, "Where Will They Go?"

70. Setegn, "Help or Hindrance?"

71. Setegn, "Fresh Neighborhood, Fresh Start"; Setegn, "Help or Hindrance?"

72. Johnson-Hart, "Residential Outcomes of HOPE VI Relocatees in Richmond, Virginia;" Setegn, "Help or Hindrance?"

73. Johnson-Hart, "Residential Outcomes of HOPE VI Relocatees in Richmond, Virginia," 65, table 5.1. Data provided Johnson-Hart by the RRHA showed that seventy-five families moved into one of the six remaining large public housing complexes (Creighton, Fairfield, Gilpin, Hillside, Mosby, and Whitcomb Courts) while twenty moved into the newly built Townes at River South in the Blackwell footprint; another thirty-four families were in various other public housing units across the city.

74. Setegn, "Help or Hindrance?"

75. Setegn, "Help or Hindrance?"

76. Setegn, "Where Will They Go?"

77. Lea Setegn, "Rebuilding Mosby South—Mosby Tenants Hope to Squelch Redevelopment," *Richmond Times-Dispatch*, February 20, 2003; Lea Setegn, "Mosby Housing Funds Plea Rejected by HUD—Housing Authority to Refile Application," *Richmond Times-Dispatch*, March 7, 2003.

78. Gordon Hickey, "Richmond Explores Creating Regional Housing Authority," *Richmond Times-Dispatch*, January 10, 1998; Setegn, "Help or Hindrance?" "Richmond," noted Curtis, "or the inner city, cannot be the only entity that is addressing the needs of poor inhabitants."

79. Setegn, "Help or Hindrance?"

80. Lauren Shepherd, "Housing Authority's Director Plans to Retire," *Richmond Times-Dispatch*, November 4, 2003: Jeremy Redmon and Gail Kelley, "RRHA Gets Acting Director," *Richmond Times-Dispatch*, January 30, 2004.

81. Michael Paul Williams, "Let's 'Walk the Walk' on Housing," *Richmond Times-Dispatch*, January 23, 2006; Will Jones, "Wilder Presents Plan to Address Public Housing," *Richmond Times-Dispatch*, January 21, 2006.

82. David Ress, "Search On to Replace Housing Czar," *Richmond Times-Dispatch*, September 28, 2006.

83. Michael Martz, "Council Approves Hill-Christian," *Richmond Times-Dispatch*, November 13, 2007; "RRHA Picks New Executive Director," *Richmond Times-Dispatch*, February 15, 2007. Hill-Christian resigned as chief administrative officer in late July 2008 after serving eight months. David Ress and Will Jones, "Top City Official Quits Post—Wilder Says He Will Not Name a New Administrator during Term," *Richmond Times-Dispatch*, July 31, 2008.

84. Michael Martz, "Redeveloping Dove Court—Richmond Is Working to Turn 'Mini Gilpin' into New Community," *Richmond Times-Dispatch*, December 26, 2007. In 2013, the first two phases of the project were completed with the opening of the 128-unit, mixed-income Highland Grove community. Zachary Reid, "Dove Court No More, Area Is Revitalized," *Richmond Times-Dispatch*, October 11, 2013.

85. Anthony Scott, Annie Giles, and Delores Robinson, "With Sound Planning, City Can Avoid Disaster," *Richmond Times-Dispatch*, March 27, 2008.

86. Zachary Reid, "Changes Planned for Richmond Public Housing," *Richmond Times-Dispatch*, September 12, 2008; Zachary Reid, "Work-in-Progress Plan for Jackson Ward Unveiled," *Richmond Times-Dispatch*, November 3, 2008; Zachary Reid, "A Plan to Revitalize Gilpin Court—Richmond Proposes Mixed-Use District," *Richmond Times-Dispatch*,

February 4, 2009. The initial Gilpin plans immediately drew comparisons to Blackwell, including from mayoral candidate Dwight C. Jones, who stated, "If you want a blueprint for how not to do it, look at Blackwell," in a September 2008 candidate forum. Michael Paul Williams, "Blackwell Ghost Haunts Gilpin Plan," *Richmond Times-Dispatch*, September 18, 2008.

87. Alex Gulotta and Cora Hayes, "Unnatural Disaster," *Richmond Times-Dispatch*, March 6, 2008.

88. Public housing residents and organizational representatives from the Legal Aid Justice Center, Richmond Jobs with Justice, Virginia Organizing, Richmond Food Not Bombs, the Richmond Peace Education Center, and the Richmond Tenants Organization, among others, set out the following bold demands in response to local and national trends seen in redevelopment and ensuing displacement and marginalization of public housing residents (see RePHRAME, accessed August 2014, rephrame.blogspot.com):

1. There should be 1-for-1 replacement of any public housing units lost through public housing redevelopment. . . . In addition, . . . newly created public housing units, and other aspects of the redevelopment process, should increase the employment, education, and other opportunities of public housing residents.
2. Current residents should have the right to return to newly developed public housing without any additional screening or requalification process. . . .
3. Public housing residents should have a meaningful voice in decisions regarding their housing and communities. . . . RePHRAME proposes 2 additional seats to the RRHA Board of Commissioners which would be filled with RRHA residents.
4. . . . RePHRAME surveyed hundreds of public housing residents in Richmond, and the overwhelming consensus is for a local rent payment option, at either the RRHA rent office in their neighborhood or at a local bank. [Tenants had been required to mail rent checks to Baltimore, risking late fees due to mail system problems or other processing delays.]

89. Council resolution 2010-R140-162, adopted October 25, 2010, City of Richmond website, https://richmondva.legistar.com/Legislation.aspx. See also Michael Paul Williams, "Residents Need More Say in RRHA," *Richmond Times-Dispatch*, September 14, 2010; and Michael Paul Williams, "Council Should Act on RRHA Panel," *Richmond Times-Dispatch*, October 18, 2011.

90. Popkin, "Hope VI Program—What about the Residents?"

91. In 2020, the Virginia General Assembly made renters' "source of funds" a protected class, in effect requiring landlords to accept Section 8 and other housing vouchers. See Housing Opportunities Made Equal, "Source of Funds," HOME of Virginia, accessed February 5, 2024, https://homeofva.org/get-help/fair-housing/source-of-funds/.

92. Lea Setegn, "City Could Lose Section 8 Funds," *Richmond Times-Dispatch*, May 5, 2001.

93. Thad Williamson and Adria Scharf, "Evicting the Poor," *Style Weekly*, September 30, 2009. See also John Moeser, "Suburban Poverty and No Place to Stay," *Richmond Times-Dispatch*, December 20, 2009.

94. Thad Williamson with John V. Moeser, *Mayor's Anti-Poverty Commission Report*, City of Richmond, January 18, 2013, www.rva.gov/sites/default/files/2019-10/Antipovertycommissionfinal1_17_2013c--printready.pdf.

95. For an extended analysis and assessment, see Mark Robinson, "To Live and Die in Creighton Court," *Richmond Magazine*, July 28, 2016; see also Dina Weinstein, "Trading Up," *Richmond Magazine*, March 30, 2018; and Nikki Patterson-Russel, "Bet on the Underdog," *Style Weekly*, November 6, 2018.

96. Jones quoted in K. Burnell Evans, "U.S. Once Again Skips Richmond for $30M Grant," *Richmond Times-Dispatch*, September 30, 2016.

97. U.S. Department of Housing and Urban Development, FY 2016 Notice of Funding Availability, Choice Neighborhoods Implementation Grant Program (Technical Correction), 23–24, accessed February 6, 2024, www.hud.gov/sites/documents/TC_CNI_FR_6000_N_34.PDF.

98. For discussion of current best policy practices drawn from Choice Neighborhoods Initiative and related programs, see Susan J. Popkin, Diane K. Levy, Mica O'Brien, and Abby Boshart, "An Equitable Strategy for Public Housing Redevelopment: Learning from Past Initiatives," Urban Institute, June 2021, www.urban.org/sites/default/files/publication/104467/an-equitable-strategy-for-public-housing-redevelopment.pdf.

99. Zachary Reid, "T. K. Somanath Brings Experience to New Role at RRHA," *Richmond Times-Dispatch*, February 8, 2015.

100. Graham Moomaw, "Plan to Redevelop Site of Former Armstrong High School Receives Backing," *Richmond Times-Dispatch*, January 6, 2015; K. Burnell Evans, "City Hopes to Make Shortlist for $30 Million Grant for East End," *Richmond Times-Dispatch*, July 5, 2016.

101. City of Richmond and Richmond Redevelopment and Housing Authority, Choice Neighborhoods Initiative Application for Creighton Court, June 2016, Exhibit H (document in Thad Williamson's possession).

102. The Community Builders, "Creighton Court Resident Needs Assessment," on behalf of Richmond Redevelopment and Housing Authority, 2014 (unpublished internal RRHA document in Thad Williamson's possession).

103. City of Richmond and Richmond Redevelopment and Housing Authority, 2016 Choice Neighborhoods Initiative application, Exhibit H; and RRHA Residents Characteristics Report, March 31, 2016 (unpublished internal RRHA documents in Thad Williamson's possession).

104. City of Richmond and Richmond Redevelopment and Housing Authority, Choice Neighborhoods Initiative for Creighton Court; "TCF Commits $750,000 to Help East End Residents Thrive," The Community Foundation of Greater Richmond news release, August 29, 2016, https://web.archive.org/web/20210414012014/https://www.cfrichmond.org/Leadership-Impact/News/All-News/Month/8/Year/2016.

105. Robinson, "To Live and Die in Creighton Court."

106. Evans, "U.S. Once Again Skips Richmond for $30M Grant."

107. HUD Applicant Notification Letter sent from HUD deputy assistant secretary Dominique Blom to RRHA CEO T. K. Somanath and Richmond mayor Dwight C. Jones, September 29, 2016 (document in Thad Williamson's possession).

108. Robinson, "To Live and Die in Creighton Court"; Patterson-Russel, "Bet on the Underdog."

109. "Richmond Residents Move into New Affordable Housing," WTVR news report, October 30, 2020, www.wtvr.com/news/local-news/richmond-residents-move-into-new-affordable-housing.

110. Richmond Redevelopment and Housing Authority, "Creighton Court Progress Update," RRHA, January 2023, www.rrha.com/redevelopment/creighton/; "Creighton Court Redevelopment—Tenants' Bill of Rights," April 2020, RRHA, www.rrha.com/redevelopment/creighton/. The "Bill of Rights" document—signed by the RRHA CEO and board chair, the mayor, the city council president, and the president of the Creighton Court Tenants Council and the Richmond Tenants Organization—committed RRHA to offering Creighton residents at least three safe and affordable housing options prior to relocation.

111. The RRHA received widespread condemnation from community leaders and elected officials in the winter of 2017–18 for its handling of widespread heating failures in units, including but not limited to Creighton Court. RRHA staff initially provided residents space heaters rather than undertake emergency repairs. Michael Paul Williams, "Lack of Heat Is a Symptom of Lack of Heart in Public Housing," *Richmond Times-Dispatch*, January 4, 2018; Mark Robinson and Ned Oliver, "RRHA Rebuked over Handling of Heat Woes—RRHA Faces Criticism over Handling of Creighton Court Furnace Failures," *Richmond Times-Dispatch*, January 9, 2018; Ned Oliver, "RRHA Knew of Heat Outages in October," *Richmond Times-Dispatch*, January 21, 2018. The episode led to Somanath's resignation in January 2018. Later that month, interim CEO Orlando Artze and other RRHA officials undertook a corrective action plan to address the heating issue but also noted the impact of federal funding cuts on the RRHA's ability to maintain its aging property portfolio. Adrianne Todman, chief executive officer of the National Association of Housing and Redevelopment Officials, noted that Richmond's problems reflected a national issue: "What happens if you can't deal with the daily maintenance is a toilet problem becomes a plumbing issue and then you've got to get behind the walls for major repairs. . . . It's a narrative that's repeated over and over again in housing authorities around the country." Ned Oliver, "Heat Problems in Public Housing Worse Than Initially Thought," *Richmond Times-Dispatch*, January 27, 2018.

112. To be sure, critical community organizations in the East End such as the Peter Paul Development Center providing services to children and families enjoyed broad philanthropic support, encouraged by frequent bus tours of the East End sponsored by Peter Paul, Communities in Schools, and prominent philanthropic supporters. But philanthropic support for East End families did not generally translate into sustained political pressure for broader changes.

113. For more information on this program, see Richmond and Henrico Health Districts' "Resource Centers" program page, accessed September 30, 2023, www.vdh.virginia.gov/richmond-city/resource-centers/.

114. Lynn Jackson Kirk, "Gilpin Court Community Plants Community Garden Initiative," *Richmond Times-Dispatch*, October 30, 2018; "Bellemeade Green Street Project," James River Association website, accessed February 25, 2024, https://thejamesriver.org/bellemeade-green-street-project/; Jeremy M. Lazarus, "Garden at MLK Middle School Is Part of New City 'Food Justice' Corridor," *Richmond Free Press*, March 15, 2019. Lillie A. Estes, who was deeply skeptical about public housing redevelopment and who played an integral role in the Gilpin Court community garden initiative, made the point this way in a May 2015 forum: "You know, we can have all concentrated black communities. I ain't trying to move in your community at all. But I want appropriate resources in my community, among my cultural people, that we deserve. That's sort of reparation." "Why Is Richmond Still Segregated?," *Richmond Times-Dispatch*, May 3, 2015.

115. The pool was closed because of maintenance needs in 2013 but, despite many years of complaints, was not reopened, due to lack of funds (or specifically, decisions made by the RRHA not to prioritize reopening the pool). Mark Robinson, "Report: Calhoun Center Repair Will Take 11 Months and Cost at Least $1.9 Million," *Richmond Times-Dispatch*, August 24, 2021.

116. On the history of gentrification, see Matthew L. Schuerman, *Newcomers: Gentrification and Its Discontents* (Chicago: University of Chicago Press, 2019).

117. Japonica Brown-Saracino, *The Gentrification Debates: A Reader* (New York: Routledge, 2010).

118. For a detailed case study, see Kathryn S. Parkhurst, "Expansion and Exclusion: A Case Study of Gentrification in Church Hill" (master's thesis, Virginia Commonwealth University, 2016), 68–91.

119. Bill Wasson, "City Outlines Goals to Improve Housing," *Richmond Times-Dispatch*, March 30, 1993.

120. City of Richmond, 2001 Master Plan, 98–99, accessed February 6, 2024, https://web.archive.org/web/20120108212114/http://www.richmondgov.com/PlanningAndDevelopmentReview/PlansMaster.aspx.

121. City of Richmond, 2001 Master Plan, 99–106.

122. Laura Lafayette, "Housing Program Is More Than Tweaking" (letter to the editor), *Richmond Times-Dispatch*, November 11, 2006.

123. Kathy Graziano and Ellen Robertson, "Affordable Housing . . . City Plan Opens New Opportunities," *Richmond Times-Dispatch*, March 6, 2007.

124. The council passed an initial version in January 2007 and then (following changes in state law) replaced it with a stronger version that September. Michael Martz, "New Way to Spur Varied Housing—Ordinance Supports Building Affordable Units in Richmond," *Richmond Times-Dispatch*, September 13, 2007.

125. City of Richmond Ordinance 2008-114-98, adopted May 27, 2008, City of Richmond website, https://richmondva.legistar.com/Legislation.aspx.

126. K. Burnell Evans, "Long-Dormant Housing Fund Paying Dividends," *Richmond Times-Dispatch*, November 25, 2015; City of Richmond Affordable Housing Trust Fund Impact Report, FY 2015–16, accessed June 3, 2022, www.rva.gov/housing-and-community-development/affordable-housing-trust-fund.

127. In 2018, the Maggie Walker Community Land Trust was designated by the city council as a land bank. The land trust sought to become the vehicle for converting Richmond's vacant properties into quality, affordable housing units. Maggie Walker Community Land Trust infographic, https://maggiewalkerclt.org/infographic/, downloaded June 3, 2022; City of Richmond Ordinance 2017-196, adopted February 26, 2018, City of Richmond website, https://richmondva.legistar.com/Legislation.aspx.

128. "The Best and Worst Places to Grow Up: How Your Area Compares," Interactive database, *New York Times*, May 4, 2015, www.nytimes.com/interactive/2015/05/03/upshot/the-best-and-worst-places-to-grow-up-how-your-area-compares.html.

CHAPTER 7

1. Richmond's Black elected leaders, spearheaded by former Governor Wilder, *did* take a significant step, with support from some white allies, to alter Monument Avenue by adding

a statue of tennis star and global humanitarian Arthur Ashe, a Richmond native, at the intersection of Monument Avenue and Roseneath Road in 1996. The decision followed a heated debate on the question of, as Chuck Richardson put it, "Do we put a black man on Monument Avenue?" "Race-Tinged Furor Stalls Arthur Ashe Memorial," *New York Times*, July 9, 1995. The city council ultimately said yes, despite considerable opposition from conservative whites in Richmond and statewide. At that point, the notion of *taking down* existing Confederate monuments was considered well beyond the limits of political possibility. For further detailed discussion, including recounting of the variety of views that Black political leaders held concerning whether Monument Avenue was in fact the best place to honor Ashe, see Matthew Mace Barbee, *Race and Masculinity in Southern Memory: History of Richmond, Virginia's Monument Avenue, 1948–1996* (Lanham, MD: Lexington Books, 2013), chap. 7.

2. In his 2018 memoir, Marsh reflected that as mayor, "I might have wanted to add a statue on Monument Avenue, but I was not in favor of taking any away." Henry L. Marsh III, *The Memoirs of Hon. Henry L. Marsh, III: Civil Rights Champion, Public Servant, Lawyer* (GrantHouse Publishers, 2018), 99.

3. K. Burnell Evans, "U.S. Once Again Skips Richmond for $30M Grant," *Richmond Times-Dispatch*, September 30, 2016. Likewise, in 2016 Delegate Delores McQuinn, longtime head of the Richmond City Council Slave Trail Commission, said that while she favored local control over monuments, she was "not interested in pulling down monuments" but rather in adding commemorations of "African-Americans who really helped build the city of Richmond" in order to "[tell] the balanced story." Graham Moomaw, "Bill to Stop Removal of Memorials Is Vetoed," *Richmond Times-Dispatch*, March 11, 2016.

4. Marvin T. Chiles, *The Struggle for Change: Race and the Politics of Reconciliation in Modern Richmond* (Charlottesville: University of Virginia Press, 2023).

5. Associated Press, "Stonewall Jackson Statue in Richmond Taken Down to Cheers," video, *New York Times*, July 1, 2020, www.nytimes.com/video/us/politics/100000007220241/richmond-confederate-monument-taken-down.html.

6. See 2018–23 Dreams4RPS Strategic Plan, RPS [Richmond Public Schools], accessed December 28, 2023, www.rvaschools.net/about/dreams4rps.

7. The proportion of RPS kindergarten students passing the PALS assessment of kindergarten readiness fell from 75.4 percent in 2016 to 71.8 percent in 2019, before a precipitous drop to 62.6 percent in 2020 (presumably as a result of the pandemic). The RPS pass rate is about 10 percent lower than the statewide average. Greater Richmond PALS Data is published by the United Way of Greater Richmond and Petersburg, accessed October 9, 2022, www.yourunitedway.org/data/kindergarten-readiness/.

8. See City of Richmond, Office of Community Wealth Building, *2019 Annual Performance Report: Making an Impact on Our Community*, accessed February 5, 2024, https://rva.gov/sites/default/files/2021-03/2019-Annual-Performance-Report.pdf.

9. Richmond Public Schools made a nod in this direction in 2021 by electing to use a significant part of its American Rescue Plan Act dollars on a system-wide literacy initiative. Bella DiMarco, "Sounding Out a Better Way to Teach Reading," *New York Times*, October 6, 2022.

10. Since 2014, NextUp RVA has developed and expanded a model for providing high-quality enrichment and academic support services to Richmond middle school students; the City of Richmond provides significant annual financial support (begun in 2014

as part of Mayor Jones's anti-poverty initiative), but most funding is from private sources. See nextuprva.org, accessed September 30, 2023, for more information.

11. David Kirp, *Improbable Scholars: The Rebirth of a Great American School System and a Strategy for America's Schools* (New York: Oxford University Press, 2013). See also David Kirp, Marjorie Weschler, Madelyn Gardner, and Titilayo Tinubu Ali, *Disrupting Disruption: The Steady Work of Transforming Schools* (New York: Oxford University Press, 2022).

12. See City of Richmond Auditor, 2022 Fiscal and Efficiency Review, June 7, 2022, http://rvagov.prod.acquia-sites.com/media/21701, for discussion, including of the need for the city to improve its internal processes.

13. See the website of STAY RVA, accessed September 30, 2023, stayrva.org, for further detail on the organization.

14. Fall Membership Reports, 2014–15 and 2020–21, Virginia Department of Education website, www.doe.virginia.gov/data-policy-funding/data-reports/statistics-reports/enrollment-demographicsdoe.virginia.gov.

15. The 2022–23 City Charter Review Commission recommended adoption of staggered terms for the city council; such a shift, if adopted, would almost certainly also lead to staggered terms for the school board. 2023 Richmond City Council Charter Review Commission Final Report, August 2, 2023, City of Richmond website, https://rva.gov/richmond-city-council/richmond-city-charter-review-commission.

16. City of Richmond, Office of Community Wealth Building Annual Performance Reports to Richmond City Council for 2019, 2020, 2021, and 2022, https://rva.gov/community-wealth-building/news.

17. Chris Suarez, "Eighteen Families to Get $500 Monthly for Next Two Years," *Richmond Times-Dispatch*, October 29, 2020; Taikein Cooper, Jesús Gerena, Valaryee Mitchell and Tyonka Perkins Rimawi, "Guaranteed Income Supports Working Families and the Economy," *Richmond Times-Dispatch*, December 20, 2020; City of Richmond, Office of Community Wealth Building Annual Performance Report for 2020, 16.

18. City of Richmond, Office of Community Wealth Building, *Social Enterprise Report*, June 2016, www.rva.gov/sites/default/files/2019-10/SocialEnterprise_6-16.pdf.

19. A 2022 report on "equitable economic development" issued by the city revived the idea. City of Richmond, Department of Economic Development, *Strategic Plan for Equitable Economic Development*, 2022, 28 (1.4.4.), https://rva.gov/economic-development/speed.

20. See The Kalamazoo Promise, accessed December 28, 2023, https://kalamazoopromise.com, for copious information about the Kalamazoo program.

21. "RVA Future Centers Open in City's Five High Schools," *Richmond Times-Dispatch*, December 13, 2015.

22. For further information on the G3 Initiative, see "Governor Northam Signs Legislation Creating Tuition-Free Community College Program for Low- and Middle-Income Students" (press release), March 29, 2021, www.governor.virginia.gov/newsroom/all-releases/2021/march/headline-894095-en.html.

23. A step in this direction was taken in April 2023, when Richmond City Council approved Mayor Levar Stoney's proposal to allocate $1.75 million in unspent FY 2022 funds to support a scholarship initiative benefiting RPS graduates. The initiative will pay for tuition and a monthly stipend for RPS graduates enrolling in neighboring J. Sargeant Reynolds Community College. Jeremy M. Lazarus, "City Approves Scholarship Program with Reynolds," *Richmond Free Press*, April 13, 2023.

24. City of Richmond, Department of Housing and Community Development, *One Richmond: An Equitable Affordable Housing Plan*, January 2022, https://rva.gov/housing-and-community-development/public-documents.

25. In 2019, the city administration advanced a $1.5 billion downtown development plan anchored around the replacement of Richmond Coliseum. The proposed development was championed by Dominion CEO Tom Farrell and (like previous proposals) had significant support from elite actors. A grassroots coalition formed in opposition to the proposal citing various concerns, in particular the fact that the proposed tax increment finance zone extended far beyond the actual project area. A review commission appointed by the city council issued a mixed but largely negative assessment of the plan. Ultimately the proposal garnered the support of only four of the seven council members needed for passage, resulting in its rejection in February 2020. Mark Robinson, "Commission: $1.5B Navy Hill Project Poses Risk to Richmond's General Fund, Schools," *Richmond Times-Dispatch*, December 22, 2019; Mark Robinson, "Richmond Council Bloc Doubles Down on Opposition to Navy Hill Plan; Consultant Praises Project," *Richmond Times-Dispatch*, February 4, 2020.

26. City of Richmond, Department of Economic Development, *Strategic Plan for Equitable Economic Development*.

27. City of Richmond, Department of Planning and Development Review, *Richmond 300: A Guide for Growth*, 2020, www.rva.gov/economic-development/richmond-300.

28. In mid-2023 there were over 2,100 tax-delinquent properties in Richmond, scattered across the city, although in many cases the taxes owed were less than $1,000 or had been delinquent less than a year. City of Richmond Data Portal, accessed August 23, 2023, https://data.richmondgov.com/Well-Managed-Government/Delinquent-Real-Estate-Taxes-Six-Months-or-More-/83t5-hbac. It would be appropriate to couple efforts to move tax-delinquent properties back on the books with assistance for long-time homeowners unable to meet rising property taxes resulting from gentrification.

29. City of Richmond, Vacant Building Information, accessed August 23, 2023, www.rva.gov/planning-development-review/vacant-building-information. See also City of Richmond, Department of Housing and Community Development, *One Richmond: An Equitable Affordable Housing Plan*, fig. 15, for a 2020 map of then-available vacant land and buildings in the city.

30. In August 2023, the City of Richmond and the Local Initiatives Support Corporation unveiled an "Equitable Affordable Housing Plan," a five-year, $100 million plan including $50 million of bond-funded city investment, matched by the Local Initiatives Support Corporation. Stated goals included 10,000 new affordable apartment units and 2,000 low- and moderate-income homes by 2033 and "transformation" of the six remaining large public housing communities by 2037. City of Richmond and LISC Housing Partnership Listening Sessions Presentation, August 16, 2023.

31. Matthew Desmond, *Evicted: Poverty and Profit in the American City* (New York: Penguin, 2016). In 2019, Richmond launched an eviction diversion program in response to a *New York Times* article, based on Desmond's research, calling attention to the city's high eviction rate. The city also used part of its American Rescue Plan Act funding to support a Family Crisis Fund providing cash relief to families in crisis circumstances. For a detailed breakdown of Richmond's usage of some $155 million in pandemic-related federal funding, which included significant investments in affordable housing, new or refurbished community centers in low-wealth neighborhoods, and the establishment of

a health equity fund, see "American Rescue Plan," City of Richmond website, accessed February 26, 2024, https://rva.gov/arp.

32. 2022–23 Richmond City Council Charter Review Commission Final Report, August 2, 2023. Thad Williamson served as chair of the nine-member advisory commission.

33. 2022–23 Richmond City Council Charter Review Commission Final Report, August 2, 2023.

34. Julian Maxwell Hayter, *The Dream Is Lost: Voting Rights and the Politics of Race in Richmond, Virginia* (Lexington: University Press of Kentucky, 2017).

35. U.S. Census Bureau, QuickFacts, accessed February 25, 2024, www.census.gov/quickfacts/. Based on U.S. Census Bureau, American Community Survey, 2018–22, 5-year estimates.

36. City of Richmond, Adopted Annual Fiscal Plan for Fiscal Year 2021–22, Section 3-3, https://rva.gov/index.php/budget-and-strategic-planning/budget-documents. In 2023 VCU's real estate footprint in the city was estimated at over $2.5 billion, equivalent to $30 million a year in foregone taxes. Scott Bass, "VCU, the Real Estate Juggernaut, Needs to Reconsider Its Mission," *Richmond Times-Dispatch*, August 13, 2023.

37. For detailed discussion and analysis of the Local Composite Index in Virginia, see, among others, Cary Lou and Kristin Blagg with Victoria Rosenboom, Victoria Lee, and Stipica Mudrazija, *School District Funding in Virginia: Computing the Effects of Changes to the Standards of Quality Funding Formula*, Urban Institute, December 20, 2018, www.urban.org/research/publication/school-district-funding-virginia.

38. See "School Construction Assistance Program," Virginia Department of Education website, accessed March 1, 2024, www.doe.virginia.gov/programs-services/school-operations-support-services/facility-construction-maintenance/school-construction-assistance-program. At the federal level, Virginia political leaders continue to push for changes in tax law to allow the use of federal tax credits in school renovations to make it easier for older cities like Richmond to address facility needs. See Michael Martz, "Kaine, Warner Try Again to Use Historic Tax Credits for Schools," *Richmond Times-Dispatch*, May 10, 2023.

39. For historical context and related discussion of the ways Virginia restricts local power, see Richard Schragger and C. Alex Retzloff, "The Failure of Home Rule Reform in Virginia: Race, Localism, and the Constitution of 1971," Virginia Public Law and Legal Theory Research Paper No. 2020-35, April 13, 2020, https://papers.ssrn.com/sol3/papers.cfm?abstract_id=3574765. Schragger and Retzloff observe that Virginia's 1971 constitution, developed when Virginia's legislative bodies were nearly all-white, had the effect of limiting the scope of Black political agency in Richmond and several other Virginia cities.

40. Wyatt Gordon, "Once Hostile to Transit, Richmond's Surrounding Counties Are Now Expanding Bus Service," Greater Greater Washington, March 24, 2022, https://ggwash.org/view/84155/once-hostile-to-transit-richmonds-surrounding-counties-are-now-expanding-bus-service.

41. For more on the 1961 merger referendum, see Christopher Silver, *Twentieth Century Richmond: Planning, Politics, and Race* (Knoxville: University of Tennessee Press, 1984), 233–49.

42. In 2020, 63.6 percent of Henrico voters and 82.9 percent of City of Richmond voters cast presidential ballots for Democratic candidate Joe Biden. Virginia Board of Elections data, Virginia Department of Elections website, accessed February 6, 2024, https://historical.elections.virginia.gov/elections/view/144567.

Index

Page numbers in italics refer to figures and tables.

Accordino, John, 160
activism: city manager, activists' conflict with, 45–46; civic activism, weak culture of, 8, 13; civil rights/Black community, 25, 34, 62, 72; community activism, anti-poverty, 177; housing activism, 24, 181, 199, 203–4; protest art, 1; and school funding, 133; and Shockoe Bottom development, 173–74; systemic racism, protests against, 1–2
Adams, Alvin, 46
Adams, John B., Jr., 119
Ad Hoc Committee on Public Education, 291n36
affirmative action, 25, 26, 38, 149
Affirmative Action and the Stalled Quest for Black Progress (Drake and Holsworth), 38
Affordable Housing Trust Fund, 177, 190, 220, 236, 238
African American community. *See* Black community
Agelasto, Parker, 82, 174
Albert Hill Middle School, 229
Allen, Bruce, 169
Allen, George F., 54, 57, 58, 104, 169

Allen, George H., 169
Altria Theater, 159
Ambler, Gordon B., 193
American Community Survey, 8
Andrews, Robin, 55
annexation policies, 10–11, 13, 23, 138
Anti-Poverty Commission (Mayor Jones), 81, 82, 165, 176, 317nn139–40; Policy Committee, 176, 317n139; Report (2013), 244
anti-urbanism, 8, 9–11, 138–39, 163–64, 245–46
Apostle Town neighborhood, 193
Appomattox Governor's School, 229, 245
Armstrong, Beverley W. "Booty," 74
Armstrong High School, 133, 211
Armstrong Renaissance Apartments, 211
arts and cultural centers, 157–59
Ashe, Arthur, 71, 328–29n1
at-large mayoral elections, 57–71
authors' methodology, 18; oral history sources, 257–60

Back to the Future: Richmond at the Crossroads (Crupi), 38–44
Bailey, A. Peter, 33, 47–48

Balanced Scorecard, Richmond Public Schools (RPS), 111
Baldwin, Davarian, 154
Baliles, Gerald, 10
Baliles, Jonathan, 82, 174
Banks, James, 61, 62
Baptist Ministers' Conference of Richmond and Vicinity, 63
Barlow, Alma, 199, 201
Baskerville, Viola, 47, 58, 63
Baugh, David P., 44
Bedden, Dana T., 132–34
Bellevue Elementary School, 99–100, 127–28
Belvidere Street Extension, 193
Bernard, Peter J., 119
Berry, Jack, 83, 172
Better Housing Coalition, 36, 209
Binford Middle School, 229, 230
BioTech Park, 153–54
Black, Harry E., 78
Black community: banking and credit institutions, 191–92; journalism, 33–34; middle class, 38; Black nationalism, 33; voting power, 68–70; majority-Black city council, 149; minority contracting policies, 46, 60; political apathy of middle class, 34–35; political wings, 32–33; and poverty, 7–8. *See also* activism; racial issues
Black Lives Matter, 1–2
Blackwell (Southside) neighborhood, 65, 160, 189, 198, 202–4; public housing, 201
Bliley, Thomas, 67
Blitz to Bloom, 65–66, 277n73
Bobb, Robert: city manager/city council conflict, 45–46, 52; city-manager position, 30–32; consultant to mayoral task force on Richmond Public Schools operations, 82, 124–25; departure from Richmond, 60, 67, 202; and development in Richmond, 154; on need for investment in the city, 32, 226; on regional tax-sharing, 32, 49

Bonner Center for Civic Engagement (University of Richmond), 176
Bon Secours Health System, 168, 169–71, 315–16n121
Boone, Raymond, 33
Bourne, Jeffrey, 125, 126, 130
Bradley, Tom, 71
Brandon, Yvonne W., 106–7, 123–24, 126
Braxton, George P., II, 114
Bridges, Kim, 125, 301n150
Bridgforth, Jeanne M., 61
Bright, J. Fulmer, 193
Broad Rock Elementary School, 128
Brown, Ernest, 68
Brown, Lucille, 99, 100
Brown v. Board of Education (1954), 90, 100
Bryant, Alton E., 56
budget process: challenges of, 11; council oversight, 240; Jones's 2014 proposals, 177–78; Richmond Public Schools, 81–82, 97–98, 112, 117, 124–25, 133; Wilder's 2005 proposal/negotiations, 76–78
Building Lives of Independence and Self-Sufficiency (BLISS), 178, 227
business community/culture, 13, 39–40; Black-owned businesses, 192; corporate power and influence, 75, 114–21; Crupi Report, 38–44; influence of, 14; investment, climate for, 31, 148–49; movement toward economic stabilization, 150–52; and racial politics, 24, 25–26, 45–48, 151; and Richmond Public Schools, 120–21; support for mayor-council structure, 71
Bus Rapid Transit (BRT) lines, 82, 177, 179, 244
Byrd, Harry F., 12
Byrd, William, II, 167
Byrd Park, 1
Byrne, Michael, 70

Cannaday, Billy, 113
Carpenter Theatre, 158–59
Carter, Wesley, 55, 56

Carver Elementary School, 230
Carver neighborhood, 153, 160
Center for Workforce Innovation, 177, 178
Central Virginia Transportation Authority, 244
Chandler, Theodore L., Jr., 119
Chapman, Peter H., 165
charter schools, 112, 127
Chavis, Duron, 177
Chavis, Larry, 47, 58–59, 275n42, 275n44
Cheek, Mary Tyler Freeman, 36
Chesterfield County: annexation, 13, 23, 138; inequality and economic mobility, 220; jobs and economic development, 142, 143, 144; population growth and demographics, 15, 27, 28; property taxes, 140; public transit, 162–64, 244, 313n89; Republican-Democrat shift, 10; subsidized housing, 205; suburban ring, 9
Chesterfield County schools, 12, 87; race and economic disadvantage, 88, 88–89, 89; student outcomes, 93
Chiles, Marvin, 264n32
Choice Neighborhoods framework, 208–11
Church Hill neighborhood, 36, 58, 99
CIAA (Central Intercollegiate Athletic Association) basketball, 102–3
City Beautiful initiative, 165
city council: Black-majority council (1977), 25; city council districts, 23–25, 57–58, 68–69, 69; Crupi Report, 43; election (1982), 25; election (1988), 28–29; election (1990), 35–36; election (1994), 47–48; election (1998), 60–63; ineptitude, charges of, 60; and prioritization of neighborhood issues, 29; and Richmond Public Schools, attempted eviction of, 121–22
city council–city manager system, 24, 30–32, 45, 51–52, 240–41; city council power divide, 45, 63–64; city/county divisions, 6, 265n38; city manager position/role, 30; Human Relations Commission divide, 45–46; and mayoral role, 65, 272n2, 276n63
city hall: council-manager model, 30–31; dysfunction, 24, 45, 47, 51, 60, 72, 75–76, 278n77; economic pragmatism, 140, 168; journalistic coverage, 33–34; reform, 66–67, 81; and school board, 111–12, 114, 121, 133
City of Richmond, Virginia, 5, 19; Black political leadership, 225–26; bond rating, 48; city/county divide, 32; city image, 32, 42; city/suburban divide, 39–40; as Confederate capital, 16; corruption, 59–60, 66–67, 82–83; cultural centers, 157–58; economic decline, 149–50; economic development, 26, 140–48, 143, 144; economic structure, suburban shift, 143–44; elitism in power structure, 74–75; history, late-twentieth-century, 27–36; history, pre-1988, 2–3; population growth and demographics, 4, 27, 28, 215, 216; property taxes, 140; public frustration with local leadership, 72–73; school zoning and rezoning proposals, 128–29; significance of, 15–17; tax base, 10–11, 139–40
City of Richmond v. J. A. Croson, 26, 149, 267n15
City of the Future initiative, 78, 114, 158
civility, calls for, 49
Civil Rights Act (1964), 100, 320–21n23
civil rights revolution, 25, 126, 136, 149, 226
Civil War, legacy of, 2, 4, 16, 31, 55, 190, 262n9
Clark Springs Elementary School, 128–29
Cleveland, Ohio, 180, 234
"cliff effect" in subsidized housing, 202, 233–34
CodeRVA High School, 229, 245
Cole, Joshua, 97
Coleman, Donald, 125, 130, 131
Columbus, Christopher, 1
Comey, James B., 65

Index 335

Commonwealth of Virginia: local government structures, 8; policy recommendations, 242–44; segregationist structures, 11–13; state laws impacting urban-suburban inequality, 10–11; state vs. regional approaches, 64
commonwealth's attorney, 44–45; David Hicks as, 47, 52, 54
Community Development Block Grants, 160
Community High School, 229
community-oriented policing, 65–66
community wealth building, policy emphases on, 232–36. *See also* Office of Community Wealth Building
Confederate memorials/monuments, 1–2, 173, 223–24, 329n3
Confederate States of America, 2
Congdon, Robert, 70
Conn, Patricia C., 101–4
Conrad, John, 47, 58, 61
Convention Center, 151, 157
Corcoran, Rob, 268–69n35
CoStar (real estate information company), 318n53
Council of the Great City Schools report, 107–10, 112, 113
COVID-19 pandemic, 226
Creighton Court neighborhood, 193, 194, 197, 198, 208, 210–11, 212, 238
crime: anti-crime activism, 62; crime rates, 32, 52, 78–79; crime summit (1994), 52–53, 272–73n6; Goins/Jones family murders, 54–56; homicide rates, 53, 54, 65–66, 78–79, 197; proposed solutions (1990s), 53–54; psychological effects of violence, 55; in public housing, 196–97; reductions (1990s), 65–66; tough-on-crime initiatives, 57; violent crime, 52
Crislip, Heather Mullins, 319n7
Cropper Analytics (consulting firm), 128, 130
Croson decision, 26, 149, 267n15
Crupi, James, 38

Crupi Report (1993), 38–44, 71; reactions to, 43–45
Crupi Report (2007), 120, 299n137
Crusade for Voters, 13, 33, 36, 46–47, 57–58, 62–63, 98, 130
Cuffee-Glenn, Selena, 82, 287n164
Cullen, Richard, 118
cultural and arts centers, 157–59
Curtis, Tyrone, 204–5

Dalal, Umesh, 114, 122
Davis, Jefferson, 1
Davis, Robin, 204
Defenders for Freedom, Justice and Equality, 173
Dell, Willie, 25
Department of Economic and Community Development, 150
Department of Housing and Urban Development (HUD), 199, 200, 203
desegregation. *See* busing; integration; segregation
Desmond, Matthew, 239, 331–32n31
development: and community wealth building, 175–82; neighborhood-level policies, 159–62; real estate tax exemptions, 159–62; Shockoe Bottom baseball proposal, 172–75; Washington NFL team training camp, 169–72. *See also* downtown development/revitalization
Devil's Half-Acre, 173
Dillon Rule, 10, 244, 264n29
direct election of mayor, movement for, 57–71
district system, city council. *See* city council; city council–city manager system
Dogwood Middle School, 229, 230
Dove Court housing development, 206
downtown development/revitalization, 151, 152–55, 331n25; Downtown Master Plan/Rachel Flynn, 165–68; retail district, 32; performing arts initiative, 157–59; Stony Point Fashion Park, 155–57

Drake, Avon, 37–38, 43, 48, 103, 291n36; critique of Richmond political leadership, 60
Dyke, James W., Jr., 124

East District Initiative, 61–62
East End neighborhoods, 8, 170–71
Echo Harbour development proposal, 167–68
Economic Development Authority, 149, 169
Edmonds, Torey, 61–62
Edney, Hazel Trice, 60
education: charter schools, 112, 127; Governor's Schools, 98–99, 245; policy emphases and future development, 226–32. *See also* Richmond Public Schools
Education Compact, 133–34, 232–33
Edwards, Ana, 173
El-Amin, Sa'ad, 33, 61, 62, 63, 66
elections, local. *See* city council; voting
elitism, 2, 3–4, 13, 42, 141, 236
employment. *See* affirmative action; jobs and economic development
Eppes, Tichi Pinkney, 130
Equality of Opportunity Project, 220
Equitable Affordable Housing Plan, 235
Estes, Lillie A., 177, 181, 207, 318–19n157
Evergreen Cooperatives (Cleveland), 180, 234

Fagan, Alexina, 101
Fairfield Court housing complex, 194, 208, 237
Fan District neighborhood, 148, 153
Farmer, Robin, 99
Farrell, Patrick W., 119
Farrell, Thomas F., II, 118
Fay, Frederic, 199
Fay Towers senior housing, 206
Federal Housing Administration, 9
Floyd, George, 2
Flying Squirrels AA baseball franchise, 172
Flynn, Rachel, 79, 165–68, 285n143

food justice, 214
Fountain Lake, Byrd Park, 1
Fourth Circuit Court of Appeals, 12
Fox Elementary School, 129–30, 229–30
Fraizer, Michael D., 118
Freeman, Lander, 204
Fulton neighborhood, 194

Galster, George, 160
gardens, community, 214
gentrification, 190, 214, 216–17; counter-gentrification, 237
Gentry, Richard C., 183, 201–2, 323n58
Giles, Annie, 206
Gilpin Court Civic Association, 55
Gilpin Court housing community, 54–55, 65, 168, 188, 193, 195–96, 198, 220, 237, 238; anti-crime team, 201; redevelopment, 206
Ginter Park Elementary School, 100
Goins, Christopher, 54–55
Golding, William, 35
Goldman, Paul, 68, 71, 80, 284n130, 286n156
Goode, Thomas E., 119
Goodwin, William H., Jr., 74, 118
Goolsby, Adrienne, 208, 209
Governor's Schools, 98–99, 245
Graham, Carolyn N., 176
Gray, Frederick T., 90
Gray, Kimberly, 125, 126, 129, 130
Graziano, Kathy, 174, 217, 220
Greater Richmond Chamber of Commerce, 153
Greater Richmond Partnership, 149, 318n152
Greater Richmond Transit Company (GRTC), 162
Great Recession (2008), 124, 137, 145, 165
greenfield space, 11
Grey, Robert J., Jr., 80, 118, 163
Griffin, Robert, III, 170

Hanover County: jobs and economic development, 142, 143, 144; population growth and demographics, 27, 28

Hardy, Eva Teig, 124
Harrell, William, 76, 77
Harris, Greta, 206
Harris, Joel, 59
Harris-Muhammed, Shonda, 130
Harrison-Jones, Lois, 85, 97–98, 200
Harvey, Shirley, 47, 203
Hassell, Leroy, 32–33, 97–98, 200, 269n36, 291n36, 321n41
Hatcher, Donald, 203
Hayes, Cora, 207
Hayter, Julian Maxwell, 191
Hazelett, Virgil, 142, 156, 205
Hedgepeth, Gwen, 47, 66–67, 278nn81–82
Henderson, Maurice, 125, 264n33
Henrico County: annexation, 139; inequality and economic mobility, 220; jobs and economic development, 142, 143, 144; population growth/demographics/diversity, 15, 27, 28, 189, 246; property taxes, 140; public transit, 162–64, 244; Republican-Democrat shift, 10; subsidized housing, 205; suburban ring, 9
Henrico County schools, 12, 87; race and economic disadvantage, 88, 88–89, 89; student outcomes, 93
Henry L. Marsh Elementary School, 214
heroin addiction, 56
Hicks, David M., 44, 47, 52, 54, 68, 276n64, 286n149, 286–87n157
Highland Park neighborhood, 65
Highland Park–Southern Tip neighborhood, 160
highway construction, 9–10, 192, 309n48, 320n14
Hilbert, Chris, 174, 285n144, 285–86n148, 300n143
Hill, C. T., 118
Hill, Oliver W., 100
Hill-Christian, Sheila, 205–6
Hillside Court neighborhood, 193, 214, 237
Historic Church Hill neighborhood, 99
historical methods, 18; oral history, 18; oral history sources, 257–60

Holmberg, Mark, 78
Holsworth, Robert "Bob," 29, 35, 38, 113
Holt, Curtis, 24
Holton, Anne, 49
Holton, Linwood, 49
homeownership assistance, 9, 235
homicide rates, 65–66, 78–79, 197
Hope in the Cities, 36, 268–69n35
housing: affordable, challenge of, 214–20; affordable, need for, 198; banking and credit institutions, 191–92; and demographic trends, 215, 215–17, 216, 218, 219; housing justice, 185–90; policy emphases and future development, 236–39; rent-to-own models, 201; Section 8 vouchers, 197
Housing Opportunities for People Everywhere (HOPE) VI grants, 202–5, 207, 323n60, 324n73. *See also* Choice Neighborhoods framework
Housing Opportunities Made Equal (HOME), 64
Howard, Amy L., 317n139
Huguenot High School, 229
Human Relations Commission, 15–16

Improbable Scholars (Kirp), 228
Industrial Development Authority, 278n82
inequality: city/county divisions, 4–6; and urban injustice, 16–17; within city of Richmond, 148. *See also* poverty
integration: and busing, 12, 90–91; failure of, 86; freedom of choice plan, 12; and Massive Resistance, 12, 16, 86, 90, 126, 189; and zoning, 229–31. *See also* segregation
interracial cooperation/coalitions, 26, 34, 35, 36, 130, 262n9

Jackson, Jackie, 78
Jackson, Jesse, 74
Jackson, Maynard, 26
Jackson, Stonewall, 2, 224
Jackson Ward neighborhood, 65, 154, 158, 160, 190, 192
Jacobs, Jane, 165

James, Allix, 44
James River as attraction, 166–67, 168
Jamison, Calvin, 63–64, 66, 67, 76, 157, 276n63, 278n78
J. B. Fisher Elementary School, 128, 229
Jewell, Marty, 46, 47, 57, 62, 82, 126, 203, 271n79, 280n100, 282n118
Jewell-Sherman, Deborah, 105–11, 112, 114, 121–22, 123, 124; departure of, 122
jobs and economic development, 142–48; and downtown revitalization, 155; educational requirements, 145–46; manufacturing decline, 144–45, 146, 147–48
John B. Cary Elementary School, 127–30, 229
Johnson, Kenneth S., 119, 204
Johnson, Stephen B., 110, 113
Jones, Albert, 98–99
Jones, Anthony, 47
Jones, Daphne, 54
Jones, David, 54
Jones, Derik, 126, 130
Jones, Dwight C., 80–83; Anti-Poverty Commission, 132, 135, 176–79, 208; on Black middle class, 34–35, 38; community wealth building, 234; Comprehensive Economic Development Strategy, 165; on direct election of mayor, 70; downtown revitalization, 168; and economic development, 149–50; and housing initiatives, 212; Jones family memorial service (1994), 55–56; mayoral race (2008), 79–80; mayoral role, 123, 124–26; Office of Community Wealth Building, 175–78; political influence (1990s), 33, 35; public housing redevelopment efforts, 198; redevelopment initiatives, 207–8; Shockoe Bottom baseball proposal, 172–75; Washington NFL team training camp deal, 169–72; on white supremacy, 224
Jones, Kenya, 54
Jones, Nicole, 54
Jones, Robert, 54
Jones, Tamika, 54–55
Jordan, Barbara, 71

Kaine, Tim: in city council, 47, 48–50; as compromise mayoral candidate, 58; criticism of, 67; on governance, 64–65; Kaine-Jamison partnership, 63–64; as mayor, 36, 62–63; Neighborhoods in Bloom initiative, 160; on public transit, 163; Richmond Redevelopment and Housing Authority regional expansion, 205; Stony Point Fashion Park, 156, 157
Kalamazoo, Michigan, 235
Kenney, Walter, 25, 33, 35–36, 47, 63, 70, 163, 200
Keys-Chavis, Edna, 59, 77
Khalfani, King Salim, 33, 68
Kilpatrick, James, 12
Kinfolk Community Empowerment Center, 214
King, Jon C., 119
Kirp, David, 228

Lafayette, Laura, 217
Lambert, Benjamin, 58
Larson, Kristen, 129, 130
Latino community: housing trends, 215, 229; population growth, 9, 88, 187; and poverty, 7–8, 189
Law, Melvin, 54, 70, 98, 101, 103
Lee, Robert E., 1
Leidinger, William, 25, 26–27, 35, 163
Libby Hill Park, 167
Lincoln, Abraham, 16
Linwood Holton Elementary School, 127, 229
Living Wage Certification program, 233
local elections. *See* city council–city manager system
Local Initiatives Support Corporation, 160, 202, 206
Lois Harrison-Jones Elementary School, 229
Lost Cause narrative, 17
Loupassi, Manoli, 76, 77, 78, 113

Luke, John A., Jr., 118
Lumpkin, Robert, 173
Lumpkin's Jail, 172–73

Maggie L. Walker Citizens Advisory Board, 177, 181
Maggie L. Walker Governor's School, 229, 245
Maggie L. Walker Initiative for Expanding Opportunity and Fighting Poverty, 177
Maggie Walker Community Land Trust/Land Bank, 190, 220, 236, 237, 328n127
Malcolm X, 33
Malone, Reggie, 58, 110
Manion, Jamison, 178
Markel, Anthony F., 119
Marsh, Henry L., III: on bus service, 163; and city council, 26, 32, 36; legal representation of Richmond Public Schools, 299n141; as mayor, 25, 30, 151, 199; opposition to direct election for mayor, 57–58, 68, 70; on Richmond Redevelopment and Housing Authority, 200; rivalry with Wilder, 73, 281n103
Marshall, Byron C., 81, 175
Mary Munford Elementary School, 123–24, 127, 129, 229
"Massive Resistance," 12, 16, 86, 90, 126, 189
Maymont Elementary School, 123, 301n154
Maymont Park and Nature Center, 123
mayoral role: Larry Chavis, 58–59; direct election, 14, 51–52, 57–71; election (1996), 58–59; election (2008), 79–80; election (2016), 83; "hollow prize problem," 264n31; Dwight C. Jones, 79–83; Tim Kaine, 62–65; Walter Kenney, 35–36; minority mayors, 264n31; and Richmond Public Schools, 87; responsibilities of, 29–30, 51–52, 71, 72–73, 79, 81, 211–12; State of the City addresses, 58, 64, 79, 124, 175–76; Roy West, 27–28; Doug Wilder, 73–80; Geline B. Williams, 28–29; Leonidas B. Young II, 52. *See also* city council–city manager system
Mayor's Anti-Poverty Commission. *See* Anti-Poverty Commission
McClenney, Earl H., 63
McCollum, Rudolph "Rudy," 62, 63, 66, 70–71, 157, 278n78, 279n83
McDaniel, Claudette, 25, 35, 62, 269n37
McDonnell, Bob, 169
McEachin, Donald, 47
McGuire Woods law firm, 70
McQuinn, Delores, 70, 78, 101, 172, 329n3
Medical College of Virginia, 152, 308–9n39
Merhige, Robert, 12, 90–95
Metropolitan Business League, 150
Miles, Chimere, 183, 210
Milliken v. Bradley (1974), 90
Minor, G. Gilmer, III, 119
minority contracting policies, 46, 60
Moeser, John, 30, 46, 68, 71, 176
Monroe, Rodney, 79
Moore, Thurston R., 119
Morris, Jean, 54
Morrissey, Joseph, 44, 83
Mosby, Michelle, 173–74
Mosby Court neighborhood, 194, 214, 237
Mosby Middle School, 97
Mosby South, 204–5
Moses, Robert, 165
Murdoch-Kitt, Norma, 125
Museum District neighborhood, 128, 129, 130

NAACP, 62–63, 101, 130
Nance, Charles, 110
National Association of Housing and Redevelopment Officials, 199
National Guard, 54
Nationwide Insurance lawsuit, 64
Navy Hill neighborhood, 192
neighborhoods: neighborhood-level development policies, 159–62; neighborhood-level policing, 65–66; neighborhood-level segregation, 193–95; neighborhood schools, 91, 229–30;

neighborhood vs. citywide issues, 29; and racial distribution, 185–88, 186–87; shifts in demographics, 215, 215–17, 216, 218, 219. *See also names of specific neighborhoods*

Neighborhoods in Bloom initiative, 64, 160–61, 217

Newbille, Cynthia, 174

Newtowne West neighborhood, 160

Nichols, Paul, 200

No Child Left Behind, 87

Northside neighborhoods, 148, 160

Northup, Solomon, 174

Oak Grove Elementary School, 112, 128

Obama, Barack, 80

Office of Community Wealth Building (OCWB), 82, 132, 175–82, 227; "community navigators," 213–14; "People Plan" and Choice Neighborhoods, 209–11; workforce programming, 233–35

Office of Minority Business Development, 150

Olds, Marilyn, 197, 209

Oliver, Jerry, 65–66

Open High School, 229

Opportunity Insights, 220

oral history, 18; sources, 257–60

Oregon Hill neighborhood, 153, 160

Page, Dawn, 125, 126

Pantele, Bill, 76, 78, 79–80, 121–22, 283n128, 285n142

parole-abolishment movement, 57

Partnership for Leaders in Education (University of Virginia), 111

Partnership for Smarter Growth, 167

paternalism, 213, 262n9, 262n12

Patrick Henry Elementary School (charter school), 127, 229

People Plan, Choice Neighborhoods, 209–11

Perkins, Charles, 35

police: community-oriented policing, 65–66; police protection and crime, 53–54; protests against police brutality, 1–2

policy development, 31–32; community wealth building, 232–36; education, 226–32; housing, 236–39

Port of Richmond, 82, 318n152

poverty: Anti-Poverty Commission (Mayor Jones), 176–79; civil rights movement goals, 135–36; "cliff effect" in subsidized housing, 202, 233–34; by council district, 137; deconcentration vs. reduction, 213; economic mobility and inequality, 220–21; and housing segregation, 189–90; impact of, 29; jobs and economic development, 145–48; and lateral movement for housing, 207–8; linked to crime, 53; neighborhood concentrations of, 184–85, 185; Office of Community Wealth Building, 175–82; and policy recommendations for education, 227–28; policy recommendations to reduce, 233–36; poverty rate, compared with other cities, 242; prevalence of, 7–9; racialized, 8, 136–39, 184–85, 185; and Richmond Public Schools, 88, 88–89, 92–96, 130; segregation and wealth disparity, 164–65. *See also* public housing

Powell, Lewis, 90

Pratt, Robert, 90

Prince, Carl, 35, 47

progressive movement, 10, 35

Project Embrace, 66

Project Exile, 65

Project One, 26

Promise Scholarships, 234–35

protest art, 1

PTAs (Parent-Teacher Associations), 228

public housing, 64, 192–95; and crime, 53, 54–55; deterioration and disappointment in, 195–98; drug activity, 201; HOPE VI grants, 202–5; redevelopment, 198, 202–4

public transit, 64, 82, 144, 162–64, 312n80; Bus Rapid Transit (BRT) line, 82, 177, 179, 244; TIGER grant, 179 racial issues: and census tracts, 186–87; housing and systemic racism, 208; hyper-racial frustrations, 37; interracial cooperation, 26, 34, 35, 130; Jim Crow racism, 2, 223–24; over-simplification of, 224–25; quotas, 26; racial clustering, 99–100; racialized housing segregation, 188–95; racialized poverty, 8, 136–39; racial tensions and cultural centers, 157–58; school zoning polices, 126–32; stereotypical views, impact of, 40–41; systemic racism, protests against, 1–2; zoning laws, 190–91. *See also* busing; integration; segregation

Randolph, James, 54

Randolph, Virginia, 194

Randolph neighborhood, 128, 194

Readjuster Party, 2

real estate tax exemptions, 159–62

Reconstruction era and segregation, 2, 190

redlining, 191

regional transit, 162–64

Reno, Janet, 54

Residents of Public Housing in Richmond against Mass Evictions (RePHRAME), 207, 325n88

retail development, 155–57. *See also* downtown development/revitalization

Richardson, H. W. "Chuck," 25, 33, 47, 56, 163, 200, 328–29n1

Richardson, Sylvia, 99–100

Richmond, Virginia. *See* City of Richmond, Virginia

Richmond 300 Master Plan, 237

Richmond Afro-American (newspaper), 33

Richmond Association of Realtors, 217

Richmond Ballet, 159

Richmond CenterStage, 159

Richmond City Charter Review Commission (2022–23), 240, 241

Richmond Coalition for Quality Education, 304n195

Richmond Economic Development Authority, 149

Richmond Education Association (REA), 101, 103

Richmond Free Press (newspaper), 33–34, 37–38; on city council elections (1998), 61–62; on city manager/city council divide, 45; on crime rates, 53; on Crupi Report, 43; on Crusade for Voters 1994 slate, 47–48; on Goins/Jones incident, 55–56; on mayoral race (1998), 63

Richmond Opportunities, Inc., 211

Richmond-Petersburg Turnpike, 192, 193

Richmond Police Department, 65–66

Richmond Professional Institute, 152

Richmond Public Schools (RPS): accreditation, 124; audits, 114, 122; Balanced Scorecard, 111; Yvonne Brandon's leadership, 123–24; budget process, 76–77, 81–82, 97–98, 112, 117, 124–25, 133; challenges and problems, 85–89; collaboration with OCWB, 179; Patricia Conn's reform agenda, 101–2; consolidation with Henrico and Chesterfield Counties, 90; corporate calls for appointed school board, 114–21; Council of the Great City Schools, 107–10; current challenges, 132–34; curriculum guides, 106–7; Education Compact, 133–34; elected school board, superintendents hired, 101–5; enrollment decline, 97; enrollment policies, 229–31; eviction from City Hall, 121–22; funding, 81–82, 86, 132–33; Jewell-Sherman's superintendency, 105–11; "memorandum of understanding," 134; model schools, 91, 289n12; open enrollment, 127; physical facilities, 123–24, 231; policy emphases and future development, 226–32; policy recommendations for, 227–28, 245; political atmosphere pre-school board elections, 96–100; pro-integration zoning, 229–31; race and economic disadvantage, 88, 88–89, 89; racial segregation and rezoning, 126–32; school board, staggered terms, 232; special education programs, 110; specialty schools, 230; Standards of Learning (SOL) tests, 104–5, 112,

124; student outcomes, 89, 93–94, 96, 104–5, 122–23; teacher recruitment and retention, 228–29; and Wilder's mayoral leadership, 111–24; Wilder's schools advisory committee, 112–14; zoning and rezoning proposals, 128–29

Richmond Redevelopment and Housing Authority (RRHA), 178, 192–94, 196, 238, 327n111; Board of Commissioners, 199–200; challenges facing, 214–20; control of as political issue, 198–201; Curtis's management, 204–5; Gentry's management, 201–2; Goolsby's management, 208; Hill-Christian's management, 205–6; HOPE VI grants, 202–5, 324n73; leadership turnover (2018–22), 211–13; one-for-one replacement policy, 206–7; Scott's management, 206; Somanath's management, 209–10; Turpin's management, 199–201

Richmond Renaissance, 26, 151, 153

Richmond School Board v. Board of Education (1973), 90

Richmond Social Enterprise Study, 180

Richmond Symphony, 159

Richmond Technical Center, 231

Richmond Tenants Organization, 197, 201, 207, 209

Richmond Times-Dispatch (newspaper): Black columnists, 34; divisiveness of, 42; power analysis of Richmond, 74–75; support for Wilder-Bliley proposal, 70

Richmond Tomorrow initiative, 31–32

Richmond Urban Forum, 36

Riddell, Joyce, 35

rights revolution, 25, 126, 136, 149, 226

Robb, Charles "Chuck," 10, 54

Robert Bobb Group, 125

Robertson, Ellen, 78, 122, 174, 176–77, 217, 220, 277n73, 287n159

Robinson, Delores, 206

Robinson, Edward, 203

Rusk, David, 205

RVA Future Centers, 235, 318n150

Ryan, James, 90

Ryan, Michael, 82

Sabato, Larry, 78

Sacred Ground Historical Reclamation Project, 173

Sales, Norman, 77

Salomonsky, H. Louis, 278n82

Samuels, Charles, 174

Schroeder, James, 113

Scott, Adria Graham, 125

Scott, Anthony, 125, 206, 208

Scott, Bobby, 70, 203

Seabolt, Robert D., 119

Section 8 housing vouchers, 198, 207, 209, 238

segregation, 8, 11–13, 319n7, 320–21n23; and busing, 12, 90–91; legacy of, 3–4; and public housing, 193–95; public transportation, 162–63; racial zoning laws, 190–91. *See also* integration

Self-Sufficiency and Community Building Task Force, 203

Sheehan, Jeremiah, 163

Shields, Tom, 68

Shockoe Bottom, 82; stadium, 168, 172–75, 316n129

Shockoe Valley neighborhood, 190, 194

Short Pump Town Center project, 151, 156–57

Siegel-Hawley, Genevieve, 91, 126–27, 130

6th Street Marketplace, 32, 151–52, 155–56

slavery, legacy of, 2, 82, 168, 172–75, 261n4, 320n10

Slave Trail Commission, 64, 277n65, 329n3

Sledd, Robert C., 119

"slum clearance," 193–94

Smith, Julious P., Jr., 119

social science methods, 18

Somanath, T. K., 194, 209–10, 212

Southern Barton Heights neighborhood, 160

"Southern Manifesto," 12

Southside neighborhoods, 8, 160

Spellings, Margaret, 112
Standards of Learning (SOL) tests, 104–5, 124; cheating scandal, 112
State of the City addresses, 58, 64, 79, 124, 175–76
STAY RVA community organization, 229
Stone Brewing, 168, 175, 317n137
Stoney, Levar M., 83, 133, 224, 231
Stony Point Fashion Park, 151, 155–57
Strategic Plan for Equitable Economic Development (SPEED), 236
Sturtevant, Glen, 129, 130
suburbanization, 136–37, 143–44, 150–51; automobiles and urban decentralization, 139; and segregation, 12
Support Richmond Public Schools, 133
Supreme Court decisions: *City of Richmond v. J. A. Croson*, 26, 267n15; district system for city council, 23; *Milliken v. Bradley* (1974), 90, 266n48; racialized zoning ordinances, 190; *Richmond School Board v. Board of Education* (1973), 90; school segregation, 12
Szymanczyk, Mike, 118

Taubman Centers, 156
tax structure: city vs. counties, 32; and downtown revitalization, 155; Earned Income Tax Credit, 233–34; public-private partnership for arts development, 158–59; real estate tax, 26–27, 76, 159–62
Taylor, Mamie, 126, 129, 130
Teams for Progress, 36, 46
Terry, Mary Sue, 95
Thomas Jefferson High School, 99, 229
Thompson, John, 35–36, 63
tobacco industry, 144
Townes, Clarence L., Jr., 101, 119
Trammell, Reva, 59, 62, 125, 174
Trani, Eugene P., 74, 118, 152–55
transportation. *See* public transit
Transportation Investment Generating Economic Recovery (TIGER), 179
Trump, Donald, 224

Turpin, Roland L., 196–97, 199–200, 213
12 Years a Slave (film), 174
Tyler, Bruce, 82, 126, 285n147

Ukrop, James E. "Jim," 44, 47, 62, 74, 75, 118, 158, 159, 282–83n122
Union City, New Jersey, 228
Union Cycliste Internationale cycling championship, 82
urban planning: economic development, 140–42; urban renewal policies, 9
Urban Strategies, 210
urban-suburban divide, 9

Venture Richmond, 172
violence. *See* crime
Virginia, Commonwealth of. *See* Commonwealth of Virginia
Virginia Commonwealth University (VCU), 136, 137, 152–55, 308–9n39, 309n46
Virginia Economic Development Partnership, 149
Virginia General Assembly, 10, 27, 70, 73, 101, 117, 138, 192, 243–44
Virginia Opera, 159
Virginia Preschool Initiative pre-K programs, 123
Virginia Union University, 152, 172
voting: Black voting power, 68–70; runoff elections, 68; voter registration and turnout, 36–37, 69–70. *See also* city council
Voting Rights Act (1965), 13, 25

Wake, Carolyn, 35
Walker, Maggie L., 191–92
Warthen, Ben, 47
Washington NFL team training camp, 169–72, 315n119
Watkins, John, 163
Weinstein, Allison P., 119
West, Roy A., 25–26, 47, 58, 93–94, 99, 199; conservative leanings, 32; leadership style questioned, 27–28; as school principal, 97

West End neighborhoods, 30, 91, 148, 169, 184
Westover Hills Elementary School, 229
Westover Hills neighborhood, 129, 188
Whitcomb Court, 194, 237
white flight, 27, 86, 89, 90, 190
white supremacy, 2, 16, 33, 224. *See also* racial issues
Wikstrom, Nelson, 67, 71
Wilayto, Phil, 173
Wilder, L. Douglas, 10, 58, 67; alliance with Raymond Boone (*Richmond Free Press*), 33; on arts and cultural development, 158–59; and BioTech park development, 154; on city council power divisions, 46; as governor, 71–72; and housing initiatives, 212, 217; as mayor, 73–80, 282nn118–20, 286n149; and public housing, 205–6; Richmond Public Schools and school improvement, 111–24; schools advisory committee, 112–14
Wilder-Bliley Commission, 67–68, 70, 111
William Fox Elementary School, 124, 127, 229, 230
Williams, Albert J., 104–5
Williams, Geline B., 28–30, 35, 47
Williams, Michael Paul, 34, 113, 173, 205–6, 269n39
Williamson, Thad, 176–77, 178, 287n161, 305n200, 317nn139–40, 332n32
Windsor Farms neighborhood, 197
Winston, Bonnie, 195–97, 220
Wolf, Carol A. O., 111, 113, 114, 284n34
Woltz, Robert W., Jr., 119
Workforce Investment Board, 150

Yancy, Preston M., 33
Young, Andrew, 26, 71
Young, Leonidas B., II, 45, 48, 52, 54; on at-large mayor, shift to, 58; election (1996), 58; federal charges and imprisonment, 59–60; Jones family memorial service (1994), 55–56; support for parole abolishment, 57

zoning: pro-integration school zoning, 229–31; school zoning policies, 126–32; racial zoning laws, 190–91

Index 345

www.ingramcontent.com/pod-product-compliance
Lightning Source LLC
Chambersburg PA
CBHW031644240226
40199CB00013B/330